£1.50

STRATUM SERIES

The Late Italian Renaissance
1525–1630

STRATUM SERIES

*A series of fundamental reprints from
scholarly journals and specialised works
in European History*

GENERAL EDITOR: J. R. HALE

The Late Italian Renaissance
1525-1630

EDITED BY
Eric Cochrane

MACMILLAN

First published 1970 by
MACMILLAN AND CO LTD
Little Essex Street London W C 2
and also at Bombay Calcutta and Madras
Macmillan South Africa (Publishers) Pty Ltd Johannesburg
The Macmillan Company of Australia Pty Ltd Melbourne
Gill and Macmillan Ltd Dublin

Printed in Great Britain by
ROBERT MACLEHOSE AND CO LTD
The University Press, Glasgow

Contents

Introduction

1525, 1527, 1529, 1530—these are tragic years in the annals of Renaissance Italy. The capture of King Francis I at Pavia crippled one of the two remaining contenders for dominion of the peninsula, and it deprived Italians of the one tactic by which they had previously maintained some semblance of independence: that of playing the foreign powers off against each other. The Sack of Rome delivered the head of one of the largest Italian states into the hands of Spanish and German soldiers, and it destroyed what remained of Italy's oft-vaunted pride in being the center of Christendom. The crowning of Charles V as emperor sealed the humiliation of the papacy and of all the other princes and magistrates who flocked to Bologna to do homage before the most powerful monarch Europe had known since the time of Charlemagne. The collapse of the last Florentine republic, after a long and heroic siege, snuffed out the last attempt to resurrect what had been the institutional matrix of so much of Renaissance culture—the commune. And it left the successors of the Florentine political philosophers with the choice of either submitting to a regime that they could no longer direct or creating Utopias that they would never be called upon to implement.

Yet the tragedies of the late 1520's were merely the culmination of the many others that had struck Italy with increasing frequency since that fatal year 1494, when the army of Charles VIII had paraded, practically without opposition, all the way to Naples. The arrival of Vasco da Gama at Lisbon in 1499 had, momentarily at least, gravely threatened the Italian monopoly of the lucrative oriental spice trade. The second French invasion of the same year had reduced the powerful duchy of Milan to the rank of a French, and then of a Swiss, dependency. The War of the League of Cambrai in 1509 had robbed Venice almost overnight of nearly all its mainland possessions and had permanently wrecked its aspirations to become the master of all Italy. The Battle of Ravenna and the Sack of Prato in 1512 had made it clear that the Spanish infantry was in Italy to stay and that its mere presence was sufficient to overthrow the government of any Italian state.

Meanwhile, all Lombardy had been laid waste. Scores of cities had been plundered. Prosperous industrial centers had been bereft of their means of support. The population of Florence had dwindled to half of what it had been forty years earlier. Venice was overrun with half-starved peasants from the continent.[1] The coasts of Puglia, Calabria, and even Tuscany were increasingly exposed to the fury of Turkish raiders. Those whom the soldiers spared, moreover, were, as often as not, struck down by other evils—extraordinary tax levies, unemployment, pestilence, and the latest instrument of divine wrath, the *morbus gallicus*, syphilis.

The witnesses to these tragedies were stunned:

> Oh Italy, you've been made a slave;
> Poor and naked, bereft of friends and arms,
> You're left in direst need.[2]

They put the blame chiefly on the "barbarians":

> Cruel, wicked, pitiless criminals,
> Rapacious wolves and dogs gone mad;
> Had I a thousand pens and a thousand hands,

---

[1] See Pietro Battara, *La popolazione di Firenze alla metà del '500* (Florence: Rinascimento del Libro, 1935), and Brian Pullan, "The Famine in Venice and the New Poor Law, 1527-1529," *Bolletino dell'Istituto di Storia della Società e dello Stato Veneziano*, V-VI (1963-64), 141-202.

[2] The three poetry selections quoted are respectively from Luigi Alamanni's *Diluvio romano*, from Celebrino da Udine's *Presa di Roma*, and from Machiavelli's *Decennale primo*. I have translated them, with due regard for the rules of poetic license, from the passages presented in Peter Amelung's *Das Bild des Deutschen in der Literatur der italienischen Renaissance* (Munich: Max Hueber, 1964), pp. 127, 125, and 104. The fourth passage is from the first page of Guicciardini's *Storia d'Italia*.

> A sea of ink and many books to fill,
> Still could I recount but part
> Of what they did to Rome.[2]

But they realized at the same time that it was they themselves who were ultimately responsible:

> When discordant Italy opened up
> Her highways to the Gauls,
> And let herself be trodden down
> By wild barbarian hordes.[2]

For some time they had been hoping that a duly placated Deity would relent in His wrath, that the present troubles would soon give way to a Joachimite "Age of the Holy Spirit," or, like Machiavelli, that a new "prince," properly instructed in the laws of politics, would summon up enough *virtù* to overcome the works of *fortuna*. Even after all seemed to have been lost, they might still hope, as did Guicciardini in 1529 and again in 1534, that wisdom, properly applied at the right place and the right moment, might at least alleviate an otherwise unbearable situation.[3] But by 1537 most of them were convinced that the *occasione* had passed forever: "From the innumerable examples [of the last thirty years] it will be fully evident that human affairs are subject to the same instability as is the sea when stirred up by winds."[2] Politics had become a matter of "vain errors" and private "cupidity," all of which usually produced just the opposite of the calculated results. Hence, politicians could do nothing but look back with nostalgia on the pre-1494 golden age that Guicciardini conjured up for them and contemplate with tragic detachment the now irremediable "calamities of Italy."[2]

Le calamità d'Italia: this became almost a commonplace among Italian writers of the 1520's and 1530's; and it is not surprising that it has since been taken as a key to a more general interpretation of the age as a whole. For Francesco De Sanctis, in the nineteenth century, the "naturalism" of Guicciardini led inevitably to the

---

[3] See Vittorio De Caprariis, *Francesco Guicciardini: Dalla politic aalla storia* (Bari: Laterza, 1950), es. dpp. 97 and 108.

"moral dissolution, without conscience and hence without remorse," of Pietro Aretino; and Italy consequently "lost completely its independence, its freedom, and its position of leadership in world history."[4] For Jacob Burckhardt, the consolidation of Spanish hegemony and the "fall of the humanists" marked the end of an age; and few of the examples with which he supported his generalizations come from the years after 1540. For Bernard Berenson, the school of painting that began with Giotto ended with Michelangelo; and he dismissed one of the founders of what is now called "mannerism" as "an academic constructor of monstrous nudes."[5] Similar judgments can be found among the most recent authorities on the Renaissance as well. Denys Hay, for instance, in his remarkably comprehensive survey *The Italian Renaissance in its Historical Background*,[6] moves directly from "The Spirit of the Fifteenth Century" to a consideration of "The Reception of the Italian Renaissance in the North"; and he includes the first three decades of the sixteenth century, not as the beginning of a new phase in the Renaissance, but as the aftermath of the preceding and final phase. Nicolai Rubinstein, similarly, looks upon Vasari's mural of Duke Cosimo surrounded by his court artists as a sign of the disappearance of Florentine political vitality. Peter Murray, in an essay in the same luxurious volume, *The Age of the Renaissance*,[7] treats Michelangelo's *Last Judgment* as a postscript to an era that had all but vanished; and he places Tintoretto, who "was almost exclusively a religious painter," in the next era, that of the Counter Reformation. Giorgio Spini, finally, who has studied the sixteenth century both in the minute detail of archival records and in the perspective of three hundred years of European history, has discerned at the time of Charles V not only an economically disastrous shift of trade from the Mediterranean to the Atlantic but also a "crisis of conscience." "The great generation of

---

[4] *Storia della letteratura italiana*, ed. Benedetto Croce and A. Parente (Bari: Laterza, 1939), Vol. II, p. 136.

[5] *The Italian Painters of the Renaissance* (London: Phaidon Press, n.d.), p. 71.

[6] Cambridge University Press, 1966.

[7] *The Age of the Renaissance*, ed. Denys Hay (London: Thames & Hudson, 1967); quoted from p. 118.

Machiavelli and Raffaello," he says, gives way "to a generation of dignified mediocrities" like Vasari, Bronzino, and Cellini. And he appropriately labels the corresponding chapter of his vast *Storia dell'età moderna* the *Finis Italiae*—the "End of Italy."[8]

That the Italian Renaissance came to an end sometime around 1530 is, in other words, a proposition that has been accepted by many students of the period for the past 150 years. Moreover, it is one which has also received support from theses and assumptions that do not derive solely from a study of the phenomenon itself. It owes much, for instance, to the interest in the medieval communes which was born with the Romantic movement of the early nineteenth century, if not with Saverio Bettinelli in the late eighteenth.[9] It owes much also to the condemnation of the Counter Reformation as a reversion to an anterior stage in the progress of human liberty or as the source of many of the more objectionable elements in the modern Church. It owes even more to the position of Tacitus in antiquity and of Leonardo Bruni in the early Renaissance—to the position, that is, according to which artistic and literary creativity depends upon the preservation of a republican constitution. Certain elements in the separate European national traditions have reinforced this proposition still further. In France the critics of the age of Louis XIV discredited all Italian literature after Ariosto:

> Évitons ces excès: laissons à l'Italie
> De tous ces faux brillans l'éclatante folie.
>
> BOILEAU, *L'Art poétique*

And Jules Michelet, a century and a half later, depicted the Renaissance as a movement of Italian origin which became wholly French after the advent of Francis I. In England, similarly, the Elizabethan Italophobes and the seventeenth-century anti-Jesuits, in spite of their occasional appreciation of Machiavelli, tended to

---

[8] I quote from Vol. I, p. 121, of the Piccola Biblioteca Einaudi paperback edition (Turin, 1965).

[9] *Il risorgimento d'Italia negli studi, nelle arti, e ne' costumi dopo il Mille* (1773); which is Vol. III of his *Opere* (Venice: Zatta, 1780).

reject of all contemporary Italian culture either as atheistic or, worse yet, as Papist. And the "Whig myth," from the eighteenth century on, made Luther and Calvin, rather than Michelangelo or Tasso, the true successors of the earlier humanists in the historical relay race toward Liberalism and parliamentary government.

The sources of these theses, then, have been different. But the conclusions are much the same. The Renaissance could not have lasted much beyond 1530—so runs the argument. For cultural vitality, of which the Renaissance was the expression at that particular moment in time, is by nature incompatible with an authoritarian state, with foreign domination, with a basically religious view of life, with "Machiavellian" amorality, or with Tridentine Catholicism. Therefore the scholars have seemed to be correct in leaving Italy after the Sack of Rome and moving off to the more pleasant fields beyond the Alps. The writers of textbooks have even further reasons for doing so. For they are seldom permitted to follow any more than one line of development for the whole of Europe; and they cannot stop for tangents and epicycles as the line moves inexorably, like that of the *Translatio imperii* of the Middle Ages, from one country to the next. At least in the United States, they are usually obliged to squeeze the traditional categories of Italian Renaissance, northern Renaissance, and Protestant Reformation into no more than three weeks of a European history course; and they have no time left for aftermaths or variants before moving on to Descartes and Cromwell.

Nevertheless, this view of the chronological limits of the Renaissance has always been faced with one serious difficulty: it does not correspond with the views of any of the direct heirs of the Italian Renaissance itself. Giorgio Vasari, in the 1550's, saw no interruption in the steady progress of the arts from Giotto to Michelangelo and beyond; and he seems to have forgotten completely the pessimism that had afflicted his compatriots just two decades earlier and to which he himself had succumbed in the spring of 1537. Scipione Ammirato, in the 1580's, looked back to the republican commune, not as an unfortunate victim of tyranny, but as a chaos onto which the new monarchy had providentially

INTRODUCTION   13

imposed some sort of order. Giovan Battista Marino, in the early 1610's, regarded the whole of the past as merely a prelude to his own triumphs in poetry and as a convenient grab bag of stimulants for his own unprecedented talent. Even Ludovico Antonio Muratori, as late as the 1710's, considered the sixteenth, not the fifteenth, to have been the great century of Italian literature; and he found no signs of decadence until the first years of the seventeenth century. To be sure, these views are no longer acceptable without severe reservations. But they are based on a knowledge of many aspects of late Renaissance Italian culture that have since been forgotten. They cannot, therefore, be dismissed as completely antiquated or superseded.

A still greater difficulty has become apparent more recently. Within some of the specialized fields of Renaissance studies, the chronology does not take account of all the known evidence. Historians of ideas, for instance, have not been able to find any abrupt break in the development of Italian thought before the end of the century at the earliest; and one of them, Giuseppe Saitta, has proposed reordering the usual periodical divisions in the direction of the one used by the older tradition of Italian literary historiography: a preparatory phase (the Quattrocento [i.e. the fifteenth century] or "Age of Humanism") followed by a phase of full flowering (the Cinquecento [i.e. the sixteenth century], or the "Renaissance" proper).[10] Historians of art, similarly, even those who cannot warm to the mannerists, have not been able to ignore the conscious revival of High Renaissance styles in the generation of Barocci and the Carracci. Thus Walter Friedlaender, among others, has implicitly rejected the notion of a decline in artistic creativity and has proposed instead a succession of two new forms of art: the anticlassical, beginning about 1520, and the anti-mannerist, culminating after 1600, each with its own masterpieces as well as its own failures.[11] Historians of philosophy, finally, have

[10] *Il pensiero italiano nell'Umanesimo e nel Rinascimento*, 2nd edn. (Florence: Sansoni, 1961).
[11] *Mannerism and Anti-Mannerism in Italian Painting* (Columbia University Press, 1957).

not been able to overlook the giants of the last decades of the sixteenth century—Bruno, Campanella, Telesio. Neither have they
been able to overlook Francesco Patrizi and his revitalization of the
Platonic tradition, which had seemed doomed to the limbo of
parlor games after the disappearance of the Platonic Academy in
Florence. Nor have they been able to forget the Aristotelians, who
had not succumbed either to humanism or to Platonism during the
fifteenth century and who did not weaken before the anathemas
of the Fifth Lateran Council. Thus Eugenio Garin, Bruno Nardi,
and Paul Oskar Kristeller, to name but three of the most prominent authorities on Renaissance philosophy, have carried their
accounts down at least until the time of Galileo.[12]

To these difficulties must be added the recent re-evaluation of
certain aspects of the sixteenth century that hitherto have been
taken as signs of decadence or retrogression. In the last fifty years,
for instance, the art of the mannerists—even such examples of it as
Pontormo's frescos for San Lorenzo, which Vasari found hopelessly extravagant[13]—has now, thanks to the advent of cubism and
surrealism, once again become appreciated by art critics, perhaps
even more so than in its own time. The artistic and literary
academies, likewise, which were long passed off as havens of
mediocrity, frivolity, and governmental thought-control, are now
being restudied in the light of their declared purposes: stimulating
constructive debate on current intellectual issues and making the
results of the debates available to an ever larger, more socially
diversified audience.[14] The work of philologians like Pier Vettori
has been reinterpreted as a means not of avoiding the message contained in the texts to be emended, but of helping students to com-

[12] I have in mind their more recent works: Garin, *La cultura filosofica del
Rinascimento italiano* (Florence: Sansoni, 1961); Nardi, *Saggi sull'aristotelesimo
padovano dal secolo XIV al XVI* (Florence: Sansoni, 1958); and Kristeller, *Eight
Philosophers of the Italian Renaissance* (Stanford University Press, 1964).

[13] See Janet Cox Rearick, *The Drawings of Pontormo* (Harvard University
Press, 1965).

[14] Armando L. De Gaetano, "The Florentine Academy and the Advancement
of Learning through the Vernacular: The Orti Oricellari and the Sacra Aca-
demia," *Bibliothèque d'humanisme et renaissance*, xxx (1968), 19–52.

prehend them better. The work of antiquarians like Vincenzo Borghini has been reinterpreted not as a rejection of the political historiography of the early sixteenth century, but as a prelude to the scientific historiography of the eighteenth. The new monarchies are now regarded, thanks to the studies of Federico Chabod, not as the destroyers of freedom, but as the creators of what has become one of the most notable features of the modern state: a permanent, independent bureaucracy.[15] The church is now regarded as a field of activity quite as respectable and as progressive as the state. The Italian patriciate is thus no longer blamed for transferring its organizational and administrative talents from one field to the other.[16] The Italian bishops who went to Trent have turned out to have been anything but rubber stamps for the Curia; and the bishops who returned from Trent have now been revealed as far more than the passive executors of a ready-made program handed down to them from on high.[17]

Finally, recent research has brought to light a number of new aspects of the age that still await incorporation into a more general conceptual framework. At least one state on the peninsula, for instance, recovered its political vitality during the course of the century, namely, Venice; and far from submitting passively to pressure from the Papacy and the Hapsburgs, who surrounded its territories on almost all sides, it proved itself determined in 1606 not only to fight for its independence, but also to regain its freedom of action as a European power. Certain forces in some of the other states, too, now appear to have been no more acquiescent—witness Cosimo de' Medici's recovery of the Tuscan fortresses in the 1540's, the rebellion of Genoa in the 1570's, the revolt of Naples in the 1580's, and the marriage of Grand Duke Ferdinando I

[15] Chabod, "L'epoca di Carlo V," in *Storia di Milano* (Milan: Treccani, 1953–66), Vol. IX, and *Lo Stato di Milano nella prima metà del secolo XVI* (Rome: Edizioni dell'Ateneo, 1955).

[16] See A. Dupront, "D'un humanisme chrétien en Italie à la fin du XVIe siècle," *Revue historique*, CLXXV (1935), 296–307.

[17] Giuseppe Alberigo, *I vescovi italiani al Concilio di Trento* (Florence: Sansoni, 1959), and Paolo Prodi, "Riforma cattolica e controriforma" in *Nuove questioni di storia moderna* (Milan: Marzorati, 1964), Vol. I, pp. 357–405.

to a French, not a Spanish, princess in 1590. The economic curve, moreover, which seemed destined to swing continually downward in the 1530's, began swinging up again in the 1550's; and by the end of the century it appears to have regained, if not to have surpassed, the level it had achieved in Guicciardini's "Golden Age" before the death of Lorenzo the Magnificent.[18] When older forms of business association were found to be inadequate, the Italians invented a new one, the *società in accomandita*.[19] When the old banks began failing in the 1580's and 1590's, they established new ones—various forms of state banks and barely disguised charitable societies, which gained considerable public confidence from their religious as well as their political associations and which proved to be very ingenious in working out more efficient kinds of savings accounts and negotiable drafts.[20] The Italians displayed their inventiveness in the more strictly cultural fields as well. As political philosophy wandered off into Utopia, they took an interest in practical piety; and their manuals were soon read in translation all over Europe.[21] As metaphysics became ever less capable of offering coherent explanations, they turned to the observation and classification of natural phenomena—like those enshrined in Andrea Cesalpino's collections of rocks and plants. As the plots of their comedies became trite and repetitive, they began experimenting with the language of the dialogues or expanding the skits between the acts, the *intermedii*. As polyphony grew too complex and too abstract, they tried out monody instead. And when monody failed to recapture fully the emotive qualities they had read about in ancient Greek music treatises, they put it together with architecture, painting,

[18] All these matters are considered at length in various of the articles included in this anthology.

[19] See Maurice Carmona, "Aspects du capitalisme toscan aux XVIe et XVIIe siècles," *Revue d'histoire moderne et contemporaine*, XI (1964), 81–108.

[20] See, for example, Carlo di Somma, *Il Banco dello Spirito Santo dalle origini al 1664* (Naples: Istituto di Storia Economica e Sociale, 1960).

[21] See Giovanni Getto, "La letteratura ascetica e mistica in Italia nell'età del Concilio tridentino" in *Contributi alla storia del Concilio di Trento e della Controriforma*, "Quaderni di Belfagor" (Florence: Vallecchi, 1948), pp. 51–77, and Massimo Petrocchi, *Pagine sulla letteratura religiosa lombarda del '500* (Naples: Libreria Scientifica, 1956).

and poetry and ended up with a wholly new form of art: the opera. Obviously a revision of the traditional periodization of the Italian Renaissance is in order; and a few historians have in the last few years proposed various alternatives. At least two of them have moved the terminal date of the Renaissance back before Machiavelli, and, putting Italy in the context of the whole of Europe, they have defined the succeeding decades as an "anti-Renaissance."[22] At least one of them, on the other hand, has cast doubt upon the very notion of an "end" of the Renaissance and has looked, rather, for a transfer of creative energies from one field of activity to another.[23] Historians of music, most notably Edward E. Lowinsky,[24] have described a continuous development beginning in the early fifteenth century and culminating with the Florentine *Camerata* and with Giulio Caccini's "new music" at the beginning of the seventeenth. Historians of literary criticism—Bernard Weinberg above all[25]—have found that this particular aspect of Renaissance culture coincides almost exactly with the hundred-year period 1500–1600. Historians of Italian literature, like Ettore Bonora,[26] have distinguished two separate, consecutive movements: one led by Ariosto and Pietro Bembo, which they call the Renaissance proper, and another, which they call "mannerism" rather than "late Renaissance" or "pre-Baroque" to emphasize its autonomy, beginning with Giovanni Della Casa, culminating with Tasso, and giving way to still another phase with Marino. Historians of piety, most recently Alberto Vecchi,[27] have placed a

[22] Hiram Haydn, *The Counter-Renaissance* (New York: Scribner's, 1950), and Eugenio Battisti, *L'antirinascimento* (Milan: Feltrinelli, 1962).

[23] H. G. Koenigsberger, "Decadence or Shift? Changes in the Civilization of Italy and Europe in the XVI and XVII Centuries," *Transactions of the Royal Historical Society*, Ser. 5, Vol. x (1960), 1–18.

[24] "Music in the Culture of the Renaissance," *Journal of the History of Ideas*, xv (1954), 509–53.

[25] *A History of Literary Criticism in the Italian Renaissance*, 2 vols. (University of Chicago Press, 1961).

[26] *Critica e letteratura nel Cinquecento* (Turin: Giappichelli, 1964). See also Ezio Raimondi, "Per la nozione del manierismo letterario," in his *Rinascimento inquieto* (Palermo: Manfredi, 1965).

[27] *Correnti religiose nel Sei-Settecento veneto* (Venice and Rome: Istituto per la collaborazione culturale, 1962), esp. ch. 1.

major break not in 1545 or 1563 but in 1600, when the typically Counter Reformation forms of religious sentiment suddenly yielded to those of the Baroque. Historians of economics have pointed to two high points, the first one in the 1480's, followed by the disastrous effects of the foreign invasions, and the second in the 1580's, followed by the great crash of the 1620's and the long depression of the rest of the seventeenth century.[28]

All these proposals have one important thesis in common: that Italian culture, however it is defined or categorized, did not suddenly lose its vitality or abandon its customary forms of expression in the 1530's, and that the study of the Quattrocento cannot be complete unless it is continued well on into the Cinquecento. Each of these proposals, moreover, provides a far more meaningful framework than the traditional chronology for the particular kinds of phenomena it refers to. What remains now to be done is to overcome the disparity between the different proposals—to bring them together, that is, into a single synthesis covering not only each of the disciplines separately, but also all of them together. Some effort has already been made in this direction, in spite of the airtight barriers that academic institutions often erect—and that academic writers all too willingly observe—between specialized fields of historiography. Riccardo Scrivano, for instance, in the brilliant introduction to his *Il manierismo nella letteratura del Cinquecento (Mannerism in the Literature of the Sixteenth Century)*,[29] has suggested that philosophy, politics, and religion follow a pattern of development very similar to the one he has described in detail for poetry and prose. And the first three papers presented at a conference of the Accademia dei Lincei in 1960 attempted to establish an appropriate terminology.[30]

Still, the effort has just begun. And one of the chief purposes of

[28] See Ruggiero Romano, "Una crisi economica: 1619–1622," *Rivista storica italiana*, LXXIV (1962), 480 ff.

[29] Padua: Liviana, 1959. Note also the introduction to his *Cinquecento minore* (Bologna: Zanichelli, 1966) and his "La discussione sul manierismo," *La rassegna della letteratura italiana*, LXVII (1963), 200–31.

[30] *Manierismo, barocco, rococo: concetti e termini*, Problemi attuali di scienza e di cultura, No. 52 (Rome: Accademia Nazionale dei Lincei, 1962).

his anthology is to contribute to a further clarification of this historical problem. It seeks to do so, firstly, by providing those historians who might otherwise be impeded by the difficulties of another language or by the inaccessibility of the relevant scholarly journals with some working hypotheses and with a sampling of recent monographic research. It seeks to do so, secondly, by providing college students with a point of view not ordinarily presented in the standard textbooks. And since students are often less inhibited than their teachers about drawing the general out of the particular, it appeals to them for insights and suggestions that may surpass the imagination of cautious specialists.

A word of warning, however. This anthology does not pretend to be complete in itself. If it is used in a college course on the Renaissance, it should be read along with such source materials as are readily available in English, e.g. Benvenuto Cellini's *Autobiography* (Dolphin), Giovanni Della Casa's *Galateo* (Penguin), Giordano Bruno's *Cause, Principle, and Unity* (New World), and Galileo's *Discoveries and Opinions* (Anchor). It also should be read along with such well-known essays as Friedlaender's *Mannerism and Anti-Mannerism* (Schocken), Kristeller's *Eight Philosophers of the Italian Renaissance* (Stanford), and Ludovico Geymonat's *Life of Galileo* (McGraw-Hill), all of which regard subjects that have, as a consequence, been excluded from this anthology.

But even with this extra reading, the whole of the sixteenth century will still be far more adequately portrayed. In selecting the following articles, I have adopted several different, and often conflicting, criteria. I have sought to strike a balance between older and younger, between well-known and "promising" scholars. I have looked for novelty of approach, profundity of erudition, and originality in documentation. I have insisted upon such literary qualities as conciseness and such purely editorial qualities as brevity. I have been limited by the necessity of keeping within the bounds of a single manageable volume. Finally, I have attempted to cover a wide diversity of specialized disciplines and of geographical areas.

Obviously I have more frequently failed than succeeded in

finding articles that correspond to all these criteria. Thus such important contributors to late Renaissance scholarship as Riccardo Scrivano, Bruno Migliorini, Gaetano Cozzi, and Marino Berengo are not included. Such important subjects as antiquarianism, poetics, natural science, and the Catholic Reform are barely mentioned. And such important places as Piedmont, Genoa, Modena, and Sicily are all but ignored. These omissions are not entirely to be blamed upon me. True, my patience did run out somewhat before I had finished paging through every *Festschrift*, every collection of essays, and every issue of every periodical that might possibly have contained something of relevance. But I am convinced that in most cases the appropriate article simply has not yet been written. And I am certain that within ten years whatever I have unwittingly overlooked will be as much in need of revision as what I have been fortunate enough to discover.

One further word of warning to those who may be doing research in this field: they should use the versions here presented only as a guide to, not as a substitute for, the original texts. Most of the articles were originally written for a professional audience. In preparing them for a nonprofessional audience, I have taken considerable liberty in abbreviating, expanding, paraphrasing, or annotating whatever I thought might otherwise not be entirely clear. I have done so, however, with the consent—sometimes tacit, but usually explicit—of all the authors who are still alive. All the passages that are mine alone, and for which I assume the total responsibility, have been placed within brackets.

PART ONE

The Problem of
Periodization

1 A Working Hypothesis: The Crisis of Italy in the Cinquecento and the Bond Between the Renaissance and the Risorgimento[1]

BENEDETTO CROCE

Benedetto Croce (1866–1952) is too well known as a philosopher in the English-speaking world to require an introduction. He is somewhat less known as a historian, since most of his historical works, and in particular the two of them most pertinent to this anthology, have never been translated, namely, the *Storia di Napoli* (*History of Naples*) and the *Storia dell'età barocca in Italia* (*History of the Age of the Baroque in Italy*). These two works have exerted a wide influence on the study of late Renaissance Italian culture. The principal theses are presented in condensed form—and without the usual explanation of Croce's philosophy of history, which it takes for granted—in this short essay of 1939.

THE causal or deterministic method is of as little help in dealing with the historical problem of the decline and revival of Italy [as it is in dealing with any other problem]; and we will do well to abandon it. This method attempts to connect events with this or that specific "fact"—with a "fact," that is, which, understood in its material sense, is actually incapable either of generating or of giving a rational explanation of reality. We must instead keep solely to the consideration of the living process of history. And this process is a spiritual one, in which explanations for a historical fact must be deduced from the fact itself [rather than from some other fact supposedly connected with it].[2]

[1] "La crisi italiana del Cinquecento e il legame del Rinascimento col Risorgimento," *La critica: Rivista di letteratura, storia e filosofia*, XXXVII (1939), 401–11. Recently reprinted by Armando Saitta in *Antologia di critica storica*, 3rd edn. (Bari: Laterza, 1959), pp. 494–508. Translated by the editor.

[2] [This in a nutshell is the theory of history Croce proposed in his *Teoria e*

A good number of "causes" [in the sense of a concatenation of "facts" in a necessary relationship] have been brought forth to "explain" the crisis of the Cinquecento; and many of them are still generally accepted today. The first of these "causes," as everyone knows, is usually identified with the failure of Italy to form itself into a unified state, one which might have taken its place among the other great states that arose and were consolidated [in other parts of Europe] at the time. The trouble with this thesis is its assumption, for example, that the formation of Spain into a large and very powerful state should have saved it from the crisis and internal decadence [which in fact took place in the following century], or that the circumstance of being small states should have prevented the Swiss Confederation and the Netherlands from making the contribution they actually did to the civil and religious revival of Europe. It fails to explain how a divided Germany managed to realize the religious Reformation in the sixteenth century and to carry European thought to new heights in the eighteenth. It is as if the unity or multiplicity of political centers were a "fact" basic to all others; whereas such phenomena really proceed rather from the expediency of adopting one or the other [constitutional] form, each of which, according to circumstances, may be more suitable and beneficial to civil life and human progress than the other. Unity, first in a federative and then in a centralized form, was felt in the nineteenth century to be the single

---

storia della storiografia (Bari: G. Laterza, 1917) and which is well known to readers of the English translation, *Theory and History of Historiography.* It may even be clear to those readers who know a bit of Hegel or Marx, in spite of differences in terminology. He is arguing against the positivistic school of historiography and against the attempt to apply in history the methods and assumptions of the natural sciences. By eliminating from the process of apprehension the logical or even temporal distinction between an object apprehended in itself and the generalizations or abstractions made about it in the mind, he ends up identifying "fact apprehended" and "explanation," and thus rules out a causal connection (in the scientific sense of one thing determining another) between individual moments or occurrences in history. Readers who do not want to be bothered with the niceties of the theory will at least see how it works in practice in the following pages; and I have occasionally elaborated on the original within brackets in order to help them out.]

necessary condition for liberty and civil life; and it was therefore tenaciously pursued and finally attained. In the sixteenth century, however, this idea [of unity] was not a driving force and had no power of moral inspiration.

The same observation can be made of the other "cause" often adduced to explain the decline, namely, the loss of national independence and the establishment either of foreign domination or of foreign hegemony. For the creation of a plurinational state, and even the subjection of several states to a foreign one, can be, according to circumstances, either useful or harmful. If Italy had really felt its subjection at the time to have been harmful, offensive, and unbearable, it would have turned against its oppressor. Thus did the Netherlands turn against the same power that ruled there as in Italy, and thus did Italy itself when the dominating power turned out to be the Austria of the Restoration.[3] These two "causal" explanations, though historically empty, were prompted by the passions of the Risorgimento, passions [that led historians] to ignore the real conditions [of life] of the leading men[4] of the Cinquecento, to reweave the events of the time into romances, dramas, and poems that served largely as a means of sketching out their own ideals, and to compose histories in the same manner.

The same kind of mythmaking is evident as well in the other "cause" usually placed beside the ones already mentioned: the loss of liberty in Cinquecento Italy consequent to the end of the medieval communal governments—and particularly of the most remarkable of them, the Florentine Republic. Hence the many other famous romances and tragedies, as well as histories, of Guerrazzi, D'Azeglio, Niccolini—to mention but a few—that were written in accordance with that theme.[5] Without doubt the

[3] [The Treaty of Vienna in 1815 awarded Lombardy and Venice to the Austrian empire, which was thus in a position to interfere in the affairs of most of the other states of the peninsula.]

[4] [*Spirito*—man in the sense of mind or spirit. I translate "spirit" later on when it makes sense, but the word is not as often used in English to denote "leading men" in this sense as it is in Italian.]

[5] [Francesco Domenico Guerrazzi (1804–73), best known for his *Beatrice Cenci*. The Piedmontese poet, novelist, and statesman Massimo D'Azeglio

question of liberty is an essential one in the life of a people, as well as in the forming of a historical judgment of a people. But what kind of liberty is meant? Is it that liberty which is intrinsic to the moral soul, which continuously varies the form it has at one moment and creates new ones at the next, and which in its political embodiment changes with the changing conditions of time and place?

In the Cinquecento liberty in its communal or medieval sense was no longer a problem of political actuality. This kind of liberty had already been overcome during the two preceding centuries by either open or disguised *signorie*;[6] and it only survived here and there in certain institutions and customs which, having lost the spirit they had once had, and having failed to engender a new spirit in its place, were incapable of further development. Certainly not all the friends and defenders of the old liberty merited the pessimistic judgment of Guicciardini and Vettori,[7] according to whom what they loved was not to live in freedom, but to keep their hands in public affairs for their own personal profit and ambition. There were among them men of generous, noble character, who felt the moral beauty of liberty and sought it disinterestedly. But such character has not been wanting even in periods of the most docile servitude—among the admirers of the

---

(1798–1866), one of the most ardent proponents of the House of Savoy in the early days of the Risorgimento, wrote among other things, *Ettore Fieramosca* and *La Lega lombarda*. The Tuscan Giambattista Niccolini (1782–1861) wrote a tragedy (1847) based on the life of the Florentine banker Filippo Strozzi, who committed suicide while a prisoner in the fortress of Florence in 1538.]

[6] [I keep the original *signorie* to denote the specific kind of political regime in many Italian city-states from the fourteenth century onward in which the constitution remained officially republican but in which all effective power was concentrated in the hands of one man or family. Neither the English terms "monarchy" and "dictatorship" nor the French equivalent *seigneurie* has this specific connotation.]

[7] [Francesco Guicciardini is too well known to need identification. Francesco (not Pier, the philologian) Vettori (1474–1539), historian and statesman, was one of his closest friends and with him one of the artificers of the new regime in Florence. See Louis Passy, *Un ami de Machiavel* (Paris, 1913).]

[great] personages of Greco-Roman history, for instance, and of doubtfully historical but sublimely ideal figures like Harmodius and Brutus. A faith capable of action, a faith that grasps reality, or those parts of reality that in given circumstances can be grasped, and a faith that imposes its own thought and its own will on what it grasps—such a faith is not apparent in the actions of any of these men of noble character. It is not apparent even in the more extreme militants of Florentine liberty, all of whom, as is clear from their political schemes and from the reasons they gave in writing for their schemes, were well disposed toward oligarchical regimes and conservative republics on the model of Venice. And the governments that actually were established according to this model in Lucca and Genoa rapidly retreated into immobility and inertia.[8] All, or almost all, of them, even the most noble and most intelligent—Segni, Varchi, Adriani, Jacopo Nardi—ended by being reconciled to Cosimo de' Medici[9] and by accepting the new [monarchical] state as the best, or least bad, alternative, now that all their hopes [for the restoration of the Republic] had been shattered.

The last bitter resistance of the Florentine Republic and then its fall[10] never became a sacred memory [among those who survived it] and never a pledge for a return of liberty in the future. In Italy,

[8] [See now Franco Gaeta, "Alcune considerazioni sul mito di Venezia," *Bibliothèque d'humanisme et renaissance*, XXIII (1961), and above all Marino Berengo, *Nobili e mercanti nella Lucca nel Cinquecento* (Turin: Einaudi, 1965).]

[9] [Bernardo Segni (1504–58), Benedetto Varchi (1503–65), and Jacopo Nardi (ca. 1476–1563) were all authors of histories of Florence written in the 1540's and 1550's. That of Giambattista Adriani (1513–79), published by his son Marcello the year after his death, does not, perhaps, belong strictly to this group, for it seeks above all to demonstrate the historical necessity of the new regime and has none of the nostalgia that creeps in even among the pages of Varchi. Cosimo de' Medici (1519–74) was elected "head of the Florentine Republic" in 1537, after the murder of the last member of the direct line of the family. Thanks to imperial help, and thanks to his own political sagacity, he soon became the absolute ruler as duke of Florence and then, after 1569, as grand duke of Tuscany.]

[10] [The republican regime was re-established upon the expulsion of the Medici following the Sack of Rome in 1527 and was abolished again after a long siege by imperial and papal forces in 1530.]

as Segni tells us, the agitations and protests of the banished Florentines in the presence of Charles V at Naples[11] occasioned laughter
and amusement. Almost the same thing occurred when Perugia,
still remembering its ancient republican spirit, took up arms against
the Pope.[12] The history of the medieval communes failed to evoke
any kind of poetic nostalgia. Indeed, it was more often viewed
with commiseration, if not covered with abuse; and it ended up,
in the following century, by becoming a favorite subject for comic
and burlesque poets.[13] The historians, even those who as citizens
had participated in the defense of the Florentine Republic, did not
know how to present the vicissitudes of liberty in Florence other
than in its negative aspect, as a series of unsuccessful tests of a
liberty that had never really been possessed or enjoyed.

A fourth "cause" proposed to explain the crisis is based on the
argument often spun out by the overly naïve admirers of the
histories of foreign [non-Italian] countries. Since those nations
most vigorous in power and civilization in modern Europe—so
the argument runs—are those which at the very beginning embraced the doctrines of Luther and Calvin, these doctrines should
have been adopted in Italy as well. And that Italy failed to adopt
them, or that it was prevented from doing so, must be regarded as
a great calamity.

Certainly the phenomenon of religious reform also is a vital and
essential one in the course of history.[14] Yet it is not one that can be
reduced to a [single] model or to a kind of *gradus* or *cursus* that
must necessarily be traversed. The paths of religious renewal are
many; and, as it happened, the particular kind of renewal in ques-

11 [But Varchi gives a much more thorough account of the audience accorded
to the Florentine exiles, and especially to their chief spokesman, Jacopo Nardi
(above, n. 8), just after the emperor's return from the Tunisian campaign in
1535.]

12 [Against Pope Paul III in 1541, because of a tax he had levied in defiance
of treaties and customs (see below, ch. 12). Ironically, it was Cosimo de'
Medici who backed up the rebels, not the exiled republicans.]

13 [The best known of which is, of course, Alessandro Tassoni's *La secchia
rapita*, though it is also a parody of Torquato Tasso (see below, ch. 5).]

14 [Croce's word *punto* has too many special overtones to be rendered simply
in English, and I have resorted to a circumlocution.]

tion did not correspond well to the intellectual and cultural level to which Italy had already risen. Indeed, it was disdained by most of the elevated and the most liberal spirits [of the time]—Giordano Bruno being the most noteworthy example.[15]

The Renaissance had exalted earthly life and had come to regard with a kind of indifference that heaven to which the Middle Ages had so long directed its eyes. But this does not mean that it was a nonreligious movement. It was religious, although rational; and indeed it was religious just because it was *seriously* rational. For reason is the eternal principle (as it may be opportune to remember these days) that rules and governs the life of man and leads it on to ever higher stages. Religions themselves, in their vital elements, positive aspects, and fruitful concepts, are nothing more than the light of reason operating in mythical forms. And the light of reason gradually wears down the forms of religion until it can shine forth in a form all its own.[16] Even though in the beginning the Renaissance did not perpetrate a revolutionary incursion into the sphere that is usually considered specifically religious, it nevertheless could not halt its own progress and relax into a sort of detachment and indifference. In carrying on the hard work of reason, it had necessarily to embrace the problems reason posed and, in time, the other problems related to them—those of the moral conscience, for instance, of freedom, of politics, of history, and, finally, of all the ways in which the Divine operates and realizes itself in this world.

All these problems were thus implicit in the Renaissance; and they were among the first to be proposed by the Reformation.[17] That Italy, more than any other country in Europe, found itself close to this transition from Renaissance rationalism to a rational religious reform is proved by the way in which it responded to the ideas of the Reformation. For when these ideas began arriving

[15] [On Bruno, see below, ch. 11.]

[16] [Here in a word is the essence of Croce's theory of historical change.]

[17] [The religious element in Renaissance humanism has been much more deeply studied since Croce wrote these lines, which must be appreciated in terms of their opposition to the then prevalent thesis of Burckhardt. See now Carlo Angeleri, *Il problema religioso del Rinascimento* (Florence: Le Monnier, 1952).]

from Luther in Germany or from mysticism under Erasmian influence in Spain,[18] they were embraced chiefly in humanistic circles and in educated society. The thesis is even more strongly confirmed by the radical turn the ideas took once they were accepted—by their running, from negation to negation, to the point where they denied[19] not only the Catholic Church but also all the myths of Christianity—the divinity of Jesus, the Trinity, the immortality of the soul, and so on. The Italian adherents of the Reformation who went into exile in Protestant countries very often awakened astonishment, disquiet, and suspicion by their overlogical rationalism. It was murmured that "when Italians start being displeased with the Church of Rome, they can no longer be pleased by any religion at all." They were among the most freethinking and fiery innovators in the countries [they settled in]. It was from them that the idea of natural religion received its first impulse and nourishment. And it was they who first proposed the other idea, closely connected with it, of tolerance, the precursor of what was later to mature as the "religion of reason."

Why did this movement, so pregnant with the future, become stifled in Italy? Why were ideas dispersed as soon as they were formulated? Why did the Italian spirit lose its impetus and enthusiasm? Why did it fall back on itself, give up [its ideals], and submit obediently to the Roman Church? Why did it become occupied with small things and amused with mere pastimes? And why did it sink into the general torpor that can be observed everywhere in the second half of the Cinquecento—in the new attitude toward life, literature, and thought that was so different from the still agile and active attitude of the early Cinquecento? To respond to such a "why" would be to go back to figuring out lists of "causes"—just the sort of thing we have shown to be empty of

[18] [A phenomenon that is described at length by Marcel Bataillon in *Érasme et l'Espagne* (Paris: E. Droz, 1937).]

[19] [I put "denied" instead of Croce's "destroyed" because it makes more sense in this context. On the Italian heretics, whom Croce credits with having alone borne the heritage of the Renaissance, see below, ch. 8.]

results. Or else it would lead to repeating in the form of an answer the statement of the fact contained in the question itself—as when it is stated that the enterprise failed because it was premature, or because it lacked the force required for its execution, or because it met with unfavorable conditions. Such is the case, for example, with the thesis that the Renaissance was a movement of aristocratic rather than of popular character, and that therefore the religious movement it engendered was very little, if at all, diffused among the people as a whole. Such also is the case with the thesis that the Renaissance allowed the seeds of the *Renovatio* and of the interior freedom that came to it from the Middle Ages to dry up and degenerate into purely exterior formalism.

History fulfills its function by ascertaining and qualifying, that is to say, by knowing what happened[20]—which is certainly not an easy undertaking; and it must know how to refrain from getting involved in fruitless questions. What has been stated above defines what the crisis and decadence of the Cinquecento truly consisted of: a halt in development, a suspension of the process of investigating more deeply the rationality that had already been asserted, a failure to accept generally the ideas and suggestions issuing from the Evangelical and Pauline elements of the Reformation and to transform and purify them in the way that several Italians had already begun to do. The morally rigid and ascetic attempt of Savonarola [at reform][21] did not touch dogma and orthodoxy; and even less did it take into account the level which Italian civilization had attained and from which it could no longer retreat now that previous levels had been superseded. Francesco Burlamacchi conceived of an alliance, in Tuscany, of the new religious movement with that of [traditional] liberty; but he conceived of it politically,

---

[20] [Croce's terms are *accertare, qualificare,* and *conoscere,* which I translate here literally because of their importance as technical terms in his epistemological system.]

[21] [Girolamo Savonarola, the preacher, prophet, and unofficial political leader of Florence from 1495 to 1498, about whom there still today rage theological as well as historical polemics. Donald Weinstein and Giorgio Spini, among others, have taken exception to Croce's thesis of a complete opposition between Savonarola and Florentine Renaissance humanism.]

as an alliance of two political forces, and he lacked the spirit of a true reformer.[22] Later on Paolo Sarpi, an ardent opponent of the Roman Curia, did not carry out, nor even wish to carry out, the great move in Venice[23]—though such a move would by then have been untimely, now that the heroic and virile age of early Protestantism was at an end.

Nevertheless, the direction implicit in the Italian Renaissance was so logically necessary that in the long run European civilization ended by adopting and following it. Such can be observed in the history of the century and a half from the Evangelical revolution of the first half of the sixteenth century to the new rationalism of the second half of the seventeenth. For the operating and driving force behind the new rationalism was still the same rational principle that the Renaissance had affirmed against the transcendental principle of the Middle Ages. It preserved the greatest and most profoundly rational accomplishment of the Reformation: the restoration of the authority of the moral conscience against the sacramentalism and casuistry of the Catholic Church. It therefore slowly rid Protestantism of the residue of medieval archaisms and of the irrational attachment to "the Book" (that is, the Bible), until it turned it into a kind of "enlightened" theology. It similarly converted the mythical concepts of Predestination, the Incarnation, and the Trinity into purely philosophical questions. It thus countered the tendencies that might have resulted in a return to ascetic rigorism. And it gave approval and sanction to a healthy economic and political life and to the cult[24] of letters and the sciences—to the expressions and instruments, that is, of civilization. Sometimes, instead of working inside the circle of religion itself, the new rationalism made use of the radical opposition to all

---

[22] [Burlamacchi was a patrician of Lucca, whose fantastic scheme, communicated only to one or two intimates before it was discovered by an agent o- Cosimo de' Medici in 1546, has most recently been discussed by Berengo in the book cited above in n. 8.]

[23] [On Sarpi, see below, ch. 15.]

[24] [Croce uses *culto*, which has the same religious significance that "cult" does in English, and not "cultivation," which might be more appropriate to the sense of the passage.]

dogma and superstition. With the help of Antitrinitarianism, Arminianism, and Socinianism,[25] with the help of the idea of natural religion, natural rights, and the social contract, rationalism asserted new intellectual positions; and it hastened, by the very contrasts of its extreme intellectualism, the elevation and intensification of the process of reason. In the more properly political field it reinforced the idea of the monarchical state against the various remnants of medieval feudalism and particularism; and in the end it led to the creation of a state that was tolerant in matters of religion. Even the beginnings of political Liberalism[26] came from the demands for freedom of thought and of its public expression, that is to say, from the supreme value accorded to the life of truth in the life of human civilization.

The course of European history here outlined did not unfold rapidly and in a straight line, but rather with many complications and exhausting detours. For it was affected by the intrusion of people culturally less advanced than sixteenth-century Italians and by long wars and revolutions. Italy to a certain extent remained apart from this process. Or rather it participated only through the last heirs and representatives of its former Renaissance—through those of its sons who escaped corruption by fleeing to Protestant lands and through their descendants who preserved the name and the memories of the Renaissance. Often thereafter Italy was to look upon that great, fervid course of history in progress elsewhere in Europe—but always as an alien spectator; and it had

---

[25] [All doctrines of the radical reformation, the leadership of which Croce has attributed to the Italian exiles. "Socinianism" derives from Fausto and Lelio Sozzini of Siena, who eventually founded the "Antitrinitarian" Church in Poland (see most recently *Italian Reformation Studies in Honor of Laelius Socinus*, ed. John A. Tedeschi [Florence: Le Monnier, 1965]). It became particularly important in the Netherlands in the late seventeenth and early eighteenth centuries and passed to England and America with the name "Unitarianism." "Arminianism" derives from the Dutch reformer Jacobus Arminius (1560–1609), who, though within the Calvinist tradition, rejected Calvin's formulation of the doctrine of Predestination.]

[26] [Croce means the Liberalism peculiar to the nineteenth century, so I capitalize the word to distinguish it from a mere adherence to the "process of liberty" he has been outlining in the preceding centuries.]

to say with a sigh, as Manzoni's verse goes, "I was not there."[27]

That century and a half thus acquired and still retains, in our history books, the designation of "The Decadence of Italy." The designation deserves to be kept, at least in the empirical and cautious use one must make of the concept "decadence," since the absence or exhaustion of an ideal is always a sign of what we call decadence. An ideal is certainly not just any image or idea for which one fights and dies; for if that were the case, fantasy, intoxication, and blind passion could function in place of it. Rather it is an essential, effective, and efficacious moral ideal, an ideal of the enlargement of life and consequently of liberty—the only thing capable of stirring up human forces. The historian, as a moral man, must listen for the sound of liberty in the various historical situations [he investigates] and make note of it. He must not allow himself to be taken in by the mere mirage of liberty or by the illiberality that marks its end. In the last centuries of the Roman empire [for instance], liberty, or spiritual progress, belonged to the sect that came from Galilee. It did not belong to the emperors or high officials who governed the state, nor to the Romans of Stoic leanings who dreamed of the old forms of Republican Rome and who still plotted—and killed themselves and let themselves be killed—for their restoration. In Italy of the Counter Reformation and Spanish domination, similarly, liberty and spiritual progress did not belong to the brave Italian soldiers and captains who fought for the king of Spain on all the battlefields of Europe, Africa, and America, nor to the obedient and zealous clergy who stood up against heresy. Many of them, it is true, were admirable and heroic, at least personally and formally, when they fell as martyrs and sacrificed themselves with pure hearts on behalf of their faith or their oaths of fidelity. But they were representatives of the past, not the creators of the future. This period was thus in Italy one of decadence. There were, if any, only a few scattered and confused apostles of the future amid the many tenacious defenders of the past.

[27] [The poet, novelist, and moralist Alessandro Manzoni, best known in the English-speaking world for his great classic *The Betrothed* (*I promessi sposi*).]

Once the last, languid voices that echoed through the schemes and writings of the surviving Florentine republicans had at last died away, there was not a sound to be heard [in all Italy] of any practical political thinking worthy of the name. Its place could not be taken by the memoranda, the pamphlets, and the books composed on behalf of the Church or of the princes and oligarchs; for this literature lacked an ideal focal point and did nothing but defend individual political interests with no regard for their more general implications. Nor could its place be taken by the generic invocations of the name of Italy, nor by the exhortations to liberate her from foreigners and make her arise great and glorious once again. Although these writings are even today admired and praised by men of letters, they are merely literary in nature and have nothing to do with real political thought, which is concrete political action *per se*.[28] The art of forming political precepts[29] did not go beyond advice on how to be astute; and the advice was no longer even adorned, as it had been in Machiavelli, by the poetic vision of the astute and violent man who drives out the foreigners and gathers Italy into a powerful state. The citizen gave way to the courtier; the desire to command and govern gave way to service for private profit; and prudence accompanied by shrewdness and deceit became a supreme virtue. A great number of handbooks were printed *De re aulica*—"Of Courtly Affairs"—and on *How to Serve at Court*. Historiography, which Machiavelli had directed away from the narration of wars and political manipulations to that of internal struggles, became military and diplomatic once again, now that those struggles had been brought to a halt. Very rarely did the ray of an ideal shine forth from the pages of the historians and of the writers of political treatises. Except for an occasional expression of regret or aspiration, except for a word of indignation or of

[28] [Like perception and generalization, true thought is for Croce inseparable from action. Hence his negation above of Utopianism as a form of political thought and his refusal to admit mere abstractions, devoid of concrete manifestations, as positive elements worthy of a historian's attention.]

[29] [*Precettistica* is an Italian historical term to describe this phenomenon so characteristic of the Seicento (like *Trattatisti*—see below, ch. 4) that has no equivalent in English.]

revulsion, which could not completely be blotted out, the nearest thing to an ideal was the *City of the Sun* of Tommaso Campanella,[30] which was really only the Utopia of a solitary man.

It is not surprising, then, that the histories written about Italian life during these centuries take the form of accounts or incidents of meanness, stupidity, sorrow, and horror, rather poorly relieved on occasions by a laugh of derision or a smile of irony. But the sole purpose of history is to describe and make understandable the works that humanity creates—institutions, sciences, systems, poetry: the positive, in other words, rather than the negative, what is done rather than what is undone, what is built rather than an accumulation of ruins. If an age offers nothing positive and constructive, it might just as well go unrecorded, in accordance with the old maxim that where nothing exists, the king loses his rights.

And yet even in ages of decadence the force of the ideal does not completely fail. It flashes and flickers in isolated individuals; and even though it cannot animate the whole, it may still operate in one or another isolated segment of life, preserving the acquisitions already made, amplifying others, accomplishing the works of truth and goodness, and preparing the elements of a future epoch in which it can at last reanimate the whole and in which general progress can again be underway. These operations [of the ideal] scattered among single segments [of a nation's total life] are exposed, it is true, to the risk of being wrecked and then dragged away in the general decadence that dominates the period. By concealing and maintaining themselves, on the other hand, they exercise a curative action, in the same manner that the healthy parts of an organism may indeed contract the malady of the infected parts, but may also contribute slowly to their cure. Their salutary power is attested by the obscure suspicions they occasionally arouse (like Caesar's suspicion of the thin and pallid Cassius), and by the threats, hostility, and repressive attacks leveled against what seems to be merely out of the ordinary and innocuous.

It is from this point of view that the period of Italian decadence must be investigated. And it was this method I endeavored to

[30] [On Campanella (1568–1639) and the Utopians, see below, ch. 6.]

follow in writing my *History of the Baroque Age*. The work aroused critical reservations (which I welcomed as praise) because I had given prominence not to what was most typical of the seventeenth century but rather to the attitudes and actions that anticipated the eighteenth and nineteenth centuries. I thus showed that Renaissance rationalism was preserved and carried forward in several areas—most noticeably in the physical and natural sciences, but also in certain phases of the speculation regarding the modes of the human spirit and the practice of politics, modes which were confirmed in their autonomy with respect to morality and freed from the imprint of perversity. I found it also in those theories of poetry and art in which new concepts of fantasy and taste were worked out. And I found it in the study of the humanities, in the appreciation and exaltation of Greek and Roman history and of the heroes of antiquity, which the Jesuits had to incorporate into their *Ratio studiorum*[31] when they realized the impossibility of pushing back current ways of life, even those of the Church, into the mold of medieval institutions and customs. The principal thread had been broken. But many lesser ones continued to be spun out, even though they remained separated from one another and hanging inertly without any prospect of eventually being brought together.

In practical matters, similarly, it can be shown that the monarchies and principalities often were capable of rationally planned and executed works of a civic nature, such as the unification and equalization of laws and customs, the demotion of an exhausted baronage to the level of a court aristocracy, and the promotion of a [new] class of industrious and intelligent men, who were already preparing, as its agents and administrators, to become the directors of the state in the following century.[32] For what is called

[31] [The *Ratio studiorum* is the basic constitution of the Jesuit educational system. It was officially adopted by the Society in 1599.]

[32] [Croce's reference is to the class of jurists and lawyers that actually was much more prominent in the kingdom of Naples than in the other states of Italy. Several different views of its function are current among historians today. The most recent is that of Salvo Mastellone, *Pensiero politico e vita culturale a Napoli* (Florence and Messina: D'Anna, 1965).]

"capability" cannot be dispensed with. And once it has been put to work, it must eventually be given a place of prominence and an opening to greater prospects in the future.

Yet from the middle of the Cinquecento up to about the close of the Seicento it is obvious that Italy was not truly alive. It lacked, that is, an elevated spiritual life, and its various spiritual forces were not drawn toward any sort of light shining in the distance nor inspired by a hope or confidence of reaching a higher goal. Italian society at the time was dominated by an otherworldly concept. It was a concept that encouraged obedience to ecclesiastical authority and kept the faithful intent in their devotional practices upon the image of dissolution and death and preoccupied solely with the salvation of their souls. The consequence was a deep pessimism. So deep was this pessimism, indeed, that not even that prodigious speculative genius who emerged from Seicento culture, one who more than any other gathered together the multiple traditions of the Renaissance and the fruits of the intense toil of the new age and who transformed them by the application of his own original concepts of the spirit and history of men— not even Giambattista Vico[33] could completely shake it off. Vico saw, or caught glimpses of, what the nineteenth century was eventually to affirm. But he did not grasp the idea of a humanity perpetually growing on itself. He meditated profoundly upon the course of history, and he came to understand its nature as a perpetual rhythm of the spirit. But he did not go on to grasp the complement of his thesis—the unicity[34] of the historical process, that is, and the element of progress inherent in it. He did not even recognize the unicity of a phenomenon

[33] [Vico (1668–1744), who provided Croce himself with some of his more important philosophical ideas, was indeed much more appreciated in the nineteenth century than in his own times. His Autobiography (Cornell) and his most famous La scienze nuove (The New Science, tr. T. G. Bergin and M. H. Fisch [Cornell University Press, 1948]) are available in English translation. For some more recent historical judgments of Vico, see Nicola Badaloni, Introduzione a G. B. Vico (Milan: Feltrinelli, 1961).]

[34] [Croce's term unicità is a technical one, and I leave to the reader the task of figuring out the meaning etymologically.]

like Christianity, even though he professed himself a Catholic.

Alongside the greatness of Giambattista Vico in the field of the intellect, the figure of his contemporary, Pietro Giannone,[35] is certainly a less distinguished one. But while Vico still represents at its highest degree the specific work of the philosophy that carried on the intellectual work of the Renaissance, Giannone is the voice of an Italy that was fashioning a whole new soul, an Italy that was renewing the moral spirit of a former age and taking up its work once again. Italy took up the work of the Renaissance, indeed, not at the level at which it had been interrupted, but at the level at which it was now accessible after the Wars of Religion—at a moment in its development, that is, in which it breathed forth the new principle of tolerance, and in which it affirmed the rationalism that had ripened in Descartes and the other philosophers of the seventeenth century and that had benefited from the contributions of the last great Italian thinkers, such as Bruno and Campanella. The occasion and the point of attack was offered Giannone by the conflict of a modern state with the persistent usurpations and the unyielding claims of the Church of Rome. The absolute monarchies of the Cinquecento had at first been the objects of terror rather than reverence. But subsequently the authors of political treatises and of eulogies of "good princes" had come to distinguish them as the very opposite of tyranny. And in the course of time they did in fact become the instruments of secularism, of progress, and, indirectly, of liberty—of that liberty which men a century and a half earlier had vainly imagined might be restored and embalmed in medieval republican forms. Toward this end Giannone, having observed how much had been accomplished by the French monarchy, took as his supporting ideal the Austrian dynasty that had succeeded the Spanish on the throne of Naples. And he was fired by the most vivid hopes for the rapid realization

---

[35] [Giannone (1676–1748) was a Neapolitan jurist and historian, whose *Triregno* is available in a modern edition (Bari: Laterza, 1940) and whose still more famous *Storia civile* was quickly translated into English as a bit of anti-Catholic propaganda. Sergio Bertelli has recently (1960) republished his *Autobiografia* in a Feltrinelli paperback edition (U.E. 297).]

of this end when Naples again acquired a king of its own, Charles of Bourbon.[36]

The author of the *Storia civile* (*Civil History*) was also the author of the *Triregno*. And fate decreed that the exile he shared with the Italian Reformers of the Cinquecento (as he later shared the martyrdom that awaited him in his long confinement and death in prison) be passed in Geneva—that it be passed in the very place where so many memories remained of the thought, the efforts, and the work of his precursors. In Geneva still lived, among other families, the descendants of Francesco Burlamacchi, who had themselves gradually corrected and elaborated their ancestor's project and who, instead of excogitating political schemes for the liberation of Italy, as he had done, had embarked upon the long, difficult road to the same liberty: religious renewal. In Geneva, similarly, a century later another descendant of the exiles, Sismondi,[37] was to bring back to the memory and the hearts of Italians, in a famous book of history, the glories of the liberty of their [medieval] communes; and he was to remind them of the fate that had overcome liberty in the Cinquecento and of the subsequent collapse of the strength and civilization of Italy during the Counter Reformation. In this way he stung them by tacit reproaches and encouraged them to push further on the Risorgimento that was already underway.

This "Risorgimento," or resurgence, thus began at the time of Giannone. And it began, though under different forms, all over Italy, not just in that part of Italy where Giannone had been born.

[36] [Austrian forces conquered Naples in 1707, during the War of the Spanish Succession, and the kingdom was awarded to Emperor Charles VI at the Peace of Utrecht in 1713. Charles (Carlo di Borbone, as he is known in Italy), son of the king of Spain, reconquered it in 1734 during the War of the Polish Succession, and resided there as king until he was called to Madrid to succeed his father in 1759. His accession marked the beginning of a serious effort at reforming the political and economic structure of the kingdom.]

[37] [Jean Charles Léonard de Sismondi (Simonde) (1773–1842), author of, among other books, *A History of the Italian Republics*, first published between 1807 and 1818. On the importance of Geneva in Italian history, see the volume of collected essays entitled *Ginevra e l'Italia*, ed. Delio Cantimori *et al.* (Florence: Sansoni, 1959).]

Once underway, the process [of historical development] was never again to be interrupted. As a consequence, Italy passed through all the progressive stages marked by the other regions of Europe, from which she was no longer divided: first anti-papal and secular monarchies, then enlightened and reforming monarchies, and finally Jacobin and democratic republics. Italy also experienced thereafter the demands for liberal constitutions and the struggles against the foreign power that sought to restrain her within the old ones, which the new Ultramontanism[38] had rendered worse than ever. And finally, with the triumph of the concepts of Liberalism, Italy arrived at one of those ideal conclusions that it is impossible to surpass. Nor, indeed, were they surpassed, for these are conclusions that admit, and indeed provide the formulas for, an infinity of innovation, development, and advance. The complications in which the Liberal movement gets entangled,[39] the obstacles which rise against it, the forces which oppress it, are not elements of a new idea, important though they may seem at the moment. They are rather the contrasts and vicissitudes of that unique ideal, an ideal that is invincible because it is one not of stasis but of the fervid labor and struggle toward higher ways of life.

As we pointed out above, the passions of the Risorgimento, by transferring its loves and hates to the past, contributed not only to putting a hiatus between the Renaissance and the Risorgimento but, above all, to making the two ages seem contrary to each

[38] [The tendency in the Catholic Church in the nineteenth century to emphasize the authority of the papal see ("beyond the mountains" or the Alps) at the expense of local or national churches. "Ultra" is here used from the French or German point of view, just the opposite of the Italian term (frequently used in the following articles) *oltremontano*, which means "beyond the Alps" from the *Italian* point of view.]

[39] [It is Croce who here shifts from the definite past to the present tense. In order to realize the full force of the argument, the reader must recall Croce's principle that all true history is contemporary history (that is, historical investigation proceeds from a meditation upon current problems and ends by offering a means toward their solution). He must also remember that this article appeared during the Fascist regime in Italy, and the censors must have been fairly dull to have missed the point.]

other. Consequently, when [men of the nineteenth century] searched for an ideal connection in the past, they found it (and their imaginations concurred in their discovery) in the medieval period and in the age of the communes. The Renaissance seemed to be the age of Italian paganism and materialism, of an Italy sensual, pleasure-loving, literary, and rhetorical—the very Italy that modern Italians had a duty to react against. The object of this paper has been to demonstrate that the Risorgimento was the resumption of the Renaissance, or rather the resumption of its rational, and at the same time religious, character, and to demonstrate that the hiatus in the intervening period of decadence is not to be understood as [a sign of] total decadence or disjunction.

2 A Case in Point: The End of the Renaissance in Florence[1]

ERIC COCHRANE

JUST when the cultural and intellectual phenomenon known as the Renaissance finally came to an end, particularly in the city that for so long had been one of its most active centers, is still an open question. Most historians of Florentine political institutions, from Lorenzo Pignotti to François Perrens and Robert Davidsohn, have assumed a connection between free political constitutions and cultural vitality, and they have thus brought their accounts to a close with the fall of the last republican regime in 1530. Ferdinand Schevill, similarly, has placed the terminal date some time in the middle of the sixteenth century, when he finds that the Counter Reformation snuffed out whatever original thought was still permitted by the newly established dictatorship of Cosimo de' Medici. Eugenio Garin, on the other hand, has insisted that many of the characteristics of fifteenth-century Florentine literature are still to be found in the writings of Galileo; and Giorgio di Santillana has moved the end of the Renaissance all the way down to 1633, when, he insists, the intervention of the Holy Office robbed even Galileo's disciples of all possibility of further work in the one field that still had seemed open to them.[2]

Some help in finding a way out of this chronological tangle might be found in an investigation of the period that falls halfway

[1] *Bibliothèque d'humanisme et renaissance*, XXVII (1965), 7–29, with minor modifications in the notes and the text. Additions to the original are placed between brackets, and most Italian quotations are translated. Reprinted with the permission of Librairie Droz S.A., Geneva.

[2] The literature here referred to is too well known to be cited. [See the Introduction to this anthology.] Di Santillana's position is stated only in passing on the last pages of his *Crime of Galileo* (University of Chicago Press, 1955 [now in Phoenix paperback]).

between the two extreme limits—that is, in the years between about 1575 and about 1600. For one thing, most of those who had been born under the Republic—the generation of Giovan Battista Gelli, of Jacopo Nardi, of Benedetto Varchi, Pier Vettori, and Bernardo Segni—most of those who had joined in founding the Accademia Fiorentina and had managed in one way or another to accommodate themselves to the new monarchy, had by this time disappeared; and their place had been taken by a new generation, which accepted the monarchy without question and which was no onger troubled by the political problems of its predecessors. Galileo, on the other hand, had not yet risen to a position of leadership in Florentine intellectual life, and few of his predecessors had any inkling of the new problems that were to arise with the discovery of the satellites of Jupiter. This period has received relatively little attention from historians, it is true, in spite of, or perhaps because of, the immense quantity of printed and manuscript material that has survived. But it is at least of potential interest to them in that a number of recent books and articles touching upon particular aspects of the period—on music, for instance, on literary criticism, and on economics—seem to confirm the thesis implicit in Riguccio Galluzzi's still unsurpassed narrative history of Medicean Tuscany: that Florence in the age of Francesco and Ferdinando de' Medici produced something more than just court scandals and empty orations. If the term "Renaissance" is taken to refer, then, as it usually is, to the principal characteristics of Florentine civilization during the hundred-odd years from the death of Giangaleazzo Visconti to the death of Niccolò Machiavelli, it may be possible, by looking for similar characteristics in the last decades of the sixteenth century, to determine how much of the Renaissance was still alive on the eve of the birth of modern science.[3]

[3] The only histories of Florence that go much beyond 1537 are Alfred von Reumont's *Geschichte Toskanas* (Gotha, 1876), Romolo Caggese's *Firenze dalla decadenza di Roma al Risorgimento d'Italia* (Florence: Seeber e Lumachi, 1912-31), and, much more briefly, Antonio Panella's *Storia di Firenze* (Florence: Sansoni, 1949), now available in the French translation of Fernand Hayward (Paris: Fayard, 1959)—all of them based largely on the still fundamental *Istoria del*

Externally, at least, the city of Florence was not too different in 1580 from what it had been in 1480—except, perhaps, that it had become still more magnificent. Just ten years earlier the last bit of scaffolding had been torn off the gracious new Ponte Santa Trinità, to the accompaniment of elaborate public ceremonies, and the new Lungarno now made it possible, on coming off the north end of the bridge, to stroll along the riverbank up as far as the Ponte Vecchio or down as far as what is now Piazza Goldoni. The Palazzo Pitti, since 1550 the official residence of the duke, had already been extended in accordance with Cosimo's sumptuous plans; and Bartolommeo Ammannati had laid out behind the palace the still splendid Boboli Gardens, which Bernardo Buontalenti was just now embellishing with his fascinating grotto. Across the river, Giorgio Vasari had finished putting stucco and gold leaf all over the interior of the Palazzo Vecchio. He had completed the vast murals in the Sala de' Cinquecento, which he

---

Granducato di Toscana sotto il governo della Casa Medici (Florence, 1781; but I use the 2nd edn. of Livorno, 1820-21) of R. Galluzzi. For Bibliographical references on the limited subject indicated in the titles, see Panella, "Gli studi medicei in Italia ed all'estero," and Sergio Camerani, "Saggio di bibliografia medicea," both in *Atti del II Convegno di studi sul Rinascimento* (Florence: Sansoni, 1940), pp. 95-105 and 115-80, to which Camerani may soon add the great number of *fiches* he has collected in a desk drawer since the publication of his *Bibliografia medicea* (Florence: Sansoni, 1964). Monographs on musicology are cited below. Most of the contemporary Florentine treatises in the field of literary criticism are summarized by Bernard Weinberg in *A History of Literary Criticism in the Italian Renaissance* (University of Chicago Press, 1961); and most of what is known today about the economic conditions of Florence at the time comes from the numerous pages on the subject in Fernand Braudel's *La Méditerranée et le monde méditerranéen à l'époque de Philippe II* (Paris: Colin, 1949), which draws largely from the careful examination of statute books in Aminitore Fanfani's *Dalla fine del secolo XV agli inizi del XVIII*, which is Vol. III in the *Storia del lavoro in Italia*, ed. Riccardo Del Giudice (Milan: Giuffrè, 1943), from Galluzzi, and from such well-documented monographs as Pietro Battara's "Botteghe e pigioni nella Firenze del '500," *Archivio storico italiano*, XCV[2] (1937), 3-28, and G. Parenti's *Prime ricerche sulla rivoluzione dei prezzi in Firenze* (Florence: Cya, 1939). These studies are not yet, however, completely in accord with one another in their conclusions and still have to be brought together with the more recent findings of Ruggiero Romano, particularly in "Una crisi economica: 1619-1622," *Rivista storica italiana*, LXXIV (1962), 480 ff., and of Domenico Sella and Carlo Cipolla for other parts of Italy.

proclaimed to be grander than anything the Venetian Senate could boast of.[4] And finally, he had joined the center of former civic life to the Arno with the long colonnade under his architectural masterpiece, the Uffizi, which had replaced one of the dankest and most crowded parts of the city, and which had since come to symbolize the final transformation of the republican commune into the capital of a bureaucratic monarchy. Meanwhile, the edict of 28 January 1551,[5] obliging owners of contiguous buildings to sell out to whoever wished to enlarge an urban residence, was bearing fruit in a vast number of stately private palaces, particularly in the now fashionable quarter around the Pitti and in the newly developed area down the river in Borgo Ognissanti; and the somewhat stark simplicity of former centuries was rapidly giving way to sumptuously decorated façades, like the one on the house of Bianca Cappello in Via Maggio and the one on the back of Palazzo Capponi in Via Santo Spirito. On the hills outside the city, similarly, from Settignano to Pratolino, suburban villas were going up faster than ever before, since the Florentine patriciate found it indispensable to imitate their sovereigns in commuting regularly between town and country. And most of the new or enlarged buildings were surrounded by the geometrically arranged hedges and cypresses, populated with appropriate figures on the model of Giambologna's outdoor statuary, which constituted one of Florence's chief gifts to France in the age of Catherine de' Medici.

Yet for all their elegant new surroundings, and notwithstanding the now distant holocaust of 1530, Florentines themselves had not changed much during the intervening century. The same crowd of ruffians and gentlemen, of scholars and wits, that Botticelli had painted into the train of the Three Wise Men and that Anton Francesco Doni had overheard as he hovered above Piazza Santa Riparata in the form of an invisible bird in 1552—the same crowd still gathered during warm summer evenings on the stone benches

[4] Vasari to Cosimo in *Carteggio inedito d'artisti dei secoli XIV, XV e XVI*, 3 vols., ed. Johann Wilhelm Gaye (Florence, 1839–40), Vol. III, p. 98.

[5] 1550, *stile fiorentino*, printed in Vol. I of the collection of laws at the Newberry Library, Chicago (Case F36.106).

around the Palazzo Strozzi or on the marble steps in front of the cathedral to pick up the latest "stories, intrigues, tall tales ... [and] jokes"[6] and to reduce the whole world to the level of the usual low-brow Florentine wisecracks. Life in Florence was still, to borrow a term from the sociologists, street-oriented. It had not yet retreated into the isolation of private homes and villas, as it would later in the seventeenth century, nor into the hubbub of inns and cafés, as it would in the eighteenth. Life in Florence was also still purely masculine: women, in general, stayed at home, even if a few of them at times grumbled about being able to read Virgil as well as anyone else,[7] while their husbands, who probably did not find their arranged marriages all that attractive, wandered about for business or pleasure and, on occasions, stopped in to brawl and gamble in the numerous night-spots that gave the police no end of trouble toward the end of the century.

Life in Florence was also one in which class differences had not yet hardened into caste barriers, however much some philosophers might rant scornfully about the vulgar populace. Indeed, the elevation of the vernacular to the level of a literary and scientific language, which the new Accademia Fiorentina had systematically promoted ever since its foundation in 1540, had obviated the once menacing split between a Latin-speaking élite and the rest of the citizenry; and yet it had not in turn introduced still another division between speakers of a national language and speakers of a local dialect, since in Florence, at least according to the lexicographers of the Accademia della Crusca, the two were just about the same.[8]

[6] Anton Francesco Doni, *I marmi* (Bari: Laterza, 1928), Vol. I, p. 6.

[7] Note Lorenzo Giacomini's distinction between men and women: only men, he insists, are intellectual, and "women are not fit [for contemplation], for they are ... continually occupied in taking care of their children and their homes": *Della nobiltà delle lettere e delle armi*, ed. D. Moreni (Florence, 1821), pp. 17–18. For a contemporary description of the city, see Francesco Bocchi, *Le bellezze della città di Firenze, dove à pieno di pittura, di scultura* ... (Florence, 1591).

[8] See Cartesio Marconcini, *L'Accademia della Crusca dalle origini alla prima edizione del Vocabolario* (Pisa: Valenti, 1910), and G. B. Zannoni, *Storia dell'Accademia della Crusca* (Florence, 1848). The chief theorist of the Crusca, Lionardo Salviati had said the same thing in one of his earliest orations (30 April 1564),

One of the most prominent authors of the period, moreover, Anton Francesco Grazzini, called "Il Lasca," set a pattern for writing, like his model Boccaccio, in a down-to-earth style that reproduced the locutions of the butchers and woolworkers as well as of the academicians and noblemen among his numerous listeners.[9] Thus the great mixed freely with the humble, who still maintained their traditional pride and self-respect; and all joined from time to time in the round of public spectacles which may originally, as Galluzzi points out,[10] have been intended as a way of ridding Cosimo's new subjects of dangerous nostalgias but which now amounted to little more than gratuitous, if expensive, entertainment, far surpassing the most lavish displays of Lorenzo the Magnificent. What, for instance, could rival the elaborate scenery put up in 1565 for the pompous procession that brought the unfortunate Giovanna of Austria in from Poggio a Caiano to the steps of the Palazzo Vecchio? And what could match the splendor of the San Giovanni parade in 1577, when three trumpeters and a mounted cupid led some twenty different floats representing the Church Triumphant, the Church Militant, and so forth, and then as many others representing the seven gifts of the Holy Spirit leading on a leash the seven deadly sins, particularly when one of the sins turned out to be a gigantic dragon spewing forth real fire?[11]

---

the "Orazione in lode della fiorentina lingua," published in his *Primo libro delle orazioni* (Florence, 1575), No. 3. For a language to be an acceptable means of written expression, Salviati insists, it must be spoken "da un popolo."

[9] On Lasca, see Luigi Russo, "Novellistica e dialoghistica nella Firenze del '500," *Belfagor*, XVI (1961), 261–83. [Michel Plaisance, "Evolution du thème de la 'beffa' dans le théâtre de Lasca," *Revue des études italiennes*, XI (1965), 491–504, suffers from the occasional attempt of the author to explain particulars in the dramas by reference to the "historical background," which he knows very little about.]

[10] *Istoria del Granducato di Toscana*, Vol. II, p. 177.

[11] Piero Ginori Conti, *L'apparato per le nozze di Francesco de' Medici e di Giovanna d'Austria* (Florence: Olschki, 1936), with complete bibliography of contemporary descriptions of the event. *Descrizzione et ordine de i trionfi mandati in Firenze per i giovani della Compagnia di San Bastiano* (Florence, 1577).

[Other contemporary descriptions of court feasts are recapitulated by A. M. Nagler in *Theatre Festivals of the Medici, 1539–1637* (Yale University Press, 1964), with illustrations.]

Florentines may no longer have had as much to do as in the days of Savonarola and Pier Capponi, when political affairs had absorbed all their leisure hours, and they may now have been spending far too much money betting on who would be the next pope.[12] But they, or at least those of them who could keep above the level of mere subsistence, certainly enjoyed themselves.

This happy existence was made possible in part by the triple blessing of peace, prosperity, and internal tranquillity. The big banking houses, first of all, were now making money again, particularly through their flourishing branches, staffed with bright young men from the best families of the city, in Lyon, Venice, Rome, and elsewhere. The wool industry, similarly, had completely recovered from the disasters of the 1520's, thanks in part to the opening of new markets in the Spanish empire and to the ruin of its chief competitors in war-torn Flanders; while the establishment of foreign commercial houses in the newly repopulated port of Pisa and in the newly constructed port of Livorno opened up still further sources of revenue from the more recent silk, glass, and porcelain industries. Even agriculture seems to have benefited from Cosimo's vast investment in drainage canals, in spite of his antieconomic restrictions on the movement of grain; and the cautious Galluzzi was probably correct when he supposed Tuscany to have been more prosperous after 1560 than it ever had been since the bank crashes of the 1340's—or at least no evidence has yet been found to contradict him.[13]

[12] The *Bando et prohibitione* of 1591 prohibited bets on papal elections, but regulated those concerning cardinals through a special commission set up in 1589 *sopra le scomesse di sede vacante et promotione di cardinali.* The argument used was that gambling of this sort was drawing money away from legitimate and productive commerce.

[13] Figures for wool production in the first three decades of the century are assembled and evaluated in a thesis recently presented to the Facoltà di Lettere of the University of Florence by R. Pecchioli, based on the Wool Guild records in the Archivio di Stato. Those for the later period and for other industries are in Galluzzi, *Istoria del Granducato di Toscana,* Vol. III, pp. 135 ff., and in Fanfani's *Storia del lavoro.* But research in this area has just begun. No one has yet tried to wade all the way through the immense quantity of papers regarding the commercial activities of the reigning house, but Richard Goldthwaite has recently studied those of some private concerns in *Private Wealth in*

The domestic turmoil of the first decades of the century, also, had apparently passed once and for all. Of the exiles who had so long threatened the security of the new regime, almost none were left; and the supposed treason of a certain Orazio Pucci in 1575 hardly warranted the brutality with which the grand duke's paid assassins tracked down the accomplices all over Europe. Florentines might grumble at times over the extravagances of their princes, and they probably were at least annoyed when Francesco's expensive mistress Bianca Cappello got her unscrupulous cousins and henchmen appointed to the most lucrative offices of the state. But Ferdinando, who succeeded his haughty and heirless brother in 1587, quickly restored the reputation of the Medici family by personally distributing the huge quantity of grain he had brought into the city during the flood of 1589—an act which produced an even greater flood of laudatory sonnets and orations.[14] Hence neither Florentines, nor Aretines and Sienese, found much reason to regret the "old days" when their cities had been "filled with towers, castles, and quarreling factions,"[15] or to complain about having been relieved of all political responsibility by an omnicompetent prince; nor did they complain when he chose to put Lombard officers in charge of his armies and to fill administrative and diplomatic posts with loyal "slaves," as they called themselves,

---

Renaissance Florence (Princeton University Press, 1968). On Livorno, see among other studies Giuseppe Guarnieri, *Il porto di Livorno e la sua funzione economica dalle origini ai tempi nostri* (Pisa: Cesari, 1931); the more recent study of Giorgio Mori, "Linee e momenti dello sviluppo della città, del porto e dei traffici di Livorno," *La regione*, III (1956), No. 12, pp. 3–44; and Fernand Braudel and Ruggiero Romano, *Navires et marchandises à l'entrée du port de Livourne, 1547–1611* (Paris: Colin, 1951).

[14] See Scipione Ammirato to Virginio Orsini, 15 November 1589, in Ammirato's *Opuscoli*, ed. S. Ammirato Jr. (Florence, 1637–42), Vol. II, p. 408. By 1603 the prominent writer Giovan Battista Strozzi was willing to scrap even a semblance of historical veracity and attribute to the Medici family the responsibility for having chased out the Duke of Athens, for having tamed the Ciompi, and for having initiated almost every happy event ever since: see *Della famiglia de' Medici* (Florence, 1610).

[15] Giovanni Rondinelli, *Relazione . . . sopra lo stato antico e moderno della città di Arezzo . . . l'anno MDLXXXIII* (Arezzo, 1755).

from subject or even foreign cities.[16] Peace, finally, had now become as permanent as war had been in the decades after 1492: for the domestic turmoil of France had eliminated the constant specter of new invasions from abroad that had so distressed the generation of Machiavelli, and the battle of Lepanto had reduced the menace of Turkish raids along the coast to nothing but an occasional rumor. Indeed, except for a few romantic adventures, like Francesco's project to corner the Portuguese pepper market and Ferdinando's plot to seize Marseilles, the foreign policy of the grand dukes was reduced to little more than quarreling with the houses of Este and Savoy about whose ambassador should precede the other in formal receptions at the imperial and Spanish courts.

Seldom, in fact, has a generation been so satisfied with itself and with the world around it. "It so happens," pointed out one observer, "that the greatness of the city of Florence and of its inhabitants has been and still is such that even the longest discourse could touch upon only a small part."[17] No hero of antiquity, continued one of his associates, could compare with the quality of those of today; for alongside the duke of Alba, why, even Achilles himself was a mere milksop.[18] Had the Florentine Renaissance begun to wane? Quite the contrary, replied another. The best kind of society, after all, is one in which virtue and letters are most fully developed. "If I were to bring forth an example of the kind of society I have been talking about," concluded Lionardo Salviati after a half hour or so of such theoretical declarations, "I would not have to go very far from the country we live in. For if literature and the noble arts have flourished in this city ever since the time of Lorenzo the Magnificent, it is clear that they are

[16] The career of Luigi Dovara is a case in point. See Guido Sommi Picenardi, "Luigi Dovara gentiluomo cremonese agente mediceo alla corte di Filippo II," *Archivio storico italiano*, Ser. v, Vol. XLVII (1911), 49–129.

[17] Lorenzo Giacomini in *Oratione . . . de le lodi di Francesco Medici* (Florence, 1587).

[18] Ammirato in "Lezione in difesa dell'Ariosto," published in appendix to Moreni's edition of Giovanni de' Bardi, *Dell'imperiale Villa Adriana* (Florence, 1825).

flourishing today more than ever before."[19] It is not surprising,
then, that those few Florentines whom business or state service
obliged to live abroad, and those whom the latest Iberian fashions
led to prefer the gravy train of some foreign prince to gainful
employment in the family firm, sent back a constant stream of
nostalgic letters. For neither colorful Madrid, nor busy Lisbon,
nor distant and romantic Goa had anything to offer like the sparkling hills and stimulating circle of friends back home.[20]

So happy, in fact, were Florentines with life in Florence that
they turned their backs completely upon what should have seemed
to them a number of rather disquieting signs. Surely they must
have known that the elaborate clothing against which sumptuary
laws railed in vain and the elaborate façades that went up year
after year were being paid for not out of profits but out of capital.
Certainly they should have realized that the failure of the grand
duke to reach an agreement with the sultan meant the end to the
still lucrative Levant trade,[21] and that the huge profits some of
them were realizing in the West would sooner or later be wiped
out by the periodic bankruptcies of the Spanish monarchy. The
big crash of the 1620's was still far off; but anyone might have seen
that the wool guild was being suffocated by its own bureaucracy,
and that the huge subsidies paid out year after year by the Medici[22]

[19] In "In lode della giustizia," published in his *Primo libro delle orazioni*, pp.
89 ff., and also in Vol. IV of the Classici Italiani edition of his *Opere* (Milan,
1809), pp. 183 ff.

[20] Besides the numerous letters of Filippo Sassetti to this effect in *Lettere*, ed.
Ettore Marcucci (Florence, 1855), see the letter of his friend, sometime ambassador to Spain, Francesco Bongianni Gianfigliazzi, to Scipione Ammirato of
18 July 1583, in Ammirato, *Opuscoli*, Vol. II, p. 345.

[21] All the negotiations are summarized by Sergio Camerani in "Sulla storia dei
trattati fra la Toscana e i Turchi," *Archivio storico italiano*, XCVII[2] (1939), 83–101.

[22] One example: the dowry of Maria de' Medici in 1601 amounted to
600,000 *scudi*, not counting the cost of transportation and festivities. Some idea
of what this sum may have meant, in a country of around 750,000 inhabitants,
can be arrived at by comparing it to 1,000 *scudi*, which was considered a very
good annual salary. But not being an economic historian *stricto sensu*, I dare
make no further comparisons. The figure is given in the *contrat de mariage*, which
I happen to have read in the Archives des Affaires Étrangères, Paris, Toscane,
II, pp. 3 ff., though there are many other copies. The similar sums paid out
almost every year in the form of "loans" to the king of Spain are recorded in

—to help the queen of France smash the Huguenots, to help the king of Spain plug up his national defense budget, and to get Neapolitan principalities for poor or shiftless relatives—were rapidly draining out of the country much of the money that came in from their well-placed shipments of surplus grain. But no one seems to have noticed any of this; and the occasional schemes of Ferdinando to recoup Florentine fortunes by capturing Chios in Greece[23] or sending colonists to South America were dreamt up wholly in the secret circles of the court, and they cannot at all be attributed to a survival of the once-famous ingenuity of Florentine businessmen.

It is even stranger that the leaders of Florentine culture should have been so oblivious to the obvious cracks in their own house. The Medici rulers would see to it that culture flourished forever, they thought.[24] But the Accademia Fiorentina, which Cosimo had established ostensibly for just this purpose, had apparently lost much of the interest it had aroused among its members back in the 1540's, and attendance at meetings had fallen off rather seriously.[25]

Galluzzi. On the extent of the Medici grain trade, see Braudel, *La Méditerranée*, p. 469. The damaging effect of political loans on institutions of public credit and the economic consequences of Alessandro's scruples are analyzed by Guido Pampaloni in "Cenni storici sul Monte di Pietà di Firenze," *Archivi storici delle aziende di credito*, I (1956), 525–60.

[23] This whole misguided and abortive adventure is recounted by Philip Argenti in *The Expedition of the Florentines to Chios* (London: John Lane, 1934).

[24] Note Salviati in *Primo libro delle orazioni*, p. 35, on Cosimo and the Accademia Fiorentina.

[25] Salviati admitted as much in his "Orazione ... nel prender del suo consolato l'anno 1566," in *Primo libro delle orazioni*, pp. 67–68; and Frosino Lapini repeated the complaint even more forcefully in his *Lettione ... del fine della poesia* the following year (Florence, 1567). Not much improvement was made, apparently, during the next twenty years, for in 1585 the Academy had to hold three elections for the consulate before it could get a candidate to accept. The account is under the article "Bernardino Neretti" in Salvino Salvini's *Fasti consolari dell'Accademia Fiorentina* (Florence, 1717), still the best source of information on the activities of the Academy [though for the earlier period, see now Armand De Gaetano, "The Florentine Academy and the Advancement of learning through the Vernacular," *Bibliothèque d'humanisme et renaissance*, XXX (1968), 19–52]. Its troubles may be also, to be sure, due in part to competition offered by the many new academies founded in the city during the course of the century.

Even the University of Pisa, which he had refounded and heavily endowed, could boast, in the letters of one student, of little but "bad air and bad teachers." Courses were usually taught, he explained, by "young jerks more fit to write sonnets and to play around with women" than to talk of philosophy; and apparently even the moral life of students and professors left something to be desired if special provisions had to be made against *assassinamenta, furta, blasphemias, raptus virginum, et violentias in feminas vel pueros per libidinem cum eis exercendam.*[26] Protection and subsidies, moreover, were all very welcome, and men of letters were grateful to Cosimo for having spared them the full rigors of the Index of Paul IV.[27] But what would happen if the protector of letters became the censor? It was bad enough when Francesco ordered a historian to fix up the genealogy of the Ricasoli family according to the preferences of one of his favorites.[28] But it was even more ridiculous that all the naughty references to monks and popes had to be torn out of Boccaccio's *Decameron* before it could be reprinted; and the editors could have gotten only momentary satisfaction out of inserting dots for expurgated passages and italicizing the word *student* whenever it replaced *priest* in the original. But except for a bit of grumbling on the part of the first unwilling expurgators, no one really protested, or ever bothered to work out principles that

[26] These comments are those of Filippo Sassetti in his letters to his cousin (and sometime employer) Lorenzo Giacomini from Pisa in 1570–74, published in the first pages of his *Lettere*, and of Giacomini to Giovan Battista Strozzi, 26 December 1568, in Biblioteca Nazionale, Florence, Mag. VIII, 1399. Chapter 80 of the *Leges* in Mag. IX, 19, is quoted by Mario Rossi in his *Un letterato e mercante fiorentino del secolo XVI, Filippo Sassetti* (Città di Castello, 1899), pp. 12–13.

[27] See Antonio Panella, "L'introduzione a Firenze dell'Indice di Paolo IV," *Rivista storica degli archivi toscani*, I (1929), 11–25. Cosimo just said yes, yes, to Paul, and then waited for him to die, to the great relief of the booksellers and of just about everyone else.

[28] Ammirato to Francesco de' Medici, 14 February 1585, *Opuscoli*, vol. II, p. 340. Ammirato must be given credit in this instance for preserving enough personal pride to refuse to go on with the project, and the Ricasoli are duly omitted from his vast *Delle famiglie nobili fiorentine* (Florence, 1616). "Mi spogliai affatto di questa impresa" ["I washed my hands completely of this work"], he wrote on 19 February 1585: *Opuscoli*, Vol. II, p. 341.

might justify their protesting; and Lionardo Salviati was even disposed to further his reputation by putting out a still more expurgated *Decameron*, even though the Holy Office gave no sign of
carrying out its objections to the 1573 edition by suspending the
imprimatur.[29] In fact, no one really complained about anything
at all. The restlessness, the dissatisfaction, and the sense of independence that may have in part been responsible for the vitality
of Florentine culture in the past had now given way to quiet,
satisfaction, and servility, and to the conviction that not much
was left to do but to sit back and enjoy what already had been
accomplished.

This self-satisfaction may have been in part responsible for the
unmistakable flatness in the personalities of late sixteenth-century
Florentines. In spite of the greater number of biographies and
eulogies that have come down from the age, it is almost impossible
to find a single portrait worthy of the pen of, say, Vespasiano da
Bisticci; and even the autobiographical passages in contemporary
treatises and orations give very little insight into the real persons
who wrote them—unless by some chance they all simply *were*
nothing but hazy images of one another. With the sole exception
of the sparkling letters of the émigré Filippo Sassetti, the private
correspondence of the time is not much better. Self-censorship
had apparently become second nature—so much that the diarist
Agostino Lapini probably erased from his mind, as well as from
the pages he wrote only for his own amusement, the whole sorry
story of that misguided and out-of-date tyrannicide Orazio
Pucci;[30] and there is not a line in the many letters of the cocky,
unscrupulous Lionardo Salviati to indicate whether he chased all

[29] That it was Salviati and neither the Holy Office nor Francesco who got
up the project for the 1582 edition has been shown by Peter M. Brown in "I
veri promotori della 'rassettatura' del 'Decameron' nel 1582," *Giornale storico
della letteratura italiana*, CXXXIV (1957), 314–32. The history of the "rassettatura"
is told by Pio Paschini in his *Cinquecento romano e riforma cattolica* (Rome: Lateran,
1958), pp. 243 ff.

[30] See the editor's note on p. 188 of Agostino Lapini (*ca.* 1515–*ca.* 1592),
Diario fiorentino (Florence, 1900). Lapini similarly skips lightly over the death
of Isabella Orsini and does not even mention Bianca Cappello until she is safely
married to the grand duke.

over Italy after various charlatans because he really thought they
had the fabulous poisons the grand duke thought they had, or
whether he deliberately duped his employer in order to prolong
his employment.[31]

The art of introspection, in other words, the art that Petrarch
had learned from Augustine and had passed on to all his successors
down to the time of Benvenuto Cellini, had disappeared. So, indeed, had the very concept of the individual human being as
something of value in itself alone, which Burckhardt a century ago
and Federico Chabod more recently have defined as one of the
chief characteristics of Quattrocento culture. All men—so Salviati
begins the eulogy of his beloved master Benedetto Varchi[32]—all
men are composed of five potential qualities. Two are bestowed
by nature (beauty and memory), and three are acquired, the first
by action, the second by contemplation, and the third by action
and contemplation together. Since these conclusions were absolutely irrefutable, all Salviati had to do was to pin Varchi up
against the chart and check off the plusses and minuses, even if
Varchi, the real man, living in a particular time and place and
responding in a particular way to specific conditions, ended up as
nothing but a collection of cellophane-wrapped "virtues" that
could be attributed as well to just about anyone else. What
Salviati did to Varchi, moreover, all his friends did to themselves.
Upon admission to the various academies they all belonged to,
each of them gave up his own for an academic name that supposedly expressed at once his dominant trait and the special
character infused in him by his new association. Bernardo
Davanzati, for instance, was "altered" by his association with the
Accademia degli Alterati into *Il Silente*, "The Silent," because he
wrote very concise Tuscan prose and because he translated the
works of the taciturn Roman historian Tacitus. The use of academic names was by no means new in the late sixteenth century,

31 Many, but not all, of his letters are published in *Lettere edite ed inedite*, ed.
Pietro Ferrato (Rimini, 1875), which supersedes earlier editions.
32 "Orazione...publicamente recitata per l'Accademia Fiorentina nell'esequie
di M. Benedetto Varchi," in *Primo libro delle orazioni*, pp. 50 ff.

to be sure, any more than were the discussions of *imprese*, of devices and mottos, that had occupied so much space in Italian letters since long before the famous passages in Castiglione's *Cortigiano*.[33] But they now acquired a much greater importance, in that they offered a way of rendering intelligible something that a generation obsessed by the neat certainty of abstract categories refused any longer to admit as unique. Trying to understand a universal category directly deducible from absolute principles and easily relatable to all other categories of the same species, after all, required far less effort than trying to understand a single whole person, inexplicable in terms of anything beyond himself. But the result was that real persons like Bernardo Davanzati, Francesco Bonciani, and Giovanni de' Bardi withered away, and their place was taken by a whole society composed of empty abstractions, like "The Sharp" and "The Pure."

What Salviati and Davanzati did to individuals, moreover, could just as easily be done to society as a whole; and society was accordingly chopped up into categories as neatly distinguished as the qualities of its single components. The lower classes, first of all, were relegated to a position of hopeless inferiority: they were completely unworthy of Machiavelli's unwarranted tributes, as Scipione Ammirato repeatedly pointed out, and they were capable of responding only to the sound of Ariosto's verse, not to the ideas the verses carefully hid from their impure gaze.[34] Whoever

[33] On the Alterati, see Domenico Maria Manni, *Memorie della fiorentina famosa Accademia degli Alterati* (Florence, 1748), and Bernard Weinberg, "L'Accademia degli Alterati: Literary Taste from 1570 to 1600," *Italica*, xxxi (1954), 207–14. The statutes prescribing the practices here referred to are in Biblioteca Nazionale, Florence, Mag. IX, 134, together with a list of members and their academic names. On the importance of *imprese*, see Mario Praz, *Studies in Seventeenth Century Imagery* (Rome: Edizioni di Storia e Letteratura, 1939); and on what became of them later on, see p. 405 of my *Tradition and Enlightenment in the Tuscan Academies* (University of Chicago Press, and Rome: Edizioni di Storia e Letteratura, 1961). (I am indebted to Ruth Prelowsky for her comments on this subject.)

[34] On Ammirato's *Discorsi . . . sopra Cornelio Tacito* (Florence, 1594), esp. Book III, ch. 7, see Alberto Alberti, "Politica e ragion di stato nell'opera di Scipione Ammirato," *Atti della R. Accademia delle Scienze di Torino*, LXVI (1930–31), pp. 598–626. The most complete life of Ammirato is still Umberto

bore a title, secondly, was put into a special race of supermen, even
if he had to be fixed up with a fictitious genealogy and endowed
with the "nobility" somehow inherent in the city of his birth, in
order to cover up the disagreeable fact that the Medicean bureaucracy provided at least a modicum of social mobility.[35] Nobility,
insisted the philosopher Francesco Verino in 1574,[36] is characterized not by service to the state or leadership in the community;
it is characterized by "light" and "virtue." It is acquired neither by
wealth, since Jesus said that camels couldn't get through needles'
eyes, nor by work, since noble parents can be its only possible
efficient cause. Nobility, he concluded, is bestowed by God—and
there is the end of some two centuries of speculation about a
"natural" nobility and of a whole school of thought based on the
assumption that social institutions are the product of human

Congedo's *La vita e le opere di S. A.* (Trani, 1904), though the old "Vita" by
Domenico De' Angelis in *Le vite de' letterati salentini* (Florence, 1710), pp.
67–116, is still useful for the earlier years. [The modern authority on Ammirato
is Rodolfo de Mattei, many of whose earlier essays and articles are now
brought together in *Il pensiero politico di Scipione Ammirato* (Milan: Giuffrè,
1963).] The comment on Ariosto is from his "Lezione in difesa dell'Ariosto,"
cited above, n. 18. Ammirato had said much the same thing as early as 1562 in
Il Rota (reprinted in *Opuscoli*, Vol. I, which I quote here from p. 466): "Thus,
similarly, do the poets, whose bark, as everyone knows, is as much of a secret
as their pith. He who would penetrate their high and profound concepts must
needs indeed be wise and learned."

[35] The Medici bureaucracy provided the most convenient, if not the only,
way of rising in society, and some of its most important officials came indeed
from very humble origins. Piero Usimbardi of Colle Valdelsa (1539–1611)
began as a poor notary and eventually became first secretary to Cardinal
Ferdinando and bishop of Arezzo (1589), dragging all his brothers and cousins
along with him. A biography is printed in the introduction to G. C. Saltini's
edition of his *Istoria del Granduca Ferdinando I* (Florence, 1880). The one apparent
exception to the refusal of the Florentine literati to recognize the validity of
social mobility proves the rule: Alessandro Minerbetti called Belisario Vinta
(for some fifty years a high administrator) worthy of special praise for having
risen without the help of a family; but then Minerbetti goes on immediately to
prove the "nobility" of his native city, Volterra, by enumerating not the heroic
deeds of the Volterrani but the number of "noble" families that made up its
patriciate: *Orazione . . . in lode di Belisario Vinta* (Florence, 1614).

[36] Francesco de' Vieri ("Verino Secondo"), *Il primo libro della nobiltà* (Florence,
1574; 2nd edn., 1577).

volition. Whoever ruled a state, similarly, was held to be not only the *prime* mover, but the *sole* mover of society, without whose free and wholly unmerited acts of grace no one could expect either bread or poetic inspiration. Occasionally an observer might express certain doubts, it is true, about the omnicompetence of a prince, as when Filippo Sassetti cautiously suggested that the Levant trade would revive only when the merchants involved found it mutually advantageous, not simply when Francesco de' Medici willed its revival.[37] But most of his associates really meant what they said when they offered to kiss the soil upon which the feet of the duke of Mantua or the grand duke of Tuscany trod in exchange for a glance of recognition;[38] and they really did consider themselves simply the tools of the one above them, relieved of all responsibility for any acts he might choose to operate through them. Hence the men of letters, who formed the last category of society, gave up any pretense they may once have had of leading society toward the goals that they, as the repositories of wisdom, might propose to it.[39] As immobility became the chief end of political action, and as political thought withered from the passion of Machiavelli's commentary on Livy to the detachment of

[37] "Sul commercio tra la Toscana e le nazioni levantine," ed. Filippo Luigi Polidori, in *Archivio storico italiano*, Appendix IX (1853), 169–84. Sassetti's position on the question of nobility, however, is very close to that of Verino, and almost as far removed, if in degree rather than in kind, from that of Baldassarre Castiglione. See, for example, *Letters*, p. 93.

[38] The expression is Ammirato's, in a letter to the duke of Mantua of 17 September 1594, *Opuscoli*, Vol. II, p. 496. Note his preface to the 1583 edition of his *Opuscoli* (which, by the way, has nothing to do with the posthumous volumes of the same name): "Hence those . . . who live on the bread of others and exist on salaries paid by others, are no longer lords of themselves, but have come, so to speak, under the lordship of another. They are thus obliged to employ themselves and all their energy and work on behalf and in the service of those by whom they are nourished."

[39] There are some glimpses of a somewhat broader concept of the social function of the literati in some of Ammirato's earlier works, but they disappear by the time he moved to Florence. In general, see Rodolfo de Mattei, "Il pensiero politico di S. A.," *Studi salentini*, III–IV (1957), 50–98. On the consciousness among late Cinquecento writers of the transformation of citizens into courtiers, see Benedetto Croce, "Libri sulle corti," in his *Poeti e scrittori del pieno e del tardo Rinascimento* (Bari: Laterza, 1946), Vol. II, pp. 198 ff.

Ammirato's discourses on Tacitus, so the broad, active class of educated and responsible citizens addressed by Lionardo Bruni and Donato Acciaiuoli hardened into an isolated, if still numerous, élite, expected to do nothing but glow like alabaster saints from behind the glass panels of academic reliquaries.

The surrender of their persons and their wills, on the other hand, by no means impaired the confidence of Salviati and his friends in having solved once and for all most of the problems that had disturbed their predecessors during the previous two centuries. The so-called language question, first of all, the *questione della lingua*, was as old as the Renaissance itself, and in its time it had provoked a good bit of valuable research into the nature of words and the function of language. The question was still far from an idle one, as the works of Antonio Sebastiano Minturno and Francesco Patrizi show. But in the eyes of Salviati it had become idle indeed, for its solution was far too simple to admit of any further debate. Language, he supposed, was a static thing existing outside of time and space; it was not the creation of men searching for a means of expression or of communication. Italian had been "discovered" by Florentines at the time of Boccaccio, just as Latin had been discovered by Romans at the time of Cicero; and anyone who wanted to write good Italian had only to copy the words and expressions of the great *Trecentisti*, which Salviati carefully transcribed into his thick *Avvertimenti* and which he then inserted in the many manuscripts submitted for his correction by all the best writers of Italy.[40] The question of what constituted

---

[40] On Salviati, whose principal interest in linguistics is reflected in most of his works but above all in his *Degli avvertimenti della lingua sopra il Decamerone*, 2 vols. (Venice and Florence, 1584–86) and in his "Orazione in lode della fiorentina lingua" of 30 April 1564, printed in his *Primo libro delle orazioni*, No. 3, see Pierfrancesco Cambi in *Prose fiorentine*, ed. Carlo Roberto Dati *et al.*, Part I, Vol. III—pp. 143–70 of the Florentine edition of 1729 and pp. 55–66 of the Venetian edition of 1751, which is the one I usually refer to. Upon this biography is based that published by Jacopo Rilli in the *Notizie letterarie ed istoriche intorno agli uomini illustri dell'Accademia Fiorentina* (Florence, 1700), as well as the *Elogio* by Giuseppe Pelli in the *Elogi degli uomini illustri toscani*, 4 vols. (Lucca, 1771–74), Vol. III, pp. 212–19, reprinted in Vol. I of the Classici Italiani edition of Salviati's *Opere*. There are no modern biographies to my knowledge,

good literature, secondly, which was perhaps the most hotly debated question of the century, was just as easy to solve. All the critic has to do, Salviati pointed out, is to start with the right principles. As soon as he realizes which of the five possible categories of human activity literature fits into, he will quickly see that the purpose of literature is nothing other than instructing by enticement, and that language is only accessory to, not essential to, the perfectly formed idea that constitutes the essence of the work of art. The critic is then in a position to apply the infallible principles either to the literature of the past—and after years of hard work Dante and Ariosto were finally squeezed into the prescribed molds—or to the literature of the present—and the quarrel over whether Tasso's *Gerusalemme liberata* could be made to fit as well made the author's own life miserable and kept the Florentine academies in a state of constant warfare for over a decade.[41]

The same approach, then, was found to be applicable to just about any other question. Why, for instance, did Rome start as a monarchy, then become a republic, and finally revert to a

but Peter M. Brown, whose articles are here cited, probably is better acquainted with Salviati than anyone else today. Among the many studies of the "Questione della lingua," one of the best is Bruno Migliorini's "La questione della lingua" in *Questioni e correnti di storia letteraria*, ed. U. Bosco *et al.* (Milan: Marzorati, 1949), pp. 1–75; though somewhat closer to the period here considered is Umberto Pirotti's article on Benedetto Varchi [included in this anthology (ch. 7)]. On Salviati's criticism of contemporary manuscript works, the best record is in his correspondence with Giovan Battista Guarini and Francesco Panigarola, some still in manuscript (Mag. IV, 63, Biblioteca Nazionale, Florence), some in his *Lettere edite ed inedite*, and some in Silvio Pasquazi's "Le annotazioni al 'Pastor Fido' di Leonardo Salviati" in the volume *Rinascimento ferrarese* (Caltanissetta, 1957).

[41] See particularly Salviati's maiden speech, "Del trattato della poetica," published by L. Manzoni in the 1873 edition of the *Opere inedite*, pp. 1–17. On the "quarrel," see ch. 19 of Weinberg, *History of Literary Criticism*; B. T. Sozzi, "Tasso contro Salviati," *Studi tassiani*, I (1951), 37–66; Umberto Cosmo, "Le polemiche tassesche: La Crusca e Dante . . . ," now republished in his *Con Dante attraverso il Seicento* (Bari: Laterza, 1954); and above all, Mario Sansone, "Le polemiche antitassesche della Crusca," in *Torquato Tasso*, published by the Comitato per le Celebrazioni di T. T. (Milan, 1957), pp. 527–74.

monarchy? Salviati had the answer.[42] There are two kinds of people in any state: those for the regime, and those against it. There are five factors involved in the mutation of any regime: occasions, accidents, passions, etc. Thus, just by juggling these categories around a bit, he managed to finish off an argument on which some of the best minds of Italy, from Coluccio Salutati to Machiavelli, had wasted so many sleepless nights. And what's more, he did it in just six and one-half pages. The approach could also be applied to the old debate between the active and the contemplative life, which was indeed resolved so successfully that no one thereafter ever had to bother reading Cristoforo Landino or any other of the Quattrocento moralists, whom not even the author of the definitive treatise on the subject had felt obliged to consult.[43] Unfortunately the approach could also be applied to such things as football games, to the famous *gioco di calcio*.[44] The final cause of the game is the passage of a ball through the goal of your opponent a greater number of times than he passes it through yours. The material cause is the players, the efficient cause is the rich noblemen who pay for their uniforms. Obviously this abuse of Aristotelian logic contributed eventually to the discrediting of the very system of thought it took for granted; and the authors undoubtedly intended their audiences to smile at the clever juxtaposition of neat logical deductions and of the rough-and-tumble brawling described in detail between propositions. But the smile is not that of a satirist; it is the smile of one who is so sure of having reached perfection that he can even afford to play for a moment with what he has achieved.

Yet there was one field in which this approach really did not work at all, namely, history. What is the purpose of history?

[42] "Discorso . . . onde avvenne che Roma, non avendo mai provato a vivere libera . . ." (1582), published in Vol. VI of the *Biblioteca enciclopedica italiana* (Milan, 1839), though I use the version published in the Appendix to Giorgio Dati's translation of the *Annali di Cornelio Tacito* (Venice, 1589).

[43] Francesco Bocchi, *Discorso . . . sopra la lite delle armi e delle lettere* (Florence, 1579), and *Discorso sopra il pregio del valore humano* (Florence, 1581–82).

[44] Giovanni de' Bardi, *Discorso sopra il gioco del calcio fiorentino* (Florence, 1580) (but I use the 2nd edn. of 1615).

Lionardo Bruni, a century and a half earlier, had offered at least
one possible answer: history makes men conscious of the relation
between past and present in such a way that they can learn how
to change what they have inherited from the past in accordance
with what they think ought to pertain in the future. Still other
answers were just then being worked out by some of the best
minds in Europe, from Francesco Patrizi in Italy to François
Baudouin in France.[45] But Florentines no longer remembered the
words of their famous ancestor, and they seem to have paid little
attention to the words of their more profound contemporaries
abroad. After all, they had learned at least some discretion about
making known just anything their fancy might lead them to in the
past, particularly after it became apparent that Duke Cosimo was
not anxious to have any of the historical works he had commissioned actually published, and after it turned out that the edition of
Guicciardini he did have published, with a good bit of flurry, was
obviously a "corrected" version of the original. Florentines had
also come to realize that it was the prince, not they, upon whom

[45] By far the best work on the subject so far is the article by Giorgio Spini
[included in this anthology (ch. 4)], although, in spite of the recent reprinting
of the volume, no one outside Italy seems to have paid much attention to it.
It is not considered either in Julian Franklin's *Jean Bodin and the Sixteenth
Century Revolution in the Methodology of History and Law* (Columbia University
Press, 1963), which dedicates a whole chapter to Francesco Patrizzi [*sic*] [pretty
much ripped out of the context of his life and times, alas!] nor in the collected
essays of Myron Gilmore, *Humanists and Jurists* (Harvard University Press,
1963), which touches on similar subjects. [It may be that Spini strays too far
from classic history-of-ideas methods for the taste of American scholars.] On
contemporary theories of history in France, see now Donald Kelley's "François
Baudouin's Conception of History," *Journal of the History of Ideas*, xxv (1964),
35–57 [and several other articles on similar subjects since, as well as the recent
studies of George Huppert, e.g. "Naissance de l'histoire de France: Les 'Recherches' d'Estienne Pasquier," *Annales E.S.C.* (1968), 69–105]. The most complete study of late Florentine historiography in particular is M. Lupo Gentile,
"Studi sulla storiografia alla corte di Cosimo I," *Annali della Scuola Normale
Superiore di Pisa*, xix[2] (1905), 1–164, which unfortunately does not go down to
Ammirato. But for the mid-sixteenth century, see the important pp. 299–341
of Rudolf von Albertini, *Das florentinische Staatsbewusstsein im Übergang von der
Republik zum Prinzipat* (Bern: Franke, 1955)—the whole book should be kept
in mind for many of the subjects considered in this paper.

all change, present and future, depended, and so Bruni's main argument would have been inapplicable anyway. And few of them would really have welcomed change, even if it proceeded from above them; for change meant chaos, disorder, trouble—and all that was just what they believed themselves to have been rescued from once and for all by the providential accession of the reigning house.

Hence history was left with a choice among much more modest ends. The first was the one proposed by Girolamo Mei: that of demonstrating, in the face of the pyrrhonists and the relativists of his age, the lasting validity of the philological methods he had learned from Pier Vettori, by applying them successfully to the records of the past. But Mei apparently found it prudent to restrict himself to moments in the past too remote to arouse much interest, and he never got around to finishing enough of his ambitious projects to inspire any successors.[46] The second was the one proposed by Vincenzo Borghini: that of clarifying passages in those products of the past—the *Decameron*, for instance—which everyone already read for other than historical reasons. But in the end Borghini himself succumbed to the prevailing antihistorical methods of literary criticism, and his occasional reflections on the utility of history remained buried in his files until the early nineteenth century.[47] The third was the one proposed by Lionardo

[46] On Mei, the only study so far is that about his musical theories in Claude Palisca's superb introduction to the *Letters on Ancient and Modern Music* published by the American Institute of Musicology, 1960 (upon which much of this paragraph is based). [See below, ch. 17.] Much of his other correspondence has been published in Part III, Vol. II. of the *Prose fiorentine*.

[47] Many of Borghini's letters on this subject are printed along with those of Mei referred to in the preceding note. But a better source are those of his papers first published in Vol. I of *Opuscoli inediti e rari di classici o approvati autori* (Florence, 1845). See M. Barbi, *Gli scritti di V. B. sopra la lingua e la storia di Firenze* (Pisa, 1889) and B. Croce, "Un critico di poesie, V. B." now in *Poeti e scrittori del pieno e del tardo Rinascimento*, Vol. II, pp. 134–54, although Croce may read a bit too much Vico back into him. The categories in this paragraph are not mutually exclusive, of course; for Borghini says much the same thing as Mei in many passages of his *Discorsi*, published posthumously in 1584–85 (I use the edition of Florence, 1755, annotated by Domenico Maria Manni), as well as in their correspondence.

Salviati: that of inciting individual readers to virtue. But in that case, Salviati concluded, history need bother only with "what is commonly thought to be true" rather than what in fact was true; and he put down the copy of Carlo Sigonio he had been paging through and took up instead a book of poetry, which, after all, served his purpose much more effectively.[48] The last was the one proposed, or at least assumed, by Scipione Ammirato. "I am so wound up in my curiosity about the past," he confessed in 1592, "that I no longer have time to worry even about my usual domestic difficulties. If you could only see me now, sitting for days on end amid the dust and mouse dung of the monasteries of Tuscany devouring the documents of the last six hundred years! Why, I've become a veritable storehouse of antiquities!"[49] History, in other words, served the sole purpose of satisfying—and stimulating— his curiosity. Ammirato had no reason to think the past at all applicable to the present. He had nothing to criticize; and he could think of nothing new to recommend to the authorities of his day except more subsidies for himself and a harebrained scheme for an Ariosto-like crusade against the Turks. And just in case he were tempted to slip, he could always recall the advice of Cardinal Azzolini: "The very charge you have received from the grand duke," the cardinal told him, "to write the history of our times, is ample indication of your ability to proceed with all the prudence and circumspection that the material requires."[50] Hence Ammirato's multivolume history of Florence turned out to be not much more than a huge mass of information, which no one read in his lifetime because he published only a part of it, and

---

[48] *Il Lasca: Dialogo cruscato ovvero Paradosso d'Ormannozzo Rigogoli* [...] "In which it is shown that it is not necessary that history be true . . ." (Florence, 1584).

[49] Ammirato to the Bishop of Isola, 27 June 1592, in *Opuscoli*, Vol. II, pp. 486 ff.

[50] Cardinal Azzolini to Ammirato, 5 April 1586, in *Opuscoli*, Vol. II, p. 425. The appeal for a crusade is repeated in a number of orations sent around by the author to the courts of Europe. The one written for Sixtus V was published in 1594 along with a similar appeal composed a century earlier under very different circumstances by Cardinal Bessarion; and a quick comparison of the two texts will reveal their basic differences in purpose and mood.

which no one read when it finally came out in 1641 and 1647 because no one really cared any longer.[51] It is thus not surprising that one of the principal fields of Renaissance culture had, in Florence at least, come to an end, and that no one would bother with either reading or writing history for the next hundred years.

What happened in historiography seems also to have happened in another field in which Florentines had once led the world, namely, the plastic arts. As late as the 1560's the future of painting, sculpture, and architecture had still looked as promising as ever. Indeed, with the vast number of commissions opened up by the new regime's elaborate building projects, with some eighty working artists able to meet the most exacting standards, and with some twenty-five students already enrolled in the new Accademia del Disegno, ready to be launched into a career by such expensive displays as the funeral ceremonies for Michelangelo, Giorgio Vasari felt justified in proclaiming that "at no time in the past" had the arts enjoyed "such greatness and abundance."[52] Yet by the end of the century all these promises had materialized in little more than a vast quantity of pale imitations of what Pontormo, Bronzino, and Rosso Fiorentino had already done fifty years before. The attempt to institutionalize and mass-produce art, for one thing, had apparently proved a failure—or at least so even Vasari suggested just twelve years after he had founded the Academy,

---

[51] *Dell'Istorie fiorentine* (Florence, 1600–47). Two editions came out in the nineteenth century: Florence, 1848–49, and Turin, 1853. [After restudying the text, I now have a much higher opinion of Ammirato as a historian, though my thesis concerning the impact of his work on his contemporaries remains unaltered; and I present this opinion in ch. 2 of my forthcoming history of Florence after the Renaissance. The more negative judgment is still maintained by William J. Bouwsma in "Three Types of Historiography in Post-Renaissance Italy," *History and Theory*, IV (1965), 304–14.

[52] Vasari to Cosimo, 14 July 1564, in *Carteggio inedito d'artisti dei secoli XIV, XV, e XVI*, Vol. III, p. 139. His reports on the Accademia to Cosimo, 1 February 1563, *ibid.*, pp. 81–85; and on the funeral ceremonies, described in detail in the *Esequie di Michelangiolo Buonarroti celebrate dall'Accademia de' Pittori in S. Lorenzo* (Florence, 1564), Vincenzo Borghini (sometime vice-president of the academy) to Cosimo, 29 December 1564, *Carteggio inedito d'artiste...*, p. 163.

when he referred to its sessions with the inelegant word *coglionerie*.[53]
The potential leaders of a new style, moreover, may have been to
some extent sterilized by the longevity of the leaders of the old,
who dominated the aging Cosimo's artistic tastes and thus kept
them working for years on the same public work projects conceived decades before.[54] The artists may also have suffered from
Francesco de' Medici's claim to competence in this as in all other
matters, since he forced them to adhere to standards of "simplicity" and "perfection" that were not necessarily their own.
And they certainly were not encouraged by Ferdinando's confes-
sion of incompetence, which resulted in their being lumped together with gardeners, goldsmiths, and distillers in one big,
efficient bureau of government contracts and deprived of the lofty
status as men of letters that they had claimed since the time of
Brunelleschi.[55] Finally, art in the mid-sixteenth century seems to
have lacked the theoretical support it had enjoyed in the days of
Leon Battista Alberti and Leonardo da Vinci. Except for Vasari in
an occasional page of his *Lives*, the practitioners talked about little
but contracts and fees, while the few theorists, before Galileo's
letter of 1612,[56] talked about categories that were not derived

[53] Vasari to Borghini, 1 March 1572, *ibid.*, p. 311. These letters, along with
many others, can also be found in *Der literarische Nachlass Giorgio Vasaris*, 2 vols.,
ed. Karl Frey (Munich, 1923–30).

[54] This at any rate is the thesis of Filippo Baldinucci in his life of Lodovico
Cigoli in *Notizie de' professori del disegno da Cimabue in qua* (I use the edition of
Florence, 1845–47), which is not too different from that of Luigi Lanzi in
Storia pittorica della Italia (Vol. I, pp. 204 ff. of the edition of Milan, 1823, which
I follow), and which is borne out by Vasari's extravagant opinion of his own
merits.

[55] Francesco to Vasari, 16 March 1567, and the order of Ferdinando of 3
September 1588, in *Carteggio inedito*, Vol. III, pp. 239 and 484–85. With one or
two exceptions, I follow the judgment of Walter Friedlaender in *Mannerism
and Anti-Mannerism in Italian Painting*.

[56] See Erwin Panofsky, *Galileo as a Critic of the Arts* (The Hague: Nijhoff,
1954). What I say here holds true not so much for the deservedly well-known
Riposo of the unfortunately little-known Raffaello Borghini, but more particularly for such bits of bombast as Lionardo Salviati's "In lode della pittura"
of 1564 (Vol. I, pp. 83–107 of the Classici Italiani edition of the *Opere*), which
mentions not one single contemporary painter except, in the very last lines,
Michelangelo, for whose *esequie*, after all, the oration was composed.

from, and that had little apparent effect on, what actually was being painted and carved at the time. Hence the style subsequent art historians have identified as "mannerism" failed to engender a new style, at the moment of its fullest development, as had the classicism of Raffaello and Andrea del Sarto at the beginning of the century. And as the few original artists of the next generation looked for inspiration not to their Florentine teachers but to the Carracci and Caravaggio, and as the major commissions went more and more to that least Florentinizable of all foreigners, Giambologna, the city that until just a few years before had still attracted imitators and admirers all over Europe dwindled to the level of a provincial outpost in a world now dominated by Rome and Venice.[57]

To the exhaustion of certain fields of intellectual activity corresponded a rapid cooling off of the intense religiosity that had so inflamed Florentines, and troubled Florentine governments, in the 1490's and the 1520's. Not that there was any grave shortage, in the late sixteenth century, of dedicated churchmen: as soon as Cosimo had permitted him to return, for instance, the long-exiled archbishop of Florence, Antonio Altoviti, summoned a provincial synod and conducted a year-long visitation according to the prescriptions of the Council of Trent.[58] The pious bishop of Fiesole, similarly, expended an immense effort in sermons, tracts, and scriptural commentaries in order to raise the spiritual level of his flock; and the regulations promulgated by the bishops of Pisa and Arezzo at the turn of the century show that even literati and bureaucrats could, when an ecclesiastical benefice came their way,

[57] [Once again, I have had to reverse my judgment—this time on the basis of further study of Florentine art in the early seventeenth century; and in ch. 3 of my history mentioned above at n. 51, I follow Malcolm Campbell in placing the "crisis" of Florentine painting in the late 1630's, when Pietro da Cortona's Roman baroque suddenly invaded the Palazzo Pitti.]

[58] Antonio di Bindo Altoviti had been elevated to the archbishopric by Paul III in 1548, but he found it tactful, especially when Cosimo confiscated his lands for political reasons, to remain at Perugia and Rome until he was invited to return in 1567. The first synod met just before his arrival, in March 1565. The first visitation began in March 1568, and it was completed the following spring. See Agostino Lapini, *Diario fiorentino*, pp. 156 and 158.

take their pastoral obligations seriously.[59] And yet all these good
intentions and all this hard work seems to have had very little
effect. Of the program set forth by Petrarch and Lorenzo Valla for
the sanctification of the Christian layman almost nothing was left,
since the reformers made no attempt to evoke the spontaneous co-
operation of those at whom the reforms were aimed. Of the hopes
expressed by Girolamo Savonarola for the realization of a Corpus
Mysticum in the New Jerusalem of Florence, every trace had been
systematically stamped out—first by Cosimo, who had thrown the
Dominicans out of San Marco on the pretext of subversive
activities in 1545, and then by the timorous archbishop Alessandro
de' Medici, who carefully combed the city for all remnants of
Savonarolism before being elevated to the pontificate as Leo XI
in 1605.[60] Hence genuine religious experience was banished to the
convents, where it became the special preserve of such wellborn
mystics as Caterina de' Ricci and Maria Maddalena de' Pazzi.[61]

[59] On the bishop of Fiesole, Francesco Cattani da Diacceto, see his *Breve
raccolto della vita et costume di suor Caterina de' Ricci* (Florence, 1592), and his
Pistole, lezzioni et vangeli che si leggono in tutto l'anno alla Messa . . . [*Epistles,
Lessons, and Gospels that are read throughout the Year at Mass* . . . *Translated into
Florentine Vernacular*] (Florence, 1578), which may be a sign of a more general
attempt to make the liturgy more intelligible to the faithful. On Arezzo: the
published *Costitutioni* (Arezzo, 1603) of the bishop, Piero Usimbardi (above,
n. 35). On Pisa: the *Sermoni* (Florence, 1585) of the future bishop, Francesco
Bonciani (d. 1620), and his subsequent order *Alle reverende badesse, priore e
monache de' suoi monasteri di Pisa* (Florence, 1619), as well as the acts of his synod
published in Pisa in 1616. Bonciani in his youth had been one of the most
active members of the Accademia degli Alterati, for which he composed a
number of discourses and orations on literary subjects. His sermons were
delivered in the several lay confraternities of the capital. Ammirato's verse
paraphrases of the Psalms show further that some literati were even capable of a
fairly intense religious piety. [. . .]

[60] The most complete source of biographical information is still the thick
manuscript "Vita del Cardinale di Firenze" in the Biblioteca Casanatense, Rome
(MS 4201) used by Pastor, but so many pages are now damaged that I have
been able to read only a part of it. The history of the campaign against Savonarola is told by Cesare Guasti in the long introduction to *L'officio proprio per fra
Girolamo Savonarola*, 2nd edn. *accresciuta* ("amplified") (Prato, 1863).

[61] On Caterina de' Ricci there is a considerable bibliography (and a certain
amount of useless hagiography), from the *Vita della reverenda* . . . by the barely
disguised Savonarolan Serafino Razzi (Lucca, 1594) and the *Breve raccolto of*

And nothing was left for the rabble outside but either to gaze in awe at the constant round of miracles that took place within the cloister or to scramble after the immense number of indulgences offered them for just about everything.[62]

Just why anyone wanted the indulgences, to be sure, is not too clear. For to the educated as well as to the ordinary Florentine of the time, the next world must have looked very much like this one. He could address the Virgin Mary in exactly the same terms that Caterina de' Ricci used in recommending worthless supplicants to the crowned adultress Bianca Cappello; he could watch young Don Garzia de' Medici, clad in garments of heavenly purple, borne aloft from a fatal hunting party to "other palaces, other cities";[63] and he could look forward to finding the Father in Palazzo Pitti placed at the right hand of the Father in Heaven, surrounded by his poison manufacturers, his assassins, his courtiers,

---

Cattani di Diacceto (n. 59 above) to *S. C. de' R.* by Guglielmo di Agresti in Collana Ricciana, *Fonti*, 3 vols. [Florence: Olschki, 1963–64]. [. . .] The classic work of M. M. Vaussard, *Sainte Marie Madeleine de Pazzi*, 2nd edn. (Paris: Gabalda, 1925), still makes very good reading, especially when supplemented by the older *Lettere spirituali e familiari*, ed. Cesare Guasti (Prato, 1861) and Vaussard's own *Extases et lettres* (Paris, 1949). [The anonymous *S. M. M. de' P.* (Rome: Presbyterium, 1960), may be useful in promoting a certain kind of pre-Vatican II piety, but it is worthless as a guide to the historical personage mentioned in the title.] The miracles are all listed in the acts of her canonization, published in Rome in 1729.

[62] The importance of indulgences is indicated by the some 164 packed pages listing those granted by Sixtus V to the new confraternity gotten together by the Franciscans of Santa Croce in 1585 and published by Fra Raffaello della Fonte: *Ritratto delle indulgenze . . . concesse . . . alla Confraternità del Cordone del serafico padre san Francesco* (Florence, 1598). The fascination for relics was no monopoly of any class: a good example is that of the wealthy and well-educated friend of Galileo, Giovan Battista Strozzi, whose reaction to a sponge once used by Charles Borromeo to wash his face and sent to him by Cardinal Federico is recorded in his letter of 18 September 15— (? — Strozzi's handwriting would tax the patience of an expert paleographer) [but in any case I would postdate the letter to 1617 or 1618, when the cardinal visited Florence]: Biblioteca Nazionale, Florence, Mag. vii, 1399, fol. 16.

[63] Such is the language of Lionardo Salviati in his three orations on the death of Don Garzia de' Medici in 1562, republished in his *Primo libro delle orazioni* in 1575.

and his *courtisanes*.[64] That anyone strove to get into heaven at all, then—and that seems to have been the only goal Christians were expected to strive for—can be attributed only to the fear of being tossed into hell, which contemporary preachers described *ad nauseam* as the scene of the most frightful atrocities. The faith, hope, and charity, in other words, that had inspired the acts of saints and martyrs for a millennium and a half had disappeared from Christianity in Florence: and all that remained was cringing fear—and a certain amount of pyrotechnics.

That historiography and Savonarolan piety had all but vanished in the last decades of the sixteenth century, that painting and architecture had lost their creative impulse, that ethics and political thought had dwindled into platitudes and arid precepts, that literary criticism had worn out the arguments it had all too long debated, and that the study of language had ended up in somewhat anachronistic word lists—all this does not mean necessarily that cultural vitality had disappeared from Florence altogether. Even within these exhausted fields, after all, it was possible to make at least a negative contribution to the future. The waning of poetics, for example, may have been in some part responsible for the subsequent revival of poetry itself; the withering of mannerism may have been a necessary prelude to what Walter Friedlaender has called the "second Renaissance";[65] and the freezing of the vernacular language may have been effective in preserving a link with the Trecento masters all during the fifty-year interval between Marino and Arcadia. Even if they were overlooked at the time, the discourses of Borghini and the *Istorie* of Ammirato provided the principal starting point for those scholars who, under the inspiration of Lodovico Antonio Muratori, were to revive

[64] The identification of the earthly and the heavenly hierarchies is present in most of the religious literature at the time, in the rest of Italy as well as in Florence, where indeed the example of none other than the famous preacher Francesco Panigarola may have had some influence, since he was a good friend of many Florentine men of letters, and since his *Orazione funerale in morte di Carlo Borromeo*, with all its rather revolting parallels between sainthood and titled nobility, was published there in 1584.

[65] Above, n. 55.

historiography in Florence in the mid-eighteenth century.[66] And even if they were regarded as mere entertainment by the populace, the public spectacles proved capable, when transferred to a more intimate court setting, of generating, or at least facilitating the generation of a completely new form of art, the opera.[67]

Furthermore, in two other fields a revolution was already well underway for which Florentines were in part responsible. It was the same Giovanni de' Bardi, the Bardi of the syllogistic football games, who gathered in his house the amateurs, the theorists, and the performers of music whose discussions led to the establishment of one of the basic patterns that Western music would follow for the next several centuries. And it was Andrea Cesalpino, the rather obscure professor of medicine and keeper of the botanical gardens at Pisa, as well as the young Galileo, just then working on his first mathematical problems in expectation of a university chair, who were laying the foundations for the world-shaking innovations in science and philosophy at the beginning of the next century.[68] These two revolutions, moreover, were being prepared in the name of precisely those principles that had inspired most of the more lasting achievements of Florentine culture during the preceding two hundred years: the principle that the chief purpose of studying ancient books, whether Archimedes or Girolamo Mei's Greek music texts, was to stimulate original thought among

[66] Note particularly the critical manuals of Anton Filippo Adami, *Prospetto di una nuova compilazione della storia fiorentina* (Pisa, 1758), and Domenico Maria Manni, *Metodo per istudiare con brevità e profittevolmente le storie di Firenze* (Lucca, 1755; 2nd edn. of Florence the same year), as well as the preface of Pietro Gaetano Viviani, largely under the inspiration of Manni, who did the annotations, to his (2nd) edition of Borghini's *Discorsi* (n. 46 above).

[67] The artistic by-products of the spectacles are now richly documented by D. P. Walker in his edition of *Les fêtes du mariage de Ferdinand de Médicis et de Christine de Lorraine*, of which Vol. I (*Musique des intermèdes de "La Pellegrina,"* ed. Federico Ghisi, D. P. Walker, and J. Jacquenot) has been published (Paris: C.N.R.S., 1963); but they are already well known from Angelo Solerti's still standard *Le origini del melodrama* (Turin, 1903). [In general, see ch. 17 below.]

[68] I have spoken of these matters at greater length in a paper entitled "The Florentine Background of Galileo's Work" [which has at last been published in the volume *Galileo Man of Science*, ed. Ernan McMullin (New York: Basic Books, 1968)].

the students, the principle that practice and theory—composition and musicology, lens-making and optics—were mutually dependent on one another, and the principle that the arts and sciences were the business of the ordinary, educated laymen, not the exclusive domain of specialists.

To be sure, both the science of Galileo and the musical theory of Bardi's *Camerata* represented new fields of thought and activity in the history of Florentine culture. In so far as they incorporated attitudes and methods previously adopted in other disciplines, they are indications of what was to be permanent in the contribution of the Renaissance to the future course of European civilization, not of what had been peculiar to Florentine literature in the Quattrocento. The substitution of new for old fields of interest may well be more properly described as a "shift" rather than a "decadence," as H. G. Koenigsberger recently suggested.[69] But at least it is clear that in those fields in which Florentines had been the most active and the most creative in the brilliant period from 1402 to 1527, the Renaissance was dead by the 1580's. It had died not only because it had been suppressed but also because Florentines were firmly convinced that it had never been more alive and because they were perfectly willing to entrust its preservation to the same omnicompetent prince to whom they entrusted all else. It had died not because something new had taken its place, but because everyone thought that the problems it posed had at last been solved. It had died not in agony, but in the pleasant amenities of one of the rare moments in history when time, with all the annoyance and insecurity it brings, seemed once and for all to have come to a halt.

[69] [See n. 23 to the introduction to this anthology.]

PART TWO

Continuation and Change
in the Humanistic Disciplines

3 Jurisprudence: The Methodology of Andrea Alciato[1]

ROBERTO ABBONDANZA

As director of the State Archives at Perugia, Roberto Abbondanza is chiefly concerned with saving Umbrian art from the mercenary and the ignorant and in restoring Florentine archival documents from oily water. But he has also discovered a long-lost autograph letter of Boccaccio. He has compiled a complete bibliography of legal history, the *Bibliografia italiana di storia del diritto medievale e moderno* (*1957–1959*) (Milan: Giuffrè, 1963). He has uncovered many new letters of Alciato beyond those already published by Gian Luigi Barni in 1953 under the title *Le lettere di A. A.* (Florence: Le Monnier). And in preparation for his forthcoming historical biography of Alciato, which is promised in the article here translated, he has written several articles in his special field of research, the history of law, e.g. "Tentativi medicei di chiamare l'Alciato allo Studio di Pisa," *Annali di storia del diritto*, II (1958), 361–403.

Along with Guillaume Budé and Ulrich Zasius, Andrea Alciato was acclaimed in his own day as one of the "triumvirate" of humanist jurisprudence. He was opposed, that is, to the ahistorical, systematic approach to the Roman law codes (*mos italicus*) which the Italian law schools of his day had inherited from the post-glossators of the fourteenth century. He called instead for the application of humanist philogical methods to the *Corpus Iuris Civilis*—the collection of all extant Roman statutes edited and published by the Emperor Justinian I in the sixth century A.D. By interpreting each of

[1] "Premières considerations sur la méthodologie d'Alciat," *Pedagogues et juristes*, Congrès du Centre d'Études Supérieures de la Renaissance de Tours: été, 1960 (Paris: Vrin, 1963), pp. 107–18. Abridged and translated by the editor with the tacit approval of the author (who happens to be a personal friend of the editor) and overt approval of Librairie J. Vrin, the publisher.

the various laws in the light of the specific concepts and institutions to which the author of the law was referring, this
approach turned the *Corpus Iuris Civilis* from the written
version of natural law which the medieval jurists had assumed
it to be into the positive law of one particular state. This
approach became particularly widespread in France (hence
mos gallicus), where it soon stimulated an interest in the
historical origins of French law and where its proponents
became known as the *Culti*. Alciato was born at Milan in
1492; and after completing his law studies, he practiced for
some years in his native city before being called to his first
university chair, in Avignon. From 1529 to 1533 he lectured
at Bourges. He then returned to Italy and taught at Pavia,
Bologna, Ferrara, and then again at Pavia, where he died in
1550. Abbondanza includes a brief biography of Alciato in
the volume containing the article here translated, *Pedagogues
et juristes*, and a more comprehensive one in the *Dizionario
biografico degli Italiani*. The most thorough biography, however, is still that of Paul-Émile Viard, *André Alciat* (Paris,
1926), though certain moments of his life have since been
studied in greater detail, e.g. by Gianluigi Barni in "La
situazione politico-giuridica milanese nella formazione di
A. A.," *Bibliothèque d'humanisme et renaissance*, XXII (1960),
7–33.

A STUDY of the juridical work of Alciato is a major undertaking.
For one thing, the quantity of his published writings is immense.
Of the five folio volumes in the Basel edition of his *Opera omnia*
(1582), only a very small part is irrelevant—and even that part
may have to be considered, given the close interdependence of all
different aspects of his thought and activity. For another, the
thousands of packed columns into which the text is divided contain tens of thousands of citations, all abbreviated according to the
custom of the common law. Every serious scholar must begin by
tracking down these citations; and he must frequently call upon
the assistance of different specialists in elucidating them properly.
There is no point in trying to approach Alciato's works through

the accompanying index, ... or even in following the systematic arrangement adopted by the sixteenth-century editors. On the contrary, it is necessary to rearrange each of the various treatises in a historical and chronological order and then to take note of the variations introduced in the original manuscript version in the course of successive editions.... In other words, Alciato's juridical commentaries must be analyzed just like any other literary document. Each part must be examined separately. The final version must be compared to earlier drafts. And the sources must be established.

Moreover, in order to comprehend the novelty of any particular affirmation or of the manner in which any particular problem is posed, it is necessary to examine the vast work of all the many commentators since the High Middle Ages. And the work of the commentators was far more varied and complex than is often realized. Alciato's methodological innovations have already been recognized. But his innovations in the realm of juridical concepts, the vitality of his interpretations, and the newness of his ideas, can be understood only after much arduous labor....

The hypotheses which I offer here, therefore, are only tentative, and I have limited myself to illustrating only certain moments in the development of Alciato's philological and practical juridical work. Not that I think that the moments I have identified are without importance: indeed, I believe that subsequent research will have to take account of them. But at present they represent a pattern that can be only very roughly traced out.

The work with which Alciato made his first appearance in the world of humanism—a world in which he was destined to become one of the most often published, one of the most read, and one of the most influential contributors—carries the date 28 July 1515. It is composed of two titles: the *Annotationes in Tres Posteriores Libros Codicis Justiniani* (*Notes on the Last Three Books of the Codex of Justinian*) and the *Opusculum quo Graecae Dictiones fere ubique in Digestis Restituuntur* (*A Short Treatise in Which the Greek Words Are Almost Everywhere Restored to the Digest*). Alciato was only twenty-four at the time; and it was probably with the assistance and on the insistence of his friend Francesco Calvo[2] that he decided to publish these works. The works are extracts from a much more comprehensive project of studies. And this project was probably already well advanced at the time, to judge by what he was to publish in the following several years and by what of it still remains in manuscript. Alciato thus came to be known among the learned even before he had obtained the degree of doctor of civil and canon law.

Alciato was indebted to his fellow student Filippo Sauli, a humanist and ecclesiastic of noble family to whom the *Annotationes* were dedicated, for much of the material he used in these two short treatises. For it was Sauli who furnished him with a copy of the *Notitia Dignitatum*,[3] which, as Alciato acknowledges in the preface, was indispensable in resolving the numerous problems he faced in his unprecedented task of "emendating" the last three books of the *Codex*. There were very few literary sources in which the laws promulgated between the reigns of Theodosius and Justinian were recorded; and neither Livy nor any of the other authors of classical antiquity could be of much help in the exegesis of texts that had been composed "when the elegance of the Latin language was perishing." For the *Digest*, on the other hand, his task was easier. More commentators had already worked on it; and in the course of developing his new approach to the text, Alciato could turn not only to the *Notitia Dignitatum* but also to the *Graecus Legum Interpres* (*Greek Interpreter*) and to "other more recent" authors, although these documents were all but unknown in an age when men of letters were interested exclusively in the classics. The *Annotationes* thus drew attention to a previously neglected historical epoch and provided materials for under-

2 [Francesco Calvo (d. after 1545), a friend of Erasmus and a frequent correspondent of Alciato, was a printer and bookdealer in Rome, part of whose business consisted in importing books—including those of Luther—from beyond the Alps.]

3 [This important document of late Roman imperial administration is discussed below. The standard edition today is that of Otto Seeck (Berlin, 1876; repr. 1962). An English translation by William Fairley was published by the University of Pennsylvania Press in 1889.]

standing it better. Alciato realized that the kind of work he had chosen would certainly draw criticism from the jurists, who were convinced of the incompatibility of humanistic and juridical studies. But what seems to have interested him most was being of service [not only to the jurists] but to all those of whatever profession who might wish to investigate a domain practically unknown before his time.

In undertaking the *Annotationes*, Alciato was provided with two models—two works which he must certainly have read and annotated. Both of them bear the same title, *Annotationes*, and both had issued from the press of Josse Bade, the former student of Guarino, professor of humanities at the University of Paris.[4] The first was called *Annotationes in Viginti Quattuor Priores Libros Digestorum* (*On the First Twenty-Four Books of the Digests*); it was written by Guillaume Budé and published in 1508. The second— though actually composed prior to the first—was the *Annotationes Doctorum Virorum* (*Of Learned Men*), published in 1511. This volume was one of the more important anthologies, if not the most important, of humanist philology. It included the *Miscellanea*, the *Lamia*, and the *Panepistemon* of Poliziano, the philological dissertations and commentaries of Sabellico, Filippo Beroaldo, Domizio Calderini, and Giovanni Battista Pio, the polemical observations of Cornelio Vitelli on Giorgio Merula, the annotations of Jacopo della Croce, and, finally, the *Castigationes in Leges* of Pio Antonio Bartolini,[5] followed by two other small writings of the same author. Most of these pieces contain some references of juridical interest, particularly those of Poliziano. But the only ones of a specifically juridical nature are those of Bartolini, which seem

---

[4] [Josse Bade (1461/62–1535), the famous printer to the University of Paris, had studied as a young man under Battista Guarini, author of one of the best-known pedagogical treatises of the Renaissance and successor to his father, Guarino da Verona, as head of the school of Ferrara.]

[5] [On the work of the Quattrocento philologians with regard to the texts of Roman law, see Domenico Maffei, *Gli inizi dell'umanesimo giuridico* (Milan: Giuffrè, 1956), and more recently Eugenio Garin, "Leggi, diritto e storia nelle discussioni dei secoli XV e XVI" in *Storia del diritto nel quadro delle scienze storiche* (Florence: Olschki, 1966).]

to have been given to a publisher in Bologna as early as 1495. In the preface, Bartolini explains that, in spite of his own limitations, he is seeking to open the way to his successors by suggesting corrections of "a good number of usually corrupt passages" in the *Digest* and the *Codex*. Several of the sixty short chapters of the book concern the texts later studied by Alciato, and he certainly had them in mind when he came to write his own *Annotationes*. But Bartolini did more than just suggest emendations. In his *Lucubratiunculae*, a brief interpretation of seven of the laws of the *Digest* and the *Codex*, he goes on to offer a juridical exegesis of the texts. And in the last of the treatises, the *Epitome de Ordine Imperatorum*, he proposes a reclassification in the usually accepted list of Roman emperors. [A full discussion of the precursors of juridical humanism would be premature at this point in the development of historical studies of the subject.] But it is difficult not to recognize in the work of Bartolini the elements of a method analogous to those which were to appear in the work of Alciato twenty years later.

That Budé had long been aware of the contents of the anthology, even though it came out three years after his own book, seems evident from the fact that he had carefully studied the Italian humanists, among whom Poliziano was the most prominent. That the two books were thought of at the time as closely related seems apparent from the fact that the copies belonging to Boniface Amerbach[6] are bound together and are all covered with the owner's marginal notes. Amerbach later studied under Alciato at Avignon. But he must have possessed the volume during his sojourn with Zasius. And Zasius[7] recognized the primarily philo-

---

[6] [Boniface (or Bonifacius) Amerbach (1495–1562) was a student both of Zasius and of Alciato and a close friend of Erasmus. He was a professor of law at Basel from 1524 to 1548. His immense correspondence has been published by Alfred Hartmann as *Die Amerbachkorrespondenz* in five volumes (Basel: Universitätsbibliothek, 1942–53).]

[7] [Ulrich Zasius, the leading humanist jurist in Germany, was born at Constance in 1461. He was employed as legal counselor by the city of Freiburg im Breisgau, where he also taught at the university, from 1503 until his death in 1535. A brief summary of his life and works is given by Hans Thieme in the

logical nature of Budé's work, ten years after its publication, by praising it as worthy of Poliziano. The famous German jurist fully realized that the juridical sciences might well profit from a philological critique of the texts of the law. But he never lost sight of their basically practical end. Poliziano had raised philology— or "grammar," as he called it—to a position of primacy among all the sciences. But to Zasius grammar was just an instrument. And Zasius correctly recognized in Budé one of the most important representatives of philology. It was a philology which drew together many different cultural experiences and one which went beyond the limits of any given field to build a new city of man upon all the concrete experiences of ancient civilization as they were preserved in Greek, Latin, and Hebrew texts. On one hand, then, Budé used the *Pandects* as a way of gaining a more complete knowledge of classical antiquity—its languages, its ideas, its customs and institutions. On the other hand, he brought to bear upon the interpretation of the *Pandects* a knowledge of a great variety of Greek and Latin authors. Budé's was a "science of serenity," as Augustin Renaudet noted; but it was also a "science of combat." For in predicting the abandonment of the glosses and commentaries [of the Middle Ages], the *Annotationes* led the fight against scholasticism in jurisprudence, just as Lefèvre d'Étaples led the fight against scholasticism in philosophy and Erasmus, with his *Enchiridion Militis Christiani*, led it in theology.[8] At the same

---

volume *Pedagogues et juristes* from which this essay is taken. See also Guido Kisch, *Humanismus und Jurisprudenz* (Basel: Helbing und Lichtenhahn, 1955), as well as Hansjürgen Knoche, *U. Z. und das Freiburger Stadtrecht von 1520* (Karlsruhe: Müller, 1957). Guillaume Budé (1468–1540), the third of the "triumvirate," wrote a number of other philological and moral works as well, e.g. the *Institution du prince* (in French) and the *Commentarii Linguae Graecae*. He was largely responsible for founding the Collège Royale (today the Collège de France), over the objections of the Sorbonne, for the specific purpose of teaching the three ancient languages. The standard biography of him is still that of Louis Delaruelle, *Études sur l'humanisme français: G. B.* (Paris: Campion, 1907).]

[8] [Jacques Lefèvre d'Étaples (Faber Stapulensis) (1461–1536), a biblical and patristic scholar, was one of the most active promoters of spiritual reform in early sixteenth-century France, and he was the chief assistant of Guillaume

time it must be admitted, I think, that the function of the *Annotationes* was basically destructive. They destroyed the patrimony of the Middle Ages, and they offered nothing to replace it. Budé was a philologian, not a jurist; and a simple return to the original reading of the texts of the law could do little to provide a new basis for the whole corpus of existing law.

Alciato was not without predecessors, then, either in Italy or in France, in his application of humanistic philology to the texts of the Law. But he was undeniably original in his choice of sources: the historians and the other writers of the late empire, the *Notitia Dignitatum*, and the *Graecus Legum Interpres*.

As Girard noticed in a very good study of the subject published some thirty years ago,[9] Alciato was the first to use and then to publish the *Notitia Dignitatum*—an "official almanack" of the empire, divided into two separate parts for the East and for the West, drawn up toward the middle of the fifth century A.D. Girard himself was a great philologian, a recognized specialist in Roman law, and an authority on the history of the various manuscripts of the *Notitia*. But he based his observations solely upon the text of the *Annotationes* published among the *Opuscula* at Lyon in 1529. Thus he did not realize that the edition he used was merely an unauthorized reprint of the Basel edition of 1523, that the Basel edition in turn was already the third edition of the work, and that the *Notitia* were referred to in a different manner both in the manuscript and in all the subsequent editions.... His oversight furnishes us with one more example of the importance of studying Alciato according to the methods of philology, in spite of the extra trouble that these methods impose upon us.[10]

Briçonnet, bishop of Meaux, in applying the reform in the realm of ecclesiastical institutions. Erasmus's *Enchiridion* is now available in English in a paperback edition by Raymond Himelick (Midland–52). On Erasmus's contribution to jurisprudence, see Kisch, *Erasmus und die Jurisprudenz seiner Zeit* (Basel: Helbing und Lichtenhahn, 1960), as well as his brief statement, "Humanistic Jurisprudence," in *Studies in the Renaissance*, VIII (1960), 71–87.]

[9] [P. F. Girard, "A. et la 'Notitia Dignitatum'" in *Studi in onore di S. Perozzi* (Palermo, 1925), pp. 59–87.]

[10] [Here I abbreviate most of a whole paragraph in the original.]

No one, to my knowledge, has yet studied or even discussed Alciato's use of the *Legum Interpres Graecus*, though it appears at least eight times in the *Annotationes*. Alciato thought this "Greek interpreter" to have been a contemporary of Justinian, though he never succeeded in identifying him. I was fortunate enough to find this practically unknown manuscript at Basel, in a copy, possibly incomplete, made by Boniface Amerbach at Avignon in 1522. It appears to be a glossary of technical Latin terms in alphabetical order drawn up for the use of Greeks—one of the kind mentioned in the still valuable works of Mortreuil and Zacharias von Lingenthal.[11]

These, then, are the principal sources of Alciato's first work that I have been able to track down so far. I will give a much more minute examination of them in my forthcoming book on the youth of Alciato. For the moment I wish to discuss merely certain characteristics of this work. When Alciato speaks of the unprecedented task he has undertaken, he is not thinking so much of the neglect of the last three books of the *Codex* among the jurists of the past—who, indeed, often detached them from the body of the *Codex*, as Francesco Calasso has shown in his study of Luca da Penne.[12] He is thinking, rather, of the humanists. The *Tres Libri* are mentioned in at least seven of the juridical treatises already in print at the time. One or two of these treatises even call for a greater knowledge of ancient authors in providing correct interpretations. But all of them are chiefly interested in applying what they find in these books to the law of their own time and place. . . . Moreover, they follow the procedure of the nonhumanist jurists in interpreting the specific points of the *Tres Libri* in the light of

[11] [Jean-Anselme-Bernard Mortreuil was a lawyer and historian of Marseilles who also wrote a *Histoire du droit byzantin* (Paris, 1843–44). Karl Eduard Zacharias von Lingenthal (1812–94), son of the law professor Karl Salomo, published many studies on Byzantine law from 1837 on, e.g. *Historiae Juris Graeco-Romani Delineatio* (1839).]

[12] [Francesco Calasso in his *Lezioni di storia del diritto italiano* (Milan: Giuffrè, 1946 et seq.). See also Walter Ullmann, *The Medieval Idea of Law as Represented by Luca de Penna: A Study in Fourteenth-Century Legal Scholarship* (London: Methuen, 1946).]

previous commentaries made upon all the other texts of the *Corpus Iuris* [—even when those texts were actually composed in response to very different historical circumstances]. This method inevitably led to gross misreadings—misreadings which became targets for the pitiless tirades of the humanists. The fundamental preoccupation of Alciato was also juridical. But it was much less immediate. Before attempting to show the relevance of the texts to current law, Alciato insisted upon getting rid of the textual imperfections which his predecessors had introduced or overlooked. He then insisted upon using all the resources of history and philology in order to provide each passage with its original meaning and to put it in the historical context [in which it was written]. He insisted, in other words, upon looking for the vitality of the laws within the laws themselves, rather than imposing upon them the norms of a completely different time and place.

Even the index shows that Alciato's first work is very different from those of the jurists in the medieval tradition. The first part is an *index dictionum*, a glossary containing more than 150 terms identified by the author. But almost none of these terms refers to a juridical concept or principle or to a point of doctrine, as did all such terms in indices destined for the use both of teachers and of practical lawyers. The second part is a brief series of passages that received a *novus intellectus*, a "new meaning.". . . The third and most important part is an *Annotationes in Varios Humanioris Literaturae Authores* (*Notes on Various Authors of Humane Letters*), which gives a good idea of the vast amount of reading that Alciato had completed by the tender age of twenty-one years.

Alciato's second work is one that so far has received almost no attention: the *Paradoxa*. It was later incorporated as the second of the books entitled *Praetermissa*. It brings the methods of the *Annotationes* to bear upon the very core of the interpretation of the law. With this book Alciato changes from a philologian specializing in juridical subjects into a professor of law.

To appreciate fully the novelty and value of the *Paradoxa*, it would be necessary to examine each of the fragments contained in each of its six books and compare them with the work of jurists before and after. I have just begun this task, realizing that it alone will enable me to escape from the usual generalizations of the history of jurisprudence. For the moment, I yield to the opinion of Viard:

> The *Paradoxa* reject the lengthy and confused discourses and the disregard for antiquity that had triumphed among the post-glossators and the followers of Bartolus.[13] In so many neat, short chapters, the work gives, with a previously unknown precision, the sense of the law under study. It cites in its support literary works which the jurists had never looked at. And it rectifies, on the basis of a more exact understanding of antiquity, the errors concerning the law then being taught. Alciato did not just display his qualities to his contemporaries. He clearly showed them the errors that his particularly rich education prevented him from ignoring—errors that he was determined to expose in an effort to change the entire direction of juridical studies. He reproached them ... for their prolixity and for their ignorance of the Latin language. ...

In the *Paradoxa* Alciato limited himself to examining isolated texts and to putting them back into their historical contexts. This procedure served him well for polemical purposes. It enabled him to strike at a great variety of separate commentaries. The next step was to present a more rigorous demonstration of his new method—to use it not only in examining certain essential chapters, but in discovering the logical and systematic connections among all the parts of the text. This is what he began doing ... in the small treatise *De Eo Quod Interest*, which concerned Justinian's constitution "De Sententiis Quae Pro Eo Quod Interest Proferuntur" (C.7.47). The idea of the treatise came to him during a visit to Venice. He borrowed what books he could, studied the text, and read the interpretations previously suggested. He then worked out a new interpretation, in good Latin, on the basis of

[13] [Bartolo da Sassoferrato (1314–57), professor of law at Perugia, was one of the greatest of the post-glossators and the author of a great number of commentaries on the law, which were brought together and printed in ten volumes at Basel in 1588–89.]

the ideas he had set forth in the prefaces to the various parts of the *Paradoxa*.

As long as he remained closed in the ivory tower of his study at Avignon, Alciato remained faithful to his philological premises; and it is the work he did there that makes him one of the pioneers of the history of law. But in the long series of lectures he delivered in the classroom, which were published under the title *De Verborum Obligationibus*, [he approaches the problem in a somewhat different manner]. As Brugi[14] pointed out over forty years ago (and no one has since followed Brugi in studying Alciato's impact upon the Italian law schools), Alciato sought not to destroy but to improve upon the older methods. He considered jurisprudence an eminently practical science; and he did not, therefore, wish scholarship to prevail over law. He was a practicing lawyer, after all, as well as a professor. He thus sympathized with the efforts of his medieval predecessors in seeking to interpret and apply the law; and he frequently attributed to their age, not to them, what appeared to be their barbarisms of expression and style. In giving his own elegant and concise commentaries, he always took care to cite the opinions of the glossators and the commentators; and he made some effort to find out what the most accepted opinion was, even while preferring the most correct to the most widely held. His own Latin was impeccable. But he always took care to write in such a way that those of his readers [who were not trained in the humanist tradition] could easily understand him. And he admitted that "every science has its own vocabulary," which must at times be used even if it seems barbarous to men of letters.

It is erroneous, therefore, to picture Alciato as one who sought to free the texts, like a pure scholar, from all previous glosses and commentaries.... The teaching and practice of law in Italy derived in large measure from the often criticized schools of Accursius and Bartolus; and it was onto their doctrines that the critical spirit of humanist philology was grafted. Alciato sought to correct and develop these doctrines. He did not seek to replace

---

[14] [Biagio Brugi, *Per la storia della giurisprudenza e delle università*, 2nd edn., with the addition of *Nuovi saggi* (Turin, 1921).]

them completely with a historical reconstruction of classical Roman law. Hence he is important not only as the founder of the history of law but also as the one who introduced a critical spirit into the great body of the common law.

Indeed, it was as a mediator between philology and the law that Alciato evoked such admiration and inspired so many disciples in Italy, the homeland of the *mos italicus*. A history of Italian jurisprudence from the sixteenth century on is long overdue. The current concept of a single historical period extending from the eleventh century to the age of codification [in the eighteenth] is unacceptable. For Alciato's contemporaries and successors were fully aware of the spirit of renovation that had penetrated all the domains of human learning. But they conceived of scholarly jurisprudence in a very special manner. Conditions in Italy were very different from those in other countries. In Italy common law was practically identical, on the normative as well as on the doctrinal plane, with the [written] law. The Italians, moreover, demanded that jurisprudence should not be separated from its practical application. Jurists should explain themselves clearly, they thought; but they should not become merely men of letters. They should avoid being too subtle and prolix. They should carefully criticize commonly received ideas with complete liberty; but they should not totally reject all those ideas. They should read both the older interpreters and the new ones.... Thus after Alciato there still remained a good number of "barbarous" authors. But Alciato gained the favor of a considerable part of the new generation. He was sought after by princes and cities. And he was cited, along with the more usual authorities, by the writers of treatises as well as by the practitioners of law. As the study of the history of the Italian universities is carried further (and this study has just begun), "Alciatans" will be found everywhere: at Padua, at Siena, at Pisa, at Bologna, at Ferrara, at Pavia, at Turin....

One final comment on Alciato's major work, *De Verborum Significatione* (*On the Meaning of Words*), which is joined to a commentary on the title of the *Digest* bearing the same name. I have just begun a systematic study of this treatise. I have found the manuscript of the Avignon lectures at Basel in the form of rough drafts. I have collected and classified the numerous editions of the complete work; and I have been fortunate enough to acquire a copy of the first edition. I am not yet able to propose any definite conclusions. But I am convinced that a study of this work, along with a study of the *Annotationes*, on the basis of all the previous commentaries of the same texts since the founding of the school of Bologna, will eventually provide us with the material necessary to appreciate fully the methodological innovations of humanist jurists of the sixteenth century.

4 Historiography: The Art of History in the Italian Counter Reformation[1]

GIORGIO SPINI

Giorgio Spini, born in 1916, began his academic career as a specialist on the sixteenth century with an annotated edition of the letters of Cosimo I de' Medici (Vallecchi, 1940) and a study of the first translator of the entire Bible into Italian, Antonio Brucioli (La Nuova Italia, 1940); and in 1945 he published his still authoritative account of the foundation of the Medici principate, *Cosimo I de' Medici e la indipendenza del Principato mediceo* (Vallecchi). In his *Ricerca dei libertini* (Editrice Universale, 1950), he moved from the sixteenth into the seventeenth century in order to follow one of the by-products of Paduan Aristotelianism down to its death at the hands of the Galilean scientists. He has since shifted his attention elsewhere: to Calvinism in Europe, to Calvinism in Massachusetts, to Protestantism in Italian nationalism of the nineteenth century (*Risorgimento e Protestanti* [Edizioni Scientifiche Italiane, 1956]), and then, after several prolonged visits in Cambridge, Madison, and Berkeley, to recent radical movements in the United States. In his monumental *Storia dell'età moderna*, first published by Cremonese in Rome in 1960 and reissued (1965) in paperback by Einaudi, he showed himself to be a master of broad syntheses as well as of detailed analyses. Yet he still has occasionally been drawn back to his earlier interests, most recently in a study of the political ideas

[1] "I trattatisti dell'arte storica nella Controriforma italiana," *Contributi alla storia del Concilio di Trento e della Controriforma*, "Quaderni di Belfagor" (Florence: Vallecchi, 1948). Translated and somewhat abridged by the editor. The author has gone over the editor's manuscript and made some corrections. However, he has not attempted to bring it up to date or to introduce substantial revisions. It therefore represents his position on this subject as of 1948, when he wrote the article, not as of 1968, when the editor translated it into English.

of Michelangelo. Spini was the first professor to hold a chair
of American history in an Italian university. He is now
professor of modern history at the Facoltà di Magistero in
Florence.

THE COUNTER REFORMATION AND THE DOGMATICS
OF HISTORY

IT is certainly not inappropriate that a study of the Council of
Trent be supplemented by a study of treatises on the art of history.
For these treatises occupy a prominent place in Italian literary production from the time of the Council down to the middle of the
seventeenth century. Indeed, the discussion of the nature of historiography, of its methods of research and manner of presentation, and of its dignity in relation to other disciplines, formed one
of the most characteristic aspects of Counter Reformation culture.
It was one, moreover, which made a considerable impact upon
other aspects of the culture and the general spiritual life of the
times. A thorough investigation [of this phenomenon], to be sure,
would require not an article but an entire volume; and it would
have to reconsider the whole vast literature of the debate between
the Tacitists and the Anti-Tacitists of the sixteenth and seventeenth
centuries. . . . This essay is limited to a consideration only of those
works that deal specifically with the art and the method of history;
and even within these limits it may still be marred by important
omissions and lacunae. Hopefully, however, it may stimulate
others to look for further elements that may serve the purpose of a
more ample treatment of the subject at another time.[2]

At least in a theoretical form, the problem of history was one
that was barely perceived during most of the Middle Ages. It was
first presented to the minds of Italians with the appearance of
humanist historiography in the early fifteenth century and of
political history in the early sixteenth. Yet in spite of some acute

[2] [The last three sentences of this paragraph appear in a footnote in the
original.]

observations in the *Actius* of Pontano,[3] and in spite of one or two suggestions by such humanists as Pico della Mirandola and Guarino, the Renaissance seems to have placed much more emphasis on the creation of new kinds of history and on the renovation of history writing itself. It had little time left for contemplating with detachment the problem of [what history was]. That was a problem it resolved in practice, in the very act of writing. Meditation upon history, and treatises and polemics upon the art of history, are thus characteristic not of the Renaissance but of the Counter Reformation and of the generation that followed Machiavelli and Guicciardini. Indeed, the problem of the art of history is one of the problems that most attracted the best minds of the age, from Patrizi to Boccalini and Campanella, not to speak of the myriad of minor writers. Discussion of the problem followed closely the spiritual evolution of Counter Reformation Italy as a whole, with its contrasts and troubles. It withered away at the same time as the Counter Reformation, with the gradual appearance in Italy of new spiritual orientations. And it vanished entirely before the Rationalism of the eighteenth century.

The relation between this treatise writing and the Counter Reformation, moreover, is not merely an extrinsic one. It is not to be explained by the fortuitous appearance in the late Cinquecento and early Seicento of a great number of books on the subject—a number, by the way, far greater than in any period before or after. Rather the first is a typical product of the second. It expresses one of the most essential tendencies of the "official" culture of the time—the culture of the academies, of the university chairs of rhetoric, and of the literary circles protected by princes or encouraged by the patronage of cardinals. And it was nourished by a general desire to establish, on the firm basis of recognized

[3] [On the Neapolitan poet and moralist Giovanni Pontano (1426–1503), who also wrote a work of history, *De Ferdinando I Rege . . . Libri VI* (a historical biography of King Ferdinando I of Naples), the most recent authority is Francesco Tateo, who published his *Trattati delle virtù sociali* in 1965 (Rome: Edizioni dell'Ateneo) and who has written several articles on him, e.g. in *Rinascimento*, v (1965), 119–54.]

"authorities," the norms for good writing and the canons of dramaturgy, prose, and oratory.

Amid so much zeal to set down exact rules for whoever sought to take up his pen or to turn toward God, it is not surprising that some people aspired to the honor of doing the same thing for present and future historians—of erecting a "dogma" of history, that is, founded on "authority" and destined to be respected without question. It is not surprising, in other words, that what the Council did in the field of doctrine and ecclesiastical discipline, others should try to do in the field of history.

THE "AUTHORITIES" OF THE COUNTER REFORMATION

The generation of the mid-Cinquecento certainly had no want of historiographical material to study. It could turn to Machiavelli and Guicciardini and to their not unworthy continuators in Medicean Florence. It could turn to the vast philological researches of the great scholars beyond the Alps as well as in Italy—of Sigonius and the Magdeburg chroniclers, of Sleidan and Baronius.[4] But reflecting upon history through an inductive examination of the works of the great historians of the past and present, and looking for the laws that had already been applied rather than for those that ought henceforth to be applied, was completely contrary to the authoritarian, dogmatic approach of the treatise-writers. The

---

[4] [Carlo Sigonio, or Sigonius, of Modena (1523–84), sometime professor of Greek and humanities at Modena, Padua, and Bologna, and author of a number of immense historical and chronological works—*Historiarum de Occidentali Imperio Libri XX, Historiarum de Regno Italiae Libri XX, Historiae Bononiensium Libri VI*, etc., republished by Argelati in Milan, 1732–37. The Centurians of Magdeburg were a group of Lutheran scholars under the leadership of Mattias Flaccius Illyricus (see below, n. 25), whose vast *Centuriae Magdeburgenses* (Basel, 1559–74) first presented a complete and well-documented Lutheran version of church history. Johann Philip Sleidanus, or Sleidan (1507?–66), wrote a history of the Protestant Reformation, the *Commentarii de Statu Religionis et Reipublicae Carolo V Caesare*. Cesare Baronio, or Baronius (1538–1607), a disciple of Filippo Neri, spent most of his life in the Vatican Library writing an answer to the *Centuriae*, the immense, heavily documented, and frequently reprinted and updated *Annales Ecclesiastici*.]

representatives of the official, orthodox culture of the Age of the Counter Reformation felt the need not for research and experiment but for "authorities" from whom they might derive absolute norms and laws. They therefore turned not to the historians but to Aristotle, the "authority" *par excellence*, or to Cicero, Livy, and Quintilian—to those "holy fathers" of rhetorical and formalistic neohumanism who corresponded, in the world of culture, to the spirit of the Jesuits in the world of religion. Historical thought went back to where Pontano and the other fifteenth-century humanists had left it. It now looked upon history as a problem of literary form and of oratorical grace rather than as one of scientific truth or political inquiry. And it put aside all the actual historical writing of the Florentine school of the first decades of the century. In doing so, it may have been partially motivated by the typical Counter Reformation desire to ignore or silence that impious Florentine secretary[5] and to banish his disquieting ghost behind a solid barrier of rhetorical, stylistic, religious, and philosophical dogmatism.

Aristotle, it is true, offered little in the way of norms for the writing of history—nothing, indeed, except a marginal comment in the *Poetics* in which he declared history to be inferior to poetry.[6]. . . But Cicero provided much more. Whereas Aristotle had treated history in the context of poetics, Cicero, with all the shiny luster of his eloquence, made it unequivocally a part of oratory and rhetoric—the *opus oratorium maximum*, in fact.[7]. . .

For us today this hunk of reverberating Ciceronian bombast seems to have very little to do with a philosophy or methodology of history. But for men of the Counter Reformation it seemed to contain all the elements necessary for constructing a complete dogmatic system. First of all, it provided them with a concept of history as a cross between rhetoric and pedagogy, as both an *opus*

[5] [For more recent literature on anti-Machiavellism, see Giuliano Procacci, *Studi sulla fortuna del Machiavelli* (Rome: Istituto Storico Italiano, 1965.]

[6] *Poetics*, IX [from which Spini here quotes at length].

[7] [Here follows in the original a long passage from] Cicero, *De Oratore*, II. 9 and 15.

oratorium maximum and a *magistra vitae*. It thus enabled them to transform history from an instrument for the scientific investigation of politics, which is what it had been for Machiavelli, into an eloquent sermon, in which the conclusions were expected only to provide concrete examples in confirmation of fixed and immutable truths about morals and doctrine.... Secondly, Cicero's statements contained . . . nothing less than the laws, the *leges*, of historiography—not very profound laws, it is true, but laws nonetheless, which his grateful Counter Reformation readers thought could be accepted as immutable. The statements also contained the rudiments of historical stylistics, or *elocutio*, as well as an indispensable outline for elegant orations *de laudibus historiae* ("in praise of history"), with a succession of grandiloquent definitions ("witness of the times," "light of truth," "life of memory," "teacher of the truth," "messenger of antiquity") that recall the invocations of the Virgin in ecclesiastical litanies. Nothing more needed to be done than to stretch out the passage from the *De Oratore* onto a hundred-odd pages, clothe it in the form of an ordered discourse or dialogue, enrich it with rare flowers of fine style, embroider it with bits of scholastic erudition, and lo! the work was done, and the new dogmatics of history had achieved its definitive form.

If what Aristotle and Cicero had said still seemed a bit modest, then it was always possible to tack on a few lines from Quintilian (like the one in the *Institutiones Oratoriae* that defines history as "near to poetry") or from Dionysius of Halicarnassus. Better yet, it was possible to add another major "authority," namely, Lucian, in his little work on *How to Write History*.[8]

---

[8] Quintilian, X.I.31: *Proxima poesi et quodam modo solutum carmen.* [The passage from Dionysius's *Ancient History of Rome* can conveniently be found in *Greek Historical Thought*, ed. Arnold J. Toynbee (Mentor Paperback), pp. 53 ff. Lucian's (*ca.* 125–*ca.* A.D. 192) *Verae Historiae Libri Duo*, or *Quomodo Historia Conscribenda Sit*, was translated into Latin by Lelio Castellano and published first at Naples in 1475. Another translation by Willibald Pirckheimer called *De Ratione Conscribendae Historiae* appeared at Nuremberg in 1515. See S. R. Forster, "Lucian in der Renaissance," *Archiv. für Literaturgeschichte*, XIV (1886), 337–63.]

In itself, Lucian's work was much more temperate than Cicero's. True, it put almost as much emphasis on the problem of historical style and narrative language. But it also made somewhat clearer the differences between history and oratory. It overlooked completely the central problem of the essence, the method, and the dignity of history. But it also posed, though with a somewhat puerile empiricism, the problem of the indispensable requisites of the writer of history. The historian must have, Lucian said, two main qualities—and he has to have them by birth, for no school can teach them to him. He must have, first, a strong capacity for political discernment, and second, an aptitude for historical narration, so that what he writes will turn out to be useful because of the lessons it teaches and pleasing because of its form and structure. The historian must also have certain qualities that may be acquired: experience in civil and military affairs, an open and impartial mind, precision in relating facts, a clear and limpid style, a sober and chaste language, and an ability to distinguish between the essential and the superfluous. But all this was presented merely by way of a preface. Having perceived a possible distinction between historiography and rhetoric, Lucian then seems not to have fully understood the consequences of his perception. He therefore drops the subject and indulges himself thereafter in an interminable list of stylistic and moralistic details.

What has appeared to later generations as Lucian's chief defect was acclaimed by his Counter Reformation readers as his chief merit. Lucian's list provided them with an indispensable corollary to Cicero's dogma, comparable to the role of moral theology with respect to systematic theology in religion. Much less agile or shrewd than their "authority," they overlooked completely his warning that none of the details would make up for a lack of natural gifts in producing good history. They thus endowed the "laws" they drew from Cicero and Lucian with an objective value in themselves, almost *ex opere operato*. The laws were thus endowed with an efficacy similar to that of baptism in Tridentine theology —an efficacy which was not compromised by the moral imperfections of the priest who administered it.

THE CICERONIANS AND HISTORY AS
Opus Oratorium Maximum

The first steps toward establishing orthodoxy in the field of historiography were taken just at the moment when the Council of Trent began its first sessions. The center of this new orthodoxy was Padua, with its university and its established interest in questions of grammar and literary form. The unrivaled luminary of academic culture of the age was also a Paduan, Sperone Speroni,[9] who already in 1542 had dedicated one of his much acclaimed *Dialogues* to the art of history. In this dialogue Speroni reviews all that Aristotle, Cicero, and Lucian had said on the subject, without departing so much as a hair's breadth from their "sacred authority." He then goes off on two interminable disquisitions to prove, first, that history is an "art" and therefore subject to certain and constant laws (the opposite opinion having been set forth by another Paduan professor, Giacomo Zabarella),[10] and second, that it can be written in the vernacular as well as in Latin. Speroni's work was continued by one of his colleagues at Padua and another star of Cinquecento pedantry, Francesco Robortello, who, in his *De Historica Facultate* of 1548, did nothing more than repeat point by point what Speroni had already copied out of Aristotle, Lucian, and Cicero, and who then plastered the Aristotelian distinction between form and matter onto the by then common distinction

---

9 [Speroni (1500–88) was born and educated in Padua, where from 1540 on he was one of the leaders of the Academy of the Infiammati. He wrote, among other things, the influential *Dialoghi della lingua*, which most non-Italian students know chiefly as one of the sources of Joachim Du Bellay's *Deffense et illustration de la langue françoise*—but which is really much more than that.]

10 Giacomo [or Jacopo] Zabarella, "De Natura Logicae," in his *Opera Logica* (Frankfurt: L. Zetzner, 1607). [But the *Tabulae Logicae* appeared in the second edition of his *Opera Logica* as early as 1586 (Venice: P. Meietum). Zabarella (1533–89) began teaching at Padua in 1564. He was the greatest of the Aristotelians in the generation after Pomponazzi and Achillini (see below, ch. 7, n. 4) and was best known at the time for his works on epistemology (*De Specibus Intelligibilibus* and *De Ordine Intelligendi*) and on the nature of the soul (*De Mente Humana*, *De Mente Agenda*, and above all, a commentary on Aristotle's *De Anima*, published posthumously in 1601).]

between chronicle and history. In 1559 the same environment of the Veneto engendered the *Ragionamento de la eccelentia et perfezion de la istoria* (*On the Excellence and Perfection of History*) by Dionigi Atanagi da Cagli, formerly secretary to Monsignor Giovanni Guidiccioni and later a collaborator of Girolamo Ruscelli in Venice.[11] And in 1568 it produced a *De Historia Liber*, which the philologian Antonio Riccoboni felt moved to tack onto his collection of the fragments of archaic Latin historians—probably for the sheer joy of being able to state the same old commonplaces once again.[12]

[Ciceronian orthodoxy soon spread to other parts of Italy.] In 1569 the Sicilian Gianantonio Viperano (d. 1610), later bishop of Giovinazzo, published his *De Scribenda Historia Liber*, which followed a treatise of almost the same name by the professor of rhetoric at Bologna, Ventura Cieco (1563).[13] In 1579 Uberto Foglietta brought forth the same classical "authorities" to justify his having put imaginary speeches into the mouths of the personages in his own historical writings—even though the humanist historians had done just that a century and a half earlier in imitation of ancient models.[14] As late as 1586, indeed, when the revolt

[11] Atanagi, *Ragionamento de la eccelentia et perfezion de la istoria* (Venice: Nicolini, 1559). [Atanagi also put out critical editions of contemporary poetry: the *Carmina* of the Neapolitan poet Bernardino Rota (Naples, 1572) and *De le rime de diversi nobili poeti toscani* (Venice, 1565). Guidiccioni of Lucca (1500-41) was a worldly prelate and an authority on the vernacular and wrote poems and madrigals. Girolamo Ruscelli of Viterbo (1500?-66), a typical Cinquecento polygraph, lived for many years in Rome as well, where he founded the Academy of the Sdegnosi. He edited the correspondence of his friends and wrote on the language question as well as on many other subjects.]

[12] [Antonio Riccoboni (1541-99), whose *De Historia Liber cum Fragmentis* appeared in Venice in 1568, also translated the *Poetics* (1579) and wrote a number of works of literary criticism.]

[13] *De Conscribenda Historia Liber* (Bologna: Rubei, 1563).

[14] "De Ratione Scribendae Historiae," in his *Opera Subsaeciva* (Rome: Zanetti, 1579). [Foglietta (1518-81) was a man of letters, a jurist, and a political commentator as well as a historian, the author of a *De Philosophiae et Iuris Civilis Comparatione* and an imitation of Paolo Giovio's *Eulogies* of illustrious men. His greatest work was a history of Genoa—the *Historia Genuensium*. His more famous *Dialogo* "On the Affairs of the Republic of Genoa," which supported the popular party against the aristocracy, led to his being first exiled from his native city, and then recalled to become its official historiographer.]

of the Tacitists was already in full swing, Ciceronian orthodoxy was still strong enough to lead Alessandro Sardi of Ferrara to dust off the same old concepts once again, although it is to his credit that he compressed them into fifty lean precepts instead of dragging them out, like his predecessors, into hundreds of pages of thundering declamations.[15]

To read one of these orthodox writers is not much different from reading them all. History is always defined as a true account of former events and is given a pedagogical purpose as the *magistra vitae*. The Aristotelian distinction between form and matter is always applied to the relationship between history on one hand and annals and chronicles on the other—the only addition being the tiny insight of Robortello into the scientific exigencies of historical method when he includes inscriptions and archaeological discoveries in the second category.... Historians are always cautioned about bestowing blame or praise; and they are warned, particularly by Viperano (whose instruction in this matter was to become one of the *loci communes* of the Ciceronians' defense against the Tacitists), about describing evil deeds and atrocities. And the lessons and directions are all put forth with the same monotony and superficiality, with the same oppressive urge to conformity, and with the same flood of words, words, and more words, as pompous and high-sounding as they are empty, useless, and insipid.

FRANCESCO PATRIZI AND THE *Cognitione del Vero*

Only against the background of this gray, mortifying orthodoxy, which continued to dominate Italian culture until the end of the century, is it possible to appreciate the really revolutionary import of the *Dell'historia dialoghi diece* (*Ten Dialogues on History*) published by the one rebel among Robortello's disciples, Francesco Patrizi da Cherso,[16] just a dozen or so years after the death of his

[15] Sardi, "Antimaco, ovvero de' precetti storici," in his *Discorsi* (Venice: Giolito, 1586).

[16] *Dell'historia dialoghi diece* (Venice: Arrivabene, 1560). On Patrizi (1413-94), see P. M. Arcari, *Il pensiero politico di F. P. da Cherso* (Rome, 1935). [Patrizi's activities as a philosopher are fully discussed in ch. 11 below. His

master. Even though he carefully disclaims any attempt to criticize Robortello in the very first lines, it is clear that the polemical arrows of this lively, caustic book are directed not against Cicero and Lucian but against the Ciceronian traditionalists of the Cinquecento, particularly against those of Patrizi's own alma mater, the University of Padua.

Patrizi's work was rich in remarkably perceptive intuitions, some of them well in advance of his age. But it was also fraught with contradictions, regressions, and almost childlike lacunae; and nothing is harder than trying to fit these devilish dialogues of his into some sort of conceptual framework. Patrizi apparently needed to fight in order to think; and he usually turns out to be original and profound only when provoked by the prospect of knocking still another venerable commonplace off the altars. He proclaims himself right from the start to be unwilling to bow before the authority of Cicero, Lucian, or Pontano. History, he says, must concern itself with an infinite number of things besides the illustrious acts of princes and republics, to which the Ciceronians had erroneously limited it. It is useless, therefore, to remain attached to these "authorities" and their talk about the virtues of the historian and the relation of history and poetry. What is needed is a dispassionate, personal inquiry toward a definition of history, a definition upon which a completely new historical methodology can be built.

It is precisely this violent demolition of the "authorities" Speroni, Robortello, and the other treatise-writers that led Patrizi to bring forth for the first time, albeit in a weak, hesitating, and incomplete form, a concept of history not as oratory, but as science. For Patrizi the problem of historiography was a problem not of style but of the proper means for searching out the truth.

Amorosa filosofia has recently been edited (Florence: Le Monnier, 1963) by John Charles Nelson, who had discussed Patrizi at length in his *Renaissance Theory of Love* (New York: Columbia University Press, 1958); and his historiographical thought has been studied by Franz Lamprecht in *Zur Theorie der humanistischen Geschichtsschreibung: Mensch und Geschichte bei F. P.* (Zürich: Artemis-Verlag, 1950).]

Philosophy, in his thought, is the science of causes and effects. History, on the other hand, is the science of effects. Historiography consists in transcribing, with the help of paintings, statues, and symbolic representations as well as of written records, what Patrizi calls "fantasies": the sensible images which the human mind has been able to form of things and events that have, do, and will occur in nature and among men. History is therefore "memory." It is the record men have made about the future as well as about the past: for prophecy and speculation on the course of the cosmos are an intimate part of human intellectual activity. Moreover, history is the "memory" not only of illustrious actions but also of the modest vicissitudes of private individuals. It is the "memory" not only of human events but also of natural events— such as those phenomena which Pliny, Aristotle, and Theophrastus set down in their books of natural history. Everything is history. Therefore, everything is [the object of science]—not only the volumes of polished stylists, as the Ciceronians would have it, but also rough "annals," which Speroni and his followers relegated to a level of inferiority, and even the diaries and personal notes that any man might jot down in order to facilitate his memory while dealing with the small events of daily existence.

Thus Patrizi courageously rescues history from the marshes of rhetoric and raises it to a category of human understanding. But there he stops—or rather at that point he seems to falter before the prospect of carrying out to its fullest consequences a vision of history that includes not only the political events of Renaissance historiography but also the very life of the cosmos. Once the stimulus of debate subsides, he loses interest in the question. He puts aside the history of nature and concentrates on the history of men (which is the terrain best suited to pursuing his adversaries); and he sets out to destroy one more Ciceronian commonplace: the concept of history as a *magistra vitae*. What *exemplum*, he asks ironically, can be gotten out of a genealogical list of Babylonian kings? And yet who can deny that such a list has historical value? The purpose of history is the apprehension of the truth (*la cognitione del vero*). History gives us knowledge, that is, of the events of

other times and peoples that lie beyond the limits of our own
immediate experience.

Then Patrizi stops again. He suddenly retreats into a discourse
about how such knowledge can help us [in establishing] a political
order capable of assuring the felicity of its citizens. He thus lets in
through the window what he has just swept out the door, namely,
the concept of history as a source of salutary examples. Piling contradiction on contradiction, he next suggests that *exempla* for good
government be drawn from states that have exercised power over
others; and he ends up right back in the Ciceronian camp, with
its preference for famous actions rather than for the more modest
events of daily life.

Yet it takes no more than a slight rattle of arms to make Patrizi
charge back into originality. His target now is none other than the
sacrosanct *leges* of Cicero about the truthfulness of history. A
history absolutely true or impartial is a chimera, he points out in a
tone of delightful irreverence. If a historian has not himself taken
part in the events, then he must depend upon the accounts of those
who have, without being able to ascertain their dependability. If
then he tries to get around the difficulty by supposing that the best
historian is one who has been the main protagonist of the event—
that is, some prince or powerful personage—he deceives himself
even more. For no one has more interest than a protagonist in
making an event appear other than as it actually occurred. After
accumulating a series of such difficulties, Patrizi cannot but arrive
at the conclusion that the exact truth is impossible to obtain and
that the most a historian can expect is a rough approximation of
the truth—something that looks more like the fantasy of poetry
than the solid truth of science.

It is obvious that Patrizi's historical skepticism comes from a
still embryonic anthropomorphic conception of the methodology
of history. But it is also obvious that Patrizi is the only writer of
his age to exhibit anything like the critical doubt about history
to be found in the works of Valla, Pico della Mirandola, and
the other humanist philologians. Yet rather than investigating
the consequences of his skepticism, Patrizi prefers to attack the

Ciceronians. He thus leaves open the question of *what kind* of truth may be obtained and turns instead to the question of how to obtain it.

The first step, he proposes, is to arrange the sources in four categories, depending upon their reliability: those composed by direct witnesses, those composed by contemporaries, those composed by later compatriots of the actors, and those composed by historians of a different time and place. The next step is to start writing with the foundation of a city or a people (since the foundation in many ways determines the future development) and then go on to its growth, expansion, and decline, according to the organic conception of the late Renaissance political writers. But then Patrizi adds an ingenious warning—one which makes him in one way a precursor of Bodin and of modern historiography. This kind of history will be fruitless, he says, unless it includes not only battles and sieges but also "four things, of which the first two have been completely overlooked by all previous historians and the other two have been barely mentioned." These "four things" are "the means of livelihood," "public income," "military forces," and "the means of government." We today would refer to them as the economic and financial conditions of the state and military, civil, and political institutions.

With all its omissions and contradictions and even with its bizarre moments, then, the work of Patrizi constitutes a fundamental milestone in the progress of Italian and European historiographical thought. Six years before Bodin published his *Method for the Easy Comprehension of History* (1566), the rhetorical, pedagogical Ciceronian tradition still dominant in the schools and the academies had already been broken. History as science had taken the place of history as *opus oratorium*. Methodology had taken the place of stylistics. And the concept of history as solely political history, which is as far as Machiavelli and Guicciardini had gotten, had given way to a consciousness of the immense breadth of historical inquiry. History could no longer overlook juridical institutions, upon which French thinkers were later to lay such emphasis. Nor could it overlook financial and economic affairs.

Although the solution was still only roughly sketched out, moreover, the problem of sources had already been perceived in all its
complexity. A truly Copernican revolution had taken place in the
field of historical theory. And the work of Patrizi was the first
manifesto of this revolution, destined to remain the necessary point
of reference for the successive evolution of Italian historical thought
until Campanella and the first decades of the seventeenth century.

In its effort, indeed, to expand upon Patrizi's concepts, to free
them of their inconsistencies, to fill in their lacunae, and to explore
the insights that had been left in the form of rough drafts, Italian
historical thought after Patrizi went in two directions. Both these
directions were implicit among the contradictions in Patrizi's
own thought. On one hand, the *Dialoghi* had made the *cognitione
del vero* the chief end of history and had put the problem of
methodology and verification of the truth in the place of the
rhetorical problem of the Ciceronians. On the other hand, the
Dialoghi had admitted the utility of history for a system of politics
based upon the concrete examples of the past rather than upon
dogmatic abstractions. The two opposing theses were left unrecon-
ciled. On one hand, then, the concept of history as a science of the
truth, enriched by the wide panoramic vision of Bodin and by the
writings of Possevino and Paolo Beni, led finally to the *Historiographia juxta Propria Principia* (*Historiography According to Its Own
Principles*) of Campanella, as well as, beyond the Alps, to the
theoretical positions of Vossius.[17] On the other hand, the concept
of history as the experimental foundations of politics influenced
all the vast political literature of the end of the Cinquecento, particularly that of the Tacitist school. From the writings of Aconcio
and Bruto it passed into those of Lorenzo Ducci and Traiano
Boccalini. And it did not finally disappear until Tacitism itself
was overcome by the Anti-Tacitist campaign launched from
Rome by the Jesuits in the first part of the seventeenth century.[18]

[17] [Gerardus Joannes Vossius (1577–1649) was one of the greatest German
scholars of his age and author of numerous works, e.g. *Etymologicon Linguae
Latinae, Ars Historia, De Historicis Graecis, De Historicis Latinis*.]
[18] [See below, pp. 114–20 of this chapter.]

"THE READING OF HISTORY": JACOPO ACONCIO
AND ANTONIO POSSEVINO

The lasting value of Patrizi's criticisms of the traditional "authorities" is confirmed by the rather pathetic testimony of another audacious rebel of the time, Jacopo Aconcio of Trent, a religious exile in England. Between one battle and another against Calvinist orthodoxy in the name of spiritual positions close to those of the other Italian "heretics" of the Cinquecento,[19] Aconcio managed to write a letter to his friend Johann Wolf in Basel, the learned and understanding companion of Bullinger and Curione,[20] praising the recently published work of Patrizi as the dawn of a new age of culture. And he added some further thoughts of his own in a brief treatise, *Observations and Warnings to the Reader of History*, which reads like a prophecy of the imminent appearance of the *Methodus* of Bodin.[21]

Through Aconcio, then, what had hitherto been a purely Italian, if not a Paduan, phenomenon spread to the whole of Europe; and it was incorporated into European philosophical, political, and even religious speculations of the age. At the same time, the discussion of how to *write* history was extended to that of how to *read* it. Then just one year after Aconcio had finished his manuscript and dedicated it to his great patron, Robert Dudley, Earl of Leicester, in 1563, out of the other end of Europe came a posthumous work of one of the champions of Counter Reformation theology, the Spanish Dominican Melchior Cano.[22] It was a work which contained a very similar discussion of the veracity of sources

---

[19] [See below, ch. 8.]

[20] [Henry Bullinger (1504–75) was the successor of Zwingli at Zürich. On Celio Secondo Curione, see the recent biography by Markus Kutter (Basel: Helbing und Lichtenhahn, 1955). Jacopo Aconcio (1492?–1566?) wrote *De Methodo* and *Satanae Stratagematum*, among other works.]

[21] Aconcio to Wolf, 20 November 1562, in Aconcio, *De Methodo, et Opuscoli religiosi e filosofici*, ed. G. Radetti (Florence: Vallecchi, 1944), pp. 324 ff. *Delle osservationi et avvertimenti che aver si debbono nel leggere delle historie* was written probably in 1562; but it remained in manuscript until Radetti published it in 1944.

[22] Cano, *De Locis Theologicis Libri XII* (Salamanca, 1563).

and of the proper reading of history. Cano had died at Toledo in 1560 and could not, therefore, have known the writings of Patrizi, much less those of Aconcio. Indeed, his spiritual position was so distant from the positions of either of them that he could find nothing better for his criteria of judgment than purely extrinsic ones—a general reputation for integrity, for instance, the "prudence" of the historian, and, finally, the approbation of ecclesiastical authorities. But the mere fact of its appearance in writers so distant from each other is an indication of the importance of the problem at the moment of the publication of Bodin's *Methodus*, where the problem is most broadly and most scientifically presented.

Thus the *Methodus*, in spite of its wide acclaim, did not obscure its predecessors; and the *Dialogues* of Patrizi continued to exercise a direct or indirect influence upon the development of historiographic thought both in Italy and abroad. The same Wolf to whom Aconcio had written published in Basel in 1579 his famous *Penus Artis Historicae*, in which the Latin translation of Patrizi was given a place of honor alongside the *Methodus*, and alongside a little treatise—of small intellectual value, if truth be told—of another religious exile and close friend of Aconcio, the Piedmontese Curione. In that same year Patrizi and Aconcio inspired another work on the art of history, the *True Order and Methode* of the Englishman Thomas Blundeville,[23] in which many passages of [both authors] are translated literally. And it was against Patrizi, who had received such acclaim in Protestant lands, as much as against Bodin himself that one of the most famous athletes of Jesuit polemics, Antonio Possevino, directed his *Bibliotheca Selecta*, a sort of anti-*Methodus*, full of scholarly details drawn from an immense amount of reading, which was later revised and expanded in his *Apparatus ad Omnium Gentium Historiarum*.[24]

---

[23] *The True Order and Methode of Writing and Reading Histories According to the Precepts of Francisco Patricio and Acconcio Tridentino* (London, 1574), on which see Radetti, *op. cit.*, p. 58 [and also the article by Hugh G. Dick in *Huntington Library Quarterly*, II (1940), 149–70].

[24] Possevino, *Bibliotheca Selecta* (Rome: Typ. Apostolica Vaticana, 1593), and *Apparatus ad Omnium Gentium Historiarum* (Venice: Giotti, 1597). The

It is not without significance that by this time Possevino had
long since given up his political and missionary activities and had
been teaching in the Jesuit college at Padua, the very epicenter of
Counter Reformation interest in the problem of historiography.
Nor is it insignificant that he turned, in seeking help for his work,
not to the Ciceronian tradition of Speroni and Robortello, but to
Patrizi and even to Bodin himself. His purpose, in other words,
was clearly that of opposing the wide diffusion of the *Methodus*
and the *Penus Artis Historicae* by offering the Catholic faithful an
expurgated version of them. Naturally the mere fact of inserting
himself into the most vital current of European historiographical
thought did not save Possevino from remaining a prisoner of those
pragmatic motives of religious propaganda and prophylaxis that
had led him to write. He had, as a matter of fact, none of Patrizi's
taste for speculation itself nor any of Bodin's insatiable thirst for
knowledge. What he really wanted to do was to erect a practical
defense against the infiltration of ideas dangerous to the Church
and to the papal *magisterium*. So little did the theoretical problem
of the nature of history interest him that he did nothing but com-
pile a list of treatise-writers, much of it apparently cribbed from
Wolf. And he put Patrizi along with Robortello and Viperano
without even mentioning the differences between their positions.
He disposed of the problem of the criticism of sources simply by
copying the criteria of Melchior Cano and by adding, in rather
disorganized fashion, a few of his own, equally puerile, such as the
need for reporting exactly the number of soldiers and human
losses in an account of a war or battle. His evaluation of the works
of ancient and modern historians, to which most of the book is
dedicated, was dominated largely by a concern to point out what
was orthodox and what had been prohibited by the Church.

With all these limitations and errors of perspective, Possevino's
work nonetheless represents a step forward with respect to the
flat rhetoric of the Ciceronians. For his very purpose of rendering

---

latter was translated into Italian by the author himself and published by Giotti
in Venice in 1598.

Bodin harmless forced him to stay close to what he was criticizing; and this purpose necessarily put him on a plane incomparably higher than that of the Ciceronians. He thus accepts Bodin's tripartite distinction of natural, human, and divine history. He then adds a fourth one—ecclesiastical history, which he attempts to differentiate from divine history, proper to the Holy Scriptures, and which he defines as the history of ecclesiastical institutions and religious thought. Although the polemics over Tacitus were already well underway when he wrote, he does not waste his energy in narrow-minded, moralistic anti-Tacitism, like his successors of the seventeenth century. Although he persists in arguing endlessly against Bodin and the Protestants, he is almost as sensitive as Bodin to the vast field now opening up to historical research; and he joyfully introduces into this panorama the contribution being made by his fellow Jesuits to the knowledge of more remote peoples. It is not improper, then, to put Possevino, too, along the line that leads from Patrizi and Bodin to Campanella.

THE LEGACY OF PATRIZI:
PAOLO BENI AND TOMMASO CAMPANELLA

The *Bibliotheca Selecta* came out in 1593, just as Campanella was completing the first draft of that part of his *Philosophia Rationalis* dedicated to history. In the very city of Padua, where Campanella was then living, that incorrigible *enfant terrible* of the age, Paolo Beni—later to become professor of literature in the same university and author of a treatise *De Historia* that was finally published just a few years before Campanella dictated the final version of his *Historiographia* in a Neapolitan prison—was rapidly acquiring a reputation. Like Patrizi, Davila, and Biondi, and, for that matter, like Vergerio, Flaccius Illyricus, and De Dominis,[25] Beni was a

[25] [Arrigo Caterino Davila (1576–1631), author of the *History of the Wars of Religion in France*, first published in Venice in 1630, was actually born at Pieve del Sacco near Padua and educated in France before he returned to assume a series of political and military offices for the Venetian Republic. But his father had been an official in Cyprus. Biondi (not the historian Flavio Biondo of Forlì, but Gian Francesco) was born at Lesina in Dalmatia in 1572 and died in

Venetian subject from beyond the seas—rather than from the
mainland, like Speroni, Robortello, and Riccoboni. And like these
other Dalmatians or Levantines, he carried in his veins a certain
amount of spiritual restlessness, of religious heterodoxy, of
irreverent iconoclasm.[26] He had left the Society of Jesus because
of a disagreement with his superiors, and he had written a theological treatise, condemned by the Church, on the burning
problem of *The Efficacious Help of God and Free Will*—as well as
another attacking the Academy of the Crusca, the linguistic
purists, the rhetoricians, and the pedants of his time.[27] He did not
even approach the speculative robustness of his predecessor. But
he joined to his rejection of tradition a good bit of solid common
sense, which permitted him to understand much better than most
of his contemporaries, even Patrizi himself, what history was and

---

Switzerland in 1644. He served for a while in the court of James I, but left
England during the Civil War. Besides the *Storia delle guerre civili fra le case di
York e di Lancastro* (1637) he wrote several romances that were widely read at
the time. Pier Paolo Vergerio (1498–1565) was born at Capodistria. He was
appointed papal nuncio to Germany in 1533, and in 1536 became bishop first
of a diocese in Croatia and then of his native city. He was accused of holding
Lutheran ideas in 1544, and in 1549 he went into exile and spent the rest of his
life as an active agent on behalf of Protestantism. Flaccius Illyricus (1520–75),
general editor of the Magdeburg Centuries (above, n. 3), was born in Albona
in Istria. Marcantonio De Dominis (1566–1624), whose theory on tides Galileo
opposed in the *Dialogues on the Two World Systems*, was born at Arba in Dalmatia in 1566. He left the Society of Jesus to become archbishop of Spalato.
When his writings on behalf of Venice during the Interdict controversy (see
n. 29, below) were censured in Rome, he moved to England and became a
Protestant. His old friend Pope Gregory XV persuaded him to return to
Catholicism (1622); but Urban VIII, suspecting the sincerity of his reconversion,
imprisoned him in Castel Sant'Angelo, where he died in 1624.] Beni's *De
Historia Libri IV* was published in Venice in 1611.

26 [Beni (1552–1627) is also well known for his *Anticrusca* (Padua, 1613 and
1619), a frontal attack on the first dictionary of the Italian language, the
Vocabolario of the Florentine Academy of the Crusca, and on its restriction of
the language to words used by the writers of the "golden age" of the fourteenth
century or by the purists of the early sixteenth.]

27 It is noteworthy that even the dedication of the *De Historia* has a polemical
overtone, in that it is dedicated to the doge Leonardo Donà and to the senators
Francesco Molino, Francesco Contarini, and Agostino Nani, all strong supporters of the Republic in its fight with Pope Paul V (see below, n. 29).

what it was not. While accepting Patrizi's thought in its general lines, and while even emphasizing its utilitarian aspects with regard to the *exempla*, he fully realized that natural history could comprehend only single phenomena, like the eruption of a volcano or an outbreak of the plague; and he excluded science in general, like zoology or botany, from the realm of historiography. He therefore rejected a tripartite division of history in favor of a simpler distinction between sacred and profane history, which actually was much closer to the reality and to the very nature of the historical sciences. While accepting, similarly, Patrizi's expansion of history to include juridical institutions, economics, and even ideas and opinions, as well as Patrizi's refusal to limit history to illustrious events, he rejected the inclusion of future as well as past events in history. Divination and prophecy, he said, had nothing to do with history, properly speaking. With regard to the criticism of sources and of historical writing, finally, he went beyond Patrizi and Bodin in putting official documents, public annals, and inscriptions second in order of reliability to contemporary witnesses, according to much more rational and reasonable criteria.

While bringing the theory of historiography down from the heavens of speculation, Beni also carried on a battle against the remaining traditionalists. He insisted energetically on separating history from poetry and oratory. He threw out Lucian's thesis about the necessity of direct experience of political and military events—as if every historian had to be another Thucydides or Caesar. He rejected the humanistic use of direct discourse. He launched a virulent attack on none other than the venerable Livy, the historian par excellence of the Ciceronians. He accused Livy of being credulous, of lacking in critical judgment with respect to his own sources, and of misusing declamations and orations in his narrative.

More than Patrizi, or even Bodin, Beni anticipated, though still somewhat obscurely, the critical and methodological exigencies of modern historiography. Unfortunately his theses in this sense consisted more of sharp intuitions than of elements in an organic concept of history. Beni lacked the speculative vigor that Patrizi perhaps had to excess. Hence he was prevented from carrying out his theses to their logical conclusions. When he attempted to descend from principles to their practical realization, or from theory to a critical examination of specific Greek and Roman historians, he was no longer sustained by the example of Patrizi, and he fell again into traditionalism, writing like a professor of stylistics. He skirmished, then, whenever he could, with the Ciceronians. But he ended up paying more attention to the way in which Livy or Caesar and Tacitus or Thucydides expressed themselves than to the reliability of what they said. And his acute and not invaluable methodological observation, as well as his perceptive corrections of Patrizi's judgments, remained isolated, without a logical follow-through.

Yet even these corrections, if they properly can be called such, are marginal rather than substantial. They leave unresolved the fundamental contradictions in Patrizi's work. A thorough re-examination of Patrizi's theories, then, and an attempt to systematize his thought, had to wait for someone much better endowed with philosophic vigor. The only trace of such an attempt in all the history of Counter Reformation Italian thought is the *Historiography According to Its Own Principles* that Campanella dictated in 1613 (just two years after the appearance of Beni's *De Historia*) to his German disciples, Rudolph of Bunau and Tobias Adami.

Campanella's work is the continuation of that of Patrizi—which he may have come in contact with during his residence at Padua in 1592–93 or through his subsequent reading of the *Dialoghi* and the *Penus* of Wolf. But it goes far beyond its predecessor. While Patrizi falls back into political history after having attacked the Ciceronians for just such a limitation, Campanella never forgets his concept of history as the "sufficient foundation of the sciences." While Patrizi, after having rejected the Ciceronians' *magistra vitae*, turns history back into a storehouse of *exempla* for an empirical political philosophy, Campanella frees history from every remnant of moral and pedagogical ends, and he constantly insists upon its exclusively scientific character.

At the same time, Campanella fails to pursue what Patrizi and Beni had made such efforts to elaborate and what he himself had pointed to in his title, namely, a methodology of history "according to its own principles"—to principles, that is, that are immanent in the nature and function of history itself. At times, indeed, he reduces his models to the level of precept-collectors; for precepts about the good historian and good historical style are what he chooses to pick out of their works, as well as out of Bodin's *Methodus*, instead of working out the canons of scientific research. The result is a list of sterile sentences unrelated to any sort of universal principles: the historian must leave out superfluous events, skip over prodigies and miracles, report exceptional natural occurrences, pay attention to economics and institutions as well as to battles, etc., etc. [And that leaves Patrizi's accomplishments deprived of the spirit that generated them.]

It is only toward the end of the treatise, when he comes to consider "how to read history" and what a historian should know, that Campanella recaptures the tone of the beginning. He suddenly comes forth with a grandiose epiphany on the immense possibilities for further knowledge now opened up to the historian and the scientist by the discovery of new worlds and new disciplines. Let the historian then read the records of the past. Let him master chronology and cosmography. Let him examine the writings of Moses, of the Greeks and Romans, of the modern historians, like Baronio, Spondano, Sigonio. Let him look into the documents of every nation and people—and not only of Christian nations, but also of the Turks, the Chinese, and the Japanese (about whom the Jesuit missionaries had recently written), the Ethiopians, and the Americans. Our knowledge of this immense field is still so limited, [says Campanella], and the need to expand it is so urgent that the help of kings is essential—most particularly the help of the king of Spain, who should commission histories of his vast new dominions. Then, on the stupendous last page of the *Historiographia*, the logical, rational theorist gives way completely to the passionate interpreter of the man's limitless longing for knowledge.[28] Campanella is the voice of the new science that has just begun to be conscious of itself and of the vast fields that await it. And his severe philosophic prose breaks out into song, into the exaltation of philosophy itself and of the effort it demands. Between fear and ecstasy he cries out: "There are as yet only partial histories. There are no universal histories, whatever the wise men may say." And the task of natural history is even greater than that of human history. God grant, [Campanella continues], that another Baronio may soon appear to do for the non-Christian nations what he has done for the Christian—a new Baronius who can embrace in one gigantic compendium all the immense sum of truths that are still hidden in the world of man and of nature.

THE TACITISTS AND HISTORY AS THE
FOUNDATION OF POLITICS

Campanella's rapture before the endless horizons open to the human mind and his burning passion for pure truth were such that he could not readily be understood by his Italian contemporaries. Seventeenth-century Italy was far too concerned with the phantasm of "reason of state" (*ragion di stato*), and it was far too obsessed by purely practical matters of religion and of politics, to be able to follow him. The defenders of orthodoxy and Spanish hegemony looked with suspicion upon every sign of philosophic thought and scientific inquiry. Hence whatever forces of renovation were still alive in Italian culture tended necessarily to become instruments in the hands of those involved in the practical political and religious issues of the day. The discussions about history had begun in university circles and had been limited to the world of the learned. When, then, they became associated with the contemporary discussions about the merits and demerits of the Roman historian Tacitus, they also were turned into a weapon of the protagonists in the chief conflict of early seventeenth-century

[28] [The passage is now conveniently printed in *Tutte le opere* of Campanella, ed. Luigi Firpo (Milan: Mondadori, 1954), Vol. I, pp. 1252–54, with Latin and Italian on opposite pages.]

Italy. This was a conflict between the Tacitists on one hand and the Anti-Tacitists on the other, between the proponents of a basically rhetorical and moralistic Ciceronianism and those seeking to renew the political historiography of the Renaissance (with all its naturalistic and Machiavellian overtones), between the supporters of Spain and the Roman Curia and the supporters of Venice and of her efforts to block the influence of the Spanish and the Jesuits.

This conflict culminated precisely in the years when Beni and Campanella were writing their historiographical treatises, when Boccalini was composing his *Ragguagli di Parnaso* (*News Reports from Parnassus*) and his *Philippics*, and when Sarpi was busy with the controversy over the Interdict.[29] But already in the 1560's

---

[29] [On Sarpi, see below, ch. 15. The following note is not in the original text. It was supplied directly by the author to the editor:] The Interdict controversy was a clamorous episode in the long struggle of Venice against the hegemony of Spain and the Curia during the seventeenth century. The Republic put legal limits on the increase in ecclesiastical property and affirmed the jurisdiction of its tribunals over members of the clergy in cases of a crime committed under Venetian law. Pope Paul V maintained that ecclesiastics were not subject to the jurisdiction of lay tribunals, and [to support his claim] he issued an interdict against Venice in 1606. On the advice of the state theologian, Paolo Sarpi, the Venetian government ordered the clergy in its territories to regard the interdict as null and void. Only the Jesuits refused to obey this order, and they were expelled. Spain supported the pope and threatened war against Venice. Sarpi hoped that the quarrel would provoke a complete religious break between Venice and the papacy, and he was encouraged in this direction by King James I of England. Mediation by France avoided a war. Venice remained Catholic, but it kept all its laws on the books and refused to readmit the Jesuits. Sarpi stayed in office; and he survived the attack of an assassin sent from Rome to kill him.

The struggle was next marked by the Monferrato War (1613–17). Monferrato was a territory of strategic importance belonging to the Gonzaga family, the dukes of Mantua and protégés of Venice. Both Spain and Savoy, under the leadership of Duke Carlo Emanuele I, tried to seize the territory and soon fell to quarreling over its possession. The war provoked an outburst of Italian national feeling; and some writers, particularly Traiano Boccalini, hailed Carlo Emanuele as the defender of the freedom of Italy against Spanish dominion. Venice succeeded in preventing the Spanish from crushing the duke of Savoy and in maintaining the Gonzagas in Monferrato. At the same time, Venice fought a war against the Austrian Hapsburgs, relatives of the king of Spain, in which it used Protestant troops from Holland. This event reawakened Sarpi's hopes for a religious break between Venice and the papacy. When these

the followers of Patrizi had begun emphasizing that element in his thought which seemed to make Anti-Ciceronianism, with its anti-Roman and heterodox tendencies, the foundation for an experimental, historical concept of politics.... Aconcio, for example, commenting in 1563 upon Patrizi's Dialogue IX on the utility of history, declared that history had three purposes:

(1) To enable us to recognize the Providence of God in the management of all our affairs. (2) To make us be guided in all our public and private actions, both in peace and in war, by the example of prudent men. (3) To inspire us to act virtuously and to dissuade us from evil actions.

The first was merely a personal addition by Aconcio to the trite commonplace about *historia magistra vitae*, and the second was essentially a repetition of what Patrizi had said about history as the basis for experimental politics. But these moralistic or religious bits were probably meant as little more than a bow to the spiritual prejudices of his environment. The rest of the short treatise is dedicated completely to Aconcio's main interest, namely, the elaboration of an inductive method for the technique of politics. In spite of his undeniable religiosity, then, Aconcio's thought in

hopes once again came to nothing, he set forth his antipapal opinions in *History of the Council of Trent*, which was published at London in 1619 under the pseudonym "Pietro Soave Polano."

Meanwhile, the outbreak of the Thirty Years War suddenly heightened the strategic importance of the Valtellina, a long, narrow valley that joined Spanish Lombardy to the Austrian Tyrol and through which Spanish troops had to pass on their way to Germany. Since 1513 the Valtellina had been under the dominion of the Swiss Grissons. Venice and France supported the Protestants in the Grissons and thus obtained the closing of the valley to the Spanish. In 1622, however, the Spanish succeeded in occupying it, taking advantage of a revolt of the predominantly Catholic population and the consequent massacre of the Protestant minority, known as the *Sacro Macello* ("The Holy Butchery"). War followed (1622–38), in which France and Venice attempted to throw the Spanish back out of the valley. [On Venetian policy in general at this period, see Gaetano Cozzi, *Il doge Nicolò Contarini* (Venice: Istituto per la Collaborazione Culturale, 1958), the articles by Luigi Salvatorelli and Ernesto Sestan in *La civiltà veneziana dell'età barocca* (Florence: Sansoni, 1959), and, most recently, William J. Bouwsma, *Venice and the Defense of Republican Liberty* (Berkeley: University of California Press, 1968).]

this matter had nothing to do with religion and morality; and it is already Tacitist or Machiavellian in its basic lines. He thus comes very close to Boccalini on the question of the political utility of history. And he is in full agreement with his successor in denouncing those who look into history for frivolous tidbits, which, compared to the kind of knowledge we are seeking, are worthy of no more attention than that which we give to the opening of the bellows when an organ is played.

The same theme was picked up again some years later by another Venetian who had gone into exile in search of religious freedom and new intellectual horizons, Giovan Michele Bruto, whose *De Historiae Laudibus* came out in distant Poland in 1582.[30] Bruto had, it is true, imbibed so much Ciceronianism that it came out in his writing style. But he noted that men of "this century" were no longer satisfied to look to the perfect republics of Plato and Aristotle for guidance. Politics must be based on history alone; and Bruto does not hesitate to praise Machiavelli for having said so. He not only rejects Aristotle's demotion of history with respect to poetry, but makes history superior to philosophy itself, precisely because of its practical value. He still insists, with a good bit of heavy erudition and a veritable hailstorm of classical examples, that history can also be effective as an incitement to virtue. But virtue to him was Senecan, and therefore Stoic (like that of the Calvinist writers in France), rather than Ciceronian and therefore oratorical and melodramatic. It was a pugnacious virtue, one which drew its stimulus and valor from being faced with difficulties. Bruto called upon historians to include examples of vices—those of the Borgias being particularly effective—along

[30] Namely, in Cracow. [Bruto (1517-94) went to Lyon in 1562 and from there, by way of almost every country in Europe, to Transylvania, where he was commissioned to write the *Historia Hungarica* (1577) that was finally published only in the nineteenth century. He followed King Stephen Báthory to Poland on his election and ended up as historiographer to Emperor Rudolph II. In the meantime he managed to stir up a considerable controversy in Italy with his attack on Paolo Giovio in his *Historiae Florentinae* of 1562. For complete bibliographical references (as well as for further consideration of other matters treated in this chapter), see William Bouwsma, "Three Types of Historiography in Post-Renaissance Italy," *History and Theory*, III (1965), 303-14.]

with examples of virtues. So far, indeed, did he push his attack on the flowery rhetoric of the Ciceronians that he ended up proclaiming ancient chronicles to be far more truthful and far more reliable than polished, carefully elaborated formal histories, precisely because of the absence of literary qualities in their style.

History as the foundation of the new politics of Machiavelli, history

> that tempers the scepter of the rulers,
> that strips its laurels and reveals to men:
> what tears and blood flow from it—

UGO FOSCOLO, Sepolcri

history in this sense is the history of the Tacitists, the history of the secret acts of religious and secular princes and of the dark misdeeds of the "reason of state."

The Tacitist position, however, was maintained not so much by those who wrote of the art of history as by those who wrote of the art of politics. More precisely, it was maintained by those who wrote history itself, like Sarpi and Davila, and like Giovan Francesco Biondi of Lesina in Dalmatia, who imitated Davila's political naturalism carefully in his *History of the Civil Wars in England*, and whose ardent support of Sarpi eventually led him to take refuge in England.[31] With their philo-Protestantism and anticlerical naturalism, indeed, with their aversion to the Spanish and the Jesuits, and with their interest in the causes and the *arcana* of history, they represented the Tacitist position with much greater force and coherence than any of the theorists, Boccalini included. Yet the mere fact that all of them lived close together, Venetians

[31] [On Biondi, see above, n. 25. The *Storia delle guerre civili fra le case di York e di Lancaster* (Venice, 1637; Bologna, 1647), later translated into English, is not mentioned in the latest work on English Renaissance historiography, F. Smith Fussner's *The Historical Revolution* (London: Routledge & Kegan Paul, 1962), perhaps because English readers paid no attention to it. Arrigo Caterino Davila (1583–1631) spent some years as a page in the court of Queen Catherine de' Medici of France before returning to Padua in the service of the Republic. His major work, the *Historia delle guerre civili di Francia*, was first published in Venice the year before his death.]

by choice or by birth, during the height of an important religious and political conflict gave their discussions of history and historiography a particularly forceful character. And it explains the split between the partisans of Venice on one hand and of the Spanish and the Curia on the other—of Strada, Mascardi, and Bentivoglio,[32] that is, who constantly opposed what had for some become the ideal capital of a free Italy during the controversies over the Interdict, over Monferrato, and over the Valtellina. The wounding of Sarpi, the poisoning of Boccalini, the exiling of Bruto and Biondi, and the condemning by ecclesiastical authority of the works of Davila, eloquently testify to the atmosphere of exasperation and dramatic dedication that these controversies aroused.

The most serious attempt, however, at a "political" anti-Aristotelian and anti-Ciceronian theory of history came not from Venice but from Ferrara, with the *Ars Historica* of Lorenzo Ducci, secretary of Ercole III d'Este.[33] Still, Ferrara was close to Venice, ideally as well as geographically, with its traditional policy of friendship for France and hostility to the Roman Curia. Patrizi himself, moreover, had taught there for a while, and it is

[32] [Cardinal Guido Bentivoglio was born in 1579, attended the University of Padua in the 1590's (during the first years of Galileo's lectureship), and rose to an eminent position in the Church through the support of the family of Pope Clement VIII. He was a close friend of Famiano Strada and Agostino Mascardi (see below, pp. 125–31), and the author of *Della guerra nelle Fiandre*. Many of his opinions on literature and historiography are set down in the *Memorie* he wrote between 1640 and his death in 1644, and which were published first at Venice in 1648 and often thereafter. An English translation was published in 1678.]

[33] Lorenzo Ducci, *Ars Historica, in Qua non Modo Laudabiliter Historiae Conscribendae Praecepta Traduntur, Verum etiam Nobiliores Historici Antiqui, Recentioresque Examinantur* (Ferrara: V. Baldini, 1604). Ducci was also the author of an *Arte aulica, nella quale si insegna il modo che deve tenere il cortigiano per divenire possessore della gratia del principe* ("in which is taught the way a courtier must follow to become possessor of the grace of a prince"; Ferrara: Baldini, 1601), which in a successive edition (Viterbo: Discepoli, 1615) is called explicitly *Opera fondata sopra C. Tacito* ("a work founded on Tacitus"), and which Giuseppe Toffanin seems to have overlooked [in his *Machiavelli e il "Tacitismo"* (Padua: A. Graghi, 1921).] On Ducci see Massimo Petrocchi, "Storia e filosofia secondo L. Ducci" in *L'uomo e la storia* (Bologna: Zannichelli, 1944), pp. 17 ff.

not surprising to find some of his audacious barbs at the "authorities" cropping up later in the treatise of Ducci, who shows his energy and originality right from the start with a call to battle against Cicero and Aristotle. Nor is it surprising to find a slight echo of another teacher at Ferrara, to find at the same time an echo of the Ciceronian's definition of history as the true account of past actions, since Ducci had probably picked it up from the *Antimaco* of Sardi,[34] who also had been at Ferrara some twenty years earlier. But Ducci was no Ciceronian; and from this definition he proceeded not toward an investigation of style and a search for moral precepts, but, like Beni soon after, toward a clear distinction between the history of man and the history of nature. History, he says, is a moral, not a natural, science. It differs both from philosophy, which serves man's contemplative faculties, and from physics, which pays no attention to his ethical faculties. The specific task of oratory is, as the Ciceronians say, that of distributing praise and reproach. But the first purpose of history, its *finis immediatus*, is the "knowledge of things done" (*cognitio rerum gestarum*), that is, the science of the past. And its second purpose, its *finis ultimus*, is *prudentia*, that is, the art of living with others in the polis. . . . History, therefore, which is as full of bad as of good moral examples, serves above all as a source for the technique of politics, to be used scientifically and dispassionately without any moralistic preoccupations. Finally, since historical politics is superior to theoretical politics, history as a discipline is far more important than the Aristotelians and Ciceronians have been willing to admit. It ought to be written with some thought of style, to be sure (though *gravitas* is preferable to *suavitas*). But stylistic considerations should never distract the historian from his chief task, which is that of uncovering the hidden "counsels," the military tactics, and the political policies of states.

[34] [Above, n. 15.]

THE MORALISM OF TRAIANO BOCCALINI AND THE
SEARCH FOR *Arcana*

This energetic re-evaluation of history found a forceful supporter just a year or so later in Traiano Boccalini. In his *Ragguagli di Parnaso*[35] Boccalini brought to bear on the Tacitist position all the warmth of his moral commitment to sincerity and seriousness and all the strength of his repugnance for hypocrisy and frivolity and for every form of tyranny—be it Aristotelian, Ciceronian, or Spanish.

Indeed, it is in this moral commitment that Boccalini made his chief contribution to the problem of historiography; for in spite of their charming humor, their gay aggressiveness, and their lambasting of the pedants and the "authorities," the *Ragguagli* have very little in the way of theoretical content. When, at a certain moment, Sire Apollo tries to show off a few general concepts about the art of history, he ends up with little more than a few commonplaces dragged out of Lucian and the Ciceronians; and he ignores completely all the polemics that had been going on since Patrizi's attack on Robortello. The speech is a shower of wisecracks and witticisms, told with all the inimitable gaiety and fluency of Boccalini's style. But whoever looks for anything substantial in it will find simply the same worn-out stage-set. Boccalini tells us that the historian "has for his principal task that of rendering eternal . . . in the memory of later generations the great acts of men." He hauls out the *leges* of Cicero on the truth of history and repeats Lucian's recommendation that the historian have direct experience in war and politics.

The only thing truly original in all this is of moral rather than

[35] Cent. I (Venice: Farri, 1612); Cent. II (Venice: Barezzi, 1613). [The author adds:] On the diffusion of the *Ragguagli* in England, see now Luigi Firpo, *Traduzioni dei "Ragguagli" di T.B.* (Florence: Sansoni Antiquariato, 1965) and the review by Spini in *Rivista storica italiana*, LXXVIII (1966), 248–51. [Boccalini was born at Loreto in 1556. He rose to important political offices in the Papal State under Paul V. In 1611 he moved to Venice in order to publish his politically hazardous *Ragguagli*. He died suddenly in 1613, probably at the hands of a Spanish assassin.]

theoretical character. Boccalini insists that history be treated as a serious discipline: not chatter and rhetoric, but facts; not the object of *a priori* rules, but the subject of careful research into the nature of politics. His moral commitment does not remain a mere abstraction in the heavens of pure speculation. Rather it falls directly into the midst of the political struggles of the moment. Boccalini launched a campaign against Aristotle, the rhetoricians, the flatterers, and the courtiers on behalf of Tacitus and political historiography—on behalf, that is, of the kind of historical study "that has the power of converting [its students] into so many Machiavellis" and of giving the sheep teeth to bite the shepherds with; and his campaign amounted to an act of war against Spain and against the gray torpor that hung over the enslaved peninsula.

Thus when Livy tries to bar Commynes from Parnassus because of his stylistic defects, Apollo bursts out violently against the rhetorical conception of historiography and accuses of self-deception those who

> study history only to savor good sentences in Greek, Latin, Italian, or French. . . . The sole purpose of this honorable discipline is to acquire that prudence which can come only from frequent reading of things past. And although I highly commend your [Livy's] pompous phrases and the terse sentences of Caesar, I want you to know that these matters, which you think are the first qualities of good historical writing, are actually the last. The soul of history . . . is the truth, and [the task of historians is] to explain the most recondite counsels and the most hidden thoughts that princes and rulers have used in governing states in the quiet times of peace and in the turbulence of war.

If they do so, they are worthy of praise and immortality even if they write in "the most vile Bartolesque Latin."[36]

36 [The reference is to the fourteenth-century jurist Bartolo of Sassoferrato, whose followers were derided by the early Renaissance humanists for their legalistic medieval Latin as much as for their unphilological methods of jurisprudence. See above, p. 87, n. 13.]

The truth that interests Boccalini, then, is one of political and moral character rather than the purely scientific truth Patrizi had envisioned. But it is still the truth; and in desiring to know and understand the truth, Boccalini remains a follower of Patrizi and Bodin, the two founders of the main line of historiographical thought in the late sixteenth and seventeenth centuries.

From Patrizi's *cognitione del vero* to Campanella's *scientiarum fundamentum sufficiens* on one hand, and from history as the foundation of *prudentia* and historical politics to Boccalini's history as the discovery of *arcana* on the other, Italian historical thought vigorously explored the fundamental theses of the two masters; and it revived the great Cinquecento tradition of history writing that orthodox Ciceronianism had sought to bury forever. Different as they may have been, moreover, the two currents of this stream of thought ended up in much the same place: in Campanella's twenty-year imprisonment and in Boccalini's tragic death. In the realm of religion, similarly, the restless ferment of reform in the Venice of Sarpi at last yielded before the rigors of the Inquisition and the blandishments of diplomacy. In the realm of politics the aspirations for overturning the lead helmet of the Spanish finally withered away, in spite of Boccalini's *Pietra del paragone politico* and his *Filippiche*. And in the realm of historical thought the quest for truth without a veil of rhetoric or adulation and the desire for moral commitment and a renovated political society finally gave way before the counteroffensive of the virtuosos of rhetoric and of the obedient eulogists of "authority" and conformity.

THE REACTION OF THE TRADITIONALISTS: LIVY AGAINST TACITUS

The return to the traditional positions of Counter Reformation orthodoxy is already evident in the work of a theologian of Urbino, Sebastiano Macci da Casteldurante, who in 1613 dedicated his *De Historia* to none other than Cardinal Scipione Borghese—to the nephew, that is, of Paul V, the most violent adversary of Sarpi and the Venetian Republic. Macci deliberately closed his eyes to the whole speculative work of European and Italian historical thought and went right back to Aristotle and the Peripatetic method. His Aristotelianism, it is true, permits him to proclaim the truth about human actions, be they bad or good, as the matter of history, of which the end is simply the conservation of the truth about the past rather than whatever eventual pedagogical value the truth may turn out to possess. Indeed, he goes so far as to argue against Cicero and the oratorical concept of history; and he distinguishes sharply between the task of the historian, which is above all the search for truth, and the task of the orator or of the poet. History is "the precise record, faithfully and splendidly set down, of things done in the past and preserved in reliable literary monuments."

The problem of history, therefore, is still one of searching out the truth, not of writing elegantly or of collecting moral lessons. But the whole framework of Macci's thought is one of opposition to scientific naturalism on one hand and to Tacitism on the other, even though he avoids a frontal attack on them. Livy is his historian par excellence, just as he was soon to be for the Jesuits of the Collegio Romano. Macci never even mentions Tacitus, and he names Guicciardini only for the purpose of criticizing him ferociously and revealing his hidden impiety. He admits the historian's obligation to seek out *consilia* and causes, be they known or hidden. But he quickly adds that neither a Turk nor a Lutheran nor a Jew can be a good historian—only a Catholic. Neither can a member of the disdained lower classes of society be one, for only a nobleman has the high spiritual qualities necessary for writing history. Nor can women—as he insists in a whirlwind of misogyny; for women, he says, along with the many other impertinent accusations he pours onto their heads, are unable to ascend to the moral dignity of history. He skims over the methodological problem of the criticism of sources with little more than a few old commonplaces about the possibility of history's being falsified through "love, hate, and self-interest." And over half the book is dedicated to an interminable analysis of historical stylistics, based, naturally, on the "authority" of the classics in general and of Livy in particular, and reinforced by the usual list of precepts regarding prefaces, digressions, orations, sentences, etc.

It did not take long for the anti-Tacitism implicit in the work of Macci to become more open and aggressive. The very next year (which, by the way, was the same year, 1614, in which Paolo Beni's work at last came out), a certain Girolamo Briani published an insipid and soporific "Addition" to the *Ragguagli di Parnaso*, in which he turned Boccalini's thesis upside down.[37] Instead of having Apollo upbraid Caesar for his stylistic criticisms of Commynes, Briani gives him the job of ridding his work, and the works of all other historians as well, of bad writing. After dividing history into four genera (topical, chronical, genealogical, and pragmatic) according to the traditional rhetorical schoolbook exercises, Caesar then charges historians with the task of selecting only nice and happy events, of staying away from questions that for the sake of convenience ought to be left in oblivion, and of avoiding precisely those *arcana* which Boccalini and the Tacitists had seen as the chief fruit of historical investigation.

But as yet the attack was still indirect, only a prelude to the great anti-Tacitist campaign that was soon to be launched from the very fortress of the Jesuit culture of the Seicento, the Collegio Romano.

THE HISTORICAL THEORY OF THE JESUITS: FAMIANO STRADA AND AGOSTINO MASCARDI

It was, indeed, a professor of rhetoric in the Collegio Romano, the Jesuit Famiano Strada, who first offered himself as a champion for the new crusade. Strada was a man so full of the spirit of devotion as to tell his biographer and fellow Jesuit that "he hardly ever made it safely through a day without having to punish himself with a whip." In 1617 he published a series of much-applauded *Prolusiones Academicae*[38] in which, while discussing various literary

[37] *Aggiunta ai Ragguagli di Parnaso* (Modena: Cassiani, 1614).
[38] (Rome: I. Mascardi, 1617.)

and moral questions, he committed himself to a battle to the finish against Tacitus and the Tacitists in the field of historiography. According to Strada, Tacitism was not only impious; it also ignored truth and led to error. And besides being "not good citizens," the Tacitists were also "not good historians." They were "not good citizens" in that they taught egoism and private interest instead of good morals. They undermined the submissiveness of subjects toward their rulers, and they disdained the firmest foundation of the authority of princes, namely, religion, which alone, "the driver, or coachman of minds," was capable of keeping subjects in obedience. They were "not good historians" because they ignored Lucian's authoritative statement about the bonds between "truth" and "pleasure" with their accounts of dreary and dreadful events, with their tyrants and crimes. Indeed, they sinned against truth itself with their exaggerated use of supposition and conjecture in trying to penetrate the *arcana* of princes.

Instead of Tacitus, then, Strada proposed Livy as a model— Livy, who was respectful of miracles and the gods, who presented so many lovely orations, and who did not try to pry too deeply into the events he recounted. True, the reading of Livy had inspired that horrible Machiavelli as well; but Strada blocked that objection by showing that Livy could provide quite different lessons to a reader properly instructed in good morals and obedient to the Church. To back up this point, he unrolled a long list of maxims he had gotten out of Livy, all of them brightly anti-Machiavellian: those who are scornful of religion, for example, are also "ignorant soldiers" who don't realize that battles are won by the fear of God; the virtues of the first seven kings of Rome are similar to those of the last seven popes. Strada then put his own ideal into practice in his *De Bello Belgico* (*On the Belgian War*),[39] which the triumphant Society of Jesus spread to the four corners of Europe. He makes history the instrument of edification, one which presents "examples" of the success of the good (that is, of those who are obsequious to religion and to the clergy) and of the ruin of the bad (that is, of those who rebel

[39] [*De Bello Belgico* (Rome, 1632); but there was already a sixth edition in 1647.]

against either or both of them). He then enhances the persuasive force of this instrument by dressing it in proper literary style. That there might be problems of research and of the critical evaluation of the sources, that there might be a speculative problem of determining the nature of history—all these are problems that fall well beyond his mental horizons. For Strada history is not a science or a work of research. It is hagiography and panegyric. He thus jumps backward over seventy years of European historiographical thought, back even beyond Possevino and Melchior Cano, back all the way to Speroni and Robortello and to the *leges* of history, the *magistra vitae*.

The vast diffusion of Strada's work is in itself a good indication of the magnitude of the victory of the Anti-Tacitists. There was only one voice of opposition in the chorus of acclamations—the biting, malignant voice of Gasparo Scioppio, an Italianate German philologian and a virulent and implacable opponent of the Jesuits, who hurled back a little work with the truly programmatic title of *Infamia famiani*.[40] With all his fury, however, Scioppio dismisses the substance of his adversary's thought and simply criticizes the formal aspects of his work, with a series of minute and pedantic notes on his Latin vocabulary and style, with a good dash of insolent shouting at the Jesuits in general, and with an equally strong dose of vituperation for Tacitus himself, whom he claims to be the real master of the Society.

The case of Scioppio—of a man, that is, who more than anyone else was in a position to understand the works of Campanella and to pick up his speculative contribution to the problem of history—the case of Scioppio is good evidence of the rapid eclipse in Italian culture of the school of historiography that had begun with Patrizi and Bodin. In fact, the *Infamia* was followed by two other works on the art of history, the *De Stylo Historico* and the *De Natura Historiae et Historici Officio*,[41] composed, apparently, in

---

[40] [Gasparo Scioppio, or Caspar Schoppe's *Infamia famiani* is published together with the three tracts cited in the next note.]

[41] Of Scioppio's three tracts [the *Infamia famiani*, *On Historical Style*, and *On the Nature and Function of History*] I have found only the edition published

a few months between 1617 and 1618.[42] Although there is no
concrete reference to it, the texts strongly suggest that the author
was familiar with Campanella's *Historiographia*. His very definition of history echoes that of Campanella, particularly in his
statements regarding the difference between human and natural
history. But the whole perspective is different; and Scioppio
forgets all about history as a portion of human knowledge in
general and makes it solely the foundation of political knowledge
—which puts him right back in the camp of the Tacitists he hated
as much as the Jesuits did. And he adds "teaching" to "narrating,"
docere to *narrare*, in order to get out of the trap. A hater of Tacitus
and a defender of Machiavelli, an opponent of the Jesuits and a
proponent of papal authority against the Protestants, a friend and
at the same time a betrayer of Campanella, Scioppio stands at the
crossroads of all the major currents of historiographic thought of
his time; and he cannot make up his mind which way to go or
how to overcome his own contradictions. He ends up forgetting
everything else and sticking to questions of style and grammar—
to the point, indeed, where his differences with the Jesuits seem to
be the product of nothing more than personal pique or disappointed ambitions rather than of conscious and deeply held ideals.

Thus the anti-Tacitist campaign rode to victory all over Italy.
Even in Padua there was a return to Ciceronian positions, encouraged by a patriotic reaction against Beni's irreverent audacities

---

posthumously by Scioppio's friend and correspondent, Giovanni Fabri (Sora:
Haubold, 1658). The *Infamia famiani* has the date, the place, and the publisher
on its separate title page. The other two follow as in an appendix without any
further indication. It is probably to this rather than to some anterior edition
without date or place, therefore, that later citations refer.

[42] In the absence of other information, the following facts seem to support
my dating of the two tracts. First, it is obvious that the *Infamia* comes after the
Prolusiones Academicae of Strada, that is, after 1617. On the other hand, in the
De Stylo Scioppio declares his wish to write elsewhere about Machiavelli.
Since [Carlo] Morandi (to whose courtesy I owe my having noticed these
works), in his study on the *Apologia del Machiavelli* of Scioppio in *Nuova rivista
storica*, XVII (1933), 277–94, shows that the *Apologia* must have been written
between 1617 and 1618, it is probable that all three were written then as well.
The stylistic and formal elements of the last two are very similar.

with respect to the Paduan Livy—first by Lorenzo Pignoria in his *Symbolarum Epistolicarum Libri* and then by Bishop [Giacomo] Filippo Tomasini in his biography of Livy, which goes right back to the theses of Quintilian.[43]

But it was in Rome that the anti-Tacitist campaign found its most favorable terrain—amid the splendid and authoritarian court of Urban VIII, where Bernini was creating his grandiose baroque stage-sets and Cardinal Bentivoglio was writing his theatrical *History of the Wars in Flanders* as an antidote to Davila's *Civil Wars in France*. And it was from Rome that came forth the work that best represented the aspirations and intentions of the Ciceronians: the *Arte istorica*[44] of Agostino Mascardi, the successor of Strada, thanks to the favor of the Barberini, in the chair of rhetoric at the Collegio Romano.

To men of the age the *Arte istorica* seemed like a masterpiece, the *ne plus ultra* of intellectual ability and learning; and it continued to be reprinted until the beginning of the nineteenth century, the sole survivor of the oblivion that soon overcame all the other treatises on the subject of the Cinquecento and the Seicento. Except, however, for a digression on style (which is important only for the history of literary criticism), the book will immediately appear to whoever is familiar with the works of Speroni and Robortello as nothing more than a huge collection of commonplaces taken from the overworked rhetorical tradition of Ciceronianism. The commonplaces, moreover, are stretched out over an interminable series of high-sounding pages and rendered unreadable by a continuous and unbearable showing-off of scholastic quotations, ancient "examples," and boring anecdotes. Mascardi is wholly unaware of methodological problems. He ignores completely everything written about historiography since Speroni. And he lacks even that certain stylistic temperance, that classical moderation, that ingenuous zeal of the faith, which makes at least not too disagreeable the

[43] Published respectively at Padua (D. Pasquardi, 1629) and at Amsterdam (A. Frisius, 1670; which is the earliest edition I have been able to find), p. 44.
[44] Rome: Facciotti, 1636.

reading of the *Prolusiones* of the candid and pious Strada. He has not even any of the orthodox Aristotelianism of Macci, at whom, indeed, he hurls abuse for permitting historians to stick their noses into the *arcana* of princes and to use history for any other purpose than good style and edifying sermons. There is nothing but rhetoric, rhetoric, and then still more rhetoric, without an idea, without a crumb of originality, without a single personal reflection.

Actually, there is no reason to read his huge volume on the *Arte istorica* to find out what Mascardi really thought about history. All his thought is contained in a much smaller book in which he sought to demonstrate his own valor as a historian. The book is his *Congiura del conte Gianluigi del Fiesco* (*Conspiracy of . . .*), which had come out just a few years earlier, and which Mascardi clearly expected to outshine the *Catiline* of Sallust.[45] The book is nothing but a series of orations, one after the other, barely held together by a thin narration of facts picked here and there out of the historians of the Cinquecento. For Mascardi, then, it is not enough to make history a problem of style, in the fashion of Speroni, Robortello, and Strada, rather than one of the search for political or scientific truth. History must be reduced still further. It must be made to serve no other purpose than that of a pretext for writing orations, just like the themes for exercises prescribed in contemporary courses in rhetoric. And thus history finally loses its identity altogether and dissolves into oratory.

It would indeed have been difficult to go much further; and the enthusiastic Romans who said the book would never be rivaled were in a certain sense correct. And everyone was truly enthusiastic. Urban VIII personally defined the work as perfect. Bentivoglio filled his *Memorie*[46] with praises of Mascardi, perhaps not without a bit of acrimony toward his rival in the history of the Flemish war, Strada. Giovan Vincenzo de' Rossi, the much-celebrated Giano Nicio Eritreo of the academies, Crasso, and a

---

[45] *La congiura del conte Gianluigi del Fiesco* (Antwerp, 1629).
[46] [See above, n. 32.]

large number of minor writers competed with one another in their eulogies.[47] The acclamation went on and on. And editions, translations, and reprintings of the *Conspiracy* as well as the *Arte* of the fortunate professor multiplied in Italy and beyond the Alps.

THE EXHAUSTION OF THE POLEMICS ON HISTORY

One after the other—Boccalini in 1613, Sarpi in 1623, Davila in 1630—all the best representatives of the ideal of a free Italy who had gathered in Venice at the beginning of the century descended to the tomb; and they were soon followed by Campanella in his retreat at Paris. In the rest of Europe their work was carried on—in France, which surrounded the work of Campanella and Davila with veneration; in Switzerland, where Sarpi's masterpiece was reprinted; in England, where Biondi had fled in search of freedom; in Germany, where Vossius returned to the thought of Patrizi in his *Ars Historica* of 1623. In Italy no one any longer read the *History of the Council of Trent*, the *Historiography According to its own Principles*, the *History of the Civil Wars in France*, or the *Dialogues on History*. Rhetoric and hagiography had at last extinguished all remnants of historiographic speculation.

Only in Paolo Pirani[48] does there reappear a small spark of criticism. In spite of his general enthusiasm about Mascardi, Pirani becomes conscious of the contradictions among the Ciceronians when they speak of history as narration and then go on to reduce it to an oratorical exercise. . . . He even attempts to return to an evaluation of history in terms of the number of true things it uncovers. He calls it "a public record of true things,

---

[47] [Giano Nicio Eritreo is really a pseudonym for Giovan Vincenzo de' Rossi author of a *Pinacotheca* published in 1643 and 1648. Lorenzo Crasso's *Elogi degl uomini illustri* appeared at Venice in 1666.] Another interesting bit of evidence of the overwhelming esteem of contemporaries for Mascardi is to be found in Fulvio Testi, *Lettere*, ed. M. L. Doglio (Bari: Laterza, 1967). [Addition by the author.]

[48] Pirani, *Dodici capi pertinenti all "Arte historica" del Mascardi* (Venice· G. Hertz, 1646).

preserved in writing for the use of the republic"; and he includes as history the unadorned chronicles as well as the polished works of the Ciceronians. But all this is merely a spark; and it is soon lost in the general mediocrity of the book, which is as wanting in originality as it is in constructive force. The whole problem of the art of history seems to have lost its charm. In 1653 the bizarre Antonio Santacroce picked up Boccalini's arrows against Mascardi himself, the pedant of the pedants of his generation.[49] Santacroce's Apollo writes a letter to the deceased Mascardi in which he refuses to force historians to read his heavy treatise, "since you have sought to appear more the learned man than the good teacher and have filled an entire volume with long and tedious talk, [which no one can get through] without wasting half a lifetime." The techniques of history and its rules "can just as well be learned from reading the good historians, with much less time and trouble; and many writers have learned to write very well without the help of your art."

But Santacroce was the last to bother himself with the argument. The age of the treatises on the art of history, of the rules for writing history and for political action, was passing away; and the mouth of the biting Neapolitan, with all its laughing at pedants, was actually announcing the first rays of a new age. The new age was to be one less inhibited in its notions and more open to the stimuli that were just beginning to reach the Gassendians and the Cartesians in Santacroce's own Naples from France. It was to be an age which would look to foreign ideas for help in shaking off the antiquated dust of rhetorical Ciceronianism, of Aristotelian *ipse dixit*'s, and of the infallible secret techniques of *ragion di stato*. The painful incubation of the new age was destined to last for another forty years. It was then to reach maturity at the beginning of the next century, when the *Storia civile* of Giannone and the *De Nostri Temporis Studiorum Ratione* of Vico were met

[49] Venice: Storti, 1653. [The author adds:] on Santacroce, see Umberto Limentani, "La 'Secretaria d'Apollo' di Antonio Santacroce" in *Italian Studies*, XII (1957), 69–90. On the Incogniti of Venice, see Spini, *Ricerca dei libertini*.

by the ponderous philological labors of Ludovico Antonio Muratori.[50]

[50] [On Vico and Giannone, see ch. 1 above. A good selection of the voluminous works of Muratori (1672–1750) are now available in the *Opere*, ed. Giorgio Falco and Fiorenzo Forti (Milan: Ricciardi, 1964). Readers who know Italian are referred to Sergio Bertelli, *Erudizione e storia in L. A. M.* (Naples: Editore Scientifiche Italiane, 1960); those who do not, to the editor's "Muratori: The Vocation of a Historian," *Catholic Historical Review*, LI (1965), 153–72.]

5 Literature: Torquato Tasso: An Introduction[1]

ETTORE MAZZALI

A former disciple of the historian of Italian literature Attilio Momigliano, Ettore Mazzali is secretary of the journal *Letterature moderne* and professor *incaricato* of Italian language and literature in the Facoltà di Magistero of the University of Bologna, as well as a founding member of the *Ente Vinciano* in Milan. He has written numerous works of literary history and criticism, from *Poeti e letterati in Valtellina* and *Critica, eloquenza, e poesia* (1954 and 1955) to *Testimonianze sul Romanticismo* and *D'Annunzio, artefice solitario* (1957 and 1962), and he has published an edition of Leopardi's *Canti* (1962). His principal contributions to scholarship on Tasso have been his *Cultura e poesia nell'opera di T. T.* (Bologna: Cappelli, 1957) and the edition of Tasso's *Prose*, with a long introduction from which this essay is taken.

THE NATURE AND CHARACTER OF TASSO'S CULTURAL FORMATION

TASSO'S cultural formation was a typical product of the late Renaissance. It fully reflects a period in which the concepts and style of the Cinquecento were being codified in treatises on aesthetics and in manuals of polite conduct.

The two principal institutions of this civilization were the court and the academy, both of which, needless to say, must be judged in their historical context. The first contained within itself the principles of political virtue and mundane courtesy. The

[1] From the Introduction to Tasso, *Prose*, ed. E. Mazzali (Milan: Ricciardi; 1959). Translated and abridged by the editor with the approval of the author and with the permission of the publisher.

second was the school of the literary and philosophical disciplines. The two complemented and perfected each other. The academy was not an apolitical and merely literary institution, nor was it merely the passive projection of the desire of princes to be patrons of the arts. It was rather the necessary complement of the court, since the man of letters was no less necessary to a harmonious and full courtly life than the gentleman politician. Indeed, the ambassador, the man of letters, and the secretary often coincided in the same person, as the art of the diplomat and the secretary took the place of the art of the orator, and as oratory moved, according to the new political conditions, from public rostra to the private chambers of the princes and to the elegant halls and gardens of the ducal palaces.

Thus between the prince and the mass of non-noble servants and common subjects was inserted a class of "noble" servants, those members of the court who concerned themselves with the liberal arts. Hence cultural activity was at once political, philosophical, and literary. It was not merely an elegant ornament. It was rather the full realization of the court; and hence courtiers could be both nobles and servants at the same time, without ever worrying about a possible contradiction between the two roles. That was something only a later democratic society would be able to perceive.

Thus Tasso never was, and never considered himself to be, a victim of the courts and the academies, for he felt himself completely a part of them. The apparently anticourt theme that turns up in one of the more famous cantos (VI) of the *Gerusalemme liberata* (but was suppressed in the revised version of the *Conquistata*) did not, and could not, represent a desire for liberty and for redemption from servitude. The shepherd in the scene puts the renunciation of court life in the form of a decorative fable, while for Erminia the pastoral idyll simply marks, with remarkable psychological coherence, a passage from the exhausting anguish of her flight to the calmer but no less gnawing anguish over Tancredi's refusal to respond to her love. So also the anticourt sentiments that recur in the letters, particularly those written after his imprisonment at Sant'Anna, during the last ten years of his life (1586–95). Far from being a serious attack on political and social institutions, these letters reveal little more than a private and sentimental rupture between the effective reality of court life and the heroic ideals that Tasso would like to have seen realized in the courts and that he still did, on occasions—whenever he was flattered by a word of praise or a monetary gift—think actually was realized in them. But Tasso's classical culture, the culture that comes through and that can be so easily documented in the *Dialogues*, in the treatises, and in the *Discourses*, is always firmly anchored in the still-flourishing Renaissance art of forming precepts and of codifying moral, religious, and literary verities. Tasso himself, when in the *Conquistata* he thought he had touched supreme perfection in heroic poetry, turned most probably for inspiration to none other than Giovambattista Giraldi Cintio, with all his classicist flavor, in evoking the "intellectual structure of his own mind."[2]

The line of demarcation between absolutism and classicism on one hand and experimentalism on the other in the Cinquecento runs through other men and other systems. It runs from Machiavelli and Guicciardini to Bruno and the philosophers of "nature." Tasso, to the contrary, is on the line of systematic and immobile orthodoxy, along with Castiglione.[3] In him the golden streams of the Renaissance tradition end up in codes, manuals, and decoration. Even Petrarchism is resolved into the abstract casuistry of a rule book of love and becomes a play of elegant and gallant variations. In Tasso the classical texts, from Virgil's *Aeneid* to Petrarch's *Rerum vulgarium fragmenta* and Poliziano's *Stanze*,

---

[2] See *Prose diverse*, ed. Cesare Guasti (Florence: Le Monnier, 1875), Vol. I, p. 493 and [Giovambattista] Giraldi Cintio, *Discorsi intorno al comporre de i romanzi, delle comedie, e delle tragedie* (Venice: Gabriel Giolito de Ferrari, 1554), p. 51. [Giraldi Cintio (1504–73), a Ferrarese nobleman and sometime secretary to Duke Ercole II d'Este, was the author of several critical works and tragedies. His relationship to Tasso is indicated by a letter to Bernardo Tasso on epic and heroic poetry of 1557, published most recently in G. Daelli's *Biblioteca rara* (Milan, 1864), Vol. LIII.]

[3] [Baldassare Castiglione, author of the *Book of the Courtier*.]

operate only through a literary filter, through the impalpable stylization of a courtly, or at least a scholarly, reading. The texts are subtly removed from the realm of experience or from the human vicissitudes actually mentioned in them. They are tenaciously and minutely subjected to an analysis for whatever abstract statements regarding moral behavior and rhetorical norms they might yield. And the results of the analysis are immediately incorporated into a learned, well-constructed treatise or memorial.

The classification and rhetorical description of literary figures are patterned after the treatises of Aristotle, the Pseudo-Demetrius Phalereus, Cicero, Hermogenes, and Quintilian,[4] and they follow a rigidly uniform order in Tasso's *Discourses on Heroic Poetry*, just as they had in the works of other Cinquecento theorists of rhetoric—Trapezunzio, Vettori, Scaliger, Minturno, Cavalcanti, and Maggi.[5] They are more than simply a form of literary technique. They are the expression of a mental habit than can be found, with the same pedantic exactitude and the same systematic rigidity, in the moral, political, and economic treatises

[4] [Those of Aristotle, Cicero, and Quintilian are well known. Demetrius of Phaleron, the Athenian orator and statesman (345–*ca.* 283 B.C.), did not write the work published under his name in the Renaissance, which is now usually attributed to a certain Demetrius of Alexandria, a Peripatetic philosopher of the second century A.D. Hermogenes wrote a number of books on rhetoric in the time of Marcus Aurelius, which were published at the Aldine Press in the early sixteenth century.]

[5] [Trapezunzio is George of Trebizond, a Greek scholar who migrated to Italy in 1395 and led the Aristotelians in their defense against the Platonists in the mid-Quattrocento. The Florentine patrician Pier Vettori became professor of Greek in Florence in 1538 and published numerous editions, translations, and commentaries on the texts of Aristotle and other ancient authors. Julius Caesar Scaliger, an Italian who spent most of his life in France and who began his career with a violent attack on Erasmus, was the author of, among other things, the Aristotelian *Poetices Libri Septem*, published in 1561, which is probably Tasso's main reference. Antonio Sebastiano Minturno (d. 1574) applied Ciceronian and Platonic concepts first to Latin (*De Poeta*, 1559) and then to Italian poetry (*Arte poetica*, 1563). Bartolomeo Cavalcanti, a Florentine exile and sometime adviser to the French governor of Siena, is better known for his political writings (*Tre trattati*, 1571); but he also did a translation of Aristotle's *Rhetoric*. Vincenzo Maggi (d. 1564), sometime professor at the University of Padua, acquired a considerable reputation with his synthesis of Aristotle and Horace.]

of the age. Behind a façade of citations and philological rigor, the transcription of poetic texts serves largely to sketch out an immobile and decorative background or to fill up little boxes labeled with analytic definitions and formulas. Each of the moral precepts that occur in rapid succession in Tasso's *Dialogues* is drawn from a specific poetic "example"; and the text of the *Aeneid* is transformed into a breviary or a rule book on how to live well and wisely.

Even Aristotelianism is reduced, in substance, to a systematic methodology. From the massive corpus of Aristotle's works are drawn not so much the particular conclusions of his analytic reasoning, but rather his system of classifying and ordering the conclusions. No one is any longer interested in the anatomical descriptions of animals, nor in the descriptions made by Theophrastus in the field of botany, by Strabo in the field of geography, by Pliny in the field of the natural sciences, by Aristotle himself in the field of meteorology, or by Aristotle and Ptolemy in the field of astronomy. No one is interested in Aristotle's description of psychic states or the minute analysis of sensory phenomenology in the *De Anima*. What is of interest now is the epistemological process set forth in his *Organon*—the *First* and *Second Analytics*, the *Categories* and *Predicaments*, the *Topoi*, *On Interpretation*— along with the problem of establishing genera, species, and definitions and of understanding the techniques of the syllogism. The process of separating experiment and analysis from the concrete things they are supposedly directed to was initiated by the Aristotelian commentators of the third to the sixth century A.D.—by Alexander of Aphrodisias, for instance, by Simplicius, by John Philopon, and even by a Neoplatonist like Porphyry, who introduced and elaborated the Aristotelian *Categories*.[6] The

6 [Alexander of Aphrodisias, the great Aristotelian commentator of the late second and early third century A.D., was particularly influential among the Aristotelians of Padua in the late fifteenth century. Porphyry (d. *ca.* A.D. 305) carried on the work of his master Plotinus and was widely read in the Middle Ages; and his work in turn was carried on by the last of the pagan Neoplatonists, Simplicius, who wrote several commentaries on Aristotle as well. John Philopon, or Joannes Grammaticus, was a disciple of Ammonius (see

process was continued in the Renaissance by the professors of logic, and the line that goes from Alexander and Porphyry and Simplicius to Aegidius Romanus[7] becomes one of the constants of the Cinquecento Aristotelians right down to Tasso.

To this systematic and categorical study of Aristotle based on logical procedures is then added the specific documentation. And that, once the categories are established, is indeed taken from the naturalists (Theophrastus, Hippocrates, Pliny), from the astronomers (Ptolemy and the many Aristotelian-Ptolemaic commentators down to Alfragan[8]), from the meteorologists (Alexander and Olympiodorus, both commentators on Aristotle), from the political and economic writers (Aristotle, Xenophon, and their exegetists). The Platonic tradition, which even in Greco-Roman times had acted as a mediator between Christianity and Aristotelianism, acted in the Cinquecento partially as a corrective to Aristotelian naturalism—by channeling it, that is, into mere logical methodology. But it also took the form of an elegant and mundane spiritualism, especially in the treatises on love, where it encouraged an eclectic combination of classical and Christian cultures (in the footsteps of Ficino and Bessarion[9]), and where it offered the prospect of escaping into contemplation to anyone upset by possible cracks in the Aristotelian system.

The so-called Aristotelian-Platonic syncretism of the High and Late Renaissance is above all an element of cultural "leveling." The Platonic impulse toward ideas that transcend nature is strictly

---

n. 16 below) and wrote commentaries in Alexandria in the seventh century A.D. that were frequently published in the sixteenth century.]

[7] [Aegidius (d. 1316) was one of the chief disciples and defenders of Thomas Aquinas, author of the still well-known *De Regimine Principum*. His commentary on the *Generation* was first published in Padua in 1480 and exerted considerable influence on Late Renaissance Aristotelianism.]

[8] [Alfragan, or Ahead Ibn Muhammed ibn Kathir, with whose work Dante seems to have been familiar, lived in Baghdad in the ninth century and wrote a book on astronomy that became very popular after its publication at Ferrara in 1493.]

[9] [Bessarion, of course, is Cardinal Basil Bessarion (d. 1492), a Greek scholar and theologian who settled in Italy and was a close associate of Marsilio Ficino as a proponent of Platonism.]

ordered within a system of Aristotelian epistemology. Plato, so to speak, gives the architectonic impulse toward a "mental or intellectual construction" that is founded firmly on Aristotle's *Organon*. Thus the symbolic dynamism of structure internal to nature (the dynamism of numbers, of polyhedrons, that operate within things), which passed from Pythagoras to Plato's *Timaeus*, is on one hand identified with the Aristotelian theory of potency and act, as in Tasso's *Malpiglio secondo, overo del fuggir la moltitudine* (*The Second Malpiglio, or On Fleeing the Multitude*); on the other hand, it is adapted to the arts of the cabala and of magic, which constitute more a technique than a phenomenon of spiritual unrest and cultural openness.

Once the "Angelic" theology or doctrine had been turned into dogma, particularly by Marsilio Ficino in his commentary on Dionysius the Areopagite, what remained open to exploration was not so much the occult zones of the soul as the wonders of nature and natural magic. This sort of magic was always concerned with doctrine and casuistry—a sort of systematic Renaissance Neopythagoreanism. Those who followed it were natural philosophers in the sense that this term had been understood in the Aristotelian tradition—philosophers like Girolamo Cardano, for instance, Martín del Río, and Giambattista della Porta.[10] As a doctrinaire exegete of Renaissance culture, Tasso never found magic completely congenial: his "demons" (*folletti*), at times cunning and malicious, at times spiteful, represented in his private life, along with the chiromancers and fortunetellers, only ephemeral expressions of his instable temperament, inclined as it was toward melancholic fantasy.[11] They never constituted the

[10] See Della Porta, *De i miracoli e maravigliosi effetti de la natura prodotti, libri IV* (Venice, 1572), as well as Eugenio Garin, *Medioevo e rinascimento* (Bari: Laterza, 1954) and B. T. Sozzi, *Studi sul Tasso* (Pisa: Nistri-Lischi, 1954), pp. 303–36. [Girolamo Cardano (1501–76) wrote extensively and very successfully about a mixture of mathematical, magical, scientific, and alchemistic subjects. His *Book of My Life* is available in English. Martín del Río, a Spanish Jesuit (1551–1608), wrote an authoritative manual of witchcraft and magic.]

[11] See Sozzi, *Studi sul Tasso*, p. 307. I believe, however, that Sozzi's judgment of Tasso's interest in magic must be modified, especially where he connects magic with Tasso's epistemological crisis and with the principle of the truly

substance of the poetry of the "marvelous" so dear to him, which was formed in virtue of another spiritual exigency—in virtue, that is, of the heroic magnificence of exemplary human situations. They never gave form and physiognomy to his fascination with landscapes of the north suggested to him by his reading of Olaus Magnus[12] or with similar ones suggested by his reading of Herodotus, Strabo, or even Aristotle's *Problems*.[13] Thanks to their humanist, or in technical matters, classical garb, moreover, the "wonders of nature" contributed, in Tasso's works, to representational clarity (which he denotes, according to the doctrine of Demetrius Phalereus, as "evidence" from a Latin root or "energy" from a Greek one). They also enhanced the flow of his narratives. And, finally, they pressed him into classical mythography, at least where this mythography does not become a means for theological exposition, as it does in the biblical and Platonic-Augustinian cosmology of the *Hexaemeron*, and as it does in the myth of the Arab phoenix in the *Mondo creato* (*The Created World*).[14]

There is, therefore, a normative, immobile base to the systematic and classicist culture of the High and Late Cinquecento, a base whose most evident qualities are abstraction and the prevalence of epistemological methodology over effectual experience, and whose most pronounced characteristics are eclecticism and structural order. As he runs through *Discorsi del poema eroico* (in so far as they are manuals of Tasso's poetical and rhetorical technique), and as he mentally puts together the conceptual procedures and conclusions [drawn from] humanistic culture in the *Dialogues* and the *Discourses*, the reader of Tasso's prose (and of

---

marvelous. In my opinion the marvelous in Tasso is basically rational in its formulation. See further Tasso's letters LXIV, LXV, XCI, and CLV, published in [Mazzali's edition of Tasso, *Prose*,] pp. 954–56, 957–61, 992–93, and 1077–78.

[12] [Olaus Magnus, archbishop of Uppsala in Sweden (1490–1558). His *Historia de Gentium Septentrionalium* (*History of the Northern Nations*) was published in Basel in 1567.]

[13] From the *Problems* Tasso took much of his information regarding "demented" poets and heroes, especially for his *Messaggiero*.

[14] [The *Hexaemeron* of St. Ambrose of Milan was one of Tasso's principal sources for the *Messaggiero*. See Mazzali, *Cultura e poesia*, p. 158.]

his *Mondo creato*) can easily perceive two processes of "leveling." First, there is that of the sciences, of politics and economics, of rhetoric and natural philosophy, which are made to correspond one to the other and which come up with basically the same conclusions. For all of them have become an art or a technique, and all, therefore, are based on a common syllogistic or apodictic method.

Second, there is the "leveling" of the authors, and even at times of original texts and commentaries. Hence Plutarch, Dion Chrysostom, and Athenaeus—writers, that is, of anecdotes and miscellaneous scholarship—acquire the same authority as that usually bestowed on Aristotle. Thucydides is made equal to Herodotus for purely rhetorical reasons, as is Polybius to Dionysius of Halicarnassus and Xenophon. Livy and Valerius Maximus are considered interchangeably as sources of historical data. Tacitus and Virgil are thought to have the same opinions. Maxims are borrowed indiscriminately now from the Scriptures, now from the Greek tragedians, now from Homer and Hesiod, now from the Seven Wise Men of Greece (on the model of Stobaeus).[15] Alexander of Aphrodisias becomes the official text of Aristotelianism, Demetrius of Phaleron the official text of Platonic aesthetics. Catholic Aristotelianism is represented by Aegidius Romanus, Catholic Platonism by Dionysius the Areopagite, Bessarion, and Ficino. Augustine and Thomas Aquinas are exalted as institutional authors. And Cicero becomes the supreme cultural and stylistic institution of classicism—Cicero, that is, in whom the epistological- and systematic-minded Cinquecento saw reflected the full flowering and the exact architectonic order of a perennial culture, and whose name became synonymous with civilization itself.

The age of Tasso is an age of anthologies, of collections of maxims, of lexicons, of *Apophthegmata*[16]—of handbooks, that is,

---

[15] Stobaeus, *Apophthegmata ex variis autoribus collecta* (Rome, 1517). [Little is known of him except as the author of this vast and valuable collection of long quotations from the works of ancient authors.]

[16] Besides the one cited in the preceding note, see the lexicons of Suidas, Ammonius, and Esichio. [Suidas wrote a dictionary sometime before Strabo, whom he mentions, which was published first in Milan in 1499 and often

on various cultural levels, which appear in response to what was considered the perfectly legitimate practice of quoting and transcribing without acknowledging the source. It is an age of storehouses of sentences, images, and poetic and literary locutions, which can be picked out as the occasion arises and inserted into an original work. It is an age in which invention—poetic creativity —is subject to the rigorous laws of artifice.

THE "PERFECT" CULTURE

Within the general framework of Renaissance culture, nonetheless, and in spite of the general tendency toward "leveling" on a theoretical plane, Tasso succeeded in working out a taste and a sensibility that was all his own. The very temporal immobility of his poetic and ideological values acquires in him an autonomous relief, precisely because he represents, much more energetically than his contemporaries, the "mythological moment" of what is spiritually perennial in the Renaissance. It is wholly consonant with his personality that he picks sentences and judgments out of Virgil or Cicero, out of Euripides or Homer, in order to provide an ideal solution to a concrete situation—that Augustus appears to him, for example, as an ideal prince for all ages and all societies, and that he follows Augustus's defense of the *Aeneid* in defending the rights of poets before the princes of his own day.[17] Indeed, it is with Aeneas's "Distribution of Awards" in Book v that he backs up the shift from justice to courtesy in his concept of the prince— a concept that in Tasso is as abstract and idyllic as it is realistic and concrete in Machiavelli.[18] There is in Tasso an implicit conviction that the Aristotelian-Platonic edifice is so perfect, so complete, and so well ordered that nothing remains to add to it but decoration and ornaments. Even more particularly Christian

thereafter. Ammonius of Alexandria was a fourth-century A.D. grammarian whose *On the Differences of Words of the Same Meaning* was well known in the sixteenth century. Esichio (Hesychius) wrote a big Greek dictionary about the same time, which was published in Venice in 1514.]

[17] See Letter xxv [in Mazzali's edition of the *Prose*], pp. 851–52.

[18] See *ibid.*, pp. 815–16.

culture, outside of the arduous dogmas that he as a believer accepts supinely from the theologians, becomes a culture of interpretation and exegesis of classical culture—a culture that is derived from another, in other words, a vast apparatus of decoration and ornaments.

Tasso is thus the interpreter of the Late Renaissance effort at re-elaborating and adorning its tradition; and his mind tends, on the cultural level, toward a decorative idealism. But to this effort Tasso adds something of his own: an intellectual freshness, which leads him to look favorably even upon the most humble grammarians and the most orthodox rhetoricians. He goes on filling his cultural baggage, he goes on tirelessly annotating poems and treatises, and he spares no pains, even in the most difficult situations and at the expense of sometimes tragic imploring, to get the texts he thinks necessary to support and to confirm the historical validity of his poems. But he does so not because of mental inertia or senile pedantry. His quotations and literary references serve him as an anchor, as a way of feeling himself fully a citizen of the universal Republic of Letters. In the cultural world of the Cinquecento as a whole, and in Tasso in particular, no single writer or school can any longer impose an exclusive dictatorship. Petrarchism, for example, is no longer a single tradition of situations and poetic language; for alongside the Petrarch of the *Canzoniere* there has now appeared the Petrarch of the *Triumphs* and the *Africa*. Alongside the precise structure and the figurative language of Dante's *Divine Comedy*, similarly, alongside the rapid discourse of Virgil and the solemn gravity of his images, there are now modulations with suggestive musical overtones, there is alliteration, internal echoes, clusters of vowels and consonants, lengthened and truncated verses, and sweetness of rime. On the level of cultural institutions the great writers, and especially the philosophers, put forth syntheses with decorations to the point of making them profuse and luxuriant.

During the period of the revision of the poem (1575–76), and later during his imprisonment and during the last decade of his life, Tasso intensifies his efforts to obtain perfect poetic forms, to

find definitive solutions, to reject earthly passions and measures
for a harmony with celestial spaces and stellar spheres, to rise from
action to contemplation, and to restate principles already affirmed,
like those of his poetics, with a new authority and with a vigor of
style capable of transmitting the absolute perfection of the truth.[19]
Even in his private life the poet reveals an increasing difficulty in
bringing what he feels into relation with day-to-day affairs and
with real men and institutions. He wanders restlessly from one
city and one court to the next. He succumbs to feverish fits of
anger and to religious crises. He accuses himself of impiety and
unorthodoxy and anxiously seeks to have himself examined by
the Inquisitors. He explodes in fury at the Este court in February
1579 and is consequently shut up in the hospital of Sant'Anna,
where he remains until 1586. What measure of spiritual serenity
he is granted during his imprisonment is accompanied by suspicions of being persecuted by men and demons, which bring
back his moments of internal anguish and his violent explosions
of anger. Upon his liberation he consumes the next ten years, the
last of his life, wandering about again without a goal, seeking
hospitality from friends, from monasteries, from courts, and then,
having obtained it, suspecting his hosts of hidden motives and
imagining foes and spies among the very persons who thought
they were offering him a sympathetic, if not always completely
disinterested, friendship. He loses himself amid dreams of glory,
which leave him pained, bitter, and tired when the dreams then
vanish.

At the same time, Tasso's cultural system makes him want to
overcome the practical and emotional vicissitudes of his life in
one leap, to shun doubt and sentimental misgivings. For him it
represents the ideal order of spirit and intelligence, one which
gives reality to all that he feels most solid and certain within
himself, above and beyond the impurities of daily life.

Tasso's idea of the "perfect" culture acts also on his Catholic
faith. In the *Gerusalemme liberata* he spontaneously and happily

[19] For a rapid sketch of the history of the fortune of the *Dialogues*, see Sozzi,
"Nota sui Dialoghi del Tasso," *Studi tassiani*, IV (1954), 67–76.

throws his native and congenial religiosity behind the Platonic-Christian synthesis that had been worked out by Ficino. But later on his religious values split. Some of them he places in contemplative theology, beyond the realm of "perfect" science; others he leaves within the realm of science, though at the very top of it. Thus he can insist, in his dedication to the *Messaggiero*, that he will fall into no heresy even when writing merely as a gentile philosopher; and in the last pages of the *Malpiglio secondo* and in the *Cataneo, overo De gli idoli,* he can acclaim the ascent of the human spirit into the sphere of pure contemplation. Celestial or human though it may be, theology is a necessary science; for it alone enables faith, which is silent without wisdom, to be expressed and to become operative. Though scholarly and syllogistic in its methods, the "perfect" culture is above all a unitary and harmonious system of true things, through which human intelligence reveals its perfectibility and in which the spirit of man can find quiet and comfort amid the tempest of doubt.

That Tasso uncovered elements of Orphic and Pythagorean symbolism in Platonism, and especially in the cosmogony of the *Timaeus*, then, is perfectly true. Indeed, he found them right in the pages of Ficino's commentary. But it is also true that the symbolism he took from Plato is not in him the sign of a spirit troubled by the prospect of God and the cosmos. It is rather the result of a desire to realize even in the geometric, incorporeal purity of "number" the objective reality of nature and of man. Tasso the philosopher beholds a triumphant God, the harmony of starry spaces, the serenity of spheres radiant before the contemplative gaze of the mortal. Dante's *Paradiso* returns in Tasso with its whole symbolic and theological frame—the paradise, that is, where the heavenly court and the spheres are light, music, and dance, geometrically constructed and theologically mediated, where ascent, though perfectly free, is still contained within an edifice built on the foundations of reason.[20]

[20] See the *Giudizio sovra la sua "Gerusalemme" da lui medesimo riformata* (*A Judgment of the "Gerusalemme" as Reformed by Himself*) in *Prose diverse*, ed. Guasti, Vol. I, p. 493.

There is still another connection between Platonism and Christianity: that which regards beauty. Yet beauty is considered to be in things to the degree that the things themselves contain an [ideal] essence. Hence even blind and lascivious lovers "desire nothing more than to enjoy the light of the Divinity," whose rays "shine through in this fallen and corruptible mass of our bodies." And these rays can be represented by "lifting ourselves up to the highest levels of imagination."[21] The connection between beauty and love is one of the most recurrent themes of Christian Platonism of the Renaissance, and Tasso took it up while still in his youth. The "Considerations on the Three Songs of M. Giovan Battista Pigno Called 'The three sisters,'" which affirm the universal harmony of love, is assigned by Serassi to 1568;[22] two years later in 1570 Tasso published—and soon thereafter read to the Academy of Ferrara—his fifty "Amorous Conclusions," elaborated according to the Renaissance casuistry of conceits. But actually casuistry, in Tasso's culture, is accompanied, or followed, by an impulse to contemplation, and systematic doctrine by a desire for an ascent to the ideal, all according to well-thought-out internal gradations. Intellectual material puts on wings for flight; but it is always a material put together by exact deductions from certain principles.

Thus his religiosity is also a combination of reason and will, and it is both programmatic and sentimental. As Tasso gradually comes to realize the impossibility of making his Platonic and religious values bear upon the political and social reality of civil and ecclesiastical institutions, he transfers . . . those values from society to a paradise which his mind imagines to be perfect, from a terrestrial sphere to a celestial one, from an Augustinian Port of Harmony to an Augustinian City of God.[23] He ends up, indeed, by looking only at the absolute goal of his quest and by ignoring or overlooking the harsh path that leads to it—or rather he looks

---

[21] See *ibid.*, Vol. II, pp. 78, 80, 86.

[22] [Pier Antonio Serassi (1721–91), one of the earliest editors of Tasso's works, cited by Guasti in *Prose diverse*, Vol. II, p. 73.]

[23] Most notably in the *Malpiglio secondo*. See p. 134 [in *Prose*, ed. Mazzali].

at the path only as a sophistical deception, like the contrasting hypotheses (which he nonetheless insists are not pure vanity) of scientific inquiry.[24]

Yet we must not concede too much to Tasso's Platonism, and we must remember two persistent and lasting elements in his culture: order and system—that is, Aristotelianism—and classicism and rationalism. The final problem for Tasso is always the problem of knowledge. And the end of his search in this life is always a court. What he looks for in the last years of his life as he wanders from city to city is not the antithesis of a court, but an ideal court, one in harmony with his longing for a "perfect" culture. When he fails to find one in this world, he takes refuge in the Court of Heaven.[25] And unsatisfied, therefore, with his terrestrial poem, he begins longing for a celestial Jerusalem; and he thinks he has found it in the *Gerusalemme conquistata*.[26]

[24] Also in the *Malpiglio secondo*.
[25] See the letter to Constantini of early April 1595, *ibid.*, p. 1142.
[26] See the *Giudizio* (above, n. 20), p. 451.

6 Political Philosophy: Renaissance Utopianism[1]

LUIGI FIRPO

Luigi Firpo, born in 1915, is best known outside Italy for his critical editions of the works, many of them previously unknown, of Tommaso Campanella, Giordano Bruno, Lodovico Agostini, Giovanni Botero, and other philosophers of the Renaissance and early modern periods. But he has also written a myriad of books and articles on many different aspects of European civilization from the Middle Ages to the present. He is general editor of the *Biblioteca bibliografica italica* series for Sansoni, director of the "Political Classics" series for U.T.E.T. and of the *Testi religiosi* for Laterza, and professor of the history of political thought at the University of Turin.

MUCH has been said of late, by those who have sought to trace the fortunes of political Utopias, about a large outcropping of works written or published in Italy from the middle of the sixteenth to the beginning of the seventeenth century. Usually these works have been interpreted as expressions of a single stream of thought, motivated by the same ideals and aspirations, and formulated in terms, often monotonously identical, of revolutionary solutions for the widespread economic and social dislocation of the age.[2] But no one has yet noticed that the supposed

[1] "L'Utopismo del Rinascimento e l'età nuova," pp. 241–61 in his *Lo Stato ideale della Controriforma* (Bari: Laterza, 1957), much of which is dedicated to a study of one of the most important late Cinquecento Utopians, Ludovico Agostini. Translated and slightly abridged by the editor. Permission to use the article was given by the author.

[2] The historiography on Utopianism, particularly abundant in the English language, usually ignores what went on in Italy and admits to citizenship among the constructors of ideal cities no one but Campanella. The following

uniformity and coherence of this phenomenon (if indeed it actually existed in fact as it has been described) makes it almost wholly irreconcilable with the ferment of ideas which characterized the Cinquecento and with the radical break in cultural continuity which occurred in the middle of the century. For the Council of Trent, the fulcrum of the Catholic Reformation, gave rise to a completely new course of thought, taste, and manners. And the Peace of Cateau-Cambrésis, which brought peace as well as servitude to Italy, also had a decisive influence in the field of political speculation. Old problems—like the card castle of the "mixed state", for instance, woich was a Utopia *sui generis*—lost their vitality and immediacy. And new problems—or old problems that suddenly seemed new—became the objects of passionate interest: the restoration of morality, for instance, and the systematic and scrupulous reduction of the humanistic values of the Renaissance within the limits set by traditional ethical and religious values.

A Utopian attitude, therefore, with its confident drawing up of plans for a perfect, self-sufficient, and happy society, contains

works should be kept in mind for what follows: Carlo Curcio's introduction to his anthologies of the Italian Utopians of the Cinquecento, *Utopisti e riformatori sociali del Cinquecento* (Bologna: Zanichelli, 1941); Adolphe Franck, *Réformateurs et publicistes de l'Europe au XVIIe siècle* (Paris: M. Lévy, 1881); Emilio Bertana, *Un socialista del Cinquecento* (Genoa, 1892); Paola M. Arcari, *Il pensiero politico di F. Patrizi da Cherso* (Rome: Zamperini e Lorenzini, 1935); Delio Cantimori, *Eretici italiani del Cinquecento* (Florence: Sansoni, 1939) [see below, ch. 8], particularly pp. 385-405 on Francesco Pucci's *Forma d'una repubblica cattolica*; Rodolfo de Mattei, *La politica di Campanella* (Rome, 1927), "Contenuto ed origini dell'utopia cittadina nel Seicento," *Rivista internazionale di filosofia del diritto*, IX (1929), 414-25, "Contenuto ed origini dell'ideal universalista nel Seicento" and "Fonti, essenza e fortuna della 'Città del Sole,' " in the same *Rivista*, X (1930), 391-401, and XVIII (1938), 405-39; Kurt Sternberg, "Über Campanellas 'Sonnenstaat,' " *Historische Zeitschrift*, CXLVII (1933), 530-71; de Mattei's introduction to Ludovico Zuccolo's *La repubblica d'Evandria* (Rome, 1944), pp. 7-30; Edith Pásztor, "La 'Repubblica cristiana' di Ottavio Pallavicino," *Rivista di studi politici internazionali*, XVIII (1951), 67-84. For the latest literature on Campanella, see [Firpo's *Lo Stato ideale della Controriforma*,] pp. 313 and 315 [where attention is drawn to the work of the other great living authority on Campanella, Romano Amerio (and particularly to his "lucid synthetic exposition," *Campanella*, of 1947)].

elements that seem to be radically incompatible with the spiritual climate [of the Counter Reformation]. It contains, first of all, a certain amount of latent Epicureanism—a search for happiness in this world—that contrasts sharply with the Christian conception of an eternal City of the Blessed [in the next world] and of a tearful vale of flesh and sin [in this]. It contains, secondly, an implicit exaltation of the autonomous human reason and an assumption that societies can subsist by themselves without presupposing any kind of transcendent power. For religion in these imaginary republics always has a rather vague character. It is usually a form of deism, which, divested of dogmatic content, is adopted solely for its moral and social value and is thus rendered capable of tolerating, as substantially equal, all particular creeds. Against such tendencies the Counter Reformation erected the complex dogmatic structure of positive Catholicism. And it extinguished what was still left of the enthusiastic faith in the achievements of human reason, which had stimulated the generous and audacious creation of new ideals during the Renaissance but which turned out to be irreconcilable with the fundamental restlessness and with the tragic sense of sin and instability inherent in all forms of profound, internal religiosity.

The Counter Reformation must not be understood [so runs the current thesis] as an external and reactionary movement or a wave of obscurantism that suddenly struck the minds of men from the outside and extinguished their creativity. It was rather a crisis of confidence that took place within those same minds, one that led them to lose faith in reforms aimed solely at the improvement of political institutions and the better distribution of material goods, and one that convinced them of the necessity of acting on souls before acting on things and of seeking the reform of morality before the reform of institutions. In this sense the Counter Reformation did in fact slow down the impulse toward political and social reform that had been present all over Italy, often in forms strikingly similar to those of the Enlightenment and the French Revolution, in the first half of the Cinquecento.[3] It looked

[3] As Curcio notes in *Utopisti e riformatori sociali del Cinquecento*, p. 28.

for schemes of social life not in human reason but in the ancient
tradition of the Fathers and the Scholastics. Hence the weakness
of Italian Utopias in the following century: for the Counter
Reformation had robbed them of all their social content.

Such is the scheme in which Utopianism has so far been placed.
But before this scheme can be fully accepted, reasonable, sym-
metrical, and almost obvious though it may seem, it must be freed
of the apparent incongruities, at least the chronological ones,
that threaten to undermine the whole edifice. The chronological
incongruities are rather notable. There is, for instance, a lapse of
some twenty-five years between the beginning of the Counter
Reformation as an effective, and even intransigent, force and the
composition of Ludovico Agostino's *Repubblica immaginaria*
(1585–90). And there is still a greater lapse before 1602, when
Tommaso Campanella wrote his *City of the Sun*, and before 1625,
when Ludovico Zuccolo's *Evandria* finally appeared in print.[4]

In order to unravel such enigmas, we must first of all recall the
principal themes, suggestions, and assumptions that the Utopian

---

[4] Because of its heretical inspiration and its immunity from the influence of
the Counter Reformation, Francesco Pucci's *Forma d'una repubblica cattolica*,
composed in England in 1581, must be assigned a place all its own. [See Firpo's
"Gli scritti di F. P.," *Memorie dell'Accademia della Scienze di Torino*, Ser. III
Vol. IV, part II (1957), 195–368. There is a short biography of Pucci, born in
Florence in 1543 and executed by the Roman Inquisition in 1597, in the preface
to his *Lettere, documenti e testimonianze*, ed. Luigi Firpo and Renato Piattoli
(Florence: Olschki, 1959), Vol. II.] A small place *within* the Italian Utopian
tradition is assigned by Curcio (pp. 175–93) to Matteo Buonamico, who in his
"fabulous disquisitions" called *Della servitù volontaria* [*On Voluntary Servitude*]
(Naples, 1572), describes a pilgrimage through imaginary countries and evokes
the lost "golden age." But his city of Narsida, with its temple of Liberty in
which visitors are miraculously freed from the dominion of their passions, has
nothing in common with political Utopianism. It is rather a kind of old-
fashioned moralizing allegory, which, after a long tradition during the Middle
Ages, was revived in Italy at the beginning of the Cinquecento by Antonio
Fregoso and Lelio Manfredi. A slight influence of allegorizing on Utopia there
most probably was; but it must not be exaggerated, as de Mattei seems to do in
La politica di Campanella (pp. 169 ff.), where he includes Fregoso's *Viaggio dei
tre peregrini* even though it has no more to do with Utopia than Dante's
Divine Comedy. On this moralizing fantasy, see my note on "Allegoria e satira
in Parnaso," *Belfagor*, I (1946), 673–99.

writers wove into their pages; and we must then distinguish those which the Catholic Restoration had necessarily to reject from those which could survive to bear fruit in a new season. We must, in other words, define the cultural climate of the first half of the Cinquecento. We must identify those social and political problems that seemed serious and urgent enough to require such radical solutions. And finally we must discover the models that inspired those solutions, either in the form of concrete [legislative] provisions or in the form of ideas expounded in books.

The most striking aspect of the spiritual climate of the early Cinquecento, the one that most affected the freer and more vital consciences of the age, is that joyous longing for human autonomy, that pride in the supremacy, if not in the omnipotence, of the intelligence, which manifested itself in a productive optimism and in an unrestrained, heroic concept of life. After centuries of measuring his actions according to the iron rule of a transcendent norm, man [in the Renaissance] was suddenly amazed to discover a sufficient reason intrinsic in the world, one capable of assuring completely its harmonious operation; and that reason was nature. Man became conscious of nature in the intimacy of his own mind, and it became the guide and the standard of his actions. "Virtue," wrote [Thomas] More, means "living according to nature. To follow nature is to conform to the dictates of reason."[5] From this confidence in being able to chart his own course in the world and to mold the world itself [in so far as it was] a creation of his own mind, arose his critical attitude toward tradition, toward historical systems of social organization that now seemed arbitrary and contingent upon specific moments in time, and toward the whole intricate complexity of positive rights and rules, from the Decalogue of the Bible to the edicts of communal governments. Reason nurtured by experience seemed able to prescribe norms for every aspect of practical action. And, indeed,

---

[5] I cite the *Utopia* always in the translation of T. Fiore (Bari: Laterza, 1942) Here I refer to p. 98. [The English translation given here is that of H. V. S. Ogden and is on p. 48 of his *Utopia* (Crofts Classics edition). The sixteenth-century English translation is on p. 85 of the Modern Library edition.]

the Cinquecento is an age replete with manuals in which principles of general and eternal value are confidently sought for and then explicated in easily comprehensible schemes.

In the realm of politics the return to nature gave rise to the concept of equality; and equality in turn brought with it the concept of legality. The uninhibited despotism of the age of the tyrants[6] and the brutal concept of the absolutist patrimonial state, completely subject to the whims of its master, offered too strong a contrast with the idyllic vision of a fraternal harmony among men. Thus while the "realistic" political writers placed their "precepts" at the disposal of the princes, the "idealist" writers kept up an incessant criticism of monarchy. And they proposed instead, not without a good bit of anachronism, a happy aristocratic republic, one usually inspired by the tenacious myth of a wise and well-balanced constitution of Venice. This aversion to the state based on nothing but force led them, in their model republics, to restore the juridical principles they felt had been obliterated by the despots and to make of them intangible rights inherent in the very nature of the human person. The Utopians thus anticipated the later theoreticians of natural law, although at the time they were merely reflecting the exhaustion of an age that had tired of uncontrolled violence and that still desired an internal and external political order capable of guaranteeing a tolerable civic life and a lasting peace.

Hence political questions were broadened to make room for social aspirations. One aspect of the irrational violence of the times was the capricious seizure of the goods of the earth and the excessive inequality in the distribution of wealth. Just about everywhere in Europe, society seemed burdened by the ills that More ascribed indignantly to the England of Henry VIII. On one side, a frivolous and avaricious nobility, a corrupt and idle clergy, in-

---

[6] [Here I preserve Firpo's expression *età dei tiranni*, even though I have referred elsewhere (e.g. above, ch. 1, n. 6) to the same phenomenon with the word *Signorie*, which is less equivocal. For *dispoti*, similarly, I generally use *signori* to avoid any confusion with "enlightened despotism" in English historical terminology.]

numerable parasites, and spoiled thieves in the guise of soldiers; on the other, the paupers and the vagabonds whom hunger forced into robbery and crime. Their love of the quiet life, therefore, must have suggested to the members of the privileged orders themselves a certain sense of moderation and a willingness to renounce a greater for a surer fortune; and they came to hope for the establishment of some sort of equality, one which might raise the poor from an intolerable state of oppression and deprive the rich of unjust privileges. Hence their condemnation of usury and idleness, their disdain for the piling up of riches, their attempt to prove that nobility was a matter of virtue rather than of birth: their philanthropic sentiments were all inspired by naturalism and by its themes of moderation, equity, and rejection of what is superfluous. Among the Utopians, in fact, social questions eventually became more important than political ones. And absolutism, which they condemned in terms of a monarchical constitution, was reintroduced under different headings, and in a form even more burdensome and inquisitorial and even less respectful of individual autonomy, solely for the purpose of blocking any possible danger to economic equality, which was the principal end of all their systems.

These ideas and aspirations were nourished in turn by a variety of specific cultural traditions, historical experiences, and literary models. Looking to nature for the norms of a perfect collective life meant refurbishing the pagan myths of a "golden age," the religious tradition of a terrestrial paradise, the popular tales of the "land of plenty" (*paese di coccagna*), the Stoic doctrine of happy innocence in the state of nature—all of which was adorned with the sensual musicality of Renaissance pastoral poetry. Plato and Virgil, Seneca and Cicero—all offered important suggestions. But Plato's *Republic* became the most typical model, since the communism it called for brought forth recollections of the religious confraternities, the chivalrous orders, and the Anabaptist communities, and since its idealization of the city-state seemed to evoke the tradition of the Italian communes and the myth of Venice. Claudio Tolomei, Ludovico Guicciardini, and Giovanni Botero, the analytic observers of reality, disputed about the best location of a perfect city. Leon Battista Alberti, Antonio Filarete, Francesco di Giorgio, and Leonardo da Vinci drew up city plans according to criteria of abstract, though functional, symmetry.[7] The dukes of Tuscany dreamed of transforming Portoferraio [on Elba] into a "Cosmopolis" and of founding a paradisiac and scholarly "City of the Sun," in which no one talked anything but Latin.[8] Indeed, the century was so permeated by reformist radicalism that Utopia often touched upon the domain of history and ideals came very close to being carried out in practice. But as soon as these dreams were put down on paper, they were shaped by literary reminiscences: by the allegorical and didactic poems of the Trecento and the Quattrocento, by the fabulous pilgrimages of the Middle Ages in search of the "Earthly Paradise," by the adventurous wanderings of the heroes of knightly epics, and, more recently, by the accounts of the travelers and navigators, often inclined to idealize the newly discovered lands beyond the seas. All these elements were fused into a new literary genre, one destined to thrive thereafter right down until modern times, and one that still gives no signs of dying out.

These descriptions of ideal cities thus represent a twofold aspiration of the Renaissance: the restoration of legality in political life and the healing of the economic ills caused by the grave inequalities in the distribution of wealth. But they are the work of isolated individuals, precursors at the best, whose voices provoked only a tenuous echo among the makers of history at the time. The social forces defending economic privilege were still too efficient,

[7] See my "La Città ideale del Filarete" in Studi in memoria di G. Solari (Torino: Ramella, 1954), pp. 11-59 [on Alberti and Filarete, with all the pertinent literature cited in the notes].

[8] [In spite of the elegant Utopian names, however, neither of these two places seems ever to have been intended for much more than a military fortress (although there was already a small town at Portoferraio), and neither Cosimo nor his ministers were the kind that would pay much attention to the ideals the names might have suggested. Such at least is my conclusion after studying the history of Florence in the 1540's and 1550's, particularly since the Florentine principate was precisely the kind of absolute government that Firpo says the Utopians most objected to, implicitly if not explicitly.]

and the course of political development toward absolute monarchies and rigidly centralized national states was too antithetical. History rejected Utopia; and Utopia in turn humbled itself—and consequently scuttled the noble themes it had taken over from Erasmian Christian humanism—to the point of drawing out vague idealizations of the pious monarch in so many unctuous "mirrors for princes."

To hold the Counter Reformation alone responsible for what was actually a general loss of nerve of Utopian idealism is to commit a hasty oversimplification. Actually the Counter Reformation aimed essentially at restoring religious values in general and those of Catholicism in particular, which Renaissance thought had denied or, still worse, had mortified by compromises. By the middle of the Cinquecento those values had taken on an intransigent and imperative character once again; and they were now juxtaposed in the consciences of men with the values of naturalistic humanism. [The Counter Reformation] at times sought to reject the one wholly and to substitute the other. But it was usually forced into making a synthesis rather than a substitution, by evaluating humanistic values systematically and by accepting some completely and reconciling others with religious ones.

The two most fundamental acquisitions of the Renaissance and the Reformation in the field of political doctrine were, first, the recognition by Machiavelli of utility as a category of values and, second, the contractualist and democratic theories of the Calvinist monarchomachs. The Catholic reaction denied neither of these two acquisitions, and it did not seek simply to return to the schemes of Thomistic political thought. It thundered against Machiavelli; but with the Tacitists[9] and the theoreticians of *ragion di stato*, it sought to reconcile utility with its new moral exigencies. It accepted the passionate demands of the Huguenot polemicists, which Mariana and Suárez[10] rendered more systematic by incor-

[9] [On the Tacitists, see ch. 4 above.]

[10] [Juan de Mariana and Francisco Suárez were the two leading political philosophers of Spain in the second half of the century, on whom see the recent monograph by Guenter Lewy, *Constitutionalism and Statecraft during the Golden Age of Spain* (Geneva: E. Droz, 1960).]

poration in the juridical schemes of their revitalized scholasticism.

Thus intransigent post-Tridentine Catholicism found nothing scandalous in the Utopians' demands either for political democracy or for economic egalitarianism. Indeed, the ecclesiastical hierarchy itself seemed to provide a concrete example of an elective republic governed by the most worthy. The Conciliarist doctrines of the Quattrocento had made government of equals by majority vote seem perfectly reasonable even in the Church. And the perennial Christian ideal of evangelical poverty seemed wholly reconcilable with what the Utopians said about wealth. What the new age could not accept, on the other hand, was their excessive rationalist optimism, as well as their tendency to degenerate into individualistic hedonism (which More, for example, tried to counter, though not without introducing disturbing antitheses, with his ethic of the collectivity) or even into gross materialism, as [Anton Francesco] Doni seems to have done.[11] The picture of man *in puris naturalibus*—as he is in nature—could shock no one, particularly a theologian who had read the sections of Thomas's *Summa* that deal with the Creation and with "the condition of man in the state of innocence."[12] What was shocking, however, was the thesis implicit in such a picture of the self-sufficiency of the *lex naturae*, to which any addition would be a deviation or at least a superfluity—positive divine law included.

The Utopians did not pick unknown islands or distant lands for their ideal cities merely in order to conform to literary models or to try out fantastic literary devices. They did so in order to rid the entire religious and ethical structure of their imaginary republics of the moral and theological dogmas of the Church, with the excuse that the inhabitants had not yet learned of Christian revelation. The simplified and generic religion of the ideal cities of the Renaissance tended inevitably toward deism. No excuses or backtracking could save it from the new intransigence of the men

[11] [The *I mondi* dialogues of the Florentine Doni (1513–74), published in 1552–53 in Venice, are discussed below. His other famous popular dialogues, *I marmi*, are available in a modern edition by Laterza (Bari, 1928).]

[12] *Summa Theologica*, I, quaest. 94–102.

of the Counter Reformation, for they understood perfectly well that the proposed political and social revolutions presupposed an analogous revolution in morals, which in turn depended upon a reformation of religion *ab imis*. It was not a question of one particular aspect of Cinquecento Utopias, but rather of one of their more constant characteristics, at least in their more extreme forms; for the transformation they insisted upon could be coherent only if it were total.[13] This was the one theme that the new age felt to be completely unacceptable, no matter how cleverly it was disguised. And a brief review of the principal ideal states of the first half of the century will show how irreconcilable the antithesis really was.

More's *Utopia* came out in 1516. . . .[14] Just thirteen years later Antonio de Guevara[15] published his celebrated *Libro llamado Relox de los principes*. In one of the episodes Alexander the Great visits the "Land of the Garmanti." There he is treated to a sermon by one of the Garmanti wise men, in which heroism, activism, and the thirst for fighting and conquering are denounced and in which peace, quiet, virtue, and moderation are exalted, along with blissful poverty, charity, and concord. The Garmanti, it seems, are ruled by few and simple laws in a regime of absolute egalitarian communism. Each one may choose the kind of religious worship he pleases, provided only that he do so with sincerity and that he recognize no more than two gods, "one of life and one of death."

[13] This seems to be a constant characteristic of Utopian literature, one destined to implicate the sphere of religion. For the period of the Enlightenment and the Revolution, see Delio Cantimori, *Utopisti e riformatori italiani* (Florence: Sansoni, 1943), pp. 17–19. Even Morelly, in the communistic state outlined in his *Code de la nature* [1758], sets forth a fundamental law prohibiting metaphysical speculation and excluding all positive religions, and admits the recognition of nothing more than a provident "Author of the Universe." See the edition of G. Chinard (Paris: Clavreuil, 1950), pp. 316–17 and 320.

[14] [I omit some two pages dedicated to an analysis of More, which does not fit strictly within the limits of this anthology.]

[15] [Antonio de Guevara died at Valladolid in 1544, after a distinguished ecclesiastical and political career. The *Relox* pretends to be the translation of a book by Marcus Aurelius and is a masterpiece of Spanish prose as well as the product of wide reading and a fantastic imagination.]

Guevara's work was translated and in part rewritten in Italy by Mambrino Rosseo in his *Instituzione del principe cristiano* (*Institutes of the Christian Prince*), which was first published at Rome in 1543. Just five years later Anton Francesco Doni put out the first Italian version of More's *Utopia*, which he had had translated by another rebel of the same stamp, Ortensio Lando.[16] And just ten years later two of the most typical Utopian works of the Italian Renaissance appeared almost simultaneously in Venice: the "Wise and Crazy World" of the *Mondi* (*Worlds*) of the same Doni, and the *Città felice* (*Happy City*) of the Dalmatian Francesco Patrizi.

The structure of Doni's imaginary world is rather roughly and summarily drawn; but it is inspired by a high degree of revolutionary extremism. The economic communism of *Utopia* becomes so radical that it corrodes even the institution of the family, which More had made the cornerstone of social life; and it ends up in sexual communism as well. The commonwealth functions solely for the purpose of satisfying bodily needs. Hence affection, which might foment unpleasant passions, is stamped out, and a crushing form of materialism rules everything. In the center of the city is a great temple, served by a hundred priests. It is they who hold whatever little is left of political power, now that collective life has been reduced to merely vegetative functions and has thus become almost completely automatic. But the priests have very few religious functions either. On every seventh day, which resembles our Sunday, the citizens "held their feast; on that day no one did anything but remain in the temple with great devotion." (They must have been hard of hearing, for their devotions were not apparently disturbed by the "hundred kinds" of music

---

[16] On the wide diffusion of the works of Guevara in Italy, see H. Vaganay, "Antonio de Guevara et son œuvre dans la littérature italienne," *La bibliofilia*, XVII (1915–16), 335–58, which furnishes a long, though still far from complete, list of Italian editions. I cite Mambrino Rosseo's reworking of the book in a hitherto unknown edition of his *Instituzione del principe cristiano* printed in Venice by Pietro de Micolini da Sabio in 1548 (pp. 8–13); but the same text is reproduced by Curcio in *Utopisti e riformatori sociali del Cinquecento*, pp. 43–55. On More, see my "T. Moro e la sua fortuna in Italia," *Occidente*, III (1952), 225–41.

that resounded at the same time under the great dome.) "Everyone visited the temple in the morning" as well, and each priest turned to the inhabitants of the street he was in charge of, teaching them "to know God, to thank Him for such gifts, and to love one another."[17] That is all. What is left, then, is a vague sort of deism, a religion deprived of dogma or of any positive content and left with a single moral law—the love of neighbor—and a single purpose of worship—solidarity among the citizens. Just as More had written: "Seeking your own advantage without violating the laws is wisdom; seeking the advantage of all is *religion*" (p. 100).

On the social level Patrizi is at the opposite extreme. His *Città felice* is interlaced with themes that are Aristotelian rather than Platonic; and he clearly takes pleasure in underlining the identity of aspirations between the oligarchy of his polis and that of the Republic of Venice. The result is an old-fashioned, if not reactionary, apologia in which the most vital force of Renaissance Utopianism, the rebellion against social injustice, seems to be brutally rejected. Rationalism in Patrizi continues to excogitate better forms of organized social life. But all of them are meant to benefit a tiny minority whom a halo of "virtuous action" gives the right to exploit the servile mob of peasants, artisans, and merchants, to leave them without a trace of civil rights, and to use them solely as a means for assuring its own sustenance and leisure. This privileged class is composed of priests as well as of soldiers and magistrates. For religion is as proper to man as social instinct, Patrizi argues, and in the perfect city the natural aspiration for the divine must be given adequate satisfaction. "For the fulfillment of the spirits of all the citizens, there are in the city persons who teach divine law, who perform the mysteries, and who with sacrifices make benign and placate the gods. Hence the commonwealth erects temples and churches where the worship of God may be performed."

[17] Most of the many reprintings of the *Mondi* after the first one [cited above in n. 11] are altered and expurgated. More correct than the text given by Curcio, pp. 1–15, is the one of G. G. Ferrero in Pietro Aretino and Anton Francesco Doni, *Scritti scelti* (Turin: U.T.E.T., 1951), pp. 478–90.

In his mystical and allegorical language Patrizi defines priests as those "who with their actions see to it that the people obtain divine favor and grace and thus escape solitude" and attain happiness.[18] The author says nothing more about creeds and worship in his happy city. But we need only read a bit further to page 136 [in Curcio's text] to find the three ways in which virtue is obtained. The means are nature, habit, and reason: and there we are, as far as ever from the essential themes of Christian morality. The rationalistic explanation of religious experience, the highhanded juxtaposition in the very same sentence of the phrases "sacrifices to the gods" and "worship of God," the essentially propitiatory and utilitarian function given to public worship and to the priesthood—all this is sufficient to reveal the composite and nebulous character of this conception of religion, in which pagan and Christian motives, naturalism and mysticism, a sense of the transcendent and an exclusive faith in reason are mixed up without being reconciled.

Renaissance Utopianism all comes to substantially the same conclusion regarding the problem of religion. Guided by the pure light of reason and by the religious instinct that is natural to him, man evolves in his religious belief according to a scheme that More traced out when speaking of the cults of the Utopians. He venerates first the stars (that is, cosmic and meteorological phenomena), then outstanding men (in the age of myths), and finally a monotheistic supreme being, one, invisible, and omnipotent, the creator of the world and the judge of immortal souls beyond the grave. This is the limit of deism; for reason can go no further. Beyond lies the realm of miracles and grace, of revealed mysteries and positive precepts.

Needless to say, these definitions of natural religion are completely free from hidden polemical themes or bits of heresy aimed

[18] Patrizi's *Città felice* was little more than a schoolroom exercise of his youth and appeared in only one edition in the sixteenth century (Venice: Griffio, 1552). It has been reprinted by Curcio (pp. 121–42; see particularly p. 134). On the religious concepts of Patrizi, see the work by Arcari [cited above in n. 2], pp. 90–91 and 135.

at opposing deism, as a form of religiosity in itself perfect and sufficient, to positive Christianity. Such ideas did not compromise the sanctity of More, the episcopacy of Guevara, or the priesthood of Doni. What they were trying to do, after all, was to ascertain in the broadest possible way the rational foundations of Christianity itself. The context is still that of Renaissance Platonism, of the attempt to establish a coincidence between reason and revelation. And the paths charted by Marsilio Ficino and Pico della Mirandola (a direct source for More) were explored with rigorous orthodoxy for the irenic hopes they stimulated in the Cinquecento among those looking for the bases of a concord among Christians. But the fissures in the religious conscience of Europe soon turned out to be irreparable; and the aspirations of Christian humanism, which found its noblest voice in More and in his friend Erasmus, were forever shattered. Rejected by history, these aspirations took refuge more and more in Utopia, in veiled suggestions for a return to the candid austerity of primitive Christianity through the simplification of theology and of the ecclesiastical hierarchy.

After a tense and dramatic debate, however, the Church of Rome went off in just the opposite direction: that of dogmatic and disciplinary intransigence, of reaction without compromise in all fields. Missionaries and apologists, diplomats and men of arms —all became soldiers in the same battle. Ignatius gave the papacy the Society of Jesus, Bellarmino the *Controversiae*, Baronio the *Annales*. Meanwhile the discontent outside the strictly theological domain was overcome by the strict measures for the selection and education of the clergy, for the assignment of benefices, for the residence of bishops, and for pastoral visitations. Even economic ills were in part palliated through immense philanthropic enterprises that reached large segments of the population. The Utopia of the Renaissance had been the result of a free search for rational solutions to the complex problems of social life. The Counter Reformation imposed upon these problems a pre-prepared solution of its own, one taken from Scripture and ecclesiastical tradition, and it removed from the realm of investigation the whole field of religion. Dogma and ethical precepts, ritual and the priest-hood were questions to be defined by a *magisterium* whose authority was absolute and whose pronouncements were not sub-ject to criticism. That narrowed considerably the field of reason alone, which was the field to which Utopia was by definition restricted. And the Utopians finally lost confidence in their own enterprise and gave up.

So much for the phenomenon. With the texts in hand we may now go on to examine some of the various theses that have been offered to explain it. With regard to Utopia in the Seicento, first of all, Rodolfo de Mattei[19] has identified as its most important model the Republic of Venice, a commonwealth so perfectly administered that it functioned with mechanical precision and regularity. He has also distinguished Seicento Utopians from those of the Cinquecento by their greater seriousness as philosophers, by their greater interest in "experiment" and in practical application of theory, and by their criticism of "doctrinal dreaming" and "academic exercises" in the work of their predecessors.

The contradictions implicit in this thesis have already been brought out by Arcari.[20] She has noticed that the thesis about the transformation of dreams into experiment and of ideals into reality is exactly the opposite of the one about the transformation of a real Venice into an ideal one. But actually neither thesis is consis-tent with what actually took place. On one hand, the myth of Venice was a typically Cinquecento phenomenon and was not peculiar to the Seicento. The books that created it are those of Gaspare Contarini and Donato Giannotti, who were the main references for the Utopians thereafter. And though the myth lived on into the Seicento, it actually faded with the declining political and economic power of the Republic and with the attacks launched against it by the ecclesiastical polemicists at the time of the Interdict.[21]

19 In the two articles on Utopianism and Universalism in the seventeenth century [cited above in n. 2].

20 In *Il pensiero politico di F. Patrizi* [n. 2, above], pp. 79–83.

21 [On the Interdict of 1606, see above, ch. 4, n. 29.] Giannotti's *Della Re-pubblica de' Veneziani* was printed at Rome by Blado in 1540 [but written in

The supposed antithesis, on the other hand, between the academic nature of the Cinquecento writers and the practical bent of those of the Seicento is essentially a return to the old thesis of A. Franck,[22] a thesis which is dubious even with regard to the only two writers it is based on, More and Campanella, and one which certainly cannot be extended to similar phenomena in the two ages of which they were not, as a matter of fact, wholly typical. De Mattei himself was aware of a certain anachronistic character in the *City of the Sun* that led him to place the work at the end of the Cinquecento rather than at the beginning of his new age. The other part of the thesis, moreover, according to which Cinquecento Utopias were merely academic exercises, is wholly unacceptable, even though it seems to be supported by Erasmus's habit of writing informal *causeries* and by More's declaration that the second book of the *Utopia* was written *per otium*—as a pastime. Such an interpretation might be satisfying to certain apologists who are afraid that More's sanctity might be compromised by his social radicalism. But all well-informed students today agree in recognizing in his work a profoundly constructive purpose, a concreteness in proposing practical reforms, and a firm grasp of the ills that actually did afflict England at the time. And no one can doubt the seriousness of his commitment to the problems he dealt with.

1526]. Contarini's *De Magistratibus et Republica Venetorum* appeared posthumously at Paris in 1543. [This is, of course, the same Gaspare Contarini (1483–1542) who was one of the leaders of the Catholic Reformation and member of the commission of cardinals appointed by Paul III on church reform. For the latest bibliography, see Hubert Jedin, *Contarini und Camaldoli* (Rome: Edizioni di Storia e Letteratura, 1953), which is also printed in Vol. II of the *Archivio italiano per la storia della pietà*.] On the idealization of the Venetian constitution, see Curcio, *Dal Rinascimento alla Controriforma* (Rome, 1934), pp. 90–109, [and Franco Gaeta, "Alcune considerazioni sul mito di Venezia," *Bibliothèque d'humanisme et renaissance*, XXIII (1951), 58–75, where it is traced back to the mid-fifteenth and up through the eighteenth century. Even better as a Utopian text is Giannotti's *Della Repubblica Fiorentina*, which was republished in Venice by Hertz in 1721; for the most recent work on him, see Randolph Starn's article in *Rinascimento*, XV (1964), 101–21].

[22] *Réformateurs et publicistes*, pp. 187–88.

The distance is great, however, between serious thought and the impulse to put it into practice. The most salient characteristics of Utopia are in fact its radicalism, its conscious separation of the schemes it proposes from any specific historical situation, and its revolutionary intransigence—an intransigence that comes not from the passions of actual political life, but from the contemplation of an ideal in the sphere of the absolute, where compromises are unnecessary. The Utopian is not interested in moderate, concrete reforms. He cannot turn his model into a goal to be realized in practice unless he changes his nature—unless he becomes active in politics and society and looks constantly in the realm of the practical for an opening through which he may connect the real and the ideal. For the Utopian the hiatus between the real and the ideal cannot be bridged: the real institutions of the real society he lives in never offer a point of least resistance where he can hope to overturn them. His only hope for action, indeed, lies in an invitation to rethink reality, to imagine the antithesis of the actual historical process, and to wait patiently until conditions change sufficiently to permit those whose minds he has affected to turn his dream into a practical goal.

The attempt to find a practical bent in Seicento Utopianism, or to sustain its transformation into an interest in reform or revolution, is a vain one—in spite of the occasional glimmers in Bacon, in Andräe, in Zuccolo, or in Vairasse d'Allais.[23] So also is the attempt to find it in Campanella, who was a Utopian and who tried, in the midst of a violent revolt, to erect his "City of the Sun" on a Calabrian mountain. The erroneous thesis started from a study of Campanella; and that is where it can best be corrected. For Campanella's faith in being able to realize his ideal is not a sign of a change in Utopianism from one century to the next. It is rather

[23] [Bacon, of course, is Francis Bacon, author of the *New Atlantis* discussed below. Zuccolo is mentioned above in n. 2. Johann Valentin Andräe or Andreae (1586–1654) was one of the fathers of the Rosicrucians. His *Christopolis* is translated and analyzed by Felix Emil Held (New York: Oxford, 1916). Denis Vairasse d'Allais, called "Le Capitaine Siden," wrote an *Histoire des Sevarambes, peuple qui habitent une partie du troisième continent*, often republished and translated in the second half of the seventeenth century.]

the product of his own individual ingenuity and of his enthusiasm
for the absurd, antihistorical conspiracy of 1599, which was conceived without a thought to political and military calculations and
sustained solely by the faith in the messianic nature of its leader
and by the expectation of an imminent cosmic palingenesis.[24]

Nonetheless, de Mattei deserves credit for being the first to point
out one other characteristic of Seicento Utopians, one which is
indeed peculiar to them: their interest in science. The experimental sciences rise to a place of great honor in the new imaginary
communities. Old problems, like that of death and economic
inequalities, are now resolved by technical improvements; and
the result is an optimistic and fervent faith in progress among the
inhabitants. Such elements are already present in Campanella;
they become the dominant ones in Bacon's *New Atlantis*. But this
characteristic must not be seen as antithetical to the Utopias of the
Cinquecento. It is rather the product of a coherent and continuous development of humanistic rationalism, which had
inspired faith in the free inquiring mind and had, by destroying
the principle of authority, opened the way for the experimental
inquiry of the new sciences. It is, indeed, in the investigation of
physical nature that the work of reason, so fiercely opposed in the
ethical and religious fields, was henceforth to be carried on.

[24] [This curious and violent rebellion against the Spanish government began,
in fact, with a series of sermons given by Campanella in Stilo in February 1599,
and was crushed the following September. Campanella escaped the death, but
not the torture, inflicted on all his associates only by feigning madness; but he
still spent the next two decades in a Neapolitan prison. See the biographical
introduction to Firpo's edition of Campanella's *Tutte le opere* (Milan: Mondadori, 1954), Vol. I. According to Adriano Seroni in his edition of the *Città del
sole e poesie* (Feltrinelli paperback 379/UE), pp. xxii ff., many of the statements
made by the conspirators during their trial sound almost exactly like passages
from the *Città del sole*, which Campanella wrote down two years later in
prison (see ch. 4 above).]

7 Aristotelian Philosophy and the Popularization of Learning: Benedetto Varchi and Renaissance Aristotelianism[1]

UMBERTO PIROTTI

Umberto Pirotti teaches in a Bologna *liceo*. He has written numerous articles on various aspects of Italian culture from the sixteenth to the ninteenth century, most of them for the journal *Convivium*. One other piece on Varchi, entitled "B. V. e la questione della lingua" ("Varchi and the Language Question"), appeared in 1960 (Vol. v, pp. 524–52). This one will soon be incorporated into a lengthy monograph on Varchi upon which the author is presently working.

I

IF those philosophers who made a valid contribution to the enrichment of the human mind were alone worthy of study, there would be little point in wasting time on Benedetto Varchi. He was born in an age which considered philosophical wisdom to be an almost inalterable patrimony, one to be acquired rather than to be added to. He himself did not hesitate to admit that the doctrines he professed were not the fruit of his own personal elaboration but were derived rather from the masters he had chosen. He proclaimed himself the debtor of Aristotle and of the great Aristotelians of the past. But above all he paid tribute to one of his contemporaries, Lodovico Boccadiferro. "I have often acknowledged, and I always will acknowledge," he declared in one of his lectures on the *Divine Comedy*, "that whatever little I know about philosophy has come almost entirely from his mouth or from his

---

[1] "Benedetto Varchi e l'aristotelismo del Rinascimento," *Convivium*, N.S., III (1963), 280–311. Translated and somewhat condensed by the editor and then corrected and amended by the author.

writings."[2]... Yet the history of philosophy would be incomplete if it included only creative geniuses and omitted those who merely received and imitated. The first, it is true, surpass the culture of their age. But the second remain within it; and studying them will enable us both to understand that culture better and to avoid misrepresenting the exception as the rule.

These prefatory remarks justify our looking into Varchi even though as a philosopher he is lacking in originality. They also justify our studying the not very illustrious personage from whom he received his philosophical formation. Who was Lodovico Boccadiferro? What lines of thought did he follow? In what way and within what limits did he exert an influence on his pupil? It is not hard to reconstruct an elementary biography.[3] He was born in Bologna in 1482; and it was in Bologna that he studied under Alessandro Achillini,[4] took his degree, and began his teaching career. Around 1524 he was invited to Rome by a member of the Gonzaga family, with which he had close personal ties; and there he lectured on Aristotle until the horrible Sack of 1527 induced him to return home. He continued teaching Peripatetic theories in Bologna to such pupils as Antonio Bernardi and Alessandro Piccolomini, who were destined for brilliant careers.[5] He himself

---

[2] *Lezioni sul Dante e prose varie*, ed. G. Aiazzi and L. Arbib (Florence, 1841), Vol. I, p. 228. [Hereafter I omit the author's references to specific passages in the works discussed unless important for the understanding of the text.]

[3] Note particularly Giovanni Fantuzzi, *Notizie degli scrittori bolognesi*, Vol. II (Bologna, 1782), pp. 210–17.

[4] [Achillini, one of the most prominent representatives of the Averroistic school of Aristotelianism, was born in Bologna about 1463 and died there in 1512. He taught philosophy and medicine both in his native city and in Padua. His many published works are described chronologically by Bruno Nardi in "Appunti su A. A." in his *Saggi sull'aristotelismo padovano dal secolo XIV al XVI* (Florence: Sansoni, 1958), pp. 226–79.]

[5] [Bernardi was born at Mirandola in 1502, became professor at Bologna in 1533, then moved to Rome under the protection of Alessandro Farnese, the nephew of Pope Paul III. In 1554 he gave up the bishopric of Caserta conferred upon him in 1552, and he died in Bologna in 1565. His works include *Eversionis Singularis Certaminis Libri XL* (1562) and *Institutio in Universam Logicam* (1545). See Bruno Nardi, *Sigieri di Brabante nel pensiero del Rinascimento italiano* (Rome: Edizioni Italiane, 1945), pp. 152–59. Piccolomini (1508–78) was a Sienese by

acquired such fame that Cosimo de' Medici, duke of Florence, tried to attract him to the University of Pisa, "on great and honorable conditions."[6] And he died on 3 May 1545.

Substantially, then, we know as much about the life of Boccadiferro as we do about the lives of such other philosophers of the age as Marcantonio Zimara and Vincenzo Maggi.[7] But if we look beyond the highlights of his life into the details of his thought, we will find that he is one of the least-known Aristotelians of the Renaissance. We must not be led astray by the eulogies heaped upon him in the sixteenth century or by the severity with which he has been judged more recently. For the judgments in both cases are always generic and elusive; and they were not then and have not since been based on a very precise acquaintance with his works. No one is really to be blamed, of course, for having avoided or abandoned this material. Boccadiferro is a minor writer among minor writers, and his books are enough to strain the patience of even the most tenacious student. They wend their way through a huge mass of theses, objections, and answers. They are constantly marred by typographical errors. And they are composed in a painfully poor, colorless, rough, and confusing language.[8] In comparison, the

---

birth; his *Annotazioni alla Poetica d'Aristotele* (1575) is one of the chief works of late Renaissance poetics.] That Piccolomini attended Boccadiferro's lectures has recently been made clear by Florindo Cerreta in his *Alessandro Piccolomini letterato e filosofo senese del Cinquecento* (Siena: Accademia Senese degli Intronati, 1960), p. 49. G. M. Mazzuchelli in *Scrittori d'Italia*, Vol. II, Part III (Brescia, 1762), p. 1373, and Johann Jacob Brucker, *Historia Critica Philosophiae*, Vol. IV, Part I (Leipzig, 1766), p. 766, as well as Fantuzzi, list Francesco, rather than Alessandro, Piccolomini among Boccadiferro's pupils. Fantuzzi includes many other disciples as well. But I would not swear that the lists are exact.

6 So says Varchi, *loc. cit.* (n. 2 above).

7 [The few sure details of Zimara's life are presented in another essay in Nardi's *Saggi sull'aristotelismo padovano*, pp. 321 ff. He took a doctorate at Padua in 1501 and became a leading proponent of Averroism in the university thereafter, as later did his equally famous son, Teofilo, born in 1515. Maggi, a native of Brescia, was one of Marcantonio's pupils and taught at Ferrara for twenty years after leaving Padua in 1542. Very few of his many works have remained, even in manuscript.]

8 One reason why Boccadiferro's works are so badly written is that they were probably put together by his students, rather than by him, from notes taken

tomes of Jacopo Zabarella are as splendidly harmonious as an Ionic temple, the writings of Camillo Porzio are interwoven with stylistic refinements, the theorems of Marcantonio Zimara are pure recreation, and the arguments of Pietro Pomponazzi are full of agile perspicuity. Nonetheless, an assiduous examination of these works can provide us with information to permit a more concrete description of the author than has previously been possible.

Boccadiferro is usually called an "Averroist." But if we take this term to mean, as Bruno Nardi insists,[9] one who habitually prefers Averroës to all other commentators when explaining Aristotle, then it should not be applied to Boccadiferro. He frequently departs from Averroës and occasionally even stabs at him with disrespectful expressions. He accuses him of letting himself be misled by his own imagination.[10] He reproaches him for putting forth fictitious and inane arguments. He says that one of his glosses on the *De Anima* is childishly erroneous. He asserts that another digression on the same treatise contains as many errors as it does words.

It is not that Boccadiferro approaches Averroës from a ready-made position of antagonism. Indeed, he frequently agrees with him, even in fundamental matters. But he does not venerate him as a supreme arbiter of, or an infallible authority on, Aristotelian controversies. He conforms to the then predominant tendency to prefer Greek to Arabic commentators.[11] It is from the Greeks, he

---

at his lectures. It was customary at the time not to write out what were improperly called *lectiones*, i.e. "readings," delivered in class: see Nardi, "Corsi inediti di lezioni di Pietro Pomponazzi," offprint from the volume *Studi in onore di Gino Funaioli* (Rome: Angelo Signorelli, 1955), p. 106.

[9] In *Sigieri di Brabante nel pensiero del Rinascimento*, p. 106.

[10] [Specific citations to Boccadiferro's main works follow:] In *Duos Libros Aristotelis "De Generatione et Corruptione" Doctissima Commentaria* (Venice, 1571), *Lectiones Super Primum Librum "Meteorologicorum" Aristotelis* (Venice, 1565), and *Lectiones super Tres Libros "De Anima"* (Venice, 1566). The date on the last work is given as MDXLVI. But that is a typographical error, which we have corrected....

[11] See Francesco Fiorentino, *Pietro Pomponazzi: Studi storici su la scuola bolognese e padovana del secolo XVI* (Florence, 1868), p. 24.

says, that Averroës takes everything good in his works. When he takes something either from his own head or from the works of his Arabic compatriots, he ends up with nonsense and chimeras.[12]

This attitude is doubtless a sign that Boccadiferro was conversant with humanistic culture. True, he looks down upon formal niceties and fails to penetrate the intimate secrets of the classical languages. Yet he pays at least some attention to the teachings of Renaissance philology. In this respect he is more modern than Achillini, who almost always follows the Averroistic interpretation and often spends a good bit of energy trying to corroborate it. Boccadiferro never displays any sign of reverence toward his master, moreover. He recalls him only in order to contradict him. And when he declares: "Many disciples have always been very ungrateful toward their preceptors," he may be thinking of his own case.

Achillini had maintained, among other things, that the active intellect is God, that the potential intellect is the "informing form" [forma informans] of man, that before death man can intuitively understand separate substances and arrive at beatitude by joining himself with the highest of all the substances—the Divinity.[13] These are the theses that Nardi attributes to Siger of Brabant. Boccadiferro does not accept a single one of them. He does not tell us what he thinks of the active intellect in his lessons on the De Anima. But he seems to combat the position of Alexander, which identifies the active intellect with the divine intellect.[14] Elsewhere he seems to approve of those Greek expositors who think that the intellective soul simply assists the body without actually informing it. The "informing form"—this is the kernel of his argument—is joined to "informed" matter in such a way that it does not perform actions all its own. But the intellective

12 *Explanatio Libri I "Physicorum" Aristotelis ex Ludovici Buccaferrei Philosophi Praestantissimi Lectionibus Excepta* (Venice, 1558), p. 53ᵛ. [The author here quotes the long passage in Latin that fully confirms his judgment.]

13 [References here to] Achillini, *Opera Omnia* (Venice, 1551). See Nardi, "Sigieri di Brabante e Alessandro Achillini" in his *Sigieri di Brabante nel pensiero del Rinascimento*, pp. 39 ff.

14 [On Alexander of Aphrodisias, see above, ch. 5, n. 6.]

soul does perform actions of its own. Hence it does not "inform" the body. It is in the body as a pilot is in a ship. With regard to the intuitive comprehension of abstract substances and to the happiness that derives from such comprehension, Boccadiferro denies both. According to Aristotle, he says, it is not given to us to contemplate such substances directly, but rather to have a discursive knowledge of them.

He is just as sharp in his divergence from Achillini over the question of whether efficient causality is to be attributed to God. In his first *Quolibetum de Intelligentiis* Achillini had answered affirmatively to this question. God moves the first heaven, he says, without the intervention of intermediate movers. Therefore he is not only the final cause, but also the efficient cause of the universe.[15] Boccadiferro, on the other hand, sustains the opinion that efficient causality belongs to God only in a metaphorical sense, as when we attribute to Him the adjective *efficiens* with the connotation of *conservans*.[16] Little does Boccadiferro care that such an opinion is hard to reconcile with the dogmas of the Church. While professing himself a Christian, he distinguishes between theology and philosophy, and he expands and even defends purely philosophical theses in a spirit of resolute freedom. We can thus find in his works,

[15] See Nardi, *Saggi sull'aristotelismo padovano*, pp. 188–89. Achillini's thought on this question is interpreted differently, and (if I am not mistaken) erroneously by Armand Maurer, in "John of Jandun and Divine Causality," *Medieval Studies*, XVII (1955), p. 195.

[16] It is not certain that on the subject of divine causality Boccadiferro may be, contrary to his usual position, more of an Averroist than his master. In fact, authoritative students have held that Averroës actually attributed creative causality to God. See Friedrich Ueberweg, *Grundriss der Geschichte der Philosophie . . . Die patristische und scholastische Philosophie*, 12th edn., ed. Bernhard Geyer (Basel, 1951), p. 317, and Fernand van Steenberghen, *Siger de Brabant d'après ses œuvres inédites*, Vol. II, *Siger dans l'histoire de l'aristoiélisme* (Louvain: Institut Supérieur de Philosophie, 1942), p. 376. It is certain, however, that on another much-debated question, that of whether substantial forms of elements remain when in mixed substances, Achillini follows Averroës, and Boccadiferro departs from him. . . . On the position of Averroës and on the problem in general, see the first study of Anneliese Maier in the volume *An der Grenze von Scholastik und Naturwissenschaft*, 2nd edn. (Rome: Edizioni di Storia e letteratura, 1952).

sometimes merely mentioned and sometimes well developed, many themes characteristic of heterodox Aristotelianism. Let us look briefly at them one by one.

The God of Aristotle differs profoundly from the God of the Catholics. He is not free. He does not possess infinite power. Since He knows nothing of single things in this world, so He is concerned with them only accidentally (*per accidens*). He does not act as an efficient cause. Hence He cannot be said to have created the world, since nothing can be born of nothing. In the opinion of the philosophers, the world is eternal. So are the abstract substances, among which cannot be included "daemons" which do not exist. It is the task of these substances to move the heavens. But it is not their task to involve themselves in earthly affairs by causing some miracle or another.

The rational soul is similarly free from generation or corruption. It is a single entity present in all members of our species. For soul is separate from matter, and matter alone is the principle of plurality. Moreover, since the rational soul does not make use of corporal organs, it is necessary to distinguish it from the sensitive soul, which can multiply and to which are entrusted the movements dependent upon the body. Neither the one nor the other confers immortality. The sensitive soul perishes with the flesh; and the rational soul is extinguished in us at the same time, since it is deprived of the means of understanding when it is deprived of the use of the senses. The philosophers, therefore, do not admit for man an otherworldly life. But they do not then consider virtue to be useless and happiness to be chimerical. Virtue is its own reward, as vice is its own penalty.[17] And happiness can be achieved on this earth through the discursive understanding of separate substances. This happiness, unlike the beatific vision of the Catholics, is not the reward of previous merit, but the result of the necessary course of nature.

[17] This is a favorite doctrine of non-Christian Aristotelianism. It is to be found much before Boccadiferro—in Siger, for instance. See Pierre Mandonnet, *Siger de Brabant et l'averroisme latin au XIIIe siècle* (Louvain: Institut Supérieur de Philosophie, 1911), Vol. I, p. 134.

No less apparent is the discrepancy between theologians and philosophers on the question of free will: the first say its roots are in the will, and the second ... place it in the intellect. ... The same discrepancy exists on the question of miracles. The theologians are obliged or willing to admit them because the Bible testifies to their reality and possibility. The Aristotelians deny them, or at least assign natural causes to them. ...

Ernst Cassirer has written that in Pomponazzi the discord between religion and reason is deliberately accentuated.[18] This thesis is valid for Pomponazzi. But it is excessive if extended ... to our little-known Bolognese. Pomponazzi ... subordinates the exegesis of Aristotle to an attempt to show that the speculations of philosophers end in results that are irreconcilable with the faith. Boccadiferro subordinates his observations on the divergence between Christianity and Aristotelianism to an attempt to clarify all the doctrines of Aristotle. He freely argues against Thomas Aquinas and Albertus Magnus. But his purpose is not so much to juxtapose points of philosophy and points of theology as to attack interpretations of Aristotle that seem to him unfounded.

Boccadiferro is still further removed from his predecessors when it comes to questions that have nothing to do with dogma. He has little faith in them or in the other Latin interpreters, even those of heterodox tendencies. ... Unfortunately, his predilection for Greek interpreters is not derived solely from a common language, culture, and spiritual orientation. It is also the result of a shortsighted, narrow hostility toward innovation. In his commentary on the *Parva Naturalia* he attacks particularly one philosopher who had departed from the Aristotelian tradition in judging memory to be an active, not a passive, faculty. "Most of these new opinions are false," he asserts. "Were they true, they would have already been adopted by one of many wise men of past ages." ... Elsewhere, to be sure, he shows himself more benign toward the

---

[18] *Individuo e cosmo nella filosofia del Rinascimento*, Ital. tr. [from the German original of 1927] (Florence: La Nuova Italia, 1935), pp. 131–32. [Eng. tr.: *The Individual and the Cosmos in Renaissance Philosophy*, tr. Mario Domandi (Harper Torchbooks 1097).]

mistreated moderns. He pays tribute to the superior competence of
Albertus Magnus in alchemy. He acknowledges the utility of the
investigation of the Latins "on reaction" and "on the proportions
of motion." But we must not be deceived by such acknowledg-
ments. He is completely certain that, in its essential structure, the
temple of the sciences must remain just as the ancients—and particularly Aristotle, the greatest of the ancients—had built it.
Boccadiferro seeks solutions to all major problems from "the
master of those who know." The borrowings from Platonism as
well as from Aristotelianism are not a sign of eclecticism, as some
have asserted.[19] The only Platonic elements in this thought are the
ones that had already been accepted and re-elaborated by Aristotle and his immediate followers. Boccadiferro's aim is to teach
the genuine doctrine of Aristotle. For he saw in it the synthesis of
all human knowledge, and he held that whoever penetrated and
absorbed that synthesis would possess philosophy itself.

It is true that Boccadiferro's Aristotelianism seems to be undermined on occasions by his realization that Aristotle did not have the
privilege of infallibility and that he occasionally put forth affirmations clearly proved wrong by successive investigation and discovery. In anatomy Aristotle was repeatedly corrected by Galen.
In mathematics he committed many errors, and he probably
never succeeded in mastering the discipline.[20] He made other

[19] So says Brucker, who also asserts (*op. cit.*, pp. 765–66) that Boccadiferro
made a compendium of Plato's *Laws*. He probably derived the assertion from
Giacomo Filippo Tomasini, *Elogia Virorum Literis et Sapientia Illustrium* (Padua,
1644), p. 118. But from a passage in the *Oratio in Funere Ludovici Buccaferrei*
(Bologna, 1545), pp. 17–18, of G. B. Camozzi, who was there at the time, it
appears that Boccadiferro never made any such compendium, since he promised
to do one, if he lived a bit longer, on his death bed. Tomasini is therefore most
probably the source of Brucker's error, which is repeated, by the way, by
Eugenio Garin in *La filosofia*, Vol. II (Milan: Vallardi, 1947), p. 64.

[20] Boccadiferro's judgment in this matter was not common in his age; but it is
similar to that of modern students of Aristotle's mathematics. See, for example,
Pierre Duhem, *Le système du monde*, 2nd edn. (Paris: Hermann, 1954), p. 192; Abel
Rey, *La science dans l'antiquité: L'apogée de la science technique grecque* (Paris: La
Renaissance du Livre, 1946), p. 64; and above all the essay of Gaston Milhaud,
"Aristote et les mathématiques," in the volume *Études sur la pensée scientifique chez
es Grecs et chez les modernes* (Paris: Société Française d'Imprimerie, 1906).

mistakes concerning the colors of the spectrum, concerning the inhabited areas of the world, concerning the positions of Venus and Mars with respect to the sun. He held that the Milky Way was caused by hot and dry exhalations and was terrestrial rather than celestial in substance, that the Danube originated in the Pyrenees, that the Red Sea communicated with the Ocean beyond the Pillars of Hercules. Sometimes, indeed, Boccadiferro is franker and more perceptive in picking out invalidated opinions in Aristotle. In his commentary on the first book of the *Meteorology*, for instance, he does not try, like Francesco da Vimercate, to pardon Aristotle's geographical enormities by referring them to the inexpert geographers of his age.[21] He resolutely rejects the Peripatetic explanation of the Milky Way that Cesare Cremonini was vainly to try saving many decades later, [after Galileo's discoveries with the telescope].[22]

While Boccadiferro must not be identified, therefore, with the more stiff-necked Aristotelians, he cannot at the same time be considered a vacillating, doubtful Peripatetic. He adhered firmly and completely to the word of Aristotle. He sought above all to overcome the objections and to parry the attacks that might have endangered the authority of that word. Some Peripatetics were rigid in their defense. They obstinately tried to hold on to solitary, poorly manned fortresses. They fought valiantly not to yield a single foot of terrain. Boccadiferro preferred a more elastic strategy. He occasionally gave up an outlying castle and evacuated a sterile or undependable province. But it never even occurred to him to retreat from a vital position; and his occasional withdrawals never weakened the strength of his defensive structure. Thus, what he puts in place of the Peripatetic Milky Way does not at all damage the fundamental principle of the inalterability of the heavens. Confessing that Aristotle was not an excellent

[21] *Francisci Vicomercati Mediolanensis In Quatuor Libros Aristotelis "Meteoro-logicorum" Commentarii* (Paris, 1556), p. 141 (16–23). [Vimercate was called to Paris by Francis I to teach Aristotle in Greek in 1540. He moved to Turin around 1561 and died there in 1570. He wrote many other commentaries on Aristotle as well.]

[22] In his *Apologia Dictorum Aristotelis de Via Lactea* (Venice, 1613).

mathematician, moreover, does little damage to his reputation
For the philosophers see little of value in mathematics—it is but
a game invented by Egyptian priests to keep them from rotting
in idleness.[23]

To whoever looks at him closely, Boccadiferro seems in many
ways to belong to the lowest class of Aristotelians. He confides in
book learning to the point of running away from sense experience.
He abuses formal logic by grasping onto minor caviling like a
lawyer. In one place Aristotle teaches that boiling water is hotter
than the flame. In another place he says just the opposite. Does he
contradict himself? No: boiling water is hotter *per se*. The flame
is hotter *per accidens*. . . . At times, indeed, he blocks the progress
of science with dialectic obstacles. He rejects the noted theory of
the Parisian school according to which the earth's center of
gravity continually moves.[24] He tries to persuade us that tides are
not caused by the sun and the moon. With a zeal worthy of a
better cause, he busies himself annulling the proofs set forth by
Galen and the Galenists against Aristotle's thesis that the nerves
proceed from the heart, not the brain.[25]

Without doubt Boccadiferro would have been as horrified as
his successors were to be eighty or ninety years later if he had seen
one of the main walls of the noble Aristotelian palace crumble.
But nothing was more foreign to his thought than a suspicion
that the human mind could erect much vaster and richer construc-
tions once the one he admired had been torn down. Though he
lived in the period of humanism, he had nothing of the humanists'
faith in the marvelous faculties of man. At times, indeed, he suggests that our knowledge consists of nothing but unsure conjec-
tures, as the thinkers of the ancient Academy would have it. . . .
We must admit, he continues, that many questions regarding the

[23] The comment is Aristotle's own, in the *Physics*, 6.
[24] See Pierre Duhem, *Études sur Léonard de Vinci* (Paris: Hermann, 1906–13),
pp. 354–56.
[25] In Francesco Puteo's *Apologia in Anatome pro Galeno contra Andream
Vessalium Bruxellensem* (Venice, 1562), Boccadiferro is portrayed as arguing
against the Galenists, holding that the heart holds a hegemony over the whole
body. Evidently he was well known for this position.

truth are beyond us: even Christ, after all, did not answer the question of what truth was.

There is a wide gulf between these propositions, which a skeptic might well accept, and the innumerable passages in which Boccadiferro, following in Aristotle's footsteps, seems convinced of being able to penetrate the intimate structure of reality. Actually his own skepticism does not contradict or weaken his dogmatism. Rather it stimulates it, it strengthens it, and it generates it. Like some Christians who take refuge in faith because they despair of reason, so Boccadiferro latches onto the principles of Aristotle in part because, in his opinion, the light of our mind is too dim. Thanks to an incomparable mind, Aristotle elaborated a coherent and profound interpretation of the universe. Let us confide in him and follow the path he has opened to us. Off that path there is naught but confusion. If we leave it, who will guide us among the thick woods of facts and problems? Not the thought of the other Greeks or Latins, nor that of later philosophers, and certainly not that of Messer Lodovico Boccadiferro....

[Unlike Averroës and Pomponazzi], for whom man could actuate his nature as a rational animal only by philosophizing... and for whom the philosophers alone can be said to possess human dignity... Boccadiferro presupposes that rationality produces philosophy rather than proceeding from it. He thus can conclude that all men are rational... and not just a small group of philosophers. Unfortunately this [thesis appears] more as an aside than [as an integral part of his thought.] Probably it is in part to be ascribed to his personal modesty. Boccadiferro seems to have been immune to professorial pride, and he was spontaneously good-natured—a person whom everyone found it easy to like. This is why Varchi was so devoted to him. That is why another, somewhat less than obscure disciple, Antonio Bernardi,[26] found "incredible pleasure" in his company.... His students must also have appreciated the dislike he often professed of subtleties. The truth, he maintained, is great and open, solid and

[26] Bernardi, *Institutio in Universam Logicam. Eiusdem in Eandem Commentarius, item Apologiae Libri VIII* (Basel, 1545), p. 228. [On Bernardi, see n. 5 above.]

clear. Subtle arguments, on the other hand, are always erroneous. . . . He loved simple theories; he did his best to follow common sense and to avoid dialectical displays. In comparison to others of his age he was little inclined to credulity; and astrology seems to have been the only one of the many superstitions current during the Renaissance that had deep roots in his mind. . . . He admits the possibility of alchemy. But he thinks that the alchemists are usually liars. He thinks it possible to determine the length of a person's life by reading his palm. But he denies firmly the scientific basis of predictions from chiromancy. . . . He follows Aristotle in seeing in nature the constant operation of laws, from which exceptions may be made only in accordance with the authority of the Church. Since the theologians teach that supernatural phenomena occur, he follows their teaching and distinguishes his position as an exegete of Aristotle from his position as a Catholic.

There is a sharp difference between Boccadiferro and the "naturalists" of his own and of the next generation.[27] The "naturalists" accept a great number of fabulous occurrences and then try explaining them without recourse to divine, angelic, or demoniac intervention. They thus end up turning nature into a capricious magician, unbound by any law. Boccadiferro, on the other hand, though he does not present a concept of natural law with clear precision, still implies such a concept throughout his writings and never takes a position that might negate it. Hence he attacks Pomponazzi's *De Incantationibus*, a book in which the theses of "naturalism" are put forth with resolute vigor.[28] Indeed, his commentary on the *De Divinatione per Somnum*, which no one has ever paid attention to, is far less distant from modern science than is the treatise of Pomponazzi, which famous critics have

[27] That is what Robert Lenoble calls them in his *Mersenne et la naissance du mécanisme* (Paris: Vrin, 1943), a fundamental work to which I owe the interpretation here given of "naturalistic" philosophy.

[28] Bernardi delivers a very harsh judgment of this work of Pomponazzi in his *Eversionis Singularis Certaminis Libri XL* (Basel, n.d.), p. 499. Since Bernardi had been a pupil of Boccadiferro, it may be his master's judgment that he echoes here.

honored with great applause. At times those modest teachers (let us take comfort in the observation!) incapable of great flights, sterile of new ideas, armed only with a bit of common sense and what learning they have acquired with much hard labor—sometimes these men come closer to the truth than the audacious and perspicacious geniuses whose names history never forgets. . . .

II

A comparison of their writings will show many similarities between Boccadiferro and his disciple Benedetto Varchi. Varchi also juxtaposes philosophical conclusions and theological affirmations. He is also convinced that reason often leads to results incompatible with the dogmas of the faith. At times he states that most philosophers usually are in agreement with religion.[29] But at others he expresses with greater exactness his own sentiment that "trying to bring philosophy into harmony with religion on many points" is impossible.[30]

To the philosophers in general, and to Aristotle in particular, Varchi attributes many of the non-Christian positions that Boccadiferro had already attributed to them. The God whose existence they demonstrate is not infinite except in respect to duration. He is not a creator, for no one can bring being out of nothing. He acts not freely, but by necessity, for freedom means potentiality and hence imperfection. He does not concern himself with the things of this world; indeed, He knows them only in their universal form. The theologians hold Him alone to be eternal. But the philosophers attribute eternity also to the stars, to the Intelligences that move them, to the sublunary world, to the human intellect. Man, however, does not enjoy true immortality. Of the two souls which philosophically must be granted man, the decrees of theology notwithstanding, the sensitive one is mortal, while the intellectual one, according to the Peripatetics, is so dependent upon the senses that once separated from them it cannot function. . . .

[29] *Lezioni* (Florence, 1590), p. 614.   [30] *Lezioni sul Dante*, Vol. I, pp. 382–83.

There is no need of further citations to show that the philosophy outlined by Varchi is resolutely heterodox. . . . Yet while some historians have, in hurried references, made Varchi an Averroist,[31] others have called him orthodox and have even maintained that he took nothing from Averroës but what had already been accepted by Thomas Aquinas.[32] It would be more accurate to say that he took nothing from Aquinas but what might have been accepted by Averroës. Varchi pours forth expressions of devotion toward the prince of the Arabian philosophers. He never misses a chance to call him "great" . . . "the only, or one of the only, true philosophers after Aristotle," the "second major Secretary of Nature."

Varchi differs from Boccadiferro, whose praises of Averroës are anything but abundant, when he shoots off these hyperboles. But this is not the only difference between them. Unlike his master, Varchi includes the cognitive soul among the interior senses. He seems to think that the rational soul does more than just assist the body; it gives it form. Worse yet, he sides with those philosophers who make God an efficient as well as a final cause. And he believes that by joining the potential to the active intellect, man can rise to an intuitive knowledge of the "final good," thus obtaining "the supreme happiness and beatitude."

Thus his late sixteenth-century biographer, Silvano Razzi, exaggerated somewhat in claiming that Varchi considered

[31] For example, Antonio Corsano, *Il pensiero di Giordano Bruno nel suo svolgimento storico* (Florence: Sansoni, 1940), p. 11, and Garin, *Umanesimo italiano* (Bari: Laterza, 1951), p. 182. [But the passage is on p. 165 of the Universale Laterza paperback edition, 1965.] A few heretical doctrines are given by Guido Manacorda in "Benedetto V., L'uomo, il poeta, il critico," *Annali della R. Scuola Normale Superiore di Pisa. Filosofia e Filologia*, Vol. XVII (Pisa, 1903), pp. 18–19, though the author is not too well informed, as would have been natural for one writing at the beginning of this century, about sixteenth-century philosophy.

[32] See Giuseppe Toffanin, *La fine dell'umanesimo* (Turin: Bocca, 1919), p. 108. Strangely enough, Toffanin's judgment is in accord with that of Giuseppe Saitta, a scholar who becomes visibly joyful whenever he thinks he can confer a diploma of heterodoxy on anyone. See his *Il pensiero italiano nell'umanesimo e nel Rinascimento*, Vol. II (Bologna: Zuffi, 1949), p. 119. With regard to Thomas Aquinas, see Toffanin's criticism of Corsano's book in "B. V. e l'aristotelesimo integrale," *La rinascita*, IV (1941), p. 14.

Boccadiferro his "oracle."[33] But Varchi himself exaggerated in saying that almost all his philosophical knowledge came from his master. Actually he had studied philosophy assiduously well before going to Bologna. Toward the end of his sojourn in Padua he had translated and done an interpretation of the *Prior Analytics*. He had commented upon the *Ethics* and had brought a number of philosophical questions to bear upon his analyses of the sonnets of contemporary poets before the Academy of the Infiammati. But he had not yet by any means reached maturity as a philosopher. Indeed, the theses he was to put forth later were often very different from those sustained by the teachers he had heard in Padua.

The first person to have given him some notion of philosophy seems to have been Francesco Verino the Elder.[34] We know very little about Verino, even though he taught at Pisa and Florence and counted among his disciples such lively minds as Giovan Battista Gelli, Vincenzo Borghini, and Pier Vettori.[35] Angelo Fabroni, [the rector and historian of the University of Pisa in the late eighteenth century,] thought him to have been an Aristotelian.[36] A modern historian, Eugenio Garin, has called him "the official continuator of the Ficinian [i.e. Platonic] tradition."[37] More

---

[33] "Vita di M. Benedetto Varchi" in preface to Varchi's *Lezioni* of 1590, p. 6 (my pagination). See further Razzi's oration in *Raccolta di prose fiorentine*, Part IV, Vol. II (Florence, 1734), p. 214.

[34] "Vita di M. B. V.," written anonymously, but probably by G. B. Busini, in Vol. I of Varchi, *Storia fiorentina*, ed. G. Milanesi (Florence, 1857), p. 25. See also *Raccolta di prose fiorentine*, Vol. IV of the Venetian ed. of 1734, p. 2, where Varchi calls Verino his "master." At least he took lessons in logic from him, as appears in a letter of Chirico Strozzi, *ibid.* (Florentine ed.), Part IV, Vol. I, p. 128.

[35] *Tutte le lezioni di Giovambattista Gelli fatte da lui nella Accademia Fiorentino* (Florence, 1551), p. 2; A. Legrenzi, *Vincenzio Borghini*, Part I (Uldine: Tip. del Bianco, 1910), p. 28; Lionardo Salviati, *Orazione funerale . . . delle lodi di Pier Vettori* (Florence, 1585), p. 15 (my pagination). [On these personages, see above, ch. 2.]

[36] *Historia Academiae Pisanae* (Pisa, 1791–95), Vol. I, p. 310. Michele Poccianti seems to agree with Fabroni, in his *Catalogus Scriptorum Florentinorum* (Florence, 1589), p. 70, for all the works he lists for Verino are exegeses of Aristotelian texts.

[37] *L'umanesimo italiano*, p. 156, and *La filosofia*, Vol. II, p. 70.

probably, Verino tended toward an eclectic position, mixing Peripatetic with Platonic elements. Such, at any rate, seems to be the
case in those of his writings that are in print: the three lectures on
Dante delivered just before his death, in 1541.[38] In these lectures
he puts forth a number of concepts dear to the Platonists. But he
also refers frequently to the authority of Aristotle, whose theories
he avoids showing as contrary to Catholicism even though he
also avoids explicitly Christianizing them.[39] With good reason
Fabroni compares him favorably with the semiheretic Pomponazzi and praises him for his modesty, his circumspection, and his
prudence.[40]

If Varchi had had no other guide than Verino, he would never
have been initiated into the mysteries of rigid Aristotelianism and
would never have come to insist so vigorously upon the contrast
between dogma and philosophy. Nor would he have made much
more progress with his second teacher, Francesco Beato, a man
hardly known today even by the best informed students of the
Renaissance. Beato was a Dominican who explained the *Metaphysics* according to Thomas Aquinas, and he therefore must have
attempted to reconcile Aristotle with Christianity. Certainly from
Beato's courses at Padua, which he attended, Varchi could not
have picked up his later preference for Averroës and Alexander.[41]

Another of his masters at that time was Vincenzo Maggi, from
whom, as recent scholarship has shown, he acquired the funda-

[38] They are to be found in the miscellany *Lezioni d'Accademici Fiorentini sopra
Dante*, Book I (Florence, 1547).

[39] Note particularly what he says about divine causality, *ibid.*, pp. 16–17.
Talking about the soul, on the other hand, he seems to be Christianizing
Aristotle: such, at any rate, is what Gelli suggests in *Tutte le lezioni*, pp. 82–83,
as well as Aonio Paleario in two letters of his *Epistolarum Libri III* (Lyon, 1553),
pp. 73 ff. Although these letters may seem at first sight to be addressed to
Verino's nephew, called Verino Secondo, they mention the study of Greek
undertaken by the recipient late in life under the guidance of Vettori. Hence, it
must be Verino the Elder who is indicated. See Salviati's *Orazione funerale*,
p. 15 (my pagination).

[40] *Historiae Academiae Pisanae*, Vol. I, p. 312.

[41] This hypothesis is confirmed by the absence of heterodox propositions
in the two lectures that Varchi gave to the Infiammati on a sonnet of Bembo
and on another of Della Casa, the only ones known to us from his Paduan period.

mentals of his theory of poetry.[42] Yet a more attentive study of the documents will show that Maggi's real influence upon Varchi occurred at a later date. Varchi has left no writings from his years at Padua and Bologna and from the first years after his return to Florence which might indicate that he was thoroughly acquainted with Aristotle's *Poetics* and had worked out a complete theory of poetry. True, he already had acquired a moralistic and intellectualistic attitude toward poetry, some of which may have come from Maggi.[43] But our evidence in this matter amounts only to a few superficial remarks. He may have heard, or read in manuscript, some of Maggi's lectures on the *Poetics*[44] around 1540; but it is probable that he did not get much out of them. Five years later, when he was already talking like a solemn Aristotelian, he confessed "to know very little" of that difficult little work of Aristotle.[45] Maggi seems not to have influenced him much in other realms of philosophy either. The only point outside the *Poetics* where it might be possible to compare their ideas is on the question of the soul. But here they differ: Maggi follows the exegesis of Alexander, while Varchi apparently prefers that of Averroës.[46]

[42] See especially J. E. Spingarn, *La critica letteraria nel Rinascimento*, Ital. tr. [from the English original: *A History of Literary Criticism in the Renaissance* (New York: Columbia University Press, 1899)] (Bari: Laterza, 1905), pp. 39, 52–53, and 78; and Toffanin, *La fine dell'umanesimo*, pp. 93–94 and 99 (to be accepted, however, with caution). [See also the numerous references to Maggi in Weinberg, *A History of Literary Criticism in the Italian Renaissance*.]

[43] In a letter to Carlo Strozzi of 8 September 1539 (Archivio di Stato, Florence, Carte Strozziane CXXXVI, cc. 95–96, of which a few passages are published in Manacorda, *op. cit.*, p. 39), he goes so far as to say that "Virgil... and Homer knew everything and knew how to teach it perhaps better than Aristotle." A few years later he called poets "moral philosophers" (*Lezioni sul Dante*, Vol. I, p. 86 . . .) and was sure of obtaining "many times . . . no less fruit from reading the poets than from reading [the same number of pages] in the philosophers": *Lezioni* [1590 edn.], p. 459.

[44] In a letter of 17 December 1541, Cosimo Rucellai asks Varchi to send him, if he owns them, the lectures of Maggi on the *Poetics*: *Raccolta di prose fiorentine* (Florentine edition), Part IV, Vol. I, p. 42. As is known, the *Explanationes* and the *Annotationes* of Maggi in *Aristotelis Librum de Poetica* were printed only in 1550.

[45] [This point is backed up by a long, detailed analysis of the relevant texts in the original, p. 294, n. 5.]

[46] Fiorentino, *Pietro Pomponazzi*, pp. 273 and 292.

More than to Maggi, who was then living, Varchi seems to have been indebted to Marcantonio Zimara, who by then had died. Varchi exalts Zimara as a "great philosopher," as "the first of those who put aside the sophisticated subtleties of the Latins and followed the Greeks." Zimara had paid more attention to Averroës than to Alexander and John Philopon;[47] and it is possible that Varchi picked up from him his own reverence for Averroës, as well as certain of his specific theses. . . .

Nevertheless, there is no reason to doubt that it was to Boccadiferro that Varchi owed his greatest debt, even after his exaggerated expressions of gratitude are trimmed down to proper proportions. After all, students of philosophy depended much more upon their teachers in those days than they do now. Any intelligent young man with a *lycée* diploma today can read the more illustrious philosophers all on his own. He has good, or at least passable, translations at his disposal. And he can turn to any number of helpful commentaries, monographs, and essays whenever he runs into major difficulties. On the contrary, in the sixteenth century anyone who tried to explore the domains of Aristotle by himself would have run the risk of understanding nothing and getting hopelessly lost. Aristotle's works had been composed in an esoteric language and translated into barbarous jargon. The most authoritative commentators were generally almost inaccessible except in just as barbarous, or at least as defective, versions, and . . . these seemed to have been made specifically for the purpose of discouraging the study of philosophy. A master was all but indispensable, therefore—a master who, by his human presence, could alleviate the aridity and the abstruseness of many of the problems and who could, by adapting himself to particular circumstances, resolve the doubts in the text itself or in the works of the many commentators.

This is the kind of teacher that Varchi found in Boccadiferro; and he drew much profit from Boccadiferro's teaching. During his residence in Bologna, from March or April 1542 to the end of

[47] [On Philopon, see above, ch. 5, n. 6].

1542 or the beginning of 1543,[48] he not only attended Boccadiferro's lectures, but he also became a close friend of his teacher and
often followed him around the streets of the city. For Varchi,
Boccadiferro was the Noah's Ark of philosophical knowledge. He
had mastered all the texts of Aristotle. He wandered securely
among the Greek and Arab commentators. He mentioned Plato
and Ptolemy. He talked of Galen. He dropped citations to
numerous [medieval] Latin authors. He seemed, indeed, to know
everything about his subject. Varchi had only to stay in his company in order to penetrate the secrets of Aristotelianism. He may
even have owed him some of the theses in which he disagreed with
him. The scholastic method was not yet dead. After hearing from
Boccadiferro's lips a counterthesis, along with the arguments
against it, Varchi may have ended by preferring it to the thesis his
teacher was maintaining.[49]

Even the considerable difference in their upbringing, their attitudes, and their tastes did not separate them. Varchi had been
raised in humanistic Florence. He had learned to write tolerable
Latin verse. He could turn out decent imitations of Petrarchan
sonnets. He could talk ably about Aristophanes and Virgil.[50] He
corresponded with Francesco Maria Molza, with Pietro Aretino,
with Ludovico Dolce. He was a close friend of Annibal Caro. He

[48] [Varchi left Florence suddenly in the spring of 1537 to avoid the disorders
in the city that were expected after the murder of Duke Alesandro de' Medicis
in January. He, like all the other Florentines in Bologna, became an active
partisan for the anti-Medici party and even, as he himself recounts in his *Storia
fiorentina*, took part in raids across the border. After some negotiating, he
accepted the offer of Alessandro's successor, the real founder of the Medicean
principate, Cosimo, to return to Florence as a sort of permanent lecturer at the
newly founded Florentine Academy. Cosimo later made him state historiographer. The author here gives more particulars about his relations with
Boccadiferro from the] *Nuova scielta di lettere di diversi nobilissimi uomini* (Venice,
1582), pp. 580–81.

[49] He may also have owed to Boccadiferro some of his attitudes toward
ancient and modern authors, for example, his slight esteem for Nifo (*Lezioni*
[1590], p. 107, and *Questione sull'alchimia* [Florence, 1827], p. 61) and his high
opinion of Gaspare Contarini (*Lezioni sul Dante*, Vol. I, p. 386).

[50] See his two letters to Carlo Strozzi of 8 September and 22 November 1539
in Archivio di Stato, Florence, Strozziane CXXXVI.

was devoted to Pietro Bembo.[51] For he was above all a man of letters, notwithstanding the jurisprudence that he had been clothed in at Pisa and the philosophy that he had been exposed to at home and at Padua. Boccadiferro, on the other hand, though he had scribbled out a few distichs in his youth,[52] carried on an old anti-literary tradition. Of the classics, which he had probably worn himself out on as a boy, he now kept on the tip of his tongue only two or three phrases, all of which had become part of common parlance. He sometimes quoted Roman prose and verse writers. But he did so only in order to expound their scientific opinions, not to rest awhile in the delightful gardens of literature. The orna-ment of style, he thought, "is not required in the sciences." And reassured by this axiom, he fulfilled his professorial functions with absolute disdain for the least bit of rhetorical finery.

Despite the freedom with which he violated the canons of harmony and beauty, however, Boccadiferro did not extinguish Varchi's ardor for philosophy. Varchi later criticized both the stylistic awkwardness of all the philosophers who had written in Latin after Boethius and the vain chatter of those who renounced matter for words alone. In his opinion words and things had to be solidly united, for "No one can be truly eloquent without doctrine, nor truly learned without eloquence." He therefore saw no incompatibility between Aristotelianism and the love of beauty in expression. He did not consider Boccadiferro and Bembo to be irreconcilable enemies. To him the divorce between physics and rhetoric was accidental and hence destined eventually to end.

It was he, indeed, who strove to bring about the reconciliation. He contributed thereby to the popularization of culture which so many of his contemporaries were interested in as well. In 1540 the Academy of the Infiammati was founded in Padua, and its guiding spirit, Sperone Speroni, insisted that all the lectures be

51 [That is, with the leading cultivators of vernacular *belles-lettres* of the age.]

52 Five poems appear in the preface to the *De Elementis* of Achillini (Bologna, 1505). Others, three brief compositions, are to be found in the *Collettanee grece, latine e vulgari per diversi auctori nella morte de l'ardente Serafino Aquilano, per Gioanne Filoteo Achillino bolognese in uno corpo redutte* (Bologna, 1503), p. 58 (my pagination).

given in the vernacular.[53] The next year, under the patronage of Duke Cosimo de' Medici, the Florentine Academy (*Accademia Fiorentina*) had been established to add luster to the Tuscan language; and more even than its counterpart in the Veneto, it actively promoted the spread of knowledge by making its lectures open to the public.[54] Varchi had participated in the assemblies of the Infiammati. After his return home he became the most assiduous lecturer in the Florentine Academy; and there he used every subject as a pretext for nourishing the unlettered with the bread of science, cutting off the hard crust of scholastic Latin and then serving it with the elegance required by those used to magnificent banquets.

Varchi's undertaking tended to transform the privilege of a caste into the possession of all. But it was not revolutionary. It did not mark the end of one age and the beginning of another. In so far as he echoed Aristotle, he repeated ideas that were centuries and centuries old. When he dressed up these ideas in harmonious Tuscan phrases, he proceeded along the furrow already dug by humanism. He sought to do what Bembo had done in his *Prose* and his *Asolani*. He sought to break down the dictatorship of Latin while appropriating its qualities. The similarity cannot be rejected as illusory just because of the difference between Bembo's Platonizing humanism and Varchi's heterodox Aristotelianism.[55] ... Varchi, after all, was a product of humanism. He himself was a humanist. And nonetheless he was a heterodox Aristotelian. His new interest in Averroës and Aristotle was not the result of a break with his humanist past. Indeed, even after becoming a disciple of Boccadiferro, he continued to pursue his older

[53] Giuseppe Gennari, *Saggio storico sopra le accademie di Padova* (Padua, 1785), p. xviii (to be found in *Saggi scientifici e letterari dell' Accademia di Padova*, Vol. I).

[54] Leonardo Olschki, *Geschichte der neusprachlichen wissenschaftlichen Literatur*, Vol. II: "Bildung und Wissenschaft im Zeitalter der Renaissance in Italien" (Leipzig and Geneva: Olschki, 1922), p. 174. [See now Armando L. De Gaetano, "G. B. Gelli and the Rebellion Against Latin," *Studies in the Renaissance*, Vol. XIV, pp. 131–58.]

[55] The radical antithesis between humanism and Aristotelianism is denied by Paul Oskar Kristeller in a very valuable study, ch. xxv of his *Studies in Renaissance Thought and Letters* (Rome: Edizioni di Storia e Letteratura, 1956).

occupations. He went on writing classical Latin songs and exercising his pedagogic functions in accordance with the models of the Quattrocento.[56]

It was just this humanistic education which enabled Varchi to make philosophy accessible to the profane. . . . "Lecturing among philosophers in the schools is one thing," he said; "lecturing in the Academy is quite another." Varchi knew his art well. Hence it is all the more surprising that he often intimidated his audience with high-sounding eulogies, and that he thus separated the philosophers and poets from the status of ordinary mortals. He even humiliated his listeners at times with such professorial expressions as "So say those who know" and "Thus the specialists; others cannot understand these matters." Instead of explaining, he often decreed. In general he avoided treating an entire subject.[57] Instead, he talked about specific questions—questions, for instance, of heat, of alchemy, of the generation of bodies. For he was loath to let outsiders visit his celebrated palace in its entirety. He preferred to admit them into this or that hall only after he had decorated it with magnificent lavishness. He then led them into a corridor of columns and dazzling mirrors, briefly mentioning the mysterious treasures in the rooms not open to the public and thus letting the fantasy of the visitors magnify the grandeur and the splendor of what they were not permitted to see. I do not wish to denigrate him. But I am led to think that he sought not so much to educate people as to display his learning and to appear to be in possession

[56] Studying philosophy seems even to have encouraged his Latin muse. Most of the poetic exercises gathered together in the manuscript collection of his "Carmina" in the Biblioteca Nazionale, Florence, MS II, VIII, 141, are certainly posterior to his meeting with Boccadiferro. One is even dedicated to his teacher (pp. 31-31ᵛ). . . . In a letter of January 1555 one of his disciples, Giulio Della Stufa, tells how he passes his day with his students, talking about the classical and humanist authors, Isocrates, Euripides, Virgil, Horace, Petrarch, Longolio . . .: Biblioteca Nazionale, Cass. Palat., II, 106. [It is the author's merit to have dug up all this hitherto unknown material. Not even Varchi's biographers have made use of it or, probably, even heard about it.]

[57] Another popularizer of Aristotle, on the other hand, Alessandro Piccolomini, willingly wrote on such general subjects as "On Natural Philosophy" and "The Instrument of Philosophy," etc.

of a vast, rich, and admirable science. He had assimilated Boccadiferro's Aristotelianism, not Boccadiferro's sincere and affable
modesty. Though he worked hard to spread culture, he was not
substantially a democrat.

These defects however should not detract from his real merits as
a popularizer. He had an admirable capacity for rethinking the
ideas of others and presenting them in an order much more comprehensible than can be found in any of his predecessors. The
tradition he followed is that of explaining, not just divulging. The
texts upon which he based his lectures were nothing like our well-
organized manuals. They were almost always a great confusion of
diverse matters which almost no one could follow. In managing
to get a coherent discourse out of them he shows an undeniable
gift for philosophy and acquires the valid title of a more than
mediocre thinker. He deserves somewhat less praise for other
aspects of his work. He may have been, as one eminent historian
has noticed,[58] the first modern writer to deny Aristotle's erroneous
theory that the velocity of a falling body is proportional to its
weight. But his statement on the matter is contained in a marginal
reference of his *Questione sull'alchimia*.[59] It is not accompanied by a
detailed criticism; and it does not lead him to propose another
theory in the place of the one he rejects. That had to wait for
Galileo. Varchi's observation does not mark, then, an advance in
dynamics.

Yet the observation does show that Varchi is not always bound
by the sentences of the Philosopher and that he freely departs
from him at times. On the question of the color of the eyes of men

[58] Olschki, *Bildung und Wissenschaft*, pp. 130–31. This work is still the best
study of Varchi as a popularizer.

[59] On p. 34. Varchi composed the *Questione* in 1544. He himself, however,
tells us that "several others," and particularly Luca Ghini and Francesco Beato,
had questioned the theory in his own day. Ten centuries earlier it had been
criticized by John Philopon and Simplicius; and it is probable that the sixteenth
century critics were not ignorant of their criticisms. By 1540 the commentaries
of both John and Simplicius on the *Physics* had become available in Latin
translation. John's, indeed, must have been considered an exciting novelty,
for it had just been published in 1539. See Pierre Duhem, *Le système du monde*,
p. 315.

and animals, for instance, he opposes Galen as well as Aristotle, and he cites the demonstrations of "the most excellent Vesalius" in his support.[60] He is much less faithful to the cult of antiquity than are most of his contemporaries. Even the ancients, he insists, were fallible, and they knew nothing of the "infinite wonders" discovered subsequently—such as the "new world" found by the Spanish and Portuguese navigators.[61] As he thought Italian more beautiful than Greek and Latin, so he thought that neither technology nor scientific knowledge had yet reached their culmination.

Boccadiferro was suspicious of new opinions simply because they were new. Varchi's judgments are often just the opposite. To authority, moreover, he repeatedly prefers experience, which he calls the "true and certain master," to be opposed only by the "thickheaded." Even when his praise of experience sounds like a commonplace, it reflects his own sincere conviction. . . . Impatient with the custom of "believing always what is found in the good authors and particularly in Aristotle," he holds it to be "surer and more delightful . . . to descend to [the level of] experience in some things." And in this belief he goes beyond his own age to announce the imminent revolution in the sciences.

Yet it would be incorrect to hail Varchi as a precursor of Galileo. . . . For a thought to be of importance, it must be thought with intensity; and before it can make a mark on history, it must make a mark on the mind of the man who elaborates it. The thoughts of Varchi that most attract attention are not of this order; and they did not affect sensibly the further development of

[60] [That is the famous anatomist Andreas Vesalius (1514–64), whose treatise *On the Fabric of the Human Body* (1543) Marie Boas Hall calls "the first real step forward from Galen," in *The Scientific Renaissance, 1450–1630* (London: Collins, 1962), p. 129. Note further: L. R. C. Agnew, "Varchi and Vesalius," *Bulletin of the History of Medicine*, XXXVII (1963), 527–31.] These demonstrations could seem to be in contrast with the Aristotelian principle according to which *omne recipiens debet esse denudatum natura recepti*. But the Peripatetics did not lack reasons or escape hatches for getting out of this difficulty. See, for example, Agostino Nifo's *Expositio Subtilissima necnon et Collectanea Commentariaque in Tres Libros Aristotelis "De Anima"* (Venice, 1559), p. 576.

[61] [This last phrase appears in a footnote in the original.]

philosophy. . . . Thus when Varchi reproaches contemporary philosophers for disregarding mathematics, we must not look in his words for a prophecy of the destruction of qualitative physics in the first decades of the next century. He does not rebel against Aristotle. Rather, he demonstrates his encyclopedic proclivities. Even though he may have translated four books of Euclid,[62] and even though he wrote a treatise on proportions and proportionality,[63] he was far from applying himself zealously to the study of mathematics. He does not include it among the higher disciplines. If it is superior to them in the certainty of its demonstrations, he says it yields to them in "the nobility of the subject," on which, much more than on certainty, depends the nobility of a particular discipline. On the question of heat, similarly, Varchi seems to anticipate Francis Bacon's major attack on the Aristotelian doctrine according to which "the heat of the sun and the heat of fire are of a completely different species."[64] . . . Alas! no suspicion that the heavens may be of the same nature as the earth ever disturbs Varchi's basic Aristotelianism. He identifies the heat of the sun with that of fire only with regard to quality, not to substance. That is his only real quarrel with Averroës on the subject. He never questions the heterogeneity of the two parts of the universe. And his solution to the problem is much the same as Boccadiferro's.

On other questions, however, he departs both from his master and from Peripatetic orthodoxy. He believes in astral influences and occult properties; and he bases his discussion of love on the

[62] So, at least, says the author of the "Vita di Messer B. V.," probably G. B. Busini [whose correspondence with Varchi on the Siege of Florence of 1529–30 is usually included in the editions of Varchi's *Storia fiorentina*, and published in *Borghini*, II (1864) [and also separately, ed. Gaetano Milanesi], 420 ff., on p. 429. I know only of Varchi's translation of the first book of the *Elementa*. It is in manuscript in the Biblioteca Nazionale, Florence, II, II, 383.

[63] Also in the Biblioteca Nazionale, II, II, 278. It is of no scientific importance. The matter explained is supposed to be made "easy . . . for those who know nothing of mathematics"; and the author compiled the book only for a few friends desirous of learning a game that was based on "proportions and the medium"—according to Varchi's prefatory letter.

[64] Cited in Bacon's *Works* (London, 1864), Vol. I, p. 1.

Platonic distinction between vulgar and celestial love. But unfortunately in these cases his independence of Aristotle does him more harm than good. More than delighting in disputes about the illusions and imaginary situations of the Platonizing Petrarchists, he turns to Platonism *tout court*. He thus makes celestial love into a sort of ethereal pederasty, for in his opinion young men are much more able to inspire love than women.[65] Instead of adhering strictly to the Aristotelian position about the constancy of nature, similarly, he admits the existence of sea nymphs. Without batting an eyelash, he tells stories about footless birds in America that remain continually in the air. He indulges in popular superstitions regarding human generation. And in spite of frequent reservations he ends by admitting alchemy as a legitimate "art."

As Varchi does not excel in discerning fact from fable, so also he does not emerge as a rigorous critic when it comes to incongruities. Some of his contradictions, to be sure, are Aristotle's fault, not his own—as when he says in one place that the multiplication of individuals comes from matter and in another place that it comes principally from form.[66] The same can be said for the contradiction he finds between sensible being and intelligible being. In a crucial passage of his *Ercolano*— in the passage where he tries to persuade us that the vernacular language should be called "Florentine" rather than "Italian"—he asserts that individuals are "incomparably" nobler than genera or species. . . . In a later lecture, on the other hand, he assures us that intelligible being "is incontestably more perfect than sensible being." This antinomy derives (if I am not mistaken) from the same antinomy that Aristotle ran into in assigning the fullness of reality in one place to form alone (the intelligible), and in another to form united with matter (the sensible).[67]

---

[65] [In this case, at least, Varchi's theory may to some extent be influenced by practice. His first trip abroad was largely made necessary by a scandal over his all-too-intimate relationship with one of his pupils in Florence.]

[66] See Léon Brunschvicg, *L'expérience humaine et la causalité physique*, 3rd edn. (Paris: Presses Universitaires de France, 1949), p. 134.

[67] On this point, see the penetrating and lucid treatise of Eduard Zeller, *Die Philosophie der Griechen*, Part II, Section II: *Aristoteles und die alten Peripatetiker*,

Other contradictions in Varchi, however, can less justly be ascribed to Aristotle. On the problem of the soul, for instance, which was one of the most hotly debated of the century, there is evidence to suggest that he accepts an Averroistic solution like the one put forth by Boccadiferro. He attributes two souls to man. He proclaims the rational soul to be ingenerate and incorruptible. Yet he also teaches that when deprived of the body this soul cannot either exist or act. It seems, then, that he is affirming that the [two souls are] one. . . . But he is not. Far from appropriating the more famous thesis of the Averroists, Varchi implicitly rejects it when he mentions the "rational souls" which "give being and action to human bodies, according to the better philosophers."[68]

It may well be that he was drawn into this incongruity by his Catholicism, which was naturally adverse to monopsychism. For though in words he carefully separates philosophy from theology, Varchi does not always philosophize without any regard to theological positions. . . . Thus in one place he is peremptorily optimistic: all things, he asserts, reach their end and hence acquire their ultimate perfection, happiness. In another place he is pessimistic, like a Christian rather than a Peripatetic: man, he says, is an exception to the law just formulated, for he usually does not arrive at beatitude.[69] Why this contradiction? Why should man be an exception to the harmony of the universe? Because, Varchi responds, man has free will. But he then follows Aristotle in putting free will in the intellect rather than, like the theologians, in the will; and he thus nullifies it. If "man cannot . . . but follow

---

4th edn. (Leipzig: Reisland, 1921), pp. 344–45 and 348. One way to get around the contradiction would have been to follow Thomas Aquinas in distinguishing essence from existence. Composite things, then, would be nobler than form because they actually existed rather than being merely an essence. But the integral Aristotelians usually rejected this distinction, since Aristotle did not admit it.

[68] Varchi is closer to Averroism when he writes that souls are "all sisters, if not one and the same thing." But it is impossible to construct completely his thought in matters of psychology, for all but one of his lectures—and there are several references to their having been delivered —have disappeared.

[69] This concept is very far from the spirit of Aristotelianism. . . . See Léon Olle Laprune, *Essai sur la morale d'Aristote* (Paris, 1881), pp. 310–11.

what the intellect presents to him as good or as apparently good," then the free will is not free, and men's actions are inevitable. The attempt to justify man's unhappiness by his freedom is thus ruined, and the attempt to unite Aristotelianism and Christian theology collapses. . . .

At other times he accentuates, rather than diminishes, the contrast between Aristotelianism and Christianity. Aristotle (if I am correct)[70] proposes the infinite periodicity of earthly affairs according to the movement of the stars. Since the sublunary world is corruptible, however, he does not insist that when the same arrangement of stars reappears, so do all the earthly phenomena from the preceding cycle. Varchi, on the other hand, in a lecture of 1553 speaks thus: "We must believe that Florence itself, the dome on our cathedral, this very academy, not to mention the printing press and artillery,[71] have already come into being an infinite number of times, according to the philosophers, and so will they reappear an infinite number of times in the future." Such a position is just about as alien to Christianity as any in the whole history of philosophy. Something of the sort had been proposed by the Pythagoreans, Plato, and a few Stoics, in antiquity, and it was to be reproposed by Friedrich Nietzsche three centuries later. Does that make Varchi a precursor of Zarathustra? Far be it from me to spruce up his sagging philosophical laurels by comparing him, even for an instant, to so much greater a personage! Nietzsche puts forth the theory of eternal recurrence with the proud and tragic pathos of his own soul. But Varchi looks at it with the tranquil, satisfied eye. He does not admit it in conscience. He therefore skips over it and relegates it to an obscure

[70] See Duhem, *Le système du monde*, Vol. I, pp. 164–68, and Rodolfo Mondolfo, *L'infinito nel pensiero dei Greci* (Florence: Le Monnier, 1934), p. 105. The necessary distinction between recurrence of the species and recurrence of the individual is omitted in two otherwise very interesting books: Abel Rey, *L'éternel retour et la philosophie de la physique* (Paris: Flammarion, 1927), and Mircea Eliade, *Le mythe de l'éternel retour*, 6th edn. (Paris, 1949) [in Eng.: *Cosmos and History: The Myth of the Eternal Return* (now in Harper Torchbooks, 2050)].

[71] [Two of the three novelties (the other one being the geographical discoveries) usually adduced in the sixteenth century to prove the superiority of modern times over antiquity.]

corner of his memory. Much the same thing happens to the other heretical ideas he comes up with. They do not become an intimate part of his soul. Like a good host, he freely lets them in and then, when it seems convenient, freely lets them go away again.

Nevertheless, Varchi's heterodoxy is perhaps the most notable part of his thought; . . . for it echoes a side of Renaissance civilization that so far has not received sufficient attention. Late Renaissance Aristotelianism took its inspiration not from Thomas Aquinas but from Alexander, from Averroës, and from the more recent Averroists and Alexandrines. Humanism provided a much more exact knowledge of Greek texts. Hence Thomas, whose reputation had already been damaged by the scholastics of the fourteenth century, now appeared to be an unreliable interpreter of Aristotle and an untrustworthy guide through the kingdom of philosophy as a whole.[72] Thomism flourished during the Renaissance only among the theologians. Although it occasionally claimed some perspicacious defenders, it lived largely in the shadow of Dominican convents, without exercising much influence on the lay culture outside. Of Thomists in the narrow sense of the term there were none. Of those who were Thomists only in the sense that they sought to reconcile the philosophers and the theologians there were only a few.[73] From Varchi to Giovan Battista Gelli, from Speroni to Alessandro Piccolomini, the

[72] That Aquinas was less faithful to Aristotle than Averroës and other non-Christian Peripatetics has been explicitly admitted or at least implied by many modern scholars of rigid Catholic orthodoxy. See, for example, P. Mandonnet, *Siger de Brabant*, Vol. I, p. 155; Franciscus Nuyens, *L'évolution de la psychologie d'Aristote*, French tr. (Louvain: Institut Supérieur de Philosophie, 1948), pp. 300 ff.; R. A. Gauthier, "Trois commentaires 'averroistes' sur l'"Éthique à Nicomaque,'" *Archives d'histoire doctrinale et littéraire du Moyen-Age* (1947–48), 187–336, pp. 335–36; and E. Gilson, "Caiétan et l'humanisme théologique," *ibid.* (1955), 113–36, pp. 130–35.

[73] Among these must be included Pierfrancesco Giambullari [another leading, and rather pugnacious, member of the Florentine Academy and author, among other things, of a *Historia dell'Europa* (Venice, 1566)], who attacked "the main belief of Averroës . . . that God pays no attention to the small things [of this world]." He claimed to be able to "demonstrate with the help of the Peripatetics that matter is not eternal, but created by God": *Lezioni* (Florence, 1551), pp. 87 and 140.

most able men of letters of the age who concerned themselves with philosophy ruled out, or tended to rule out, the possibility of an accord between reason and dogma, between Aristotle and the Bible.

A few passages from the less-read literature of the sixteenth century will suffice to illustrate this phenomenon.[74] Unfortunately an explanation of the phenomenon is somewhat more difficult. The first explanation that comes to mind is the simplest one: these so-called philosophers have secretly opted for rationalism, and their occasional expressions of respect for the faith are merely put into their texts to ward off the hostility of ecclesiastical authority. Yet a reading of their biographies and their works makes it clear that some if not all of them were in fact devout Christians. Gelli, for instance, in the same *Capricci del bottaio* in

[74] In the *Capricci del bottaio* Gelli maintains that "The theologians, in order not to admit that they do not understand what belongs to the faith by natural reason, have let themselves be led . . . into trying to prove [the faith] with propositions drawn from philosophy. That is contrary completely to the faith, for [philosophy] proceeds according to the order and the principles of nature, while the faith wholly exceeds and is superior to nature": *Opere*, ed. Agenore Gelli (Florence, 1855), p. 225 [but now more easily available in the new edn. of Ireneo Sanesi (Turin: U.T.E.T., 1952)]. Elsewhere he affirms "that the human intellect, proceeding with its own light and according to natural discourse, becomes a rebel and contrary to divine law—which is what [Aristotle's] genius demonstrated": *Letture edite de inedite sopra la "Commedia" di Dante*, ed. Carlo Negroni, Vol. 1 (Florence, 1887), p. 138. There is no doubt that in philosophy the good cobbler is much more in agreement with his opponent Varchi than with his friend Giambullari. As for Speroni, Tomitano, who knew him well, puts into his mouth the following words: "Theology discourses with principles, bases, and conclusions that are completely dissimilar to those of philosophy. Indeed, if I were to call them wholly contrary and repugnant to each other, I would not be erring excessively"; *Ragionamenti della lingua toscana* (Venice, 1545), p. 92. As is known, sixteenth-century authors put into the mouths of the interlocutors of their dialogues opinions that the corresponding historical personages actually held. There is no reason to think that here Tomitano is an exception to the rule—even less so considering that several of Speroni's own dialogues show that, at least for a certain period, he himself professed concepts that could not be harmonized with theological teachings. Piccolomini, finally, even while never proposing a strident contrast between theologians and philosophers, presupposes and suggests such a contrast frequently. See his *Della filosofia naturale*, Part I (Venice, 1560), pp. 166–66ᵛ, and Part II (Venice, 1565), p. 194 *et al.*

which he juxtaposes philosophy and theology, expresses a very sincere religious mentality. Varchi, similarly, ends his life in a fervor of piety; and there is no evidence of any conscious break between his earlier and his later years.

The collapse of religious faith during the Renaissance is nothing but a myth, one which has been spread about largely upon the authority of Burckhardt. Lucien Febvre, admittedly with occasional exaggerations, has shown that Rabelais and his contemporaries were anything but nonbelievers.[75] Many more recent studies have backed him up by restoring a Catholic physiognomy to personages previously hailed as the heralds of free thought. The cultural revolution known as the Enlightenment has thus been taken away from the late Middle Ages and the early modern period and restored to its proper place, the eighteenth century.

The first interpretation is therefore fallacious. Is its opposite any better? Is it possible . . . that the integral Aristotelians, in expounding doctrines contrary to Christianity, are seeking merely to reconstruct the philosophy of Aristotle? Are they really not philosophers at all, but merely historians of philosophy? This explanation has the advantage of taking into account the claim of many [medieval] Latin Aristotelians to be no more than interpreters of Aristotle. But it is impossible to consider this claim as completely sincere. For they always refer to Aristotle as the Philosopher, not just as one of the philosophers.[76] If we look carefully at their works, we will realize that they propose to do much more than merely cast more light on one or another chapter of the history of philosophy. Born in an age completely alien to historicism, they aspire rather to acquire the whole of knowledge; and knowledge they find most completely revealed in Aristotle.

What is true for the medieval Aristotelians is true also for their

[75] *Le problème de l'incroyance au XVIe siècle: La religion de Rabelais* (Paris: A. Michel, 1942). . . .

[76] This objection has already been made by Gilson in "Caiétan et l'humanisme théologique," p. 131. See also Anneliese Maier, *Die Vorläufer Galileis im 14. Jahrhundert* (Rome: Edizioni di Storia e Letteratura, 1949), p. 251, and *Metaphysische Hintergründe der spätscholastischen Naturphilosophie* (Rome: Edizioni di Storia e Letteratura, 1955), pp. 26–27.

sixteenth-century successors. To cite but one of them: Piccolomini, in his *Filosofia naturale*, puts forth Peripatetic theses, not
because he wishes to explain them historically, but because he
thinks they get at the essence of nature. If occasionally (and it
happens rarely) one or two theses seem unacceptable to him, he
substitutes other theses that seem to be better supported by reason
or experience. Varchi, similarly, does not hesitate to assert that
Aristotle is always right and that (Aristotelian) philosophy is the
same thing as Truth. Someone may object that such affirmations
are of little importance, that they are not to be taken in their literal
sense, that they are contradicted by other passages in which
Varchi dissents from Aristotle. But such affirmations are perfectly
consonant with what Varchi says elsewhere. When he speaks of
the theory of eternal recurrence he calls it "necessary." When he
refers to "many" heretical propositions, he says that the philosophers are obliged to accept them. After admitting that the most
rigorous demonstrations, those which proceed from the cause to
the effect, are unusual even in Aristotle, he then adds that Aristotle
defends his own theses with arguments that are "necessarily
conclusive."

Some medieval Aristotelians held that philosophy did not go
beyond the realm of the probable. Hence they could easily
abandon any thesis that came into conflict with religion. For
Varchi, on the other hand, philosophy proceeds, frequently if not
constantly, according to the law of rational necessity; and he has
no logical reason for making it bow before the dogmas of the
Church. Necessary conclusions cannot but be true. That, after
all, is what Thomas Aquinas declared against the Averroists.
Opposing Thomas's declaration would amount to despairing of
human reason itself. And this Varchi refuses to do. For although
Aristotle did not ignore the weakness of our intellectual faculties,
he still professed a vigorous faith in them. As a good Peripatetic,
Varchi never refers to Tertullian's dictum: "It is credible because
it is ridiculous." Nor does he ever write a phrase like Pascal's: "To
make fun of philosophy is truly to philosophize." If, at the beginning of a lecture on Dante's *Paradiso*, he concedes a point to the

negators of the sciences, he quickly turns against them and compares wisdom, or philosophy, to the sun: "What would happen
to our eyes if the sun were removed from the sky is what would
happen to our intellects if philosophy were removed from the
earth."

Philosophy, then, is light. So is theology, to which Varchi
willingly pays homage. But philosophers and theologians hold
irreconcilably different opinions on many problems of fundamental importance. How can their differences be explained?
What becomes of the undeniable axiom that the truth is one?
Varchi does his best to answer these grave questions by distinguishing between natural light, which belongs to philosophy, and
supernatural light, which belongs to theology. One has its origin
in the senses and is guided by reason. The other depends upon
divine revelation. Their principles and their methods are different.
Hence it is inevitable that they should arrive at different results.
In an absolute sense the results furnished by theology command
our assent. But within the domain of natural light philosophy
never leads us astray.

Reduced to its essentials, Varchi's answer is deceiving. In vain
does he fit it out with citations to the philosophers and the poets.
The distinction between natural and supernatural knowledge
gets him nowhere. If the principles and methods of both are
equally valid, it is impossible that their conclusions with regard
to the same subject should differ. . . . Piccolomini, in answer to
the same question, tries an Occamist procedure. He refers to the
sovereign power of the divinity. Some philosophic theses, he
says, which contrast with theology, are founded upon the order
of nature. But nature is not absolute and necessary. For God
transcends nature; and He is free to break the laws that He imposed
upon it. These theses, then, do not transcend the limits of con-
tingency and relativity. They are exact as long as the present
natural order endures. They are false when God interrupts that
order.[77] This answer is less superficial than Varchi's, and at first
sight it seems to resolve everything. . . . But if we look more

[77] *De la seconda parte de la naturale filosofia*, pp. 238–39.

closely at the text, we will notice that Piccolomini opens himself to strong objections. . . . When he tries to prove, for instance, that "Being that can be generated is the same as being that can be corrupted" and "Being that is not generated is being that is incorruptible," he relies not on the natural order and experience, but upon the *a priori* principle of noncontradiction. Unless it is vitiated by some error, therefore, the thesis has the force of absolute necessity. But so also does the thesis that inexorably descends from it: if the human soul can be generated, then it is corruptible; if it is incorruptible, then it cannot be generated. Can Piccolomini really deny, then, that philosophy supports theses which are heterodox and which at the same time are necessary and absolute? The only way out is to appeal to divine power and say that God is not forbidden to confer incorruptibility upon a generated substance. And yet he also insists that "God with his immense power" cannot do things that "include self-contradictions."

The fact is that the Renaissance Aristotelians, who professed themselves Christians and who nonetheless sought to follow Aristotle, got themselves involved in a logical dilemma from which no dialectical expedient could free them. None of them had the vigor and the courage to push on to the ultimate consequence: a double truth. For even Aristotle had insisted that the truth is one. We must be very careful about taking too seriously the few passages in their works that seem to indicate such a direction. Speaking of geological mutations, for instance, Boccadiferro points out which causes the Christians and which causes the Peripatetics assign to them. *Secundum fidem et veritatem Catholicam* ("according to Catholic faith and truth"), they are produced by the will of God. *Secundum veritatem philosophicam* ("according to philosophical truth"), they derive from the movement of the heavens. Such a passage suggests that Boccadiferro admits the existence of two contrary truths. But then why does he not bother to justify theoretically an admission so alien to the teachings of Aristotle? And why does he elsewhere recognize that "truth does not contradict the truth"? It may be, in the passage here cited, that Boccadiferro endows the term "truth" with the meaning not of effective truth but of a concept defended as true. Or it may be that having used the term in its accepted meaning to designate Catholic theology he then, drawn by the force of his discourse, uses it in an improper sense to indicate Aristotelianism.

As many great historians have maintained, the doctrine (sometimes called Averroist) of the double truth belongs in the category of a scholarly legend.[78] The Latin Averroists and, in general, all the strict Peripatetics were satisfied with affirming that philosophy was irreconcilable with the dogmas of the Church. That such an affirmation undermined the dogmas is not what they said, but it is what the theologians of the second half of the thirteenth century said in their attack on Siger of Brabant and his followers. Actually, however, the Sigerians never formulated a theory of double truth. But they seem to presuppose one. . . . Perhaps they were not too different from the philosophizers in all ages who proclaim the singleness of the truth and then go on behaving as if the truth were sometimes double anyway.

Our sixteenth-century Peripatetics were sons of the Renaissance, and they share at least one thing with the artists and the humanists of their age. Except for Pomponazzi, who is occasionally overcome by a bitter uneasiness of religious origin, most of them do not seem to be very disturbed about the contrast between philosophy and Christianity. The one promises a life beyond the grave. The other denies it. The difference between the two theses is radical, and those who are both Christians and philosophers should be perplexed, if not pained, by the difference. Surprisingly enough, however, these Peripatetics view the dilemma with immaculate serenity. Some of them regard it as part of the nature of things. A few of them, like Varchi, judge it to be actually beneficial, for it serves to distinguish philosophical from theological speculation, whereas the useless attempt to put them back

[78] First of all Gilson, in his work specifically concerned with the theory, *Études de philosophie médiévale*, and then Nardi, in his "Intorno alle dottrine filosofiche di Pietro d'Abano," first published in 1920–21 in the *Nuova rivista storica* and now reprinted in his *Saggi sull' aristotelismo padovano*.

together is productive only of "infinite numbers of heresies."[79]
It is Thomas Aquinas and his disciples, then, who endanger the
faith; and it is the Averroists and the Alexandrines who protect
its integrity.

Does this conclusion, then, assist Varchi and company in
quieting their Christian consciences? Possibly: people often put
their faith in the most fragile of arguments. But much as we may
reflect on their work, the attitude of Renaissance Aristotelians
toward the antinomy between intellect and dogma remains un-
intelligible to us. We can understand Siger, whom this antinomy
troubled right to the end of his days.[80] But we cannot understand
Varchi, Boccadiferro, and Piccolomini, who show no signs of
being disturbed by it at all. It is as if they belonged to a different
species. Actually they simply belonged to another age, an age that
was as untroubled by internal conflicts as it was rich in unresolved
contradictions. Its painters took delight in Venus, and at the same
time they glorified Mary. Its poets wrote devout verses opposite
pages of sensuality; and while affirming the immortality of the
soul, they sought to enjoy the fleeting moment. Its wise men
celebrated fame, pleasure, and avarice, the mundane virtues and
the goods of the world; but they also paid homage to the Gospel
and worshiped the transcendent God of the Church. They could
not bring concord to the discord within their own spirits. But
they were not therefore upset.[81] Their world was far from being
brought together in a credible organic synthesis. But their works
seem to reflect a harmony of spirit that few men of other ages
have ever approached.

With a bit of retouching, this paradox could be just as well
applied to our philosophizers. Integral Aristotelianism has usually
been seen as completely separate from humanism. But at least in
one sense philosophy was a close cousin of humanism in its
attempt to restore and to take possession of a great monument of

---

[79] A similar opinion is in Bernardi, *Eversionis Singularis Certaminis Libri XL*,
pp. 261–62.

[80] Van Steenberghen, *Siger de Brabant*, Vol. II, p. 690.

[81] So says Febvre, in *Le problème de l'incroyance*, p. 488. . . .

pagan antiquity—and to do so without denying the Catholic religion or being bothered by the contrast between the two. Though it was born in the Middle Ages, Aristotelianism is to some extent a typical expression of the Renaissance. The hierarchical spiritual unity of the Middle Ages is well reflected in Thomas, who rigorously subordinates everything to the faith and who reconciles philosophy and theology with tireless acumen. The untormented acceptance of contradictions by the Renaissance is well reflected in those thinkers of the sixteenth century who recognized that Aristotle could not be reconciled with the Bible, but who went on imperturbably venerating both Aristotle and the Bible.

Pushing these men back in time is as misleading as pushing them forward. At least one well-known historian has tried to enroll Varchi, for example, in the army of the Counter Reformation and has altered his physiognomy to the point of disguising him as a Thomist. He has been led to do so by the proud moralism of Varchi's poetics; and noticing that Varchi's pronouncements often sound like those of an inquisitor, he has concluded that all Varchi's thought corresponds to the criteria of the Inquisition. In spite of his independence of Croce, he has fallen victim to a tendency among many followers of Crocianism to identify philosophy with aesthetics. But the truth is that Varchi belongs to Renaissance culture, even if at times he puts forth ideas that later were to become dear to post-Tridentine literature. Neither his Aristotelianism in particular nor heterodox Aristotelianism in general were in accord with the spirit of the Counter Reformation. When they came into contact with it, they suffered a setback and were forced to arm themselves with ever greater precautions.[82]

[82] In his *Saggi sull'aristotelismo padovano*, p. 453, Nardi writes: "Whoever thinks that the spirit of the Counter Reformation and ecclesiastical prohibitions contributed to the fall [of integral Aristotelianism] is wrong." I cannot accept this judgment. Nardi would, in my opinion, be completely right if he had limited himself to showing that "Averroism [and, we might add, heterodox Aristotelianism in general (author's comment)] was buried under the ruins of Aristotelian physics" (p. 454) and that a mortal blow was dealt it by the new science. But he goes on to maintain that post-Tridentine Catholicism was not a fearful adversary of that philosophy. This opinion is contradicted by many facts

Toward 1550, before the Catholic reaction was able yet to display all its forces, Aristotelianism seemed to be on the verge of conquering Florence. Varchi popularized it, Gelli accepted it, and one of Varchi's disciples, Lelio Bonsi, echoed its themes. But two decades later it was in retreat. About 1575 the most representative philosophizer of Tuscan culture was not an integral Peripatetic. He was Francesco de' Vieri, called Verino Secondo, who did his best to persuade us that, properly understood, philosophy is not in contrast with the faith.[83]

The air [of the Counter Reformation] was no more benign to heterodox Aristotelianism when Varchi's *Lezioni* were finally printed in 1590. In order to uproot the damnable plant of philosophical heresy, the Jesuits in 1586 instructed their masters to play down "these interpreters of Aristotle who have harmed the Christian religion."[84] For much the same reason the inquisitor Tommaso Buoninsegni did not permit the *Lezioni* to appear without the addition of marginal glosses that severely censured the doctrine of eternal recurrence proposed in them. Yet the rigors of the Catholic reaction did not prevent Varchi from effectively spreading about Aristotelian theories. When Galileo rose up to

---

which, taken together, are rather striking as evidence for the opposite hypothesis. Let me add a couple to those already given in the text, since they are relatively unknown. In 1570 Tomitano republished, with considerable revisions, his *Ragionamenti della lingua toscana*, which had first appeared in 1545. A comparison of the two texts will show that in the second edition he took out the passage in which Speroni affirms the irreconcilability of philosophy and theology. It is difficult not to suppose that Tomitano made the change out of fear of asserting something unacceptable to ecclesiastical authority. For the same reason Zabarella, in a passage of his celebrated comment on the *De Anima* (Venice, 1605), Book III, fol. 23, col. b [I omit the long Latin passage to be found in the original on p. 310, n. 1], opposes not theology and philosophy, as Pomponazzi or Boccadiferro had done, but good philosophy and bad philosophy. He certainly seems to have been trying to please someone in power who would have been offended by hearing that intellect was opposed to the faith.

[83] [On Verino Secondo, see above, ch. 2. He does so by trying out one more big experiment in reconciling Aristotle with Plato.]

[84] These words are taken from the *Ratio Studiorum* of 1599. But the concept is already expressed in the instructions of 1586. See *Ratio Studiorum et Institutiones Scholasticae Societatis Iesu per Germaniam olim Vigentes*, ed. G. M. Pachtler, S.J., Vol. II (Berlin, 1887), pp. 132–33 and 330–32.

combat them, he was able to find support in a vast and interested public that could follow his arguments because it was well informed about the arguments he was combating.[85] And it is probable that he owed his success partially to the work of a clear and elegant popularizer such as our Varchi.

This, then, is the most valuable contribution that Varchi made to scientific progress. Is it too small a contribution for a man who claimed to be a philosopher (i.e. a scientist) as well as a poet? Without doubt. But the path he took, the one which it was almost necessary to take in his age, did not lead, in the field of science, to heights from which new horizons could be contemplated.

What discoveries, then, can justly be ascribed to Aristotle's Renaissance disciples? Their most sagacious apologist, a learned American scholar, has come up with many subtle arguments to show that a few of them, particularly Agostino Nifo and Jacopo Zabarella, contributed much to the development of modern science by elaborating a methodology to which Galileo was considerably indebted.[86] But his thesis, although it has seemed convincing to several prominent students of the age,[87] is, if I am not mistaken, vitiated by one basic defect. It is founded on the erroneous presupposition that a methodology can be considered of great importance completely apart from its practical application. As the authoritative writer Paul Tannery has pointed out,[88] a method can be assimilated by the mind of a scientist only after it has been illustrated by a few examples.

Tannery's judgment was intended as a way of diminishing somewhat the role generally accorded to Francis Bacon. But it

[85] As observes Olschki, in *Bildung und Wissenschaft*, pp. 284 and 300.

[86] J. H. Randall, Jr., "The Development of Scientific Method in the School of Padua," *Journal of the History of Ideas*, I (1940), 177–206.

[87] Namely, to Hiram Haydn, *The Counter-Renaissance*, p. 87; to A. C. Crombie, *Histoire des sciences de Saint Augustin à Galilée*, French tr. (Paris: Presses Universitaires de France, 1959), Vol. I, pp. 235–37; and to Herbert Butterfield, *The Origins of Modern Science*, 2nd edn. (London: Bell, 1958), p. 49.

[88] Cited by Lenoble in his essay "Origines de la pensée scientifique moderne" in *Histoire de la science*, ed. Maurice Daumas (Paris: Encyclopédie de la Pléiade, 1957), p. 423.

much more effectively diminishes that of such inferior geniuses as Nifo and Zabarella, who never bothered to relate their methodological excogitations to the concrete reality of scientific research. After all is said, their contribution to the progress of science is not much greater than Varchi's. They may surpass him as philosophers. But they yield to him as writers of prose. And once in a while (unless I am misled by my proclivities as a student of literature) a good work of popularizing prose is no less useful to the sciences than the work of an ingenious, but abstract, philosopher.

PART THREE

Reformation and Counter Reformation

8 The Problem of Heresy: The History of the Reformation and of the Italian Heresies and the History of Religious Life in the First Half of the Sixteenth Century—the Relation Between Two Kinds of Research[1]

DELIO CANTIMORI

Delio Cantimori was professor of modern history, first at the Scuola Normale of Pisa and then, from 1951 until his sudden death in 1966, at the University of Florence. He was interested in a great variety of philological, philosophical, and political as well as historical subjects, some of which are treated in such collected volumes as his *Studi di storia* (Turin: Einaudi, 1959). His *Utopisti e riformatori italiani* (Florence: Sansoni, 1943) established him as an authority on the early Italian Risorgimento. But his principal field of endeavor has been the history of religion in the sixteenth century. His *Eretici italiani del Cinquecento* (*Italian Heretics of the Sixteenth Century*), first published in 1939 and republished in Florence (Sansoni) in 1967, is now a classic. A more general survey was published posthumously: "Le idee religiose del Cinquecento: La storiografia" ("The Religious Ideas of the Sixteenth Century: Historiography") in Vol. v of the Garzanti *Storia della letteratura italiana* (Milan, 1967). For a short biography in English, see Eric Cochrane and John Tedeschi, "Delio Cantimori, Historian," *Journal of Modern History*, xxxix (1967), 438–45. For a complete bibliography of his published

---

[1] Cantimori was working on a revised version of this article as a personal favor to the editor at the moment of his death. Unfortunately the revisions were lost in the proverbial chaos of his study. Hence this translation follows, with small stylistic modifications, the original text: "Studi di storia della Riforma e dell'eresia in Italia, e Studi sulla storia della vita religiosa nella prima metà del '500 (rapporto fra i due tipi di ricerca)," *Bollettino della Società di studi valdesi*, LXXVI (1957), 29–38. The article is used with permission of the publisher.

works, see *Rivista storica italiana*, LXXIX⁴ (1967). Excerpts from this article were republished as ch. II of his *Prospettive di storia ereticale* (Bari: Laterza, 1960).

THE term "Reformation," or "Protestant Reformation," has been used in many different senses. I use it here to signify a movement in the sixteenth century which drew support from churchmen and men of letters, from patricians and artisans, from princes and peasants. It was a movement which emerged from many different local historical circumstances, but which sought to reform both the dogmatic principles and the chief institution of all Western Christian society, the Church. Finally, it was a movement which resulted in the concrete action of Luther, Zwingli, Calvin, and their friends and followers for the renovation of doctrine, institutions, sentiments, and customs within the churches they founded; and it was one which exerted a considerable influence within the Anglican Church as well. The term "heresy" is also equivocal. I mean by it those doctrines, groups, tendencies, and movements aimed at Christian renewal which sprung up spontaneously from various sources all over Europe after Luther's initial blow to the Church and which remained detached or excluded from all established Christian communions, Protestant as well as Catholic. These "heretics"—men and women from every class and occupation—considered themselves to be the only truly reformed Christians. They organized themselves into many different groups and were given many different names—the various kinds of Anabaptists, the Mennonites, the "Spirituals," the followers of Thomas Müntzer, and the Christian rationalists who eventually assumed the name "Socinians."²

With these definitions, and with Giorgio Spini's just criticisms of Italian Reformation scholarship in my generation . . . in mind,³

² [The name derives from the founders, Lelio and Fausto Sozzini of Siena. See ch. 10, n. 6, below. The most comprehensive survey of what Cantimori calls "heresy" north of the Alps is now George Williams's *The Radical Reformation* (Philadelphia: The Westminster Press, 1962).]

³ Spini, "Storiografia moderna," *Il ponte*, III (1947), 382–86. [See n. 14 below.]

I seek to emphasize the conscious action consciously undertaken by the men of the Reformation. I am aware, moreover, of the apparent similarity of certain of our own interests today with those of the Italian reform movements of the past; and I seek also to . . . avoid the modern overtones of the word "heresy." Heresy is a word which has come to mean simply dissent and nonconformity and the defense of the right to voice dissent publicly. It is a convenient, broad, and generic term that embraces numerous different "heresies." But, unlike the term "Reformation," it was not one that was used by the agents and promoters of the movement it designates. Indeed, the term was applied to the so-called heretics by their enemies; and at least until the twentieth century almost no one ever boasted of being a "heretic" in the same way as those who proudly call themselves *les gueux*. Future students of the Reformation and of the Italian heresies should at the same time take note of Gerhard Ritter's criticisms of my attempt to reduce all the various manifestations of heresy at the time under the common denominator "Anabaptist."[4] For that amounts to repeating the sixteenth-century error of calling all Protestants "Lutherans." We must distinguish carefully one group from the others. And when we do not have enough information to permit distinctions, we do better to use the broader term "heresy" [rather than to extend the proper name of one of them to all the rest]. If we are to maintain a strictly historical point of view, we must keep our studies of the Reformation in Europe and in Italy and the "heresies" carefully within the bounds of these definitions.

By "the history of religious life" as distinguished from "the history of heresy" or "of the Reformation" I mean the history of the expression of religious sentiment in its traditional forms, in so far as these forms were not tied directly to ecclesiastical institutions. I mean the traditional forms of Christian life that continued to exist or were only gradually modified beyond and beneath the

---

[4] Ritter, "Wegebahner eines 'aufgeklärten' Christentums im 16. Jahrhundert. Bericht über neuere italienische Forschungen," *Archiv für Reformationsgeschichte*, XXXVII (1940), 268–89, esp. pp. 272–73.

conscious efforts of the Reformation leaders or by that movement usually called the "Catholic Reform."

There has recently been published in Italy a new work, original both for the questions it asks and for the way it seeks to answer them, which has shown us what richness of tone and nuance the history of religious life is capable of, even when it is limited to the various denominations and confessions of Christianity. The work is Alberto Tenenti's *Il senso della morte e l'amore della vita nel Rinascimento* (*The Sense of Death and the Love of Life in the Renaissance*).[5] It is a work inspired by the teaching of Lucien Febvre[6] and Fernand Braudel, and it seeks to account for sentiments and affections and for that religious sensitivity and basic morality that are so important a part of religious phenomena, at least from the historian's point of view.

This is the kind of history that one Catholic scholar, Giuseppe De Luca, has called "the history of piety"—in an excellent article[7] that has been unjustly neglected, perhaps because of its rather unacademic form of presentation. The history of piety covers such phenomena as wills and testaments, literature, the fine arts, philosophy, theology (for example, the fate of Erasmus's *Praise of Folly*), the *danse macabre*, sermons, signs of satisfaction with earthly life and of the horror of death. All these are phenomena that can be studied historically—phenomena, that is, which can be differentiated and specified in space and time. They are phenomena which developed in the sixteenth century on a plane all of their own. It was a plane on which the theological and dogmatic differences of the age had little importance. It was a plane on which the antagonisms and bloody struggles had little apparent effect until later in the sixteenth century, when the consolidation of both the new churches and of the old one produced new forms

---

[5] (Turin: Einaudi, 1957).

[6] [The essay of Febvre here and later referred to is his "Une question mal posée: Les origines de la Réforme française," *Revue historique*, CLXI (1929), 1–73. It has since been republished in his *Au cœur religieux du XVIe siècle* (Paris: S.E.V.P.E.N., 1957).]

[7] De Luca's introduction to Vol. I (1951) of the *Archivio italiano per la storia della pietà*, pp. xi–lxxvi.

of religious sentiment, like Puritanism and Spanish rigorism, and new versions of old orthodoxies.

The study of the relationship between the history of the Reformation and the history of heresy has only recently been formulated as a genuine historical problem. For only recently have historians ceased to consider Anabaptism, Spiritualism, Socinianism, and Arianism as products of the internal difficulties of the reformed churches. And only recently have they begun considering them in a way different from Ernst Troeltsch and Wilhelm Dilthey—as the only genuine representatives, that is, of the spirit of the Protestant Reformation. Not until the appearance of studies like those of Roland Bainton in the United States and of Walter Köhler in Germany[8] did anyone realize how diffuse these movements were or how great a proselytizing force they engendered. Nor did anyone realize the necessity of studying them for the purpose of attaining a more adequate historical understanding of the whole campaign of the sixteenth century to renovate Christian society. Whenever the question of the relationship between heresy and the Reformation has been considered from a rigorously historical point of view, it has been posed only as a way of overcoming the limits of particular orthodoxies and dogmatic patrimonies. But sixteenth-century heresy represents in part a reappearance (perhaps after a temporary underground existence?) of some of the themes of medieval heresy. It also represents in part a development of new themes. At the present stage of historical research it seems even more to represent an attempt to pursue to their utmost limits the themes originally posed by the Lutherans and the Zwinglians. It seems, therefore, to have remained within the great wave of the Protestant Reformation and to have considered itself consciously a

---

[8] [Bainton has written many works on this subject; but Cantimori is referring specifically to his *Bernardino Ochino* (Florence: Sansoni, 1941), which for some reason has never appeared in the original English text. Köhler (d. 1946) edited the works and correspondence of Acontius (n. 9 below), of Erasmus, and of Johann Brenz, and wrote numerous books on the Reformation.]

part of the Reformation even when it was rebuffed by the established churches. Luther, Zwingli, and Calvin, [so runs the argu-
ment], did not proclaim themselves Protestants. Fausto Sozzini,
similarly, did not call himself a heretic, but simply a "true
Christian."

The historian, of course, cannot ignore the distinctions hidden
beneath the term "true." Nor can he overlook the validity of the
desire to be "true Christians" among those who called themselves
such. The historical problem must not be formulated in such a
way as to perpetuate the differences willed and carried out by
individual reformers, big and small—differences which can best
be attributed partially to particular circumstances of ecclesiastical
and political organization. The various heresies were single
aspects of one great movement; and they cannot be separated
from the whole even (if I may be permitted a bit of irony) for
the purpose of setting up a "dialectical" relationship among the
artificially distinguished parts. At the same time, just as the
movement of the Reformation was divided within itself among
Lutherans, Calvinists, *et al.*, so heresy also was divided among
various groups and tendencies. Hence, it is impossible to study
Zwingli correctly [—to put the conclusion in the form of an
example—] without considering his relations with the Anabaptists, just as it is impossible to study Jacopo Aconcio[9] without being familiar with the Calvinist doctrines to which he
referred.

One of the most important problems remaining to be solved
regards the connection between the various movements we call
"heretical" in the sixteenth century and the "heresies" of the
Middle Ages. At present a solution is still far off; for the field
remains almost wholly unexplored. But at least some indications
have been given by Augustin Renaudet and by Vladimiro

---

[9] [On Jacopo Aconcio (or Acontius), who fled Italy for England upon the
accession of Pope Paul IV and who subsequently wrote an appeal for religious
toleration, see the biography by Charles O'Malley, translated into Italian by
none other than Cantimori himself and published in Rome by Edizioni di
Storia e Letteratura, 1955.]

Zabughin[10] in their studies of religious humanism. A study of
ascetic and mystical literature, both popular and learned, may
reveal some others. To cite one example: in his reprinting of the
humanist translation of the *Theologia Germanica*, the "arch-
heretic" Sebastiano Castellione put in appendix the mystical
directions of a certain *idiota*, who may well be Giovanni Pico
della Mirandola. A study like that of Renaudet has not yet been
done for the various groups in Italy—with the exception of
Roberto Cessi's *Paolinismo preluterano*,[11] which I hope will soon be
expanded further. An investigation of the writings of St. Lorenzo
Giustiniani,[12] for instance, may reveal hitherto unsuspected links
with the *Devotio Moderna*. The exemplary researches of Eugenio
Garin in 1948, which, in characteristic fashion, touch upon a
broad range of subjects—from moral reform and clerical corruption to rhetorical themes and demands for a greater interiorization
of religious sentiment[13]—have not been followed up. Neither
have the equally suggestive researches of Spini, published the
same year.[14] To be sure, such researches involve a patient and
adventuresome search through the archives for traces of fourteenth-century heretical ideas during the fifteenth and sixteenth
centuries, as well as the discovery and organization of unknown
material and the critical restudy of what material is already

[10] Particularly Renaudet's *Préréforme et humanisme à Paris pendant les premières
guerres d'Italie, 1494–1517*, 2nd edn. (Paris: Champion, 1953) [and Zabughin's
Il cristianesimo durante il Rinascimento (Milan: Treves, 1924).]

[11] "Paolinismo preluterano," *Rendiconti dell'Accademia nazionale dei Lincei*
(Classe Scienze morali, storiche e filologiche), Ser. VIII, Vol. XI (1957).

[12] [Lorenzo wrote a great number of spiritual works, which were published
in his *Opera* in Brescia in 1506, and often thereafter. He died in 1455. He should
not be confused with the equally famous Blessed Paolo Giustiniani, whose
retreat to the hermitage at Camaldoli in 1510 was such an important event in
the development of the Counter Reformation in Italy. See now Jean Leclercq,
"Le Bx. P. G. et les ermites de son temps," *Problemi di vita religiosa in Italia nel
Cinquecento* (Padua: Antenore, 1960), pp. 225–40 (a volume which contains
many other articles relevant to this subject).]

[13] "Desideri di riforma nell'oratoria del Cinquecento" in *Contributi alla storia
del Concilio di Trento e della Controriforma* (Florence: Vallecchi, 1948), pp. 1–11
[the same volume from which ch. 4, above, is taken].

[14] "Introduzione al Savonarola," *Belfagor*, III (1948), 414–39.

known. The report of E. Pommier on "The Idea of the Church Among the Italian Anabaptists"[15] of 1957 shows how much has to be done and how much actually can be done. Similarly, if we look a bit beyond the strict limits of the sixteenth century we will find ourselves obliged, as the studies of Gaetano Cozzi[16] and B. Mianach have shown, to revise radically what hitherto has been said about Sarpi. Here we are no longer at the bottom of theological, ecclesiastical, and political consciousness, as we are with the Anabaptists, but at the apex. We must reread *ex novo* the *History of the Council of Trent* in relation to Sarpi's other activities during the years in which he was writing it.

Another example: the most important and comprehensive study published so far on Juan de Valdés is the one by the Carmelite Father Domingo de Santa Teresa,[17] a work founded on a complete knowledge of the major and minor works of Valdés, as well as on much hitherto ignored unpublished material. Nor is it limited to the theoretical positions of Valdés: the author follows the spread of his ideas during his lifetime and in the years after his death and has discovered many of these ideas still operative (occasionally disguised in such works as the *Beneficio di Cristo*)[18]

---

[15] "L'idée d Église chez les Anabaptistes italiens au XVI siècle," *Relazioni del X Congresso Internazionale di Scienze Storiche* (Florence: Sansoni, 1955), Vol. IV, pp. 75–110.

[16] Cozzi, "Fra Paolo Sarpi, l'anglicanesimo e la 'Historia del Concilio Tridentino'," *Rivista storica italiana*, LXVIII (1946), 559–619.

[17] *Juan de Valdés . . . Su pensamiento religioso y las corrientes espirituales de su tiempo* (Rome: Gregoriana, 1957). [Valdés (1498?–1541) was a Spanish Erasmian who moved to Naples in order to avoid persecution in 1534 and who became one of the leaders of Italian spirituality. Many of his ideas were eventually denounced as heterodox. His followers Cantimori calls "Valdesians." They must not be confused with the medieval heretical sect, the *Waldensians* (from Waldo, the founder—*Valdesi* in Italian), who became associated with Calvinism in the sixteenth century, and whose descendants today, still inhabiting the same Alpine valleys west of Turin (referred to as the "Valleys" in ch. 10, below) as they did in the Middle Ages and the Renaissance, publish the review *Bollettino della Società di studi valdesi*, in which this article appeared.]

[18] [This famous treatise on piety, which has now been almost definitively attributed to the Benedictine monk Benedetto da Mantova, was widely acclaimed by reforming Catholics as well as Protestants and "heretics" when it was first published in 1543. Salvatore Caponetto ("Benedetto da Mantova" in

right up to Trent and beyond. The work of Father Domingo has shown (at least by example) how much still has to be done in this kind of research. It has also shown that such problems must be treated in the context of history—and of the history of all European Christendom, not just of Italy. It has shown that they must be treated in the context of "spirituality" and religious devotion, not just that of doctrine, and in the context of intellectual religious thought, not just that of popular piety. On the other hand, all that regards the participation of the Valdesians in the Reformation is pushed into the background. Thus in the work of Father Domingo the history of religious life ends by obscuring both the history of the Reformation and the history of the heresies.

This same tendency is characteristic also of many passages in such promising historical studies of the Catholic Reform as Hubert Jedin's life of Cardinal Girolamo Seripando and his essay "Catholic Reformation or Counter Reformation."[19] These studies have certainly done much to clarify and renovate the historiography of the Catholic Church in the Tridentine and post-Tridentine periods. But we must beware of the danger, both in the Protestant and in the Catholic camps, of overemphasizing the elements common to all of the confessions of the time. For we

---

Dizionario biografico degli Italiani) calls it "the greatest work of the Protestant Reformation in Italy." See the notes by C. Ginsburg in Rivista storica italiana, LXXVIII (1966), 184 ff. It has been translated into English with annotations by Ruth Prelowski in Italian Reformation Studies in Honor of Laelius Socinus, ed. J. A. Tedeschi (Florence: Le Monnier, 1965), pp. 21–102. The latest study of the treatise is by Valdo Vinay, "Die Schrift 'Il Beneficio di Giesu Christo' und ihre Verbreitung in Europa nach der neueren Forschung," Archiv für Reformationsgeschichte, LVIII (1967), 29–72 (which, however, does not mention the Tedeschi volume). The latest, and apparently definitive, word on the relations between Benedetto and Valdés is by Philip McNair, Peter Martyr in Italy (Oxford University Press, 1967), ch. 6.]

[19] [Jedin's Girolamo Seripando was first published in Würzburg in 1937. His Katholische Reformation oder Gegenreformation (Lucerne, 1946) was translated into Italian and published by Morcelliana in Brescia in 1957. See Cantimori's review in Studi di storia, pp. 537–53. On the history of the historiography of the Catholic Reformation, see Pier Giorgio Camaiani's "Interpretazioni della Riforma Cattolica e della Controriforma" in Vol. VI of the Marzorati Grande antologia filosofica (Milan, 1967).]

may end up transferring modern ecumenical tendencies to an age of violent struggles, inexorable persecutions, and neat, though sometimes tacit, distinctions. If we go too far on this road, we may end up teaching children that the Reformation was the work of Leo X in the Fifth Lateran Council or of Cardinal Morone, rather than of Luther and Calvin; and we may transform the perpetrators of burnings, persecutions, desecrations, and insurrections into nice people who were really good religious Christians at heart.

Here we must make one further reservation. The celebrated and now truly classic article of Lucien Febvre[20] has certainly given an important and fundamental impulse to studies of this sort; and the report on it given in Italy by one of the greatest Italian teachers of history, Carlo Morandi, may well have encouraged the multiplication of proposals for research and investigation.[21] But, notwithstanding Morandi's intentions, it has also encouraged certain deviations. True, it has opened the eyes of many, and I am the first to acknowledge my debt to it. It has done much to overcome the antiquated formulas derived from confessional apologetics—formulas like "Precursors of the Reformation in Italy," "Martyrs of the Protestant Reformation in Italy," and "Heroes of the French Reformation." It has encouraged us to look into the reform movement and the religious life of the Italian sixteenth century for its own specific historical characteristics, and not for martyrs of free thought or for acts of heroism in resisting oppression.

At the same time the work of Febvre belongs to a great tradition of historical scholarship. It followed upon the accurate and rich research into the Protestant Reformation undertaken in the nineteenth century, often for religious as well as for purely historical motives—research which still preserved echoes, though by then attenuated and at times largely rhetorical, of the great struggles of the past. The ideas and suggestions of Febvre were born in a

[20] [See n. 6 above.]
[21] [Morandi, "Problemi storici della Riforma," *Civiltà moderna*, 1 (1929), 668–80.]

humus that was profoundly Catholic, though devoid of confessional bias—just as Morandi was a devout Catholic without
letting his Catholicism slant his historical work. The perspective
of history shifted from old controversial questions to questions
regarding the whole of Christian religious life in all its manifestations; it shifted from churches and confessions to religious feeling,
from external struggles to interior preoccupations. The framework of history shifted from a topical one (political or ecclesiastical history) to a geographical one (France and Europe, though
with emphasis on France). The most important Protestant historian to follow Febvre's lead was Émile G. Léonard, whose *Le
Protestantisme français*[22] seeks to define a "French Protestant
type."

Febvre's suggestions have had little effect in other countries,
particularly in Italy—though I myself have used them extensively
in my own researches. But even I have had considerable difficulty
in my attempts to carry on my work in this direction. Historical
studies in Italy had not arrived, when Febvre first became known
there, at anything like the level of maturity that they had reached
in France. Neither in quantity, nor in the systematic character of
research undertaken, nor in the critical evaluation of what had
been found, could Italian historians rival their French colleagues.
The conscientious, though rather restricted and still somewhat
apologetic, work begun by Gustav Adolf Benrath and Emilio
Comba, by Domenico Berti and Giacomo Manzoni and their
followers, was picked up and endowed with a real scientific
and historical spirit by Francesco Ruffini, by Monsignor Francesco Lanzoni, and finally by Alfredo Casadei and Federico
Chabod. This endeavor has come to a halt—at least in so far as it
was directed to the Italian sixteenth century—with Chabod, with
Spini's life of Brucioli,[23] and with Benedetto Nicolini's studies of

---

[22] (Paris: Presses Universitaires de France, 1953.) [More recently the same
author has published a three-volume *Histoire générale du Protestantisme* (Presses
Universitaires de France, 1961–64), which has been translated by J. M. H. Reed
as *A History of Protestantism* (London: Nelson, 1965).]

[23] [See above, introduction to ch. 4.]

Ochino.[24] Only a few, like Arturo Pascal and Salvatore Caponetto, have continued to carry on research in the archives and
libraries. Spini has since turned to other periods and other problems—to the Libertines [of the seventeenth century] and to the
Protestants of the Italian Risorgimento.[25]

Some people apparently thought that there was nothing more
to do: that instead of deepening the research begun according to
Febvre's indications, they could now widen it and change its
point of view. Hence the case, typical in its paradoxical nature,
of a work produced by one of Morandi's pupils (but without any
responsibility on the part of Morandi, needless to say, and certainly not on the part of Febvre) which sought to demonstrate
that Aonio Paleario[26] was in fact a good Catholic. The way to
overcome the old-fashioned apologetic historiography about the
"witnesses of the truth" . . . does not lie in formulating precise
programs for the study of popular devotions, life in the convents,
and witch trials (though there is still very little systematic research
in these areas). Nor does it lie in concentrating exclusively on the
Catholic Reform—even though that is a very promising field and
one that merits considerable discussion. It lies rather in continuing
the inquiry into the history of the reform movement. The reform
movement was one which was common to all Italy, just as the
Protestant Reformation was common to all Europe. For like the
itinerant preachers of other ages, the Anabaptists, Calvinists, and
Waldensians wandered from one part of Italy to the other. The

[24] [Nicolini's most recent work is his *Aspetti della vita religiosa, politica e
letteraria del Cinquecento* (Bologna: Tamari, 1963).]

[25] [Spini, *Ricerca dei libertini* (Rome: Editrice Universale, 1950) and *Risorgimento e Protestanti* (Naples: Edizioni Scientifiche Italiane, 1956).]

[26] [Aonio Paleario (1503–80) was professor of eloquence in Milan until 1567,
when he was arrested on a heresy charge and taken to Rome. He finally
recanted; but refusing to abjure publicly, he was hanged and burned in 1570.
He wrote a number of religious treatises; but he did not write the *Beneficio di
Cristo* (n. 18 above), as was once believed. Cantimori tactfully does not
mention the scholar here referred to, and the editor will not do so either. On
the Counter Reformation in general, see the editor's own essay by that name
first printed in *Essays in Western Civilization in Honor of Christian W. Mackauer*
(College of the University of Chicago, 1967), pp. 19–32.]

various communities frequently changed their pastors. And often the single groups of reformers were more closely connected with groups in other states than they were with those in the places they sought to work in.

The attempt to fit single, local situations into a more comprehensive survey can at times lead us to forget something that I think no historian should ever forget: the actions, theoretical formulas, and conscious doctrinally defined tendencies which movements on a local level contribute to those on a more general level, and which provide a certain cohesion to the peculiar religious life of the various single localities all over Europe. The tendency to introduce subtle deformations into the study of these phenomena may be stated in this manner: the sixteenth century is the Age of the Reformation; and to study the Reformation we must study the whole sixteenth century. Consequently, we should no longer concentrate on Calvin until we have learned all there is to know about St. Charles Borromeo.

The same error has sometimes been committed by students of the Risorgimento in amalgamating the history of a specific movement with the history of the entire peninsula. The amalgamation results in diluting and denaturing the movement itself. In his exemplary researches Federico Chabod has never once overlooked the Italian and European ramifications of the Protestant movements in the various parts of the duchy of Milan.[27] He has never overlooked the doctrinal consciousness of those movements and the real struggles, persecutions, expulsions, and resistance that they endured. Just because these things have been recounted over and over again, sometimes with rather pathetic overtones, is no reason for the historian not to keep track of them in pursuing his original research. After all, even in striking off into wholly new fields he inevitably runs into the difficulty of having no preparatory work to which to apply his new questions. To give one example: Casadei's proposal to distinguish the religious life of all

[27] Chabod, *Per la storia religiosa dello Stato di Milano durante il dominio di Carlo V*, 2nd edn., ed. Ernesto Sestan (Rome: Istituto storico italiano per l'età moderna e contemporanea, 1962).

Christians from that of ecclesiastics in particular is a very useful
and suggestive one.[28] But except for a few specialists in ecclesiastical history, no one has yet provided us with any specific information about the actual distinctions between the secular and the
regular clergy in the various dioceses of Italy in the sixteenth
century. Even such distinctions, moreover, may obliterate the
organic bond that seems to have been effectively established in the
Lutheran and Zwinglian as well as in the Waldensian and Calvinistic communities between pastor and flock. The bond may have
been much looser in many parts of the Catholic church. But it is
one thing to say that the bond was loosened and another to ignore
it and to consider as wholly separate groups those who were and
wished to be united.

There is still another field of history that I think should be
looked into: the history of theology. By that I mean the projection
of the various theological positions of the age in elementary and
popular form and in images. I also mean the conflict of ideas
which, in this period, began to be capable of arousing a spirit of
sacrifice without having to be projected in the form of symbols
and myths. To be sure, theology concerns ideas and doctrines;
and today it often seems as if ideas and doctrines count for nothing
before economic and social structures, customs and popular feelings. But such methodological assumptions are not acceptable for
the history of the sixteenth-century reform movement. We must
not forget that the theologians intended their formulas as a way
of expressing and of directing the interests and the sentiments of
their flocks. They were neither blind to the realities of their social
environment nor unwilling to face up to those realities. And they
did not waste their time arguing about the sex of angels.

Even while admitting, however, the social content and implications of sixteenth-century theology, we must remember that
its main purpose was purely religious. The religious struggles of
the age were carried on *religionis causa*—for the sake of religion,
for the sake of salvation, for the sake of conscience. An Erasmian
theologian might well treat the problem of caring for the poor

[28] [See below, ch. 10, n. 6.]

from a completely new point of view. The artisan and peasant class composition of the Anabaptists may well explain why their doctrines were considered so subversive at the time, and historians of economic and social movements and of anarchical ideas have done well to pay attention to them. Still, we must proceed with caution. We must avoid the temptation to identify the Anabaptists with a sort of proletariat, the Calvinists with a bourgeoisie, etc. Luther was not merely the product of the peculiar conditions of Saxony. Zwingli and Calvin were not merely reflections of Zürich and Geneva. And what the Anabaptists said cannot be regarded merely as an expression of the social classes to which they belonged. Thus, when studying someone like Matteo Giberti of Verona,[29] we must remember to look carefully into the administrative structure of his diocese[30] and into the customs and religious traditions of his flock—even those that touch upon magic, superstition, and witchcraft. But we must also remember Giberti's connections with Rome, with Erasmus, with the Italian evangelical humanists, and even with the Protestants. Since we are dealing with struggles that were primarily religious, we cannot subordinate the religious, and hence the theological, elements to the nonreligious elements within them.

[29] [Giberti was a humanist and papal secretary under Pope Clement VII, who retired definitely to his diocese of Verona after the Sack of Rome in 1527 and became the first of the great "model bishops" of the Catholic Reformation. Much of what he worked out in practice was eventually incorporated into the reform decrees of the Council of Trent, which began meeting two years after his death in 1543. See ch. 3 of Jedin, *Das Bischofideal der Katholischen Reformation*, now in the Italian of E. Durini (Brescia: Morcelliana, 1950); and Enrico Cattaneo, "Influenze veronesi nella legislazione di San Carlo Borromeo," *Problemi di vita religiosa in Italia nel Cinquecento*, pp. 123–66.]

[30] [That is precisely what Paolo Prodi does in ch. 9 below.]

9 The Application of the Tridentine Decrees: The Organization of the Diocese of Bologna During the Episcopate of Cardinal Gabriele Paleotti[1]

PAOLO PRODI

After leaving the Catholic University in Milan in 1954, Paolo Prodi did graduate work at the University of Bonn under the direction of the leading modern historian of the Catholic Reformation, Hubert Jedin. Since 1962 he has been professor of modern history in the Facoltà di Magistero of the University of Bologna as well as, since 1954, one of the directors of the Istituto per le Scienze Religiose (Institute for the Religious Sciences), one of the most complete and most active libraries of ecclesiastical history in the world. Prodi has written many articles and essays on the sixteenth century. Some of them are monographic, e.g. "Relazioni diplomatiche fra il ducato di Milano e Roma sotto il duca Massimiliano Sforza," *Aevum*, xxx (1956), 437–94, and "San Carlo Borromeo e il cardinale Gabriele Paleotti," *Critica storica*, III (1964), 135–51. For those who do not read Italian, one of these articles is available in French: "Charles Borromée . . . et la papauté," *Revue d'histoire ecclesiastique*, LXII (1967), 379–411. Others seek to give a broad synthetic view of the whole epoch, like "Riforma cattolica o controriforma" in *Nuove questioni di storia moderna*, ed. Luigi Bulferetti (Milan: Marzorati, 1964), Vol. 1, pp. 357–418, and *Diplomazia del Cinquecento: Istituzioni e prassi* (Bologna: Patron, 1963). He has collaborated in editing the now indispensable *Conciliorum Œcumenicorum Decreta* (Freiburg im Breisgau: Herder, 1962). His principal work so far is his two-volume biography

---

[1] "Lineamenti dell'organizzazione diocesana in Bologna durante l'episcopato del card. G. Paleotti (1566–1597)" in *Problemi di vita religiosa in Italia nel Cinquecento*, "Atti del Convegno di Storia della Chiesa in Italia: Bologna, 2–6 Sett. 1958," (Padua: Editrice Antenore, 1960), pp. 323–40. Translated and slightly altered by the editor and then corrected and amended by the author; used with permission of the publisher.

Il cardinale Gabriele Paleotti (1522–1597) (Rome: Edizioni di Storia e Letteratura, 1959 and 1967), in preparation for which he wrote the article here translated.

THE period immediately after the Council of Trent was one of profound evolution in the structure of the Church. New institutions were created to accomplish the new tasks of reform and centralization. Old institutions were given new form by the more zealous pastors for the purpose of restoring them to their former functions. This evolution was particularly important in the reorganization of the diocese. Yet whoever attempts to study the Catholic Reform within the limits of a single diocese inevitably finds himself in a labyrinth of offices, officers, central and local authorities, from which it is very hard to extract a clear pattern.

This study of the diocesan bodies that collaborated with the bishop in running the diocese does not pretend to be definitive. It seeks only to indicate the lines of future research into diocesan organizations and to draw attention to the importance of such research. For most studies of the Catholic Reform have generally touched upon these organizations only marginally, and they have regarded the activities of synods, visitations, and so on, principally in relation to the religious situation of the diocese.[2]

This lacuna, to be sure, extends far beyond the limits of the period here considered. Indeed, we must turn far back in history to find an adequate panorama of the development of ecclesiastical institutions.[3] But the lacuna is particularly grave for the period of the Catholic Reform, which was essentially a period of the transformation of such institutions. Even the most famous *exemplum* of ecclesiastical reorganization, that of Charles Borromeo, which the personal prestige of the author and the publication of the *Acta*

[2] Giuseppe Alberigo, "Studi e problemi relativi all'applicazione del Concilio di Trento in Italia (1945–58)," *Rivista storica italiana*, LXX (1958), 285.

[3] For a bibliography on the history of diocesan ecclesiastical institutions, see W. Ploechl, *Geschichte des Kirchenrechts* (Vienna and Munich: Herold, 1953–55), ch. 6 of Vol. I, and Vol. II: "Regierung und Aufbau der Diözese."

Ecclesiae Mediolanensis (*Acts of the Milanese Church*) spread through-out Catholicism, has not received due attention from modern historians.[4] The same is true—even more so, indeed—for the work of the other leading pastors of the Catholic Reform, who at the same time, and often in contact with the archbishop of Milan, faced many of the same problems and arrived at similar, or at times different, solutions.[5] Projecting Borromeo's "model" upon the whole reform movement has unfortunately, and in-correctly, deprived the movement of the multiplicity of forms that are almost always the principal expressions of vitality. While recognizing, then, the profound influence of Borromeo upon his contemporaries, we must not overlook the way in which the different personalities of other pastors affected the movement within their respective jurisdictions.[6] The career of Gabriele Paleotti is a case in point. He was bishop (and after 1583 arch-bishop) of Bologna from 1566 until 1597. He was an intimate friend of Borromeo and carried on an intense correspondence with him on pastoral matters. Yet his character, his spiritual life, his cultural formation, and the actions of his administration were often very different. . . . This difference is particularly apparent in the kind of organizational structure he created for his diocese.

It is this structure, rather than his character and his administra-

---

[4] There are numerous references to Borromeo's diocesan organization in M. Bendiscioli, "Carlo B. cardinale nepote arcivescovo di Milano e la riforma della Chiesa milanese," in *Storia di Milano*, Vol. x (Milano: Treccani, 1957), pp. 119–99, and in E. Cattaneo, "La religione a Milano dall'età della Controri-forma" in Vol. XII of the same *Storia*, esp. pp. 294–98. For a more detailed analysis of the various parts, we must go back to Louis Thomassin, in *Vetus et Nova Disciplina circa Beneficia et Beneficiarios* (I use the edition of Venice, 1752), who bases himself largely on the *Acta Ecclesiae Mediolanensis* [see n. 16 below] for the evolution of diocesan institutions [in general] in recent times. The most up-to-date and complete bibliography on Borromeo is to be found in the article "Charles Borromée" in *Dictionnaire d'histoire et de géographie ecclésiastique*, ed. R. Mols, who also wrote "Saint Charles Borromée, précurseur de la pastorale moderne," *Nouvelle revue théologique*, LXXXIX (1957), 600–22 and 715–47.

[5] Alberigo, "Studi e problemi," p. 246.

[6] [Here I paraphrase, rather than translate directly, from p. 324 of the original, out of respect for the peculiarities of English style.]

tion in general, that I wish to discuss here.[7] I have based my conclusions on two principal sources. One of them is in print: the
Archiepiscopale Bononiense of 1594.[8] The other, which I was fortunate enough to find in manuscript in the archiepiscopal archives
of Bologna, is the "Governo archiepiscopale di Bologna" ("Administration of the Archdiocese"), which can be dated at about
1584.[9] The first is somewhat burdened with generalizations and

[7] There are brief biographical sketches in the articles "Paleotti" of the
Dictionnaire de théologie catholique and the *Enciclopedia cattolica*. [But see now the
full biography by the author mentioned in the introduction to this chapter.]
I wish here to express my gratitude to the Isolani family of Bologna, who
kindly permitted me to examine the Paleotti papers in their family archive,
which was very seriously damaged during World War II. At the very beginning of his term as bishop, which coincided with that of Borromeo, Paleotti
sent his friend several criticisms: "I do not wish to omit pointing out to you,
to fulfill the obligations of my servitude, what I hear: The first is that you never
spare yourself, nor ever take rest; and in this way you will not last long. The
second is that you are too austere and rigorous toward others and that you know
little of clemency and leniency. That is what I hear on all sides. Finally, some
say that you seldom consult others but do everything by yourself and according
to your own will. Undoubtedly you do so with most holy zeal; but you would
do well to communicate with persons of experience ...": Biblioteca Ambrosiana
[Milan], fol. 37 inf., fol. 447: G. Paleotti a C. Borromeo, 5 December 1566
(orig.). The difference between the two pastors was noticed even by contemporary biographers, e.g. A. Bruni, "Vita Gab. Paleotti" in Edmund
Martène's *Amplissima Collectio* (Paris, 1729), Vol. VI, col. 1412.

[8] *Archiepiscopale Bononiense, sive De Bononiensis Ecclesiae Administratione
Auctore Gabriele Paleotto . . . Opus Septem Partibus Distributum* (Rome, 1594).
A provisional and unorganized collection of decrees was published in Bologna
in 1580 called *Episcopale Bononiensis Civitatis et Diocesis*.

[9] Archivio Arcivescovile di Bologna (hereafter referred to as A.A.B.), H.537.
The long preamble to this document occupies fols. 1–90 and is published [in
appendix to the Italian text of this article]. Fols. 91–188 contain instructions
for the individual collaborators of the bishop and various notes concerning
diocesan administration. Some parts of the manuscript go back to the period
before the elevation of the Bolognese Church into a metropolitan see (1583);
but the whole document, in the hand of different secretaries, was put together
between 1584 and 1586. The "Governo archiepiscopale" is incomplete. The
two last sections on the administration of the province and on the life of the
archbishop, mentioned in the index at fol. 1r, are missing. Each part was copied
separately and has its own pagination along with the new pagination of the
whole work added subsequently. The work was not destined for publication
and is thus totally different from the above-cited *Archiepiscopale Bononiense*,
which is a true treatise on diocesan administration. [The author cites Latin

theories intended to promote its diffusion outside the diocese. Hence it is not always faithful in its reflection of the particular conditions of Bologna. The second is a memo for the bishop's collaborators to be used in case of his absence; and it contains an on-the-spot analysis of the situation of the diocese. For the purposes of this study I use only those parts of these two documents which directly concern the structure of the organizations that participated in the episcopal administration, and I leave out those parts that concern the purposes and the specific activities of the organizations.

After having spoken, in the first part of the *Archiepiscopale Bononiense*, of the spiritual love for souls that should keep the bishop in a state of continual tension and vigilance, Paleotti says: "Just as merchants never leave idle the money they have invested in business, but rather keep strict track of time and calculate their money accordingly, so much more should the bishop, who concerns himself with the business of all businesses and the science of the sciences, namely, the governing of men, the most varied and many-sided of all animals. . . ." This "mercantile" wisdom, of which the conclusions are "proved by long experience and by careful study accommodated to human actions," is the foundation of Paleotti's pastoral activity. He did not seek to turn the existing situation upside down overnight nor to impose reform by force and violence. He chose rather to call upon all the elements of the diocese that still had some life in them to assist him in the construction of a new kind of Christian society. At the base, or "grass roots" level, he found a network of associations that extended all the way from the "Society of Perseverance," composed of bright students from the university, to the "Corpus Christi" societies of the country parishes. At the top he placed his immediate collaborators. For the art of government, he held, consisted in large

---

passages in the original, but I have rendered them all into English without distinction. I also omit hereafter footnote references to specific passages in the two documents.] Compare the modern organization of diocesan chanceries in Eduard Eichmann and Klaus Moersdorf, *Lehrbuch des Kirchenrechts auf Grund des Codex J. C.*, Vol. III, 8th edn. (Paderborn, 1957), pp. 59 ff.

measure in knowing how to choose collaborators and in establishing among them a harmonious distribution of tasks.

First of all, then, let us examine the work of the chancery
officials. . . . In the fourth part of "Governo Archiepiscopale,"
entitled "Of the Tribunal and Its Officers," are described the
fourteen principal chancery officers and their respective charges.
. . . In the first place we find, naturally, the *Vicar General*, who
watches over the entire administration of justice and who is
ultimately responsible for the overall application of the decrees of
the Council of Trent. He signs edicts and extradiocesan permits
and attestations. And in case the bishop is absent or prevented
from acting, he receives still more ample powers over those
responsibilities expressly reserved for the ordinary. The *Suffragan
Bishop* has as his principal task the celebration of religious services.
But he also, in his capacity as visitor general, supervises the application of reform measures in the city, in which task he is assisted
by four prefects for each of the four urban quarters. He is responsible for issuing licenses to confessors and to curates and for
granting leaves of absence. He grants permissions for preaching
not only in the city but also in the country—or in the "Diocese,"
as the country is often called to distinguish it from the urban parts
of the diocese. The *General Auditor and Commissary* has the
traditional task of expediting all the affairs of the diocese and of
taking direct care of those special affairs that do not fall within
the normal scope of the other officers, like the "episcopal table," or
household. He is also charged with assembling preparatory
material for the synods and congregations, and he takes over the
visitor general's responsibilities in the country whenever the latter
is away on business. Indeed, the *Visitor General* is away most of
the time, for he is charged with "going about" whenever he can
to supervise in person the application of the reforms and to report
back to the general auditor (*Uditore Generale*) in the city. Beneath
him are several subordinate visitors. The *Representative (Vicario)
to the Inquisition* has functions that were established in a treaty
signed by the archbishop and the Father Inquisitor in 1584, after

years of arguing about the participation of the bishop in the activities of the Inquisition.[10] Finally, a number of minor officers have tasks that are described by their very titles—the *Vicar of the Nuns*, the *Prefect of Examinations*, and so on. . . .[11]

The archbishop reserves to himself all appointments to benefices and all exchanges of benefices from one holder to another. He alone permits the creation of new "patronages,"[12] the presentation of candidates for ordination, the concession of indulgences, the union or suppression of benefices, the erection of new confraternities, the succession of a candidate designated by a preceding benefice-holder, the acceptance of extradiocesan benefices by those within his jurisdiction, absolution in reserved cases, resignations from benefices, and the revocation of confiscations ordered *ex officio* for the repair of churches.

According to the decrees of the Council of Trent, several *Examiners* are to be appointed at the annual synod for promotions to parish churches, as well as several *Judges* for any disputes that might arise over such promotions.[13] Following the example of Borromeo,[14] Paleotti added to these officers several *Synodal Witnesses*, whom he appointed at each synod, without revealing their names, for the purpose of furnishing him information regarding the more serious abuses to be remedied in the reform

---

[10] A.A.B., L.59 (118): "Memoria di alcune cose che parrebbe bene s'havessero da servare tra il Padre Inquisitore et Vicario Archiepiscopale per maggiore servigio del S.to Officio." At the end of this (original) document appear the autograph signatures of Paleotti and Fr. Eliseo Capys, the Inquisitor, approving the convention of 12 October 1584. . . . The convention provides for joint approval of all major decisions by the Inquisitor and the vicar general. The convention was renewed in identical terms with the successor to Capys in 1585. A. Battistella, in *Il S. Officio e la riforma religiosa in Bologna* (Bologna, 1905) overlooks these documents and affirms simply (p. 50): "The bishops and archbishops had some relations with the Inquisition, but never one of supremacy...."

[11] [I omit the rest of the list, which is not complete in the original either.]

[12] [*Giuspatronati*. Third persons could "own" a benefice with the right to appoint the incumbent.]

[13] Compare modern law on this matter: Eichmann and Moersdorf, *Lehrbuch*, Vol. I, p. 404, and Vol. III, pp. 48–59.

[14] Thomassin, *op. cit.*, Vol. II, p. 627.

decrees. The persons appointed at the synod also have control over the activities of the archiepiscopal tribunal. We possess a detailed list of instructions for the three persons appointed in 1583 —two cathedral canons and one doctor of civil and canon law. They must hold frequent meetings and be present during the discussion of cases in the tribunal to make sure that all the rules are properly followed. To permit recourse to them [in case of a complaint about the rules], their names are written on the wall of the courtroom.[15] At the synod are also appointed two *Extraordinary Visitors* from the clergy to supervise the prisons; they are distinguished from the *Ordinary Visitor*, who is a chancery officer and a member of the archbishop's household.[16]

Having described the functions of the chancery, we must now examine the functions of the external, or peripheral, bodies,[17] limiting ourselves for the moment, however, to those bodies more closely connected with diocesan administration and omitting those on the parish level. These are the bodies indicated by the expression in the *Archiepiscopale Bononiense* "you who are called to responsibilities in the [various] parts of the diocese."[18]

The city, the suburbs, and the country (*contado*) were organized separately. Following the traditional division of the urban clergy into four sections, Paleotti divides all the curates of the city according to the four quarters. Every six months the curates of each quarter elect a prior, an underprior, and two elders, who

---

[15] A.A.B., H.537, fols. 146ᵛ–147ᵛ: "Instruttione per i Deputati et, revisori sopra le tasse del Tribunale, et mercede degli essecutori della Corte archiepiscopale (1583)."

[16] A.A.B., H.537, fols. 147ᵛ–148: "Instruttione per i visitatori delle carceri dell'arcivescovato di Bologna (1584)." The orders given by Borromeo in his first provincial council do nothing but prescribe that visitors are to be appointed by the bishops. In the fifth provincial council it is specified that the visitor ("protector") must be a canon of the cathedral (*Acta Ecclesiae Mediolansis*, ed. A. Ratti, Vol. II [Milan, 1890], pp. 88 and 694). The provincial constitutions of Milan say nothing about officers to oversee the work of the tribunals.

[17] For the history of peripheral diocesan institutions, see Thomassin, *op. cit.*, Vol. I, Book II, and Paul Hinschius, *Das Kirchenrecht* (Graz, 1869–97), Vol. II, pp. 261–90.

[18] The Augsburg synod of 1536 uses the same expression for the archpriests: Thomassin, *op. cit.*, Vol. I, p. 170.

have the specific task of organizing and presiding over the "congregations." These are the clerical assemblies, one in each quarter, called for the purpose of discussing cases of conscience and other pastoral problems. Four prefects appointed by the suffragan bishop oversee the whole of religious life in each quarter. Later on, however, the four congregations were united into a single one for the whole city and took place in the presence of the archbishop.[19]

In the country Paleotti keeps the traditional subdivision into *pievi*, or rural parishes, each of which is composed of several churches with a care of souls. The head of the *pieve* has the title of archpriest and the powers of a visitor for his *pieve*. The documentation on this office furnished by the "Governo archiepiscopale" shows it to be a good example of the peculiar nature of Paleotti's reform program, which sought, whenever possible, to respect the traditions of the ancient [Bolognese] church rather than starting from scratch.[20] Borromeo took a much more revolutionary line. He put the single districts under the direction of rural vicars (*vicari foranei*), whom he appointed at his own pleasure and whom he could transfer [at will] from one church to another.[21] Paleotti

[19] The regulations given by Paleotti at the beginning of his tenure were printed in 1568 as *Modo che avranno ad osservare i curati della città di Bologna in fare le loro congregationi* ... (A.A.B., Editti, I, no. 61).

[20] [This sentence appears in a footnote in the original (p. 331).] See Tommaso Casini and R. Della Casa, "Pievi e vicariati foranei del Bolognese," *L'Archiginnasio*, XIII (1918), 157–76, and XIV (1919), 38–53. Concerning the *Vicariati foranei*, this study is based almost wholly on F. Galinetti, "I vicari foranei nella nostra diocesi," *Bollettino della diocesi di Bologna*, I (1910–11), 72–74, 330–33, and 479–84. This article, however, gives only a general panorama and an indication of research still to be done. For the organization of the diocese in the Middle Ages, see T. Casini, "Sulla constituzione ecclesiastica del Bolognese (studi storici)," *Atti e memorie della R. Deputazione di Storia Patria per le Provincie di Romagna*, Ser. IV, Vol. VI (1916), 94–134 and 361–402, and Vol. VII (1917), 62–100. See also P. Sella, "La diocesi di Bologna nel 1300," *ibid.*, XVIII (1928), 97–155 (republished in the collection "Rationes Decimarum Italiae," *Aemilia* [Vatican City, 1933], pp. 197–270); A. Sorbelli, "La parrocchia dell'Appennino emiliano nel Medio Evo," *ibid.*, Ser. III, Vol. XXVIII (1910), 134–279; and G. Fasoli, "Sui vescovi bolognesi fino al sec. XII," *ibid.*, Series IV, Vol. XXV (1935), 9–27.

[21] *Acta Ecclesiae Mediolanensis*, Vol. I, pp. 79–80. The Ravenna provincial council of 1568 transcribed almost literally the Milanese prescriptions: G. D.

also appointed rural vicars; but he gave them, at least in the beginning, a charge very different from those of Borromeo: they were judges in the episcopal tribunals with jurisdiction "up to a certain sum" in two border areas that were difficult to reach.[22] They subsequently were given responsibilities for carrying out the reforms in those areas as well. Their numbers grew as they gradually took on some of the tasks once assigned to the heads of the *pievi*. And the office eventually became very similar to the one known by the same name today.[23] The archpriests of the *pievi* (there are forty-eight of them) are obliged to visit frequently the churches subject to them and bring the curates together for a meeting three times a year . . . while they themselves are to attend two annual congregations in Bologna. These congregations in turn function as a sort of "archpriests' synod" in which the bishop confers with

Mansi, *Sacrorum Conciliorum Nova . . . Collectio*, 53 vols. (Florence *et al.*, 1759–), Vol. xxxv, pp. 609–10. For the opposition incurred by Borromeo and for the practice he instituted in nominating the rural vicars from among the archpriests, see Thomassin, *op. cit.*, p. 171.

[22] The "Governo archiepiscopale," Appendix, fol. 47, already expresses the intention of giving the rural vicars charges concerning reform. It must be pointed out, however, that rural vicars can be found in Bologna (and a similar office had long been used in the field of civil jurisdiction) before the arrival of Paleotti, even though little is known of their functions. Speaking of the reform activities of Fr. Francesco Palmio, of the Society of Jesus, and the work done by him during the visit he was charged with in the diocese of Bologna in 1555 on behalf of Bishop Giovanni Campeggi, Polanco [the historian of the Society] writes that "many vicars" of this sort had already been assigned [I abbreviate the long quotation]. See his *Chronicon Societatis Jesu* (Madrid, 1897), pp. 123–24. For the reforming activities of Palmio in 1555, see his important letter to Fr. Ignatius [of Loyola] of 14 January 1556 in *Litterae Quadrimestres* (*Monumenta Historica Societatis Iesu*," Vol. IV (Madrid, 1897), pp. 58–63. On his visit of the diocese, see L. Vezzini, "La diocesi di Bologna nel 1555 secondo le visite pastorali," *Memorie dell'Accademia dell'Istituto di Bologna*, Classe di Scienze morali, Ser. IV (1943–44), pp. 81–136.

[23] . . . For the later development of the office of rural vicar, see Galinetti, *op. cit.* (in n. 19 above). It seems clear that these charges did not emanate from Paleotti, who had no intention of putting these vicars over the *pievi*: A.A.B., uncatalogued papers in the file of the archivist: "Nota della divisione delli vicarii foranei della diocese [*sic*] pubblicati nella congregatione de pievani sotto li 7 di marzo 1596." Here the rural vicars appear as links in the chain between the head of the diocese and the single *pieve*. Each one (sixteen of them) has several *pievi* within his jurisdiction.

all his collaborators. The acts of several of these congregations were printed, and they contain perhaps the best of Paleotti's pastoral legislation. They provide for "lecturers on cases of conscience" in each *pieve*, charged with conducting monthly meetings among the priests, and masters of ceremonies. All these officers meet during diocesan synods under the presidency respectively of the *Penitentiary Theologian* of the Cathedral and of the *Prefect of Ceremonies*, to whom they must make regular reports during the year.[24] ...

The fifth part of the *Archiepiscopale bononiense* deals with congregations and confraternities. The term *congregationes* is taken here in its largest sense to mean a group that assembles periodically. It thus includes congregations on cases of conscience and congregations of the archpriests of the *pievi*, even though these groups do not form a true "body" or collegiate organization. But I will confine myself, in accordance with the purpose of this study, to those congregations that were permanent organizations and that collaborated directly in the administration of the diocese. Such, for example, are the congregations that assist the officers of the chancery who are mentioned in the instructions for the vicar general. They have considerable administrative authority, except for those affairs "that require summons, decrees, confiscations, and other judicial acts of this sort," which can emanate only from the tribunals. Each of these congregations has its own internal bylaws, which are kept in the archives along with the names of the members and the presiding officers.[25] Each, moreover, is charged with a specific task: reform, inquisition, visitations, convents, examinations, catechumens, the seminary, etc.[26] They

[24] [The last three sentences appear in a footnote (p. 332) of the original.]

[25] ... From November 1568 to February 1569 a diary kept by the secretary to the cardinal, Nucci, records the activities of these congregations and is full of interesting details: Archivio Isolani, F. 31, Minutario ii, fols. 303–22.

[26] A list of the congregations that more closely collaborate with the [central] administration is found in the *Archiepiscopale bononiense*, Part vi, 436[a]. An earlier version of the list (A.A.B., H.537, fol. 99[v]) contains as well the congregations of Christian doctrine and of the nurses, which were probably crossed off because of their nonadministrative functions. Extraordinary congregations were created from time to time to meet specific needs, e.g. one for the plague.

all follow a pattern of organization similar to that of the *Congregation on Reform*, which includes the suffragan (in the absence of the bishop himself), the vicar general, the archdeacon, several canons, several regular and secular priests, and occasionally even laymen, "depending on the matter under consideration." It makes recommendations for edicts concerning everything pertaining to reform, for example, the revision of titles to benefices, the residence obligations and moral conduct of the clergy, the rules on Easter communion.[27]

Alongside these congregations, which are true organs of administration, there are others defined more precisely as "congregations or sodalities." These are spiritual or charitable organizations whose activities are not limited to the members themselves, but extend beyond the membership in the service of the church as a whole. The most important of them is without doubt the *Congregation for the Teaching of Christian Doctrine* in the city, with six hundred members and forty schools.[28] The *Congregation of Perseverance*, which carries on its activities among university students, is also very active. There are also congregations for prisoners, for the sick—and for so many similar tasks that they cover almost every spiritual and material need of the population. In the structure of the social body of Christians as envisaged by the Tridentine restoration, the confraternities are much more than merely a link between the top and the bottom of the church. They are the first step toward the creation of bodies endowed with a spontaneous vitality of their own and charged with representing the community of which they are part. Of the two lay overseers to be elected by each church in Bologna, for example, one is appointed by the bishop and the other by the community

[27] I believe that this congregation developed out of a *consulta segreta* composed of the bishop, the vicar, the visitor general, the secretary, and the Jesuit Fr. Palmio, which already existed at the beginning of Paleotti's tenure. Palmio reported on this body in a letter to Father General Borgia of 8 July 1570: Roman Archive of the Society of Jesus, Epistolae Italiae, 139, fol. 83. . . .

[28] This organization deserves a study in itself because of the abundance of material it might furnish regarding the youth of the age. There are many documents concerning it in the Archepiscopal Archive.

in which the church is located. If, as in the city, an organized community does not exist, they are elected "by the Society of the Holy Sacrament or by some other lay congregation."[29] The Company of the Name of God, similarly, has the functions of a preparatory tribunal for resolving disputes before they appear in court. And the members meet at headquarters in the archbishop's palace three times a week to hear and discuss cases.[30]

A special emphasis on the social aspects of Christian life, therefore, is characteristic of the Bolognese diocesan organization. All the faithful are usually considered as members of certain social groups; and these groups, organized into specific associations, constitute the means whereby the bishop reaches the souls of individuals. Hence Paleotti's tendency to call to his side as collaborators the representatives of the various bodies of Christian society.

One of the most important collegiate organs of administration is the *Congregazione dell'Economia*, or finance board. Paleotti was moved both by his desire to dedicate himself completely to the care of souls and by the canonical provisions for maintaining control of the property entrusted to him for the service of the church and of the poor.[31] He therefore did not just appoint a financial officer (*economo*), as did Borromeo at exactly the same time and with his advice. He also created a collegiate body. In the first project, drawn up probably in April 1579, the congregation is given powers of decision as well as the task simply of over-

---

[29] The statutes Paleotti wrote for the Society of Corpus Christi also mention the particularly active role of the laity, especially in Part v: "De pauperum custodia aliisque Parochiae necessitatibus" (*Archiepiscopale bononiense*, Part II, fol. 135). Vezzini, *op. cit.* (above, in n. 22) p .107, mentions these confraternities, which were already very numerous in Bologna before the advent of Paleotti. But he considers them to be totally subject to the ecclesiastical hierarchy.

[30] "Capitoli et regole sopra l'audite, trattare et concordare lite et differentia per gli huomini della Compagnia del Santissimo Nome di Dio in Bologna," by A. Benacci, 1575 ("Governo archiepiscopale," fol. 32ᵛ).

[31] *Decretum Gratiani*, dist. 89, c. IV, *Corpus Juris Canonici*, ed. A. Friedberg (Leipzig, 1879), Vol. I, p. 312—from canon 26 of the Council of Chalcedon. Thomassin, *op. cit.*, Vol. III, Book II. . . .

seeing, in whatever regard, the financial aspects of the tribunal and of the maintenance of the cardinal's household. Its members are to be chosen from among the officers of the *Monte di Pietà* (state bank). The criticism of this project by the Jesuit Francesco Palmio, one of Paleotti's principal collaborators, has survived. Instead of a congregation, Palmio calls for the appointment of a domestic financial counselor, who should be completely subject to the bishop and whose work should not be regulated by any formal rules by which the bishop might be bound. Evil tongues, says Palmio, there will always be. "[But] it does not seem to me that you need take such precautions about limiting yourself in the realm of finances, though of course I am very pleased that you should do all you can to justify your actions." The institution of financial advisors according to the project, continues the Jesuit, would certainly furnish a good example to other bishops. But the "reasons for a negative judgment" are weightier:

1. It [i.e. the reform] should not be done, because the canon law mentioned is not in use, and other good and holy bishops do not do it, and therefore many will judge this action as an extraordinary departure from normal practice.
2. Because the Council of Trent has not restated or confirmed the said canon, although it has been most precise, as may clearly be seen, on other matters of reform.
3. Because this action may not be pleasing to many prelates, and above all, it may not be approved by the Court of Rome. By common consent, it seems well to abide by what is decided in Rome [even] with regard to things that are good or indifferent or that are not binding under sin. Hence it would perhaps be better, before putting this project into practice, to send it around to the better and more prudent prelates of that Court.
4. It would give occasion to laymen, particularly of the lower classes, to criticize other bishops who do not act in this manner.
5. Many simple persons, and others who are not very well disposed toward ecclesiastics and especially toward rich prelates, may get it in their heads that the heretics are right when

they falsely say that the goods of the church should be distributed to the poor and that bishops and other prelates should live in poverty as they do.

6. Electing the financial advisors in the way projected will subject the bishop to them; and even though they are bound to administer the goods of the church according to the will of the bishop, nonetheless it might easily come about that they censure him when he does something they do not approve of.

7. This may turn out to be prejudicial to your successors, whom you should take into consideration.

8. Because it is possible to fulfill both the prescriptions of the canon and the obligations the canon laws on the bishop without putting yourself so much into the hands of the financial officers. Speaking generally, therefore, I do not think it good to commit this matter to the officers of the *Monte di Pietà*. It would be better to appoint directly several clergymen, who would be totally dependent upon the bishop and thus pleasant and trustworthy as well, of course, as good, prudent, and diligent—these being qualities necessary for such an office—and they would be known as such by everyone in the city. So much for the matter in general.[32]

Paleotti accepted only a few of Palmio's criticisms, namely, those which corresponded to the ones Borromeo also brought up in a letter,[33] and those which regarded the details, rather than the substance, of his idea. In the synod of June 1579 he proceeded to set up the congregation and to establish, though somewhat loosely, its powers:[34]

Judging that the matter should be allowed to mature, His Lordship does not intend at present to do other than provide

[32] The text of the project that Palmio criticizes has been lost. His criticisms are preceded by a letter to Paleotti and followed by "several reasons that show why it is not fitting that the Most Illustrious and Reverend Archbishop eat every day with the members of his household": A.A.B., G.537, fols. 154–59ᵛ. [Palmio continually mixes Latin into the basically Italian text.]

[33] Only Paleotti's answer to Borromeo, of 19 September 1579, has survived: Biblioteca Ambrosiana, Milan, F. 74 bis., inf., fol. 420....

[34] "Instruttione per gl'Economi deputati al governo delle cose temporali del Vescovato di Bologna ordinata nella Sinodo diocesana del mese di giugno 1579": A.A.B., H.537, fols. 142ʳ–46.

the basis for what day-to-day experience may show to be the best. . . . He has thus set down the following bylaws, which will be altered or changed from time to time according to whatever future practice may show to be expedient.

On the basis of these instructions, and from the description of the office written several years later in the "Governo archiepiscopale," it is possible to draw a complete picture of the activity of the congregation. There are four finance officers: two cathedral canons, one canon from St. Petronius, and one "wise clergyman." Their responsibility is collegiate. They meet at least once a week in the episcopal palace to discuss all matters regarding the "table" (*mensa*), of which they administer, under the supreme authority of the bishop, the entire endowment. All the income must be exchanged for money and deposited in the *Monte di Pietà*, the officers of which are advisors for technical questions. No money may be withdrawn from the *Monte* without an authorization by two of the officers; and sums superior to 100 *scudi* require the signature of the bishop as well. Even the officers in charge of the expenses of the bishop's household, though their responsibilities were not, in the end, turned over to the finance officers as called for in the original project, must request disbursements in the same manner so that the most minute payments can be checked. The same applies to the priest in charge of distributing charity. Beyond the expenses that are absolutely necessary for the maintenance of the church and the episcopal palace, all income belongs to the poor and to charitable institutions. Hence the finance officers "are in all expenditures to avoid any excess, which would do nothing but rob the poor and other worthy works of what is rightly theirs." The bishop reserves the right to withdraw certain sums by his own personal authority for the assistance of the "poor and miserable." "Nonetheless," points out the "Governo archiepiscopale," "this has never been done except in very small quantities, since the archbishop wishes them [the officers] to be informed of everything."

Still in 1590, in the report on the state of the diocese presented to the Congregation of the Council [in Rome] on the occasion of the archbishop's visit *ad limina*,[35] it is noted: "The entire income of the archiepiscopal table is administered by the four ecclesiastical finance officers; and all affairs are executed, looked into, and treated through instructions signed by them."[36] In the summary of the rules printed in the *Archiepiscopale bononiense* of 1594, the power of the finance officers seems to be in decline. The drafts [now] "are prepared by a financial specialist (*ratiocinatore . . . scientibus œconomis*) and countersigned by the "Illustrious Archbishop," as well as by one or the other of the said officers, when they exceed sums ordinarily expended by twenty-five pounds." Only for sums inferior to twenty-five *scudi* are the signatures of the officers alone sufficient. Evidently the *ratiocinator*, or technical advisor, has risen in importance as the congregation on finance has declined. In fact, the congregation disappeared entirely shortly after the death of Paleotti. In a report of 1610 on the state of the table we find simply these words:

> Cardinal Paleotti formerly set up a congregation with the name of *Economia* to handle the administration of income, and [he charged it] with reporting on the state of property and income and on contracts for rents, etc.; but for the last seven or eight years it has not functioned, and the accounts are kept by a secretary.[37]

The difficulties I have encountered during my research on the Catholic Reform in Bologna have led me to trace out these short outlines . . . and to pose the question once again: what was the evolution of diocesan organization in the sixteenth century? A lacuna on this point can compromise a complete understanding of the Catholic Reform. Certainly a study of the earlier period

[35] [The periodic visits to Rome of all bishops required by the decrees of Trent (but not very frequently observed in practice).]

[36] "Relatio Status Ecclesiae Archiep. Bonon. Facta Sacrae Congregationi Ill. morum DD. Cardinalium super Rebus Concilii. Die 8 Februari 1590"; A.A.B., uncatalogued papers in the file of the archivist (in copy).

[37] "Relatione dell'Arcivescovo di Bologna," fol. 4: A.A.B., L.54—a manuscript of the seventeenth century of 182 fols. The passage is taken from a report presented to Cardinal Scipione Caffarelli Borghese upon his appointment as archbishop of Bologna.

will be necessary to fill it up. Only much more careful attention to the history of ecclesiastical institutions can enable us to understand a movement that affected the entire structure of the Church at the time. Particularly important for this purpose are the years immediately following the Council of Trent—years in which the individual pastors who felt themselves responsible for, and jointly the creators of, the reform movement most vigorously imposed their own particular personalities on the instruments that they themselves forged. Their action in those years was not yet incorporated into the rigid juridical formulas which were soon to crystallize from what they—and especially the greatest and most significant of them, Charles Borromeo—had worked out in practice. In this short examination of the diocesan organization of Bologna, I have tried to bring out those elements that seemed to be original. . . . These elements may be an example of the vitality that the Tridentine Reform manifested, even in the rather limited field of ecclesiastical reconstruction.

10 Submission and Conformity: "Nicodemism" and the Expectations of a Conciliar Solution to the Religious Question[1]

DELIO CANTIMORI

AMONG those Italians of the sixteenth century who accepted the new doctrines of the Protestants, the heretics, or the Valdesians,[2] there were many who assumed an attitude that was largely practical, though it was occasionally provided with a rudimentary theoretical justification. This attitude was called "Nicodemism." In France and also in Italy two distinct groups participated in one way or another in what was for a long time thereafter called—without much thought being given to the propriety of the term—the "Reformation." On one side were the audacious preachers of the new faith. On the other side [in the words of Adolfo Omodeo] were

> those who preferred to disguise their convictions behind an outward conformity to Catholic rites. The name given them, "Nicodemites," was coined by one of their most vigorous opponents, Calvin. Calvin borrowed the name from the lawyer in the Gospels, Nicodemus, who visited the Lord at night for fear of the Jews and who thus, in Calvin's commentary, devalued Christianity, the religion of the light and the truth.[3]

[1] " 'Nicodemismo' e speranze conciliari nel Cinquecento italiano," first published in *Contributi alla storia del Concilio di Trento e della Controriforma*, "Quaderni di Belfagor" (see above, ch. 8, n. 13), pp. 14–23, and then reprinted in Cantimori's *Studi di storia*, pp. 518–36. The title is extended somewhat in translation to make it clearer to the English-speaking reader.

[2] [Somewhat abridged in translation, since these terms, defined by examples in the original, have already been explained in ch. 8.]

[3] Omodeo, *Giovanni Calvino e la Riforma in Ginevra* (Bari: Laterza, 1947), p. 47; see Robert Nigel Carew Hunt, *Calvino* (Bari: Laterza, 1939) [from the original *Calvin* (London: Centenary Press, 1933)], pp. 33 and 267.

Calvin's two treatises against the Nicodemites are full of harsh sarcasm. He calls them "cultivated notaries," and he accuses them of talking Christianity with the ladies, with spinning out Platonic Ideas, and with sitting by idly in the hope that "some good reform will be adopted" instead of openly bearing witness to their faith. The French Nicodemites belonged, as Calvin pointed out, to the educated circles of the courts and universities. They did not belong to the lower classes, which were more easily impelled to action and less able to hide personal convictions.[4] The Italians who assumed such attitudes also belonged to these circles. Casadei says that even the Valdesians fell into this category, although he does not think that Calvin's terms are applicable to them. "Calvin," says Casadei, "called Nicodemites those believers who remained attached to the old superstitions, out of fright, calculation, or interest, even though they had been enlightened by the light of grace." But he thinks they should more properly be called "reformists," since they sought to mediate between the old and the new, between tradition and revolution. Casadei's reservations seem to be valid with regard to the Valdesians and to the many friends and followers of Erasmus. These men were much more interested in mediating between conflicting forces than in [upholding] specific doctrines. They were more logically coherent than Calvin's "cultivated notaries." They were also more coherent than that very cultivated notary Pietro Carnesecchi[5] and the great ladies of the early Catholic Reform movement. And when the moment of combat arrived, they were denied justice. "Counter Reformation Catholicism," Casadei continues, "fought the Valdesians with the same fury it fought the Protestants; and the Protestants in turn had little but disdain for the Valdesians, even

[4] Omodeo, *op. cit.*, pp. 45 ff.

[5] [Carnesecchi (1508-67) was a Florentine patrician and long-time secretary to the second duke of Florence, Cosimo I de' Medici. After protecting him for years, in spite of his known heterodox religious views, his patron finally yielded him to Pope Pius V, partly out of a conviction that Carnesecchi actually was a heretic and partly in exchange for the title of grand duke of Tuscany. The latest, although not yet completely satisfactory, biography of him is by Oddone Ortolani, *P.C.* (Florence: Le Monnier, 1963).]

while appreciating their intelligence, their honesty, and their spirit of toleration toward dissidents."[6] It is, moreover, much easier to understand the efforts of the Erasmians on behalf of reconciliation and compromise than to understand the casuistry of the true Nicodemites as it is expressed, for example, in the questions Lelio Sozzini posed to Calvin in 1549.[7]

Calvin's treatises against the French Nicodemites were written in 1543 and 1544. Just as the second, and more famous, of them was being published, many of the accused had begun seeking the opinion of Luther, Melanchthon, and Bucer, since they thought Calvin's opinion too severe and too inhuman.[8] In 1549–50 Calvin replied, in response to a request from the French Calvinists, by publishing a Latin translation of his two treatises (along with an appendix which repeated his arguments and his call for firmness and coherence); and he added the opinions, not of Luther, who had died in 1546, but of Bucer, Melanchthon, and even Pier Martire Vermigli.[9] The book is best known by the title *On Avoiding Superstition—De Vitandis Superstitionibus*. The presence

---

[6] ["Juan de Valdés," *Religio*, XIV (1838)], p. 121.

[7] Cantimori, *Eretici italiani*, pp. 134 ff. [Lelio Sozzini, son of the famous jurist Mariano, was born in Siena in 1525, studied at Padua, and subsequently traveled all over Europe, engaging in theological discussions and writing a number of treatises. He died at Zürich in 1562. From him and from his more famous nephew Fausto (1539–1604), who finally emigrated to Poland, derives the sect of Anti-Trinitarians originally known as Socinians and then, in its English version, as Unitarians. See above, ch. 1, n. 25.]

[8] *Correspondence des réformateurs dans les pays de langue française* . . . , ed. Aimé Louis Herminjard, Vol. IX (1543–44) (Geneva: H. Georg, 1897), pp. 310, 313, 340, 348, and 444. Cf. Calvin, *Opera Omnia* (Brunswick: Schwetschke, 1863–1900), Vol. XX, p. 579; Vol. XI: Letter of Capsius to Calvin at the end of 1544; Vol. VI, cols. 596 and 638. The *Excuse* was republished in 1921 in Paris; the *Traité du fidèle parmi les Papistes* appears in Calvin, *Homme d'Église* (Geneva, 1936), pp. 192 ff.

[9] [Vermigli (1500–62) was a humanist and religious leader in close contact with Valdés and his circle and actively engaged in practical reform within his Augustinian order. He left Italy during the first wave of persecution in 1542 and resided at various times in Strasbourg, England, and finally Zürich, where he was professor of Hebrew and theology. He became a staunch Calvinist and represented the Calvinist position at the Conference of Poissy in 1561. See now the book by McNair cited above, ch. 8, n. 18.]

of Vermigli seems to reveal an intention to spread the work in Italy. For the Italian Reformers were just then being troubled by the case of Francesco Spiera [an Italian Lutheran who had abjured in 1548 and who had then so repented of his abjuration that he became certain of being among the damned].[10] Vergerio drew from the case a special lesson for them:

> And it must be noted carefully that Christ and the Truth can be denied in many ways. This is precisely the lesson that Spiera used to teach us. We deny Christ when, having been called before the courts of the Pharisees, we deny Him when we know the Truth and yet by our presence consent to and approve of forms of worship that are false and illicit. And we deny Him when, having felt within us the divine regeneration, we still willingly remain submerged in vice and sin, thus soiling the temple of the living God which we are.[11]

To know the truth and still go about consenting and approving false and illicit forms of worship—that, in its most general form, was the phenomenon of Nicodemism.

SOME ITALIAN NICODEMITES

Nicodemism in its more specific, conscious form appeared in Italy about five years after the publication in Latin of Calvin's

---

[10] [The clause is added to explain what is merely referred to as the "case" in the original.]

[11] Quoted in E. Comba, *I nostri protestanti*, Vol. II: "Durante la Riforma nel Veneto e nell'Istria" (Florence, 1897), p. 281. See the "Storia di Francesco Spiera" in *Biblioteca della Riforma italiana: Raccolta di scritti evangelici del secolo XVI*, Vol. II (Rome and Florence, 1883). Spiera was a chief citizen of Cittadella, near Padua, and had a wife and eleven children when he was summoned before Della Casa [the same Giovanni Della Casa (1503–56) who was papal legate to Venice and author of the famous guide book to good manners, the *Galateo*]: "At times he seemed to want to declare his opinions openly and hide nothing. At other times he thought rather of saving us from this danger by going as soon as possible out of the country, leaving his property and children behind. Finally, after a long internal battle, he decided upon dissimulation. He would keep his opinions firmly but secretly in his heart and with his mouth say something else, namely, exactly what the legate wished him to say. And so he did." (p. 113.)

treatises. . . . We have three clear indications of its existence. First, there is the letter of Celso Martinengo to the Genoese Carmelite Angelo Castiglione of 1554. There are the references of the old historians of the Waldensians to the danger of persecution around 1555. Finally, there is the small controversial treatise of a Waldensian pastor and chronicler of the persecutions, the Neapolitan Scipione Lentulo. This treatise, unknown until now, presents us with many of the arguments used by the true Nicodemites to justify their positions.

Martinengo, the pastor of the Italian community at Geneva, mentions Nicodemism at the very beginning of his letter. He reproaches his friend, who eight years before seemed to have accepted the new faith but who now has openly preached against it:

> And you think that you can make us believe you are a Christian when you constantly deny [being a disciple of Christ] and when you remain within the halls of Papism! You deceive yourself! If you did not deny it, you might possibly pass, though falsely, as a Nicodemus, behind whose mantle so many witless men do [not] blush to hide themselves! But you deny Christ openly. . . .[12]

And he explains further:

> The preachers of Italy (and I also have been one) live in that error, thinking to be excused for these two reasons. One, that they may help their brothers who live in the states of Italy.[13] The other, because they say they insist upon the affirmative [i.e. upon positive points of doctrine], even though they say nothing about the negative [i.e. ways in which their doctrinal position differs from the Catholic]. As for the first, I say: Cursed be that charity which destroys the faith! We must help our neighbors, true, but we must not thereby dishonor God. . . . As for

[12] A. Pascal, "Una breve polemica fra il riformatore Celso Martinengo e fra Angelo Castigliono da Genova," *Bulletin de la Société d'histoire vaudoise* [now the *Bollettino della Società di studi valdesi*], xxxv (1915), 77 ff. [The emendations in brackets are Cantimori's, who explains:] I have inserted the "not"; for otherwise Pascal's text does not make sense. . . .

[13] [*in quel stato*. Here as elsewhere in this passage I paraphrase a bit in order to make the meaning clearer to the modern reader.]

the second, I say that there was once a time when our enemies permitted it. But no longer: for they now prescribe the subjects of our sermons. Hence this loophole has been closed. The only explanation left is that these men are held back either by ambition or by an attachment to earthly comforts. This motive has long been there and has acted like so many chains, even though they were not visible because they were covered up by professions of the first two reasons. But the knife of persecution has revealed the secret motives of many. . . .[14]

In other words, Martinengo reproaches Castiglione for not even being a Nicodemite any longer—for going completely over to the enemy camp and for now preaching against Protestant doctrine. At the same time, Martinengo takes the opportunity to criticize Nicodemism as being no longer in accord with the times. To be sure, he may well have been sympathetic to Nicodemism before his flight from Italy. His criticism of it, indeed, rests on two arguments. One argument is religious and is typically Calvinistic: "Cursed be that charity which destroys the faith! We must help our neighbors, true; but we must not thereby dishonor God. . . ." The other argument may be called political in the broad sense of the term. Given the situation in Italy—so the argument runs—it may have been useful to insist solely on the affirmative and drop for the moment the negative—to talk positively about the new truths, that is, and put aside denouncing errors and superstitions. But the situation has now changed. The enemy has begun to counterattack. It is he who now establishes the subjects of discussion, and we, dragged onto his terrain, must face them openly. Hence the tactics of setting forth the positive principles of the new faith without drawing from them the consequent criticism of the old faith is no longer viable. If we try applying it now, we will be forced to adapt ourselves to the affirmative arguments of our enemies—to the point, indeed, of accepting their arguments in substance; and the tactic will thus be robbed of all effectiveness. Hence, utility can no longer be used to justify a Nicodemite position. And those who remain Nicodemites do so for two

[14] Pascal, *op. cit.*, p. 84.

reasons only: ambition and an excessive regard for personal convenience. There is no longer any need to hold back denunciations of the Roman Church and of "Papist superstition." There is no need to disguise references to Luther and Calvin and to avoid open, explicit formulations of the faith. And the only reason that can be assigned to those who continue to do so is that of personal egotism.

Egotism, of course, had been there all along—so Martinengo seems to confess. We simply did not notice it because it was hidden behind expressions of charity for others, of a desire to avoid scandalizing the weak of spirit, of a plan to penetrate sections of society [that might have been offended by open polemics]. Martinengo might well have cited some of the most famous writings of the Italian heretical movement as examples of this "only affirmative" approach: the *Beneficio di Cristo* and the *Alfabeto Cristiano* (*Christian Alphabet*) of Valdés.[15] In the *Alfabeto*, after all, the purpose of attendance at Mass and the other sacraments is skillfully reduced to that of providing an occasion for interior spiritual exercises.... Often in such treatises charity is made superior to faith. Charity is defined in its broadest sense as the love of one's neighbor and the practice of evangelical virtues according to the theme of "imitation,"[16] and faith is defined as the knowledge of religious truths. So it is in the polemical treatise of Giorgio Siculo against the Protestant interpretation of the Spiera case: the treatise sets forth the doctrine of Nicodemism without actually mentioning the name.[17]

About the same time as Martinengo's letter, we have information from Pierre Gilles[18] about letters from the pastors of Geneva

[15] [See ch. 8, n. 18, above.]

[16] [Cantimori uses the Latin word *imitatio* here in its Renaissance sense to mean not copying or following uncritically, but taking inspiration from another through contact with him as a person, in order to stimulate one's own creativity.]

[17] See Cantimori, *Eretici italiani*, pp. 57–70.

[18] [This Pierre Gilles is not the specialist on the topography of Constantinople, but a Reformed pastor whose only published work (1st edn., Geneva, 1644) is cited below at n. 20.]

to the Waldensians of the Valleys,[19] some open letters and others addressed to individual persons. These letters were intended as a refutation of the "vain reasons and pernicious opinions" of a priest who had accepted the reformed doctrines but who, when the persecutions came, "tried to turn whomever he could away from Christian zeal." Zeal, said the good Calvinist Gilles, meant "never disguising the known truth, but rather making an open profession of it and persevering in it until death." We have no other information about these letters except what is in Gilles and in the early historians of the Waldensian persecutions. Apparently the author was a certain Domenico Baronio, a Florentine who taught at Valgrana under the protection of Massimiliano, the lord of Valgrana and Cervignase and a relative of the marquis of Saluzzo.[20] This Baronio supposedly published many anti-Catholic polemical writings. Many of them he distributed under the name of his protector; and in one of them, the *Constitutions humaines*, he included a sharp condemnation of the Mass. But at the same time he held that in moments of great danger one might disguise one's true thoughts and even attend Mass, though without approving in one's heart of the errors one beheld. In such moments a minister of the Truth should teach his disciples to distinguish the chaff from the grain, to hate the one and love the other. But he should also teach them to leave all overt action and exterior expressions of religious conviction to the Lord, without exposing themselves and others to danger. . . .

It is impossible to tell from Gilles's account whether Baronio was a priest who tried to adapt, as a first step toward an open profession, some of the exterior rites of the Reformers, or whether he was a Reformed minister who set forth a Nicodemite doctrine. Nor is there evidence to justify the judgment of Giovanni Jalla. "This was a commodious doctrine," Jalla declared. "So well did it reconcile the pleasures of life with the dictates of conscience that it

---

[19] [The valleys of the Piedmontese Alps, where the Waldensians had taken refuge during the persecutions in the Middle Ages. See above, ch. 8, n. 17.]

[20] [Saluzzo lies to the south of the Waldensian regions of Piedmont. It was under French control during much of the sixteenth century.]

won him many disciples, especially among the well-to-do." There is no evidence, that is, except the continuing benevolence of Baronio's protector and Martinengo's condemnation, in terms similar to those of Jalla, of ambition and comfort-seeking under the guise of religion. What is certain, however, is that doctrines like those of Baronio acquired a considerable following in the Waldensian Valleys—in an area, that is, where resistance to religious oppression had so long a tradition. They were first introduced, moreover, not by a "beard," as the Waldensians of the Valleys were called, but by a foreigner, a "Florentine."[21]

What might have been his more detailed arguments may be gathered from the *Risposta*—"Reply according to the Pure and Sole Word of God to the False Arguments and Objections Made by the Prudent and the Wise of This World Against the True Faithful"—inserted by Scipione Lentulo in his *History of the Great and Cruel Persecutions Done in Our Times in Provence, Calabria, and Piedmont Against the People Called Waldensians [. . .]*.[22] We cannot and we ought not to resist persecution—so says the *Risposta*. It is useless even to flee; for abandoning goods, family, fatherland, and friends is hardly a sign of Christian charity. Actually, we are not asked to deny Christ, like the early Christians. We are only asked to accept one form of the worship of Christ rather than another. We have never studied theology and certainly cannot know more about it than the theologians. But we need not be deceived. If God granted salvation only to those who fled from persecution and gave up Catholicism, it would be a great cruelty on his part. Not

[21] Gilles, *Histoire ecclésiastique des églises vaudoises*, Vol. I (Pinerolo: Chiantore e Mascarelli, 1881), pp. 100–5 and 412–13; Jean Léger, *Histoire générale des églises aevangéliques des vallées de Piémont, ou vaudoises* (Leiden, 1669), Part II, pp. 52 ff. Léger's account differs from that of Gilles, which I have followed, in some particulars. Léger goes so far as to mention "many famous Nicodemites." Baronio, he says, used all his eloquence "to persuade those of the Religion that they could in good conscience pretend [. . .] that they wished to be good Roman Catholics when it came to saving thereby their lives and their goods.' Jalla accepts this judgment in his *Storia della Riforma in Piemonte fino alla morte di Emanuele Filiberto (1517–1580)* (Florence: Claudiana, 1914 [–36]), [Vol. I], p. 271.

[22] Published by Teofilo Gay (Pinerolo, 1906).

even the Protestants, after all, are of holy and irreprehensible life. Hence their religion is no better than the old one. Where, moreover, are the miracles that attest the truth of the new doctrines? Abandoning father, mother, brothers, and country is inhuman: "and what is it to you to kneel at Mass, doing as the others do, when you may believe in your heart what you please?"

Lentulo's answers are the usual ones of Protestant controversial literature, and they need not be repeated here. They do, however, have a particular vivacity, as when the author replies to the observation about the morality of Protestants. "It is true," he says, "and it cannot be denied that there are some who act like good companions when they first come among us, some out of fear, some because they are libertines, some because they are hypocrites. But when we discover them, we castigate them severely; [while among you such people are pardoned and justified.]"

The following words from the reply to the last, and typically Nicodemite, objection are worth quoting.

> We who follow the doctrine of the Holy Scriptures pay no attention, in matters of religion, to crowns, scepters, purple vestments, or human knowledge. St. Paul says: For you see, brothers, our vocation. Among us there are not many who are wise according to the flesh, not many who are powerful, not many nobles. But God has chosen the foolish things of the world to put the wise to shame. God has chosen the weak things of the world to put to shame the strong. And God has elected the lowly things of the world, and those that are considered as nothing [...] to annul those things that are considered of worth. All this [He has done] so that nothing of the flesh will be glorified before Him. The same Apostle affirms that the doctrine of the Holy Gospel he preached was wisdom not of this world, nor of the princes of this world: for none of the princes of this world has known it. And experience shows us that almost always the princes of this world and the wise have persecuted the true religion, while the humble and the ignorant have embraced it with all their heart. . . . It is true that today there are princes who call themselves Christians and who have given themselves titles that express not only excellence and sublimity,

but also special piety. One calls himself "Most Christian," the others "Catholic," "Defenders of the Faith," and what not. If the name alone of religion were sufficient, you would be right: that we err in not obeying their commands in matters of religion. But the Word of God teaches us that not those who say, "Lord, Lord" will enter into the Kingdom of Heaven, but those who do the will of the Heavenly Father. . . . Hence, when they command us to act contrary to piety and honesty, we must follow the rule of St. Peter, to obey God rather than men. We do not mean that subjects should revolt and rebel against their princes; but we say that pious subjects must rather die or go into voluntary exile than obey their princes who order them to do impious and immoral things.[23]

Lentulo's argument seems to justify what has been said above about the character of Baronio. In fact . . . it could apply just as well either to those ordinary believers who have let themselves be carried away by Nicodemite tendencies or to those who have been persuaded by Catholic preachers. That it did so apply seems to be corroborated by the probable policy of the civil and political authorities to prevent the depopulation of the Valleys.

The Exhortation to Martyrdom, as it is commonly called,[24] of Giulio Della Rovere is much vaster in extent. It was accompanied by a small treatise on a theme that Vermigli had also written about: "Whether It is Permitted to Flee from Persecution for Reasons of Faith." The question is similar to the one considered in the conclusion of the treatise by Lentulo. But Della Rovere decides against flight. Then he goes much further:

This is no longer the time to dispute and to argue about the faith. By now each of us should be a doctor [of theology]. Now is the time to do deeds, to follow Christ with the cross on our shoulders and prepare ourselves to go resolutely to martyrdom.

[23] Bern, Stadtbibliothek, Cod. Bernensis 716, fol. 112ʳ ff. [I translate directly from Lentulo's version of the biblical passage, needless to say, rather than inserting a modern English version.]
[24] Comba, *I nostri protestanti*, p. 167.

Instead, he continues, our Italians deny Christ as soon as they are in trouble. They deny him "with all their force." And they then go back to confessing Him—that is, to professing Calvinist doctrines —as soon as they arrive "in the cantons" [of Switzerland]. There are examples of Italian martyrs, to be sure; and even Della Rovere admits having gone into exile rather than facing martyrdom. Yet notwithstanding strong suggestions that he withdraw from the debate, he also brings up the difficult question of whether and when a Christian might flee in case he is threatened with persecution because of his faith. His answer is this: Those preachers who are itinerant may justifiably flee; but those who have a fixed residence may not abandon their churches. The faithful, moreover, should follow the example of the pastors. Yet because of the particular conditions of their country, this severe rule cannot be rigorously applied to Italians:

> The Christians of Italy are like dead and scattered members, without guidance and without a head, since the Italian churches are neither organized nor regulated according to the Word of God. [. . .] The Gospel is banished among them; and they see little sense in suffering persecution when they do not feel the living Christ in their hearts. [. . .] If the Italians got together, if they were united into a body regulated according to the Word of God, they also would be inflamed by the faith. . . .[25]

But rarely is the Word of God, the soul and the life of the Church, preached in the Italian Reformed congregations, nor are the sacraments, the backbone of the Church, regularly administered.

> How then can these congregations take up arms to fight for Jesus Christ? That the greater part of Italy is devoid even of a trace of the Church gives rise to this disorder, in which everyone thinks himself permitted to live as he pleases. [. . .] It is not surprising, then, that at the slightest breath of a contrary wind, the Italians tremble, became frightened, and voluntarily deny their faith.

[25] *Ibid.*, p. 174.

WHAT THE NICODEMITES HOPED FOR FROM A
CHURCH COUNCIL

It was not only a question of abjurations, of repeated and insistent negations, of the use of generic and evasive formulas like the responses to the questions of the Inquisitors. Often, as Comba has noted, "in this drama of the Reformation, the Alps appeared to be a curtain, with the actors on one side and the spectators on the other. Lucio Paolo Roselli, who encouraged the Reformers to persevere, providing that he be allowed to follow them with his eyes only, is typical in this respect."[26] Roselli's letter to Melanchthon is sonorous and solemn. But his positive action consisted in a few little pamphlets that proceed in the usual "affirmative" manner without a word of polemics or open declarations. And when a number of Protestant writings, some of which he had translated, were found in his house, he retracted and abjured.

The situation, then, was one of disorder: congregations without pastors to preach the word and administer the sacraments, the absence of a hierarchy capable of bringing together the various congregations, uncertainty about doctrine and little consciousness of the importance of theoretical formulations, confusion about what action to take in critical moments, the sort of indifference that evoked Calvin's wrath, a spirit of resignation before the inevitable, a tendency to engage in subtleties, a feeling of satisfaction with a private, personal, "interior reformation" on the level of piety and morality. These were the elements of Nicodemism in the strict sense, and the substance also of Nicodemism in the more general sense. The same impulse that drove some into exile abroad or into an "exile" at home of carefully disguised convictions and false abjurations—this same impulse led others to look for a way out of suffering and persecution through the intervention of an exterior force. For those who lost hope in a sudden change in the general political situation or a sudden action by some powerful personage, or for those who never had nurtured

[26] *Ibid.*, pp. 185 and 642.

any such hopes, there remained the hope in a council—the hope in eventual action from the more moderate and theologically more "modern" elements of the Council of Trent, the hope that the council, however it might be assembled, would resolve the conflicts, make the "true faith" win, or at least put an end to the persecutions.

They first placed their hopes in the Council of Trent. Giorgio Siculo proposed bringing his revelations before the Fathers; and far from fearing to attract restless spirits and future heretics, the Inquisitor of Ferrara seems even to have approved of him.[27] The hopes of the visionaries and the prophets, moreover, were shared by the great ladies Giulia Gonzaga and Vittoria Colonna, by prelates like Carnesecchi, and by the well-known circles of the Valdesians and the Erasmians. These hopes did not vanish after the disappointment over the way in which the first sessions of the Council were being conducted. They did not vanish even after the close of the Council in 1563, even though the more moderate Fathers had been forced to yield, either before overwhelming theological arguments or before political pressure and considerations of opportunism.[28] We need only remember what Comba has written about the last part of Bartolomeo Fonzio's *Fidei et Doctrinae Ratio* (*An Explanation of Faith and Doctrine*), a work first sketched out in Rome about 1540 at the request of the commission of cardinals charged with examining Fonzio's doctrine, and elaborated during his imprisonment in Venice, just before the execution of his death sentence, in 1562.

The religious career of Fonzio was constantly tormented by uncertainty and moments of repentance, by trials and abjurations; and it is similar in many ways to that of Carnesecchi. Toward the end of his *Ratio* he takes up the question of the council. He suggests

[27] Chabod, *Per la storia religiosa dello Stato di Milano durante il dominio di Carlo V* (Bologna, 1938), p. 204 [p. 244 of the 2nd edn., cited above, ch. 7, n. 27. The report on the Inquisitor's attitude is from the abjuration of Pietro Bresciani, dated 1552.]

[28] B. Croce, introduction to his edition of the *Alfabeto Cristiano* of Valdés [(Bari: Laterza, 1938)]. Jedin, in *Girolamo Seripando*, also gives a good picture of the Valdesian circles and includes a bibliography.

the election of the members by a more direct participation of the faithful and a provision for making it permanent, either through continuous sessions or through regular reconvocations. He does not think that it is infallible or that its authority should be exaggerated. But he does think that the council can be rendered perfect. Yet from what Comba says, it seems as if Fonzio's hopes begin to turn, toward the end, not so much toward Trent as toward another council, a council which he expected to be very different from the one actually in session. "Unless this is merely an echo of former aspirations," says Comba, "the first disappointments did not shatter the eternal mirage of the conciliators. . . . What is certain is that he looked now for something better than the Council of Trent."29

THE SUBTLETIES OF THE "NOTARIES"

The question placed in the mouth of one of the interlocutors in Aconcio's *Dialogo del Riccamati* is characteristic [of late Nicodemism]. Since exile, he says, is extremely painful and full of perils and uncertainties, "would it not be less bad to avoid all these calamities (each one of which is very great) by waiting until a free and holy council is assembled which might clarify the truth without exposing us to danger? For sooner or later such a council will have to be called."30 After all, men like Morone,31 dear to the

29 Comba, *op. cit.*, pp. 85–114. Quoted from pp. 111–13 [but I have modified the quotations slightly to make them fit together. The word *conciliatori* I take to mean "those who look toward reconciliation" rather than "those who are proponents of a council."]

30 For Aconcio, see ch. 8, n. 9, above; "Acontiana," in *Abhandlungen der Heidelberger Akademie der Wissenschaften*, Phil.-Histor. Klasse, VIII (1932), p. 20, line 10 (but see also line 35). Aconcio, *"De Methodo" e opuscoli religiosi e filosofici*, ed. Giorgio Radetti (Florence: Vallecchi, 1944), pp. 200–1.

31 [Cardinal Giovanni Morone (1509–80) rose to eminence as a legate of Pope Paul III to some of the most important meetings with the German Protestants. Pope Paul IV (1555–59) threw him into prison on suspicions of heresy, from which Pius IV absolved him. He was president of the first and last sessions of the Council and was seriously considered as a candidate for the papacy in 1565 and 1572. He was closely associated with another leading reformer, Reginald Pole, who, after years of exile, assisted Mary Tudor in restoring

hearts of the moderate Reformers, took part in the last phase of
the Council, and so did others who were eventually to be famous
as Reformers or heretics, men like Andrea Dudith.[32] But the hopes
placed in these theologians and in the conciliating tendencies supposedly inherent in Christianity and Catholicism were not fulfilled.
In retrospect, the marchesa di Pescara[33] seemed to have been correct
when she rejoiced in the absence of [Cardinal Reginald] Pole
from the deliberations on the decree concerning justification.
Carnesecchi had frequently feared that Pole and Morone would
have let themselves, out of timidity, be "corrupted." He feared
that they might make concessions to the "world," to exterior
forms, to tradition, to ecclesiastical authority, and to the opposition.[34] For in the generally Nicodemite circles of Italian society—
among the better-educated, that is, who knew how to distinguish
between "affirmative" and "negative" arguments, who knew how
to talk vaguely about religion and to express themselves by signs,
by inference, by implications, by inconclusive demonstrations—in
these circles men were walking on a razor's edge. They were the
circles for which so many pages of Calvin's exhortation seem

Catholicism to England, only to be undercut by the hysterical wrath of the
same Paul IV.]

[32] Pierre Costil, *André Dudith, humaniste hongrois* (Paris: "Les Belles Lettres,"
1935), pp. 111–16. [In his *Eretici italiani* Cantimori also refers to C. Juhasz,
"A. Dudith. Ein Beitrag zur Geschichte des Humanismus und der Gegenreformation," *Historisches Jahrbuch*, LV (1935), 55–74. Dudith lived between
1533 and 1589.]

[33] [The "marchesa di Pescara" is the famous Vittoria Colonna (1492–1547), a
close friend of Michelangelo as well as of Pole, Morone, and the rest of the
leaders of the early Catholic Reform in Italy. She is one of the "ladies" referred
to rather disparagingly by Protestant opponents of Nicodemism.]

[34] "Estratto del processo di Pietro Carnesecchi," published by Giacomo
Manzoni in *Miscellanea di storia italiana*, edita per cura della Regia Deputazione
di Storia Patria, Vol. x (Turin, 1870), p. 549: "During the time when the Council of Trent drew up the decree on justification [1546], the Cardinal of England
of happy memory was ill . . . and hence had retired outside of Trent. . . . The
marchesa of Pescara expressed her joy to me, as if [his illness] had been turned
admirably to his own advantage. She said that God had almost miraculously
disposed and ordered this matter [so that the Cardinal would not take part] in
the discussion of [the said decree.]" [Emendations by the editor solely for the
sake of greater clarity.]

specifically to have been written; and their attitudes are well documented in the records of the trial of Carnesecchi. It was all too easy for them to pass from one side to another. It was easy for them to fall into ambiguities, not only into intellectual and doctrinal ambiguities, but also into psychological ones. The distinction between the "affirmative" and the "negative" easily led to doctrinal ambiguities. For one could always take refuge in generic statements about an elementary and undefined faith according to which "believing in one way" was much the same as "believing in another," providing only that one remain "always inside the Catholic faith."[35]

These are the two questions, along with the answers, that the Inquisitors posed to Carnesecchi concerning the problem of exile "for the sake of conscience":[36]

Q. Why did you not go to Geneva, as you had planned?

A. The reasons that impelled me to depart are much more difficult to state precisely in such deliberations than those that held me back. Exile would have been very unreasonable and very inconvenient, for one thing. There were many reasons for not taking so precipitous a step. But I think the most important was that I was not wholly resolved in my heart to accept that religion [Calvinism].

[35] *Ibid.*, pp. 332-33: "I did not at that time understand that that term in religion included anything beyond 'justifying faith,' in which I thought consisted salvation and consequently the whole force of the Christian religion. Nor would I have held that opinion for a good or true one if I had then believed that it was opposed to the Catholic faith, since I have never by the grace of God had any intention of departing from the Catholic faith. But I have been tempted into thinking that the faith consisted rather in believing more in one way than in another . . . and I say temptation, for although I assented to this article more than to any of the others regarding that doctrine . . . I have never held so firmly to my opinion that I would not be disposed to abandon it. . . ." Cf. p. 494: "Indeed, we did talk about religious matters; but we talked about them in general, discussing, for example, the Providence that God has for his own and praising humility as the foundation of all the other Christian virtues, as well as the mortifications that Christians must expect, *et similia.*"

[36] [I have to recast Cantimori's prose (although without changing any words) in dialogue form to facilitate reading. In the original the answers are between quotation marks, but the questions are not.]

Q. But then why have you praised and exalted those who have emigrated "into the lands of the heretics"?[37]

A. It may be that I have praised the resolution of some who have gone off into those countries in that they placed the satisfaction of their consciences, and living according to their consciences, above all other interests and human considerations.[38]

This undeniable presence of human considerations, of [material] interests, of reasonableness and a sense of propriety ... and this indirect, oblique manner of speaking, together with a consciousness of being among the elect, explains the essentially political or tactical character of the action undertaken by the groups favorable to the new doctrines. Their members never felt any qualms of conscience, not even when dissimulating and making tortuous denials of a general nature—the sort of talk Calvin would have called hypocrisy—before the Inquisition. They went even so far as to acclaim the concession of an ecclesiastical benefice to one of them as a fortuitous grant of assistance to the good cause. This is [Carnesecchi's] comment: The abbey has been given us, with a considerable pension attached to it. Notwithstanding all the Reformers' attacks on the benefice system, God is to be thanked as the "direct agent" of this grant. "You cannot have flesh without bones; and God does not bother about these tiny details, being satisfied in this case more with the appearance than with the substance, so that those who have eyes to see and ears to hear may glorify His divine Majesty."[39] Making good a claim is a triumph for the good, even if the advantage is more apparent than substantial. It is the effect that counts, for the effect amounts to a recognition of the "good cause."

[37] [Latin in the original.]
[38] *Estratto del processo*, pp. 278–80. But see the letter he wrote to Giulia Gonzaga on 31 January 1559, on pp. 282–83, and his willingness to accuse himself of hypocrisy in order to disculpate Morone: "Whence I have resolved to confess that I have used the name of both these gentlemen [Pole and Morone] as a pretext for my own indecision, hoping thereby to gain praise from that lady as a good servant and friend both of the living and the dead. . . . If Your Lordships wish to say that this is a sin of hypocrisy, I will not deny it."
[39] *Ibid.*, pp. 488–89.

THE SURVIVAL OF NICODEMISM

It was in this climate of opinion that the Nicodemites awaited the decisions of the Council of Trent. When the decisions were at last promulgated, they then professed to accept them, though with the tacit reservation that they might interpret them as they saw fit. "The only article that gave any trouble in religious matters," said Carnesecchi, "was the one about justification. It cannot be said that divergent opinions were previously heretical, since the Council had not yet determined what should be believed on that subject."[40] Still, many continued to hope right to the end that the more moderate tendencies in the Council would succeed in giving broader definitions of the faith and less specific condemnations. In the meantime they went ahead with the method of "interior reformation," which in substance was the same, even with differences in matter and content, as the position of those who had looked forward to a reform of the church without doctrinal changes. It was the same, that is, as the position of the Catholic Reformers. For the [Protestant] Reformers, for those who were not content with the Nicodemism of the Waldensians or the declarations of faith in eventual reforms by a council, the answer was this: "Do you know how this council ought to be accomplished? In many pieces. Today, you and I will do our part. Tomorrow, two or three friends will do theirs. And eventually all those who esteem the honor and glory of God will do their 'Council'."[41]

"The honor and glory of God": that formula in that age is typically Calvinistic. It was one that led those who professed it directly to martyrdom or exile. And it was very close to the one that led the Jesuits to persecute the heretics. It was a formula which

[40] *Ibid.*, pp. 334–35. But see p. 563 and p. 569, where the Inquisitors contest these distinctions and where they question the way used by Carnesecchi to save himself from condemnation as well as the concept he had of the role of the Council.

[41] [I.e. the "council," and hence reform, was to be purely interior.] "Acontiana," p. 21, lines 28 ff.; and Aconcio's *De Methodo*, p. 201 [both cited in n. 30, above].

in all its versions led to conflict—and to the consciousness of the necessity of conflict on behalf of clear-cut decisions. Even the Nicodemites, in their own way, shared this consciousness. They too longed for a final solution to religious questions, even though they did not succeed in defining it very clearly. As Carnesecchi said:

> You Lordships accuse me of having approved of the religion of Caracciolo and Brisegna[42] simply because they fulfilled the dictates of their conscience. But the accusation is not exact. [. . .] For I did not say simply that I approved of their opinions. I said that since they had such opinions, it seemed to me that they acted properly. That is, I said it was less bad for them to go off to a place where they could live according to their conscience, wishing to suggest that those who live according to their conscience and who walk sincerely in the ways it prescribes can more easily hope for the mercy of God, at least at the end of their lives, than those who stumble on one side or the other or on both sides at the same time. And to respond to the rest of the interrogation, I say in conclusion that those erroneous opinions I have held, I have held with the supposition that they would be proposed and disputed at the Council; and I always intended to adhere to whatever the Council should determine with the consent and approbation of the pope.[43]

This faith in the Council, which was very real and which Carnesecchi made use of in his defense, was accompanied by a kind of millenarianism:

> And when it pleases God to make of all of us one flock with one pastor, and it looks as if the time is approaching when He will do so; for there are many Jews who have been enlightened,

[42] [Galeazzo Caracciolo, marchese of Vito, was a Neapolitan nobleman who experienced his first religious conversion after listening to a sermon by Pier Martire Vermigli at Naples in 1540. He fled suddenly in 1551, followed by the Spanish noblewoman—and sister-in-law of the Inquisitor of Spain—Isabella Breseña (Brisegna), first to the imperial court, and finally to Geneva, where he became a firm follower and friend of Calvin. B. Croce has written a biography of him in *Vite di avventure di fede e di passione* (Bari: Laterza, 1936), pp. 179–281.]

[43] *Estratto del processo*, p. 340.

but who have not yet resolved to be baptized, for they prefer to wait until the controversies that they see raging among us Christians concerning the faith have been ended. We must now wait to see what God will do, and devote ourselves to praying to His Divine Majesty to give us a pastor who is capable of gathering and uniting the poor lost sheep, of bringing in those who are still outside and drawing back those who have gone outside into the good pastures of salvation. I am able to teach whoever is fitted for this task, though I am not able to help him to succeed. . . .

These hopes flowered for a moment when the rumor spread of the possibility of Morone's election to the papacy; though even then there was some doubt about Morone's courage.[44]

These hopes continued to be nourished, even after the closing of the Council of Trent, by one of the exiles who professed to admire Giorgio Siculo. He was Francesco Pucci of Figline, who, after an adventurous life, ended his days in the obscurity of Castel Sant'Angelo.[45] Pucci also expected the imminent establishment of the Kingdom of God, the unification of all Christians and of all nations hitherto outside the Christian communities; and he thought that the miracle would be accomplished by a general council convoked by a pope. This council, enlightened by natural and rational revelation of which he, Pucci, had made himself a

[44] *Ibid.*, p. 382. [The last sentence of the quotation is not very clear: "per il che fare saprei ben io insegnare chi sarebbe a proposito, ma che giova, non potendo io aiutarlo a riuscire. . . ." But such is often the case with transcriptions of oral testimony, taken down word for word exactly as delivered, before the Inquisition.]

[45] Cf. *Eretici italiani*, pp. 370 ff., and 385 ff., and the texts there cited. On Pucci's unhappy end, see Angelo Mercati, *Il sommario del processo di Giordano Bruno, con appendice di documenti dell'eresia e l'inquisizione a Modena nel secolo XVI* (Vatican City, 1942), p. 124 (Francesco Filidino). [Pucci has since become much better known, thanks to the publication by Luigi Firpo and Renato Piattoli of his *Lettere, documenti e testimonianze* (cited above, ch. 6, n. 4). Pucci (1543–97), a Florentine patrician, was one of the last Italians to go abroad for religious reasons. He returned to Catholicism at Prague in 1587; but doubts about the sincerity of his conversion led to his arrest at Salzburg six years later and his transportation to the famous prison in the Castel Sant'Angelo ("Hadrian's tomb"). After a long trial he was decapitated and burned.]

proponent, would certainly overcome the resistance not only of the various Christian churches but also of the synagogue and the mosque. At times Pucci thought this council ought to be prepared under the auspices of a pope—specifically, Clement VIII (1591–1605). At other times he thought it should be composed of a much wider membership than what the Holy See might countenance—of all "spiritual persons" and "lovers of truth," that is, whether approved of by the Curia or not. It should reform the church and re-establish the spirit of a "Society of Prayer" (*Societas Oratorii*). Pucci's lucubrations may well represent a visionary's re-elaboration of the hopes and aspirations of the Catholic Reform that had been so alive in the first decades of the century and about which he may have had some vague information. He may have imagined that he could now bring those desires and those aspirations to fulfillment.

The hopes, then, still survived; and in France they were exploited at times for political reasons by the pamphlet-writers. But in Italy, and particularly as they were reflected in Pucci and in the author of the *Forma d'una Repubblica Catholica* (*Constitution of a Catholic Commonwealth*), these hopes amounted to little more than the expression of dissatisfaction with what the Council of Trent had accomplished. Such expressions remained isolated and without energy. And so also did Nicodemism in its two principal forms—that of the Waldensian Valleys and that of the Valdesian intellectuals.

11 The Flowering and Withering of Speculative Philosophy—Italian Philosophy and the Counter Reformation: The Condemnation of Francesco Patrizi[1]

LUIGI FIRPO

BY THE middle of the sixteenth century the Church of Rome was deeply engaged in a campaign of restoration and reaction against the forces that had assailed and so much weakened it during the previous decades. It was just then that the Church brought forth a new weapon: the Index of forbidden books. The Holy Office intensified its efforts to repress the heretics, the living rebels against orthodoxy. But the Index sought to silence the voices of the dead, which the invention of printing had multiplied and spread, openly or clandestinely, throughout Catholic Europe.[2] The first list of condemned books, subscribed by Pope Paul IV in 1559, awakened considerable discontent among men of learning because of its extreme harshness. The list comprised two main categories. One set down the titles of works condemned according to specific doctrinal criteria. The other category included indiscriminately everything published anonymously. And it included also all books ever put out by a number of specified writers [whether these books had anything to do with theology or not]. It thus comprehended in one vast condemnation not only known heretics, but also the

[1] "Filosofia italiana e Controriforma," Introduction and Part II, *Rivista di filosofia*, XLI (1950), 150–53 and 159–73. Translated and slightly emended, with the addition of first names and a few explanatory asides, by the editor. Permission to use the material was granted by *Rivista di filosofia*.

[2] For the history of the Index in general, see Heinrich Reusch, *Die [Indices Librorum Prohibitorum des sechzehnten Jahrhunderts]* (Bonn, 1883–85) [now reissued in photo-offset, Nieuwkoop, 1961], and Joseph Hilgers, *Der Index der verbotenen Bücher* (Freiburg im Breisgau, 1904).

subtle Machiavelli, the mild Erasmus, the festive Boccaccio, and even the skeptical, mystical Gelli.[3]

Harshness, however, soon gave way to moderation and discrimination. The Council of Trent approved, on 26 February 1562, a revised version, which Pius IV published in March 1564. The new Index transferred many authors, Erasmus in particular, from the second to the first class. It introduced the clause *donec corrigatur*—prohibited until corrected—a clause which permitted many works to be salvaged, even though in mutilated form. It laid down general criteria by which the orthodoxy of a book might be ascertained. And it ruled out in advance all unauthorized translations of the Scriptures and theological works, and all books of divination, pornography, and journalistic scandal.

In the initial phases this repressive action tended to be sweeping and comprehensive, for it sought to erect a defensive dike as quickly as possible, and it had no time for subtle distinctions and emendations. Later, during the pontificate of Pius V, it became implacably severe. Pompeo De' Monti in 1566, Mario Galeotta and Pietro Carnesecchi in 1568, Aonio Paleario in 1560—one by one the victims were sent to the gallows or the stake. The survivors, now that even the most cautious form of Nicodemism[4] had become untenable, fled across the Alps: Fausto Sozzini in 1574, Giordano Bruno in 1578, Alberico Gentili in 1579. Pope Pius changed the nature of the Index. He intended it no longer as a fixed list, to be published once and for all, of writings condemned to destruction. He intended it, rather, as a continuous action of vigilance and censorship, both as a way of executing the special decrees of the Inquisition and as an instrument for rooting out other books for condemnation. He thus set up a special Congregation of the Index in March 1571. At first the new Congregation limited itself, according to the criteria of moderation adopted at Trent, to putting previously condemned works back into circulation after proper precautions had been taken; and it authorized expurgated editions of Boccaccio, Erasmus, Castiglione, and Machiavelli. It attempted, in a manner that was as annoying at

[3] [On Gelli, see above, ch. 2.]   [4] [See above, ch. 10.]

times as it was ingenious, to restore to the European cultural patrimony those works that had long been an essential part of it. It ended, unfortunately, by betraying all too often the intent of the Reformers themselves—as it did most notably in Lionardo Salviati's "Assassination" of the *Decameron*, which appeared cleansed of its anticlerical satire but still rich in scenes and situations that . . . could sow dangerous germs of religious indifference.[5]

What Pius V had started, another rigid monk carried on: Sixtus V, who as a cardinal had been a member of the Congregation of the Index. In a *breve* of 20 June 1587, he called upon the learned men of safe orthodoxy in all the great universities of Europe to cooperate in systematically reviewing all the books ever printed for a new Index; and on 9 March 1590, he signed the introductory bull. The severe criteria laid down by the pope caused considerable uneasiness. For they brought down a condemnation upon one of the main proponents of the Counter Reformation, Roberto Bellarmino, because of the theses on papal authority in his *Controversies*. The death of Sixtus (August 1590) led to the suspension of the printing of the Index; and that very year his successor, Urban VII, ordered it to be emended in a less rigorous sense, though without satisfying all the complaints that had been raised against it.[6] Though it was finally printed, then, both in a quarto and in an octavo format, the new Index was never published. Not until May 1596 did a fully revised version finally come out, with the approval of Clement VIII.

[5] ["Assassination" is the term used by Traiano] Boccalini in his *Ragguagli di Parnaso*, Cent. III, 15 [But I find the passage in *Pietra del paragone politico* ("Cosmopoli," 1615), no pagination; for some editions of the *Ragguagli*, e.g. the 7th edn. of Venice, 1637, do not include a third "Century." The whole story of the censorship is told by Pio Paschini in *Cinquecento romano e riforma cattolica*, pp. 165 ff., and in two articles by Peter M. Brown in *Giornale storico della letteratura italiana*, CXXXIII (1956), 544–72, and CXXXIV (1957) 314–32. For the context, see above, ch. 2.]

[6] The protests of the printers were particularly vociferous—and some of them were listened to. Enforcement of the Index in Venice would have meant the destruction of great quantities of merchandise and the ruin of one of the principal commercial enterprises of the city.

Much time had elapsed between the Index of Trent and the Index of Clement VIII. Thirty years earlier the Church was faced above all with the task of suppressing the Protestants and the Libertines, of putting an end to polemics about grace and indulgences, and of trimming down the frank language of Aretino[7] and his imitators. It had no time for the subtleties of the philosophers and the possibly heterodox implications of what they wrote. In the last decade of the century, however, the political and religious situation had changed radically. Popular heresy had been suffocated in Italy.[8] The Turk had been stopped in the East. France had been pacified, and its new king, Henry IV, had been readmitted to the Catholic Church. The old religious orders had been reformed, and the new ones were busy with their apostolic endeavors. The Church had come out of [the struggle] with renewed vigor; and it could now adopt an attitude of intransigence that was a consequence, not an instrument, of its success. It continued to keep an eye on the theologians, as it did in the case of Baius and Carranza.[9] But it now extended its vigilance to all manifestations of social and spiritual life—not only to religion, but also to ethics, to politics, to philosophy, to art, and even to the manners and customs of the people.

The consequences of this extension are well known, at least in

[7] [Pietro Aretino (1492–1557) was the son of an Aretine artisan who rose to fame, power, and wealth through his writings, many of which verge on the pornographic, and through his voluminous letters. The *Dubbi amorosi* and the *Ragionamenti* have recently been republished in paperback by Sampietro in Italy; and the latter has appeared in an English paperback edition (Brandon House, 1966).]

[8] [The author here (p. 152, n. 2 of the original) quotes at length from a document in the Archives of the Holy Office (Sant'Uffizio) in Rome of 10 July 1597 to illustrate] a particularly late, and therefore significant episode in the spread of Protestant ideas in Italy.

[9] [Michel Baius (1513–89) was a professor at Louvain whose extreme Augustinian position on the doctrine of grace was condemned by Pius V and attacked thereafter by Bellarmino. Bartolomé de Carranza (1503–76), a Dominican and archbishop of Toledo, was one of the leaders of the Catholic Reformation in Spain until 1559, when he was suddenly arrested and carried off to a secret prison. His seventeen-year confinement and eventual condemnation in Rome is one of the sorriest stories of the Counter Reformation.]

part. Religion, first of all, degenerated into artificial devotional practices often tainted with an unctuous hypocrisy. Morality, secondly, withered into exterior show and caviling casuistry, which in turn were bereft of spontaneity and robbed both of their educational function and of their ability to engender a sense of individual responsibility. Morality was then subjected to a purely verbal and largely deceptive reconciliation with Machiavelli's amoral utilitarianism in the form of what was called "reason of state." Philosophy, finally, entered its most dramatic moment. Or at least that is what happened to the "new" philosophy which had been born of the rebellion against conventional university Aristotelianism and which Bernardino Telesio, Francesco Patrizi, and Giordano Bruno[10] were preparing for the soaring metaphysical heights of Campanella's *instauratio scientiarum* ("establishment of the sciences") and of Galileo's "new science." Free philosophical speculation in Italy fought its decisive battle during the pontificate of Clement VIII, in the last decade of the century. It suffered the condemnation of Patrizi's *Nova Philosophia*, of Telesio's *De Rerum Natura*, and of all the works of Bruno and Campanella. It was crippled by the investigations opened against Giambattista Della Porta, Col'Antonio Stigliola, and Cesare Cremonini,[11] by the beginning of Campanella's long imprison-

[10] [On Telesio, who was born in Cosenza in 1509 and died there in 1588, and whose major work, *De Rerum Natura Iuxta Propria Principia* (*Nature According to its Own Principles*) was published in Naples in 1565, and on Patrizi, sometimes called "of Cherso" from the town in Istria where he was born in 1529, to distinguish him from the Sienese writer of the preceding century by the same name, see now ch. 6 and ch. 7 in Paul Oskar Kristeller, *Eight Philosophers of the Italian Renaissance* (Stanford), where further bibliography is given in an appendix. On Bruno, see ch. 8 in Kristeller, *op. cit.*]

[11] [The famous philosopher, magician, and inventor of Naples, Della Porta, later to become head of the Neapolitan branch of the Lincei Academy to which Galileo belonged (after contesting Galileo's priority in the invention of the telescope), has recently been studied from a previously little-known angle by Louise George Clubb, *Giambattista Della Porta, Dramatist* (Princeton University Press, 1965). His *De Telescopio* is now available in an edition by Vasco Ronchi and Maria Amalia Naldoni (Florence: Olschki, 1962). Cremonini is best known today as the obdurate Aristotelian at Padua who refused to look through Galileo's telescope, though he always remained on friendly terms with his younger colleague.]

ment, by the execution of Francesco Pucci, and by the burning of Bruno.[12] And finally, it was completely destroyed, in spite of the heroism of its martyrs. Its last, posthumous act was played out thirty years later, in the silence of Arcetri.[13]. . .

In a lively, polemical passage of his dialogues *On Cause, Principle, and Unity*[14] Bruno contrasts the "most judicious" Telesio, the champion of the "honorable war" against Aristotle, with an Italian whom he does not deign to mention but whom he castigates as a "pedantic dung heap," a "bestial and asslike" scribbler. This man, he insists, cannot be said to have either understood or misunderstood Aristotle, for he has done nothing but read and reread his books, cut them up and sew them back together with pieces from a thousand hostile and friendly Greek authors . . . without any profit at all; in fact, with considerable lack of profit. He has simply shown "how far a pedantic garb can make one fall into madness and presumptuous vanity."[15] Yet the *Discussiones Peripateticae* of Francesco Patrizi da Cherso, published in part in Venice in 1571 and then in a definitive edition in Basel ten years later, represent the only battle actually won in the Late Renaissance by the opponents of Aristotelianism. These discussions may have bewildered readers with their mass of scholarly citations. But they opened to the anti-Aristotelians the one sure path to their goal—the path of internal criticism, based on philology and philosophy, and directed toward exposing the contradictions and weaknesses implicit in the system rather than toward proposing another system to take its place. . . . Patrizi may possibly have realized that men of his generation would never

[12] See my two studies, "Processo e morte di Francesco Pucci," *Rivista di filosofia*, XL (1949), 371–405, and "Il processo di Giordano Bruno," *Rivista storica italiana*, LX (1948), 542–97, and LXI (1949), 5–59.

[13] [The villa outside of Florence to which Galileo was confined after his condemnation by the Holy Office in 1633.]

[14] [Now available in English in paperback as *Cause, Principle, and Unity*, tr. Jack Lindsay (New World Paperbacks, NW–39).] The first Italian edition was published in London in 1584.

[15] I cite the edition of G. Gentile in *Dialoghi* (Bari: Laterza, 1925), Vol. I, pp. 202–3.

have followed him beyond a work of mere destruction. Such, at
any rate, is suggested by the rigorous methodology and the
conscious limitation of scope in the *Discussiones*. But actually he
did nothing of the sort. Instead, he embarked on an ambitious
speculative venture of his own: an artificial and complex metaphysical system which he called the *Nova Philosophia*.

In the eyes of Patrizi's contemporaries, the very barrage of
pedantic erudition that Bruno could not put up with was exactly
what gave the *Discussiones* their title of nobility. Free of the
gratuitous pride that usually accompanies a revolutionary view of
the universe and full of incontrovertible citations, the book com-
bated Aristotelianism on its own ground. It struck repeatedly at
vital points, and it came out of the fight uninjured, precisely
because it did not offer opinions of its own which could be con-
futed rationally or dogmatically. A few Aristotelians tried to
ignore these pages, so laden with the poison of doubt. But none
of them dared counterattack even the grosser historical misstatements, like the denigration of the man Aristotle as an immoral,
untrustworthy plagiarist—misstatements which left them helpless
and which were picked up and amplified by their opponents.[16]

After many years of restlessness and wandering, Patrizi had just
settled down, at the age of almost fifty, to teaching in Ferrara in
1577.[17] He was to remain there, engaged continually in research
and polemics, for another fifteen years. He had originally been
invited only to comment on the *Republic*. But he soon set out to
expound the entire philosophy of Plato. And, with a chair specifically erected for this purpose, he proposed a revival of Platonism—

[16] Campanella as a young man was much inspired by the *Discussiones*, as he
confesses in several passages of the preface to his *Philosophia Sensibus Demonstrata*
(Naples, 1591), which I have published in Italian translation in *Rivista di filosofia*, XL (1949), 182–205. On p. 196 there is a reference to the course on Platonic
philosophy given at Ferrara, though without specific mention of Patrizi.

[17] Paola Maria Arcari, *Il pensiero politico di F. P. da Cherso*, p. 50, assigns the
beginning of Patrizi's teaching at Ferrara to 1578. But Patrizi's own record is
explicit, in the *Autobiografia* edited by A. Solerti in the *Archivio storico per
Trieste, l'Istria e il Trentino* (1886), Vol. III, p. 280. See E. Solmi, "Nuove
ricerche su F. Patrizio," *Atti e memorie della R. Deputazione di Storia Patria per le
Provincie Modenesi*, Ser. v, Vol. VII (1913), p. 114.

of a Platonism that might inherit the fame, though perhaps not the tradition, of the Florentine Academy, that might be enriched with logical and scholarly subtleties, though without Ficino's flights of religious feeling, and that might serve as a counter-altar to the temple of the Aristotelians.

At first this program did not encounter much resistance. Perhaps the common opinion about the "Christian Plato" calmed the suspicious. Perhaps Patrizi's armor of history and philology frightened them away. Only a certain Teodoro Angelucci, a physician from the Marche, dared attack Patrizi, in a short work entitled *Quod Metaphysica Sint Eadem Quae Physica Nova Sententia* [. . .] (Venice, 1584). Patrizi promptly replied with an *Apologia contra Calumnias* [. . .] (Ferrara, 1584), dedicated to his young colleague, Cesare Cremonini. When Angelucci repeated his attack, with his *Exercitationes cum F. Patritio* (Venice, 1585), he ignored it himself and turned over the task of writing a rebuttal to a minor, though not obscure, proponent of the new philosophy, Francesco Muti, a Calabrese from Aprigliano and a fervent follower of Telesio.[18] Muti's collaboration marked a sort of public announcement of an informal alliance between Ferrarese Platonism and the naturalism of the Academy of Cosenza. It established, beyond particular divergencies, a solidarity among all the innovators against the guardians of authority and tradition. Patrizi's letter to Telesio from Venice of 26 June 1572 is written in a respectful tone, free of the slightest polemical sharpness. So also are the *Solutiones* that Telesio dictated in response to the letter, as well as Antonio Persio's *Apologia pro Telesio adversus F. Patritium*, still unpublished.[19] When later, in 1590, Persio published in

---

[18] Muti, *Disceptationum Libri V Contra Calumnia Theodori Angelutii in Maximum Philosophum F. Patritium* (Ferrara: Galdura, 1588), dedicated to Telesio. Nothing is known of Muti except the bare notes of the scholars of the seventeenth and eighteenth centuries, which have been repeated by others more recently [the author gives a long list of them]. For Patrizi's Polemics, F. Fiorentino, *B. Telesio, ossia Studi storici su l'idea della natura nel Risorgimento* [i.e. Renaissance] *italiano* (Florence, 1872–74) is still fundamental.

[19] The first two writings were published by Fiorentino, *op. cit.*, Vol. II, pp. 375–98. On the third, which is in manuscript in the Magliabechiana collection of the Biblioteca Nazionale, Florence, see *ibid.*, pp. 1–19, as well as Garin,

Venice Telesio's posthumous *Varii de Naturalibus Rebus Libelli*, which he had procured through the efforts of Muti, he dedicated the fourth section, the *De Mari*, to Patrizi. And Patrizi, the following year, paid tribute to "Bernardino Telesio, that admirable man, and Francesco Muti, his disciple."

Patrizi was certainly fascinated by the rigorous naturalistic monism of Telesio. He appreciated that vision of nature living in an organic unity that Telesio explained "according to its own principles." For his own philosophy tended toward the same end through the meanderings of Hermeticism and the Cabala. The enlarged Neapolitan edition of the *De Rerum Natura* in 1586 may well have been the spur that drove him out of the closed terrain of historiography and aesthetics and onto the highway of metaphysical speculation. The two "decades" of his *Poetica* were published at Ferrara in 1586, and his literary polemic with Jacopo Mazzoni came to an end in the middle of the following year. He thus wrote to Baccio Valori, the learned librarian of the Laurenziana library in Florence, in November 1587: "I have taken up philosophy again this month... and I can already inform you that as Aristotle found the Prime Mover through motion, so I have found it through light in the *Panaugia*, and by the Platonic method of descending to the production of things in the *Pancosmo*."[20] Writing the work took him a little less than two years. The *Panaugia*, the metaphysics of light, with a title borrowed from Philo, bears the final date of 1588, while the three remaining sections, the *Panarchia*, the *Pampsychia*, and the *Pancosmia*, put into final form during a hundred days of feverish labor, were finished on 5 August 1589.[21] Publication took another two years, perhaps because of the usual financial difficulties; and not until 1591 could Benedetto Mammarelli put out in Ferrara, with the title *Nova de*

"Nota telesiana: Antonio Persio," *Giornale critico della filosofia italiana*, xxvIII (1949), 414–21 [now republished in his *La cultura filosofia del Rinascimento italiano* (Florence: Sansoni, 1961), pp. 432–41].

[20] Solerti, *op. cit.* [above, n. 17], p. 280.

[21] The dates are given explicitly in the printed version. See Fiorentino, *op. cit.*, Vol. I, p. 382.

Universis Philosophia, the vast treatise, dedicated to Pope Gregory XIV, decorated with the pope's coat of arms, and adorned not with an explicit ecclesiastical imprimatur but only with an ambiguous *Superiorum consensu*.

Minor polemical skirmishes had no part in a work of such speculative commitment, and Patrizi was apparently not bothered by the implications of his new metaphysics for Catholic theology. He asked the pope's protection, in the dedication, for Platonic philosophy, which, he said, had been called to rid the schools of impious Aristotelian doctrine and which was capable of reconverting the dissidents in Germany. Moreover, either caution, or else ambition, led him to assemble a distinguished gallery of influential cardinals in the dedications to the eleven separate parts of the work; from the cardinal-nephew Paolo Emilio Sfondati to Federico Borromeo, the nephew of St. Charles. Some of them, indeed, had been fellow students of his, some forty years earlier, in the halls of the "artists" at Padua: Ippolito Aldobrandini, Scipione Gonzaga, Agostino Vilier, Girolamo Della Rovere, and even the pope himself.

The initial reception of the work was encouragingly favorable. There was not a dissenting voice either among the Aristotelians or among the prelates. The dedications were accepted with pleasure. On 3 October 1591, Cardinal Aldobrandini sent Patrizi a letter in praise of the new philosophy, "which accords perfectly with Christian piety." He invited him to his own house in Rome. He then informed him of negotiations underway with the pope and several other cardinals to procure him a chair at the Sapienza —the University of Rome.[22] Meanwhile, another eminent cardinal, Pietro di Norres, son of the famous Giasone, "mentioned Mr. Francesco Patricio and said that he ought to be in Rome," as Gian Vincenzo Pinelli heard in a letter of December 12.[23] Then two months later, on 30 January 1590, Aldobrandini himself

[22] Cf. G. Fontanini, *Biblioteca dell'eloquenza italiana* (Venice, 1753), Vol. I, pp. 226–27. The "Epistolae Due ad F. Patricium" by Ippolito Aldobrandini are in the Vatican Archives, Cod. Ottoboniano, 1088.

[23] A. Solerti, *Vita di Torquato Tasso* (Turin: Loescher, 1895), Vol. I, p. 735.

became pope, as Clement VIII. Duke Alfonso II d'Este gave his consent to the appointment on March 25.[24] By April 10 Patrizi was in Imola, where Pietro di Norres found him full of enthusiasm, "great hopes and great plans."[25] And by the first of May he had completed the prescribed complimentary visits about the city and had settled down in the house of Cinzio, later Cardinal, Aldobrandini, the son of one of the pope's sisters and a noted patron of the men of letters and artists who gathered in an academy under his sponsorship. Thus Patrizi found himself "most honorably ascribed in the household of the papal family." He began immediately to lecture on the *Timaeus* at the university, with a large concourse of students. He was provided with a high salary of 600 *scudi* a year. And he was courted and revered by a great number of old and new friends, whom the open favor of the pope had attracted to him.[26]

Meanwhile the work was spreading about among the learned. The first judgments were varied. Some admired "the antiquity and the novelty of the contents." Others disapproved of the emphasis on Plato and the marked disdain for Aristotle. A few

[24] The letter is published by Solmi, *op. cit.*, p. 134. See also Solerti, *Vita di Torquato Tasso*, Vol. I, p. 730, and the "Avviso di Roma" of 2 May 1592, in the Vatican Archives, Cod. Urbin, Lat. 1060, Part I.

[25] On the stop at Imola, see Solerti, *Vita di Torquato Tasso*, Vol. I, p. 730. On May 5 Cardinal Lancellotti reported to the duke of Ferrara that Patrizi had visited him and could be assured of his favor. The letter is in Arcari, *op. cit.*, Vol. I, p. 730.

[26] On this moment in Patrizi's life there are precious reports in the unpublished "Declarationes F. Patritii in Quaedam Suae Philosophiae Loca Obscuriora," fourteen closely written pages with corrections, additions, and the signature of the author, in the Vatican, Cod. Barberini Lat. 318. . . . On his salary, see P. Serassi, *La Vita di Iacopo Mazzoni* (Rome, 1790), p. 108, and Arcari, *op. cit.*, p. 68. The latter says by mistake that with the money he thus acquired Patrizi was able to have his *Magia Philosophica* printed at Hamburg in 1593. But after his misfortune with the Congregation of the Index, Patrizi would never have taken the risk of publishing anything philosophical. The Hamburg edition is just a reprinting of his *Zoroaster et Eius 320 Oracula Chaldaica*, which he had sent to Germany as early as 1585. See Solmi, *op. cit.*, p. 124. On Cardinal Aldobrandini's academy, in which Tasso also participated, see the two letters (15 May and 6 June 1592) of Patrizi to Orazio Ariosti in Solerti, *Vita di Torquato Tasso*, Vol. II, p. 340.

readers objected to the excessive obscurity of some concepts that were either too ancient or too new, and they invited the author to give an explanation of the more difficult passages. So at any rate Patrizi claimed in the preamble of his subsequent *Declarations Regarding Certain Obscure Parts of His Philosophy*—though the little work was really intended not to rebuff purely philosophical objections, but to silence the accusations of heresy that had already begun to spread about the Roman Curia. Indeed, the packed list of citations to the Fathers and the Scriptures and the attention to the theological aspects of the supposedly "more obscure parts" in the *Declarationes* make it clear that by the middle of 1592[27] Patrizi had already felt obliged to defend his work against the suspicions of ecclesiastical authorities. Hence his profession of orthodoxy and submission; and hence the last words: "I submit all that I have written to the judgment of the Holy Church."[28]

That Bellarmino was behind the attack on Patrizi, as P. M. Arcari has affirmed on the basis, probably, of a misunderstood passage in Tiraboschi,[29] is improbable. In 1592 Bellarmino was the confessor and hence the rector of the Collegio Romano of the Society of Jesus; but he did not yet enjoy any particular influence in the hierachy, and he certainly was not in a position to oppose the new pope's known sympathies for Platonism.[30] Two years later Patrizi was still high in the favor of Cinzio Aldobrandini, as we learn from a letter of the Ferrarese diplomat and amateur

[27] The little work [above, n. 25] is not dated. But it appears to have been written in Rome, certainly before the Congregation of the Index took up the question, which occurred at the end of the year. Arcari gives the wrong call number for the document and then attributes the anti-Patrizi campaign to a certain "Friar Pietro di Saragozza, Master of the Sacred Palace." But actually Patrizi's defense seems to be a purely preventative measure rather than a reply to specific censures. Moreover, the Dominican Pietro Giovanni Saragozza never was the Master of the Sacred Palace, but only an associate of Bartolomeo de Miranda, who was Master from 20 March 1591, to 7 June 1597.

[28] *Declarationes*, fol. 14ᵛ.

[29] Arcari, *op. cit.*, p. 69; Girolamo Tiraboschi, *Storia della letteratura italiana* (Florence, 1809), Vol. III, pp. 451–52. . . .

[30] I have already exposed the romantic myths that have grown up around the supposed role of Bellarmino in the trial of Bruno in my "Processo di Giordano Bruno", [above, n. 12], pp. 89–92.

philosopher, Antonio Montecatini.[31] Five years later he was still teaching Plato in the university, in spite of the condemnation of his work; and the course was interrupted only by his death, in February 1597. Only then, while Clement was considering the appointment of a successor, did Bellarmino, who had just been called from Naples as papal theologian and counselor for the Holy Office, enter the scene. When, according to a biographer, the pope asked his opinion, he responded that Platonism contained many more insidious subtleties than Aristotelianism. It did so not because it was more erroneous but rather because its deceptive affinity with Christianity could more easily lead minds from the straight path. Platonism, therefore, was more dangerous than Aristotelianism for the same reason that heresy was more dangerous than paganism. And Bellarmino recommended that the chair be suppressed.[32] Patrizi's successor thus became his eclectic rival, the same Jacopo Mazzoni of Cesena whose attempt to reconcile Plato with Aristotle, the *De Comparatione*, had been sent to the press in April of that same year, 1597.[33]

It was, then, not the generic Platonism of the *Nova Philosophia* that stirred up the murmuring of Patrizi's opponents in mid-1592. It was rather a group of specific assertions that might be suspected of heterodoxy. On November 7 he was called before the Congregation of the Index to give an account of these assertions. There was nothing he could do but offer to retract whatever turned out to be erroneous;[34] and of his own initiative he quickly presented, in his own handwriting, an "Emendatio."[35] But even that did not

---

[31] [The author here quotes from Montecatini's letter in] Garin, *La filosofia*, Vol. II, p. 63.

[32] See I. Fuligatti, *Vita Roberti Bellarmini Politiani, S.J.* (Antwerp, 1631), pp. 189–90.

[33] See P. Serassi, *op. cit.*, pp. 105 and 108 [and above, ch. 2]; Mazzoni's salary was raised to 1,000 *scudi*.

[34] Vatican Archives, "Archivio della Congregazione dell'Indice, Diari," Vol. I, at the date 7 November 1592. [I omit the long quotations from the Holy Office records that appear in the footnotes of the original from this point on.]

[35] *Ibid.*, "Protocolli," Vol. I, fols. 376–79. The date is missing but can be easily deduced from the letter quoted here below. I was not able to make a copy of this document.

satisfy the censors; and from then on the title *Nova Philosophia* always appeared in the printed versions of the Index as condemned "until corrected by the author and printed at Rome with the approval of the Master of the Sacred Palace." Patrizi therefore turned for help to one of the most authoritative cardinals on the Inquisition, the Dominican Girolamo Bernio, bishop of Ascoli:[36]

MOST ILLUSTRIOUS AND REVEREND LORD: I have been told that, in spite of the corrections I presented to Your Most Illustrious and Reverend Lordship, and in spite of my offer to emend the whole of my book, the book is still to be put on the Index "until expurgated." This seems incredible, for I am still working on an expurgation and expect to have it finished next week. I therefore beg you not to let me be given this perpetual infamy of being put on the Index, since I am most ready to obey that most holy tribunal. I would have come myself to present this petition to you, but the bad weather frightens me. I humbly kiss your hands and commend myself to your Grace.

At home, the 4th of December 1592.

Of your Most Illustrious and Reverend Lordship,
    the devoted servant,

FRANCESCO PATRICIO

[Superscription:] To my Most Illustrious and Reverend Lord Monsignor the Cardinal of Ascoli.

Patrizi's prompt obedience and his fear of "perpetual infamy" did him little good. On the same sheet with the letter is written: "The Congregation holds that no injury has been done [to Patrizi], since much more illustrious men have been put on the Index pending expurgation [of their works]."[37] These were harsh, disdainful words for the aging philosopher; and except for the Biblical solemnity of the "pending expurgation" phrase, they seem to reflect an attitude of inexorable intransigence, deaf to the least worldly consideration.

[36] Autograph letter in the same "Archivio dell'Indice, Protocolli," Vol. I, fols. 465–68.

[37] There is a similar note on the exterior side of the sheet [quoted in the original] and in Vol. I of the "Diari," December 5.

Seven days later Patrizi kept his promise and presented the Congregation with a hastily emended version of his text and with a request that it be turned over to authoritative judges. Instead, and without telling him what they were doing, the cardinals decided to leave the examination to the Master of the Sacred Palace and to keep unchanged the condemnation pronounced upon the printed version.[38] Completely unaware of what had happened, Patrizi addressed another petition, three months later:[39]

MOST ILLUSTRIOUS AND REVEREND LORDS: Francesco Patrizio requests that, having many days past, before Christmas, presented to this most holy tribunal his book emended, and having asked that it be given to review to a person competent in the subject and in the confidence of the tribunal so that he could, if necessary, emend it still further: having then learned that it had not been given to anyone, he now petitions once again that it be given to be reviewed as soon as possible in order that it may be published and that copies presently in the hands of the bookseller can be properly altered. And he will regard this as a singular favor.

[Superscription:] Pro Patritio. Die 23 martii 1593.

From the context it appears that the distribution of the Ferrara edition had been suspended, that many copies were still in Mammarelli's offices, and that Patrizi hoped to "alter" the work by replacing not too many pages with others duly corrected. Thus on the twenty-seventh of the same month he decided to hand over the text he had already emended, along with the censured portions, to the general of the Jesuits, who was then Claudio Acquaviva, so that a father in the general's confidence might conduct a conclusive examination.[40] The father selected was the Genoese Benedetto Giustiniani, a man of great authority and learning, but certainly not one to judge a philosophical work,

38 "Diari", 12 December 1592....
39 "Protocolli," Vol. I, fols. 464 and 469, original but not autograph.
40 See the instructions written onto the memo. The same words are in the "Diari" at 27 March 1593....

given his substantially juridical education.[41] Poor Patrizi's situation seemed now improved. He warmly recommended his cause to Clement in an audience he obtained on 23 April.[42] The opinion of Giustiniani, moreover, after a close examination, cannot have been too harsh, for at the end of June Patrizi sent another memorial to the cardinals of the Index in this vein:[43]

MOST ILLUSTRIOUS AND REVEREND LORDS: Several days ago the Very Reverend Father General of the Jesuits returned to Father Friar Pavolo,[44] secretary of this holy Congregation, the correction made by me of my philosophy along with another one made on commission of His Reverend Lordship by Father Benedetto Giustiniano. I, Francesco Patricio, now petition Your Most Illustrious and Reverend Lordships to deign to order that Father Giustiniano's correction be given to me in order that I might finish correcting my philosophy in its entirety and that the work might come out corrected and expurgated according to the decree of his holy tribunal. Which I will receive as a singular favor.

[Superscription:] To the holy tribunal on the Index. For Francesco Patricio.

It is clear that Patrizi, in referring to the condemnation "until corrected," hoped to republish his emended text before the publication of the Index of prohibited books then being prepared. He must have been consoled, then, by the decree of 3 July, which ordered Giustiniani's criticisms turned over to him and invited

[41] Giustiniani was an outstanding canon lawyer and an auditor of the Rota. He later distinguished himself with an influential "Parere" ("Opinion") on the annulment of the marriage of Henry IV of France (Vatican, Cod. Ottoboniano, 2423). He died in 1622.

[42] Patrizi gained the audience as bearer of a message from the duke of Ferrara (see Solmi, *op. cit.*, p. 135).

[43] "Protocolli," Vol. 1, fols. 466–67, original but not autograph. The date is missing, but it must have been written a few days before the deliberation of July 3 referred to below.

[44] Paolo Pichi, a Dominican from Borgo San Sepolcro, and secretary of the Congregation of the Index from 1593 until 1613, when he was made bishop of Volterra. He died in his sleep in 1622. See I. Taurisano, *Hierarchia Ordinis Praedicatorum* (Rome, 1916), p. 115.

him to get together with his censor on a final redaction of the emended passages.

Evidently the task of polishing the text included a fairly deep investigation of the very structure of the work, for it took almost a year to complete. Finally, on 3 June 1594, Patrizi was able to return to the Congregation with a written defense of the theses that had been censured and with a certificate favorable to publication signed by another learned Jesuit, the Spaniard Juan Azor, a teacher of moral theology in the Collegio Romano.[45] Instead of granting his request, the cardinals called in the censor they had appointed and invited Giustiniani to present his own opinion. Giustiniani appeared eight days later with a response that must have been rather ambiguous. For the cardinals decided not to rely upon it completely, and they referred the matter for final decision to Cardinal Toledo, who was forthwith furnished with all the pertinent documents.[46]

Thus Patrizi's fragile little boat, which until then had had at least a slight hope of arriving in port, suddenly crashed into the intransigence of the rigid Jesuit Cardinal Toledo. In the session of 2 July 1594, Toledo's conclusions were heard and discussed; and they resulted in the prohibition of the whole work. Patrizi in person was called before the Congregation to hear a recitation of a list of his errors, which, he was told, ought never to be held or taught by a Catholic, particularly in Rome. The obstinate pride of the polemical scholar vanished. Humiliated and frightened, he submitted himself and his work to the correction of Holy Mother Church and of the Holy Congregation in particular. He asked pardon for his errors. He insisted that he had committed them solely out of ignorance. And he declared, as an obedient son of the Church, that he had never really held and taught as true what was written in his book. The judges then reprimanded him, first harshly and then mildly. They ordered him to gather up scrupulously all the copies of his work that could be found and to hand

---

[45] Azor, a native of Lorca, died in Rome on 19 February 1603.
[46] [Long passages from the documents are quoted in the notes to pp. 170–71 of the original, here omitted.]

them over for destruction to the secretary of the Congregation. The copies that could be found in Rome were quickly deposited with the Master of the Sacred Palace. A few escaped through the "treason" of Mammarelli, who fled to Ravenna, where a good number of the volumes he had printed were stored, in order to escape total financial ruin.[47] Mammarelli sent the sheets to his colleague Roberto Meietti in Venice, who put up what few mutilated copies he could for sale with the publication date of 1593.

In spite of his prompt and humble submission, which at least one contemporary historian thought worthy of record, Patrizi did not succeed in avoiding the "perpetual infamy" of being included in the Index. He was spared only the harsh formula "completely prohibited"; and in the Index of Clement VIII published on 27 March and distributed on 17 May 1596, the milder formula used in the first condemnation was repeated, leaving open a hypothetical emendation in the future.[48]

[47] The first work Mammarelli had printed in Ferrara was indeed another work of Patrizi, the *Milizia romana*, dedicated by the printer to Alfonso II d'Este, on 23 March 1583. . . . One of his later productions was a reprinting of the *Filosofia morale* of Anton Francesco Doni. Bibliographers have assigned the date 1610 to the edition from the "MDCX" printed on the title page and in the dedication. See S. Bongi, "Catalogo delle opere di A. F. Doni," appended to the Florence, 1863, edition of the *Marmi* (Vol. II, p. 289). But it certainly is of 1590, as can be seen in the arabic numerals in the colophon. The printer apparently reversed the "C" and the "X" in the Roman numeral. Besides the *Nova Philosophia*, he also published, in 1591, with the title *Exordium Lecturae*, the inaugural lecture of Cesare Cremonini at the University of Padua, delivered on January 26 of that year. In 1592–93 he did the first reprinting of Parts I and II of Giovanni Botero's *Relazioni universali*, which had appeared in Rome for the first time in the same year, 1592. His device was the pelican, who tears her breast to nourish her children, and the motto *Quid non cogit amor*.

[48] J. A. de Thou, *Historiarum Sui Temporis Libri CXIX* (London, 1733), Cap. 17, Vol. V, p. 716 (from the first, posthumous, edition of 1620): "He had many adversaries, and just before his death he retracted the new philosophy that had been censured." From de Thou derives clearly the later mention of the affair by a historian of the University of Padua, N. C. Papadopoli, in *Historia Gymnasii Patavini* (Venice, 1726), Vol. II, p. 258. . . . From the Index of 1593, which was printed but not published, derives probably the Venetian edition "apud Floravantem Pratum, 1595," cited by Guerrini, *op. cit.*, p. 218. It is anterior to the official Index of Clement VIII, but it already notes, on p. 55, the condemnation of Patrizi.

Disappointed in his hopes for success and glory, and profoundly humiliated by the destruction of his greatest work, Patrizi was forced to give up metaphysical speculation and take refuge in technical and scholarly researches in military science.[49] It was not, then, "old age and an improper environment" that reduced the philosopher to silence, as F. Fiorentino has supposed. It was rather the harsh condemnation and the threat of still harsher punishments. Indeed, his theoretical bent was as alive as ever: as late as spring 1596 he was "completely taken up in ideas about how to bring to an end his entire philosophy," as he told his friend [Baccio] Valori [in Florence] on April 20 of that year.[50] But he never emerged from that cloud of fears and unrealized ambitions. He continued his public teaching, which was attended somewhat less now by the adulators and dilettantes of former years, but which was still followed with great interest by young students. A certain Giovanni Zarattino Castellini, recalling many years later his sojourn in Rome during the first months of 1595, wrote: "I attended the university in those days, when Francesco Patrizi was lecturing on Platonic philosophy. He also wrote against Tasso, who nevertheless went to see him. . . . I often joined a group of instructors and young students after the lectures, in which even Tasso took part."[51]

The two old adversaries were thus reconciled in the bitterness of old age; and the common destiny that had brought them from the Este court to a sad twilight in the house of the cardinal-nephew was now preparing to join them in the tomb as well. On 7 February 1597, less than two years later than Tasso, Patrizi closed his eyes for ever. The Fathers of St. Onofrio buried him under the high altar of their church, in the same anonymous grave in which lay the remains of the poet of the *Gerusalemme*.

[49] His last work, the *Paralleli militari*, came out in two folio volumes in Rome in 1594–95.

[50] In Solmi, *op. cit.*, pp. 139 and 143, justifying his refusal to write a biography of Marsilio Ficino, which he himself had proposed to Valori the year before.

[51] Letter to an unknown correspondent from Faenza, 8 October 1611, in Solerti, *op. cit.*, Vol. II, p. 388.

PART FOUR

Political Vitality
and Economic Recovery

12 Rome: Political and Administrative Centralization in the Papal State in the Sixteenth Century[1]

JEAN DELUMEAU

Jean Delumeau, a former fellow of the French Academy in Rome, is now professor of modern history and director of the Institut de Recherche Historique at the University of Rennes. He is also *directeur d'études* at the École Pratique des Hautes Études in Paris (Section VI). Besides his monumental *Vie économique et sociale de Rome dans la second moitié du XVI*e *siècle*, of which the present article is a continuation and an elaboration, he has written two books in the field of economic history: *L'Alun de Rome* (Paris: S.E.V.P.E.N., 1962), and *Le Mouvement du port de Saint-Malo: Bilan statistique, 1681–1720* (Paris: Klincksieck, 1966). He is also author of a general survey of the Reformation, *Naissance et affirmation de la Réforme* (Presses Universitaires de France), which is now being translated into English, as well as a synthetic study of the Renaissance, *Civilisation de la Renaissance* (Paris: Arthaud, 1967). He is currently writing a general history of the Catholic Reformation.

CARDINAL ALBORNOZ[2] had dreamed in the fourteenth century of creating a large Italian state, effectively, and not just nominally,

[1] "Le progrès de la centralisation dans l'État Pontifical au XVIe siècle," *Revue historique*, CCXXVI (1961), 399–410. Translated by the editor with the approval of the author and the permission of the publisher, Presses Universitaires de France.

[2] [Cardinal Gil Albornoz was the legate for the Avignon popes at Rome from 1353 to 1365. He attempted to reduce all the areas nominally subject to the pope to papal control, and to this end he published his famous *Constitutions* in 1357. His aggressive policies provoked a counterattack by a league of free cities under the leadership of Florence in 1378; and most of his accomplishments were undone during the last phases of the Great Schism.]

subject to the pope. But only in the sixteenth century was his dream finally realized.[3] This realization has frequently been obscured by a more traditional thesis, one which can be traced back to the reports of the Venetian ambassadors of the age[4] and which emphasizes the political and administrative weaknesses of the Papal State at the beginning of modern times. [But this thesis overlooks a number of significant events;] and it is the purpose of this brief, synthetic essay to rectify the thesis accordingly.

Actually, the century that opened with Julius II saw the extension of the frontiers of the Papal State to the north, the incorporation of many of the autonomous enclaves within its frontiers, and the reduction of the power of the feudal nobility. Here are the principal dates:

1506: the defeat of the Bentivoglio and the occupation of Bologna by the armies of Julius II.
1509: the recovery of the cities in the Romagna—Faenza, Ravenna, Cervia, and Rimini—which previously had fallen into the

---

[3] On the subject of centralization in the Papal State, the following can be consulted: Niccolò Del Re, *La Curia romana* (Rome, 1941); Jean Delumeau, *Vie économique et sociale de Rome dans la seconde moitié du XVIe siècle* [hereafter referred to as *Vie économique*], 2 vols. (Paris: Boccard, 1957–59); G. van Gulik and C. Eubel, *Hierarchia Catholica Medii et Recentioris Aevi* (Münster-in-W., 1901), especially Vol. III; G. Moroni, *Dizionario di erudizione storico-ecclesiastica* (Venice: Emiliana, 1840–61); P. Pecchiai, *Roma nel Cinquecento* (Bologna: Cappelli, 1948); E. Rodocanachi, *Les institutions communales de Rome* (Paris: Picard, 1901); A. Serafini, "Le origini della Segretaria di Stato" in *Romana Curia a Pio X . . . Reformata* (Rome, 1952); . . . W. V. Hofmann, *Forschungen zur Geschichte der kurialen Behörden vom Schisma bis zur Reformation* (Rome: Loescher, 1914). [To this list may now be added Giampiero Carocci, *Lo Stato della Chiesa nella seconda metà del sec. XVI* (Milan: Feltrinelli, 1961), though unfortunately the author did not see fit to postpone publication in order to take advantage of Vol. II of Delumeau's *Vie économique*, which covers much the same ground more thoroughly.] Much information is still to be found in Ludwig von Pastor's monumental *History of the Popes*, of which the Italian translation by Angelo Mercati and Pio Cenci, *Storia dei Papi* (Rome, 1942 *et seq.*), is preferable to the German original or the French translation.

[4] *Relazioni degli ambasciatori veneti al Senato*, ed. Albéri, particularly the report of Marino Giorgi (1517) in Ser. II, Vol. III, p. 55; that of Luigi Mocenigo (1560) in Ser. II, Vol. IV, p. 28; that of Girolamo Soranzo (1563), *ibid.*, pp. 88–89; and that of Paolo Paruta (1595), *ibid.*, pp. 388 ff.

hands of the Venetians, although some of these cities had to be retaken in 1529.

1532: the seizure, by surprise, of Ancona.[5] This mercantile city, which previously had enjoyed considerable liberty, was henceforth kept under control by a powerful fortress, and its population was disarmed. The capital of the Marche, which normally should have been established at Ancona, was established instead at Macerata.

1540: during the so-called Salt War[6] the Baglioni were finally defeated, and a fortress was built to keep Perugia thereafter in subjection.

1542: the victory of Paul III over Ascanio Colonna, who also had risen in revolt over the salt tax. The chief fortress of the Colonna at Paliano fell into the hands of papal troops.

1545: Camerino was incorporated into the Papal States.

1585: Count Pepoli of Bologna, the most respected nobleman of the city,[7] was condemned to death and executed for refusing to hand over a bandit who had taken refuge in his palace. This execution provoked as much emotional stir in Italy as

[5] See the account of this event by Giuliano Saracini, *Notitie historiche della città d'Ancona* (Rome, 1675), especially pp. 337–42.

[6] [The autonomy of Perugia had been guaranteed at the end of another Salt War in 1379. When Paul III unilaterally raised the price of salt, which Eugenius IV had prevailed upon them to buy solely from the Apostolic Chamber, the Perugians rebelled and recalled the chief member of the Baglioni family, Rodolfo, who was then in the service of Cosimo I de' Medici. The salt tax, needless to say, was the last straw: Paul had already imposed four special *decime* in the first six years of his pontificate.] See also Pastor, *Storia dei papi*, Vol. v, pp. 216 ff.

[7] [The name of the family is associated with a small town on the Apennine border of Tuscany, where the Pepoli possessed an autonomous feudal domain. It served as a gathering point for Florentine exiles in the mid-1530's. According to Pastor, Giovanni Pepoli was the victim of the machinations of one of his enemies, who prevailed upon the cardinal legate to entrust him with the criminal proceedings. What really sealed Pepoli's fate was not so much his refusal to give up the bandit as his reluctance to acknowledge the authority of the pope over his previously free imperial fief. After his enemies produced "proof" that he had referred to Sixtus V as a "tyrannical friar," there was nothing even the duke of Ferrara could do to save him; and he was quietly strangled in prison. This bit of semilegal injustice had the desired effect of frightening all the nostalgic citizens of Bologna out of any further opposition to the commands of the pope.]

the execution of the duke of Montmorency was to provoke
in France in 1632.[8]

1578–1595: the defeat of those feudal nobles (Paolo Giordano
Orsini, Alfonso Piccolomini, Ramberto Malatesta, and
Marco Sciarra)[9] who had encouraged or actually led the
groups of bandits that then infested much of the Papal
State.

1598: the last great event on this list—the recovery of Ferrara and
the flight of Cesare d'Este from the city of his ancestors.

This is an imposing list of successes. But it must not be permitted to hide the fact that the antifeudal policy was frequently
checked, stalemated, and even forced into significant retractions.
Clement VII was defeated by an imperial army allied with the
Colonna in 1527. Leo X was not seeking to incorporate the duchy
of Urbino into the Papal State when he started the War of 1517,
but rather to give it as a fief to his nephew Lorenzo. The same
Paul III who humiliated the Perugians and the Colonna also
invested his son Pier Luigi with Parma and Piacenza and his grand-
son Ottavio with the duchy of Castro—presents of which he
repented only after it was too late. Paul IV followed his predecessor in pursuing the Colonna; but he seized their fiefs of Paliano,
Marino, Nettuno, et al. only for the purpose of creating a duchy
in 1556 for his nephew, the count of Montor (who, nevertheless,
did not succeed in keeping it very long). Finally, all the popes had
to fight until the end of the seventeenth century against the right

[8] On bandits and their protectors, see my *Vie économique*, Vol. II, pp. 529–66.
[Henri de Montmorency was one of the last great proponents of the independence of the feudal nobility in France. In 1632 he led a rebellion against Richelieu
and the royal government in the province of Languedoc, of which he was
governor and one of the greatest landowners. He was defeated, tried before the
Parlement of Toulouse, and then, in spite of the pleas of his many influential
friends, executed.]

[9] [Sciarra was the "Robin Hood" of the kingdom of Naples in the latter
sixteenth century, rather than a feudal baron, and he identified himself more
with the peasantry than with the aristocracy. His romantic career and tragic
end are fully described by Rosario Villari in *La rivolta antispagnola a Napoli*
(Bari: Laterza, 1967, pp. 58 ff.); see ch. 13 below.]

of asylum,[10] which nobles, cardinals, and ambassadors insisted upon maintaining for their residences.

Yet in spite of the obstacles, the moments of weakness, and the concessions, the general line of development remains clear. Its high point is marked by Pius V's bull *Prohibitio Alienandi Feudi* (*Prohibition Against Granting Fiefs*), which later provided the legal basis for the recovery of Ferrara and Urbino.[11] It is significant that Gregory XIII refused to grant a papal fief to his son, Giacomo Boncompagni, in spite of the great affection he bore him. And Giacomo had to be furnished with domains outside of the Papal State—the *marchesato* of Vignola near Mantua, and the county of Arpino and the duchy of Sora in the kingdom of Naples. In 1578 the same pope ordered the verification of all feudal titles[12]—an order which it was hoped would restore some fifty castles to the Apostolic Chamber (*Camera Apostolica*). The order itself [was galling enough to the barons. But since it] was issued in the wake of particularly bad harvests, it brought about a renascence of banditry as well. One of the leaders of the feudal opposition to this latest effort at centralization was Alfonso Piccolomini, duke of Montemarciano, who revolted in 1578. But he revolted in vain: his castle had already been razed, and now he himself was executed.

To be sure, banditry never completely disappeared from the Papal State: it had existed before, and it continued to exist after the sixteenth century. But between 1578 and 1595 it became extraordinarily virulent. At certain moments the bandits managed

[10] [The right of asylum was usually accorded to churches in secular states until most of them abolished it in the eighteenth century. The institutions or places which enjoyed it were exempt from the jurisdiction of the local administration of justice. Hence, anyone sought by the police could escape arrest by getting inside one of them.]

[11] Bull of 29 March 1567, in *Bullarium Diplomatum et Privilegiorum Summorum Romanorum Pontificum* (Turin, 1860 *et seq.*; hereafter cited as *Bullarium*), Vol. VII, pp. 560 ff.

[12] Confirming the measures already taken [in this matter], Gregory XIII published the famous bull on the rights of the Apostolic Chamber on 1 June 1580: *Bullarium*, Vol. VIII, pp. 336 ff., and Augustin Theiner, *Codex Diplomaticus Dominii Temporalis S. Sedis* (Vatican, 1861–62), Vol. III, pp. 547 ff.

to cut off communications between Rome and Naples; and the gates of Rome were closed as in wartime. On many occasions the city authorities had to treat with the bandits and sign temporary peace pacts. To be sure, these pacts could never be more than truces, for the Papal State was too committed to a policy of consolidation to tolerate these anarchical forces indefinitely: hence the victorious campaign conducted under Clement VIII between 1592 and 1595. [But banditry was merely the most obvious manifestation of much more complex phenomena.] It represented a rebellion of the country against the rapidly growing city. It represented an upsurge of centrifugal forces,[13] particularly in those provinces with a long tradition of insubordination like the Marca d'Ancona and the Romagna. And it represented an attempt by the peripheral areas of the Papal State to escape increasing control by the capital. From this point of view the end of the sixteenth century marks a real victory for Rome. True, the war between Hungary and the Turks greatly facilitated the task of Clement VIII by permitting him to ship a good number of outlaws off to Central Europe. Still, during the last years of the century the temporal domain of the popes enjoyed a greater interior calm than it had ever before known. The harvests of Romagna and the Marche increased notably.[14] Pilgrims traveled with relative safety along the highways during the Holy Year of 1600. And Botero could write [as early as 1595]: "The Ecclesiastical State is more peaceful today than formerly and the authority of its prince is greater than it has ever been."[15]

[13] See Braudel, *La Méditerranée et le monde méditerranéen au temps de Philippe II* (1949), pp. 643–60.

[14] Delumeau, *Vie économique*, Vol. II, pp. 539 and 629.

[15] Botero, *Relazioni universali* (Rome, 1591–96), of which many other editions appeared during the lifetime of the author: "Discorso intorno allo Stato della Chiesa," pp. 33 and 37. [(Part II, Book IV of the Venetian edition of 1605, pp. 145–52.) Giovanni Botero, born in Piedmont in 1544, was one of the most prolific and popular writers, particularly on political subjects, of the Counter Reformation. He served as secretary to several princes, most notably to his own, the dukes of Savoy, and to Charles and Federico Borromeo, archbishops of Milan. He died in 1617, leaving his property to the Society of Jesus. He is best known today for his attempt to overcome Machiavelli's antinomy

This notable achievement was in great part the work of an internal administration which, in spite of its frequent (and to us today rather strange) confusion between the spiritual and temporal spheres, was relatively well-developed for the age. Regional administration became increasingly docile toward central authority. The administrative offices in the capital became increasingly specialized. Something like a prime minister emerged, in the person of a cardinal-nephew or, when there was none, in the person of a secretary of state. This prime minister was the predecessor of Olivarès, Richelieu, and Mazarin in the following century. His chief duty was the supervision of foreign policy.

The third most important figure in the state (or the second, when both functions were given to a cardinal-nephew) was the cardinal-chamberlain (*camerlingo*), who was the head of the entire administration of the temporal domain. The administration in turn was subdivided into legations or "presidencies": The Patrimony [Latium], Campania (including [the pocket of] Benevento in the kingdom of Naples), the Marche of Ancona, Bologna, Romagna, and Avignon. The legate of each of these circumscriptions was a cardinal. But the legates seldom resided there, and the actual power in each province was exercised by a vice-legate. At the beginning of the century the vice-legate was almost always a creature[16] of the legate, though he was less often so at the end. At Bologna the vice-legate was chosen directly by the pope from a list of several names submitted by the legate.[17] The vice-legate in turn named the governors of the principal

---

between politics and religion, the *Ragion di Stato* (first published in Venice in 1589), of which the title quickly passed into current usage in all European languages ("raison d'état," "reason of state") to designate a particular set of political doctrines. The most recent edition of his works is the *Della ragion di Stato . . . con tre libri Delle cause della grandezza delle città*, ed. Luigi Firpo (Turin: U.T.E.T., 1948).]

[16] [From the Italian *creato* (not from *creatura*, to which corresponds the English "creature" in the usual sense). The term designates one who owes his promotion (or, in the case of cardinals, "creation") to another; and this debt was usually prolonged by feelings of personal obligation.]

[17] According to the Venetian ambassador Giovanni Dolfin: Albéri, *Relazioni*, Ser. II, Vol. IV, p. 460.

cities and the commissioners or *podestà* of the smaller ones. As delegates of the central government, these governors and commissioners took part in the deliberations of the municipal government and were represented in all judicial decisions. The collection of direct taxes was in the hands of treasurers appointed from Rome.

To be sure, the various cities of the state still maintained the exterior vestiges of their former autonomy. But no one at the time was fooled. The political and financial authority of the commune of Rome was no longer anything but a memory. The city was guarded by the *castellano* of the Castel Sant'Angelo, who was appointed by the pope; and the chief of police was the governor himself, who at the same time was the vice-chamberlain. The same was true for Bologna, the second city of the state. As he was passing through Bologna in 1574, the French traveler Nicolas Audebert noted, in a fragment of a journal still unpublished:[18] "The governor must discuss the affairs of the city with the *gonfaloniere*. On such occasions they both reside in the city hall. And although such are the ancient customs, nonetheless the governors honestly dispense with them, so that of the Republic there remains nothing but the name and certain ceremonies." At the end of the sixteenth century all the higher officials of the state, including the governors, were ecclesiastics; and although they were certainly not always excellent administrators, they enjoyed the significant advantage of being more docile than laymen to the orders of a theocratic government. Paul II was the first pope to put the fortresses under the control of ecclesiastical dignitaries (1464); and he did so for the purpose of making sure that the fortresses remained loyal to him.[19] By 1600 the term "ecclesiastical state" had become a very appropriate term for describing the temporal dominion of the Church. The Roman nobility complained bitterly of this "tyranny of priests"; for even in local government their authority had been taken over by representatives of the Roman court.

[18] British Museum, London, Landowne MS 720, fol. 67.
[19] Moroni, *Dizionario*: article entitled "Governatore."

Still more important than the docility of the provincial administration was the increasing specialization of the central offices. This development is already fully visible in the division of work in the Apostolic Chamber at the end of the century. The cardinal-chamberlain, the treasurer-general, and the auditor were assisted by the clerks of the Chamber (seven before Sixtus V; twelve thereafter). The departments dependent upon some of them merit special mention: the Roman Bureau of Coinage, Civitavecchia, the Tolfa mines, highways, prisons, Roman river tolls, land tolls, and the food supply of the capital.[20] The congregations of cardinals, which became permanent in the sixteenth century and which became increasingly numerous from the time of Gregory XIII and Sixtus V on, also functioned as specialized governmental commissions. Usually they met once a week. The earliest of these congregations were limited in competence to religious questions. Others straddled both spiritual and temporal matters. Still others concerned themselves with nothing but the administration of the state. Of this last group one was in charge of food supply, another of highways and bridges, another of the navy, another of the University of Rome, another "for the decrease in taxes." There was a Congregation of the *Consulta*—a kind of general administrative tribunal. And there was a Congregation of Good Government (*Buon Governo*), created by Clement VIII in 1592, charged with proposing all kinds of improvements in the interest of the subjects and soon charged also with going over the financial accounts of the communes—a task of considerable importance.[21] Did the French government at the time of Henry IV possess central administrative organs of so high a degree of specialization?

[20] See the manuscript collection entitled "Avvisi d'Urbino," especially Cod. Urb. Lat. 1042, fol. 8A, 20 January 1571; 1054, fols. 12B–13A, February 1586; 1055, fol. 389B, 5 September 1587; and 1056, fol. 18A, 9 January 1588, in the manuscript section of the Vatican Library.

[21] *Bullarium*, Vol. IX, pp. 603 ff. See also [Petrus Andreas] De Vecchis, *Collectio Constitutionum, Chirographorum, et Brevium Diversorum Romanorum Pontificum Pro Bono Regimine Universitatum ac Communitatum Status Ecclesiastici*, 3 vols. (Rome, [1732–43]), and A. Lodolini, "L'amministrazione pontificia del Buon Governo," *Archivi italiani*, VI (1919), 181 ff., and VII (1920), 3 ff.

Certainly the development of a spirit of methodical administration took place all over Europe toward the end of the sixteenth
century. It was perhaps farthest advanced in Spain and in Spanish
America under Philip II. But it was also present in such different
decisions of the papal government as the creation, in 1562, of
local archives for the preservation of legal contracts,[22] the sub-
ordination of notaries to the Apostolic Chamber,[23] and Gregory
XIII's organization of a regular diplomatic corps, with a hierarchy
of subordinate offices.[24]

In spite of what has been said to the contrary, then, the Papal
State was not behind the other states of Europe in 1600, at least
from the point of view of the centralization of administrative
authority.

The transformation of the temporal domain of the Church
into a centralized state is important for another reason: it is closely
connected with the renascence of the city of Rome during the
sixteenth century. Albornoz had managed to impose his will for a
moment on the feudal nobility—but on behalf of a pope who
resided at Avignon. He had tried to create a state without a
capital. From the time of Nicholas V, and above all of Julius II,
the popes adopted a different policy. They sought to transform
Rome into a large and beautiful city; and this new city then
imposed itself, by the force of circumstances, as the natural center
of the temporal domain. From this point of view even those popes,
like Leo X, who pursued a family policy hardly compatible with
the interests of the Papal State, still contributed effectively to the
consolidation of the state through the money they spent in Rome
and for Rome. During the course of the century the city rose in
population from about 30,000 to about 100,000.[25] It was filled

[22] Romolo Quazza, *La preponderanza spagnuola (1559–1700)*, "Storia politica
d'Italia," 2nd edn. (Milan: Vallardi, 1950), p. 146.
[23] *Loc. cit.*; cf. *Bullarium*, Vol. VII, pp. 285 ff.
[24] Pastor, *Storia dei papi*, Vol. IX, pp. 47–49.
[25] On the growth of Rome and on the other subjects treated in the following
paragraphs, see my *Vie économique*, Vol. I, pp. 280–81 and 469–85, and Vol. II,
pp. 751–845.

with sumptuous public and private palaces, with majestic and luxurious churches, with new streets and new quarters, with reconstructed aqueducts and gracious fountains that assured it an abundance of good drinking water. Rome grew rapidly just as Bologna entered a period of stagnation and Ancona lost much of its wealth. At the same time, it became more Italian—not because of its ever more numerous visitors from abroad, but because of its growing resident population; and consequently it became much more connected with Italy. At the end of the century, thanks largely to the example of the Medici popes, the language of administration had become Tuscan. Thus to a large extent it was Rome itself which created the modern Papal State.

Rome played in the Papal State a role comparable to the one Versailles was to play in France. For reasons of prestige the nobles left their medieval *castelli* and established themselves in the capital. There they rivaled one another in the display of luxury: palaces, hunting expeditions, carriages, and enormous dowries—all of which devoured their capital and left most of them, by the end of the century, heavily in debt. The Colonna, the Orsini, the Savelli, the Caetani had to sell much of their rural property; and if they managed to preserve a position among the upper Roman nobility, it was now thanks to the favors of the popes, upon whom they became closely dependent. Rome thus transformed bellicose barons living in country fortresses into civilized, and subject, court nobles.

The Colonna had to sell Nettuno, and the Savelli had to give up Castel Gandolfo[26] at the time of Clement VIII. At the same time, other new nobles without a military tradition arose to challenge their position of pre-eminence: the Boncompagni, the Peretti, the Aldobrandini, and the families of the other Catholic Reformation popes. The resistance of the feudal nobility [to Papal authority] was thus weakened just at the moment when the popes were forced, for financial reasons, to tighten their hold on the state.

It was not by accident that the revolt of Perugia and of the Colonna in 1540–42 broke out as a protest against the increase in

[26] [Well known today as the summer residence of the pope.]

the salt tax. The Councils of the fifteenth century and the secession of the Protestants had cut into the resources of the Apostolic Chamber in a very disquieting manner. It was just at this time, moreover, that the introduction of artillery increased considerably the cost of warfare; and like all the other states of Europe the Papal State found itself in need of new revenues for military purposes. The Urbino War of 1517 and the war against Spain in 1557 were very costly. At the same time the popes sought to assist the Catholic princes of Europe in their struggles against the Turks and the Protestants; and money thus poured out of Rome to Hungary, Malta, and France. Sixtus V, moreover, found it necessary to construct a navy. To military expenses were added those of turning Rome into a grandiose capital city. The reconstruction of St. Peter's alone, from 1506 to 1626, required more than forty-four tons of pure silver—which is the equivalent of the gross receipts of the Holy See during an entire year in the period around 1590.

Where could all the money be found? [As foreign sources of revenue dried up,] the popes were forced to find new ones in their own domains; and, indeed, by the end of the century some three-quarters of their income came from the Papal State, which now paid three times what it had in 1500. Taxation became much heavier, notably on wine and meat: hence the constant complaints reported by the Venetian ambassadors. At the beginning of the century the Papal State was the least-taxed state in Italy. But by the end of the century it was probably the most heavily taxed. It was largely, then, in order to find the money they needed that the popes were led to reduce their previously insubordinate territories to obedience.

But papal income still remained insufficient to cover the immediate needs of the popes; and from 1526 on, and particularly after 1550, they had recourse to massive loans. They created a public debt; and through the intermediary of the great banks they floated papal bonds (*luoghi di monte*) all over Italy and even abroad. Rome thus became a center of high finance; and Genoese and Florentine bankers fought among each other for the privilege of buying up blocks of papal bonds. Within the short span of half a century, Rome borrowed more than 380 tons of silver. Only the backing of a pope could have permitted, in the Papal State of the sixteenth century, so great an appeal to private investors. Rome thus achieved a financial primacy that crushed out all its rivals in the rest of the state; and this primacy was fully recognized by the other cities and by the feudal barons.

The other cities, also, had need of money, usually to pay the taxes they owed to Rome; and Ancona, Perugia, Orvieto, and Bologna obtained permission as well to float *monti* on the Roman market with the backing of the Apostolic Chamber. So did the great barons; and the Colonna, the Savelli, the Cesarini, and the Muti similarly received permission to create a public debt with government support. The most heavily indebted member of the upper nobility in the seventeenth century was Odoardo Farnese;[27] and his conflict with Urban VIII was in large measure provoked by his inability to pay the interest due on his *monti*.

Rome's predominant place in the Papal State was further encouraged by its position as a monetary capital.[28] In this regard the struggle was just as intense against what remained of the right of the other cities to coin money. Besides Avignon, there were four state mints: at Bologna, Ancona, Macerata, and Castro. But Perugia, Camerino, Fano, and even, under Sixtus V, Montalto in the Marche frequently issued coins. Controlling the issuing of money in the provinces was more difficult than in Rome; and

[27] [Urban's second (if not first) motive in this dispute was his desire to carve out a feudal domain for his own family, the Barberini, similar to the one procured for the Farnese family by Paul III a century earlier. Odoardo, duke of Parma and Piacenza, was excommunicated after expiration of an ultimatum about settling his debts in 1642, and Urban confiscated the feudal domain he held inside the Papal State, Castro. As a consequence Tuscany, Venice, and the Farnese declared war on the pope and forced him to give Castro back; and it was finally incorporated into the state only during the pontificate of Urban's successor—who did not feel obliged to hand it over to the Barberini.]

[28] Information on monetary questions is to be found essentially in B. Garampi, *Saggi di osservazioni sul valore delle antiche monete pontificie* (a rare book, left unfinished, and printed around 1766), and E. Martinori, *Annali della Zecca di Roma* (Rome: Istituto Italiano di Numismatica, 1917–22).

decentralization of coinage increased the risk of differences in quality among pieces that theoretically were of the same value. Sixtus V seems to have decided, for the first time, to suppress the provincial mints in 1589. His successor, Clement VIII, made a serious attempt in 1595 to close all of them except the one in Avignon. But even in the seventeenth century the popes were forced to authorize the coining of money at Bologna, at Ferrara, and even, occasionally, at Gubbio, though the amount of money thus coined was relatively unimportant. Here again the Papal State compares well with the rest of Europe. In France at the same period Paris was the principal mint for gold; but silver coins were more often produced by the other twenty-two mints of the kingdom.[29] In the Netherlands each province, and indeed each city, jealously maintained its rights of mintage; and the Estates General never succeeded in suppressing them. There were fourteen local mints at the beginning of the seventeenth century.[30] In Spain the silver brought in from America was coined not at the capital but at Seville, at Segovia, and at times at Barcelona.[31] One more significant fact: in 1595 the whole Papal State was forced to adopt the system of weights and measures used by the capital.[32]

Another reason for Rome's increasing supremacy is to be found in the exigencies of food supply. As the city increased rapidly in population and visitors from abroad became ever more numerous, the problem of food supply became much more severe. This situation was made still worse by the fact that the surrounding countryside was more and more turned over to pasture, deforestation, and malaria. Until the middle of the century at least, the land of the Campania and the *Patrimonio* easily managed to keep the

[29] F. Spooner, *L'économie mondiale et les frappes monétaires en France* [1493–1680] (Paris: Colin, 1956), esp. pp. 215–75.

[30] J. V. Dillen, "The Bank of Amsterdam" in *History of the Principal Public Banks* (The Hague, 1934), p. 81.

[31] Earl Hamilton, *American Treasure and the Price Revolution in Spain* (Harvard University Press, 1934), p. 27, n. 2.

[32] Aminitore Fanfani, *Storia del lavoro in Italia*, 2nd edn. (Milan: Giuffrè, 1959), p. 44. Rome's example was followed by Milan in 1604 and by Piedmont in 1612.

capital supplied and even to furnish foodstuffs for exportation. But in the second half of the century, and particularly after 1580, local production became incapable of supplying even Rome; and the city turned to Sicily and perhaps even to the Marche of Ancona for supplements. Between 1554 and 1599 the Apostolic Chamber made fourteen different contracts for special importations of grain . . . and it placed progressively stricter controls on the exportation of cereals from the state. A fundamental date is established by Pius IV's letter of 13 August 1562.[33] The principle set forth in this letter (which is actually a piece of legislation) is that as a general rule the extraction of cereals is forbidden without authorization, and that this prohibition applies to the whole Papal State, not just to the provinces near Rome. Thus in the area of the grain trade central authority took the place of local authority, even in the Marche and the Romagna. In 1566 Pius V extended this control from cereals to all food products.[34] In 1578 Gregory XIII ordered that exportation licences bear the signature of the pope himself.[35] In 1588 Sixtus V tripled exportation taxes—to the great detriment of Ravenna, which had always sold much of its harvest to Venice.[36] At the same time, the Apostolic Chamber set up a number of grain depots in the Romagna and the Marche for the purpose, apparently, of assuring provisions for the capital.[37]

The dependence of the state upon Rome was encouraged in still another way: through the improvement of postal services. In the sixteenth century Rome was probably the most important postal center of Europe. It was furnished with regular couriers to all the major cities of Italy and Western Europe. Toward the end of the century the Master of the Papal Post Office sought to create a similar system of regular service between Rome and the cities of the state. Thus, while in France Paris shared its importance in the

[33] *Bullarium*, Vol. VII, pp. 386 ff.
[34] *Ibid.*, Vol. VII, pp. 848 ff.
[35] *Ibid.*, Vol. VIII, pp. 215 ff.
[36] Vatican Library, Manuscript Section, Cod. Urb. lat. 1056, fol. 124B, 19 March 1588.
[37] Col. Urb. lat. 1055, fol. 333B, 1 August 1587.

postal system equally with Lyon, in the Papal State Rome was without a rival. The routes from Rome to Bologna, to Loreto and Ancona, to Alatri, and to Benevento were traversed several times a week by the *ordinari* of the Papal Post Office;[38] and other localities were served by those on the routes to Naples and Florence. It thus became far easier for the authorities at Rome to keep check on the whole domain.

By the end of the century, then, the popes disposed of a state that administratively was the equal, if not the superior, of any other state in Europe. They thus possessed a number of important trump cards in the game of international politics, especially in Italy. And not the least of these trump cards was an economic one, namely, the alum mines at Tolfa. The papal government had bought the mines from the Frangipani shortly after they were discovered in 1462;[39] and far from decaying after the death of Agostino Chigi in 1520,[40] as some historians have held, they continued to prosper for a long time thereafter.

Yet as a political entity the Papal State seldom exerted any attraction upon foreigners or upon other Italians during the course of the sixteenth and seventeenth centuries. To be sure, pilgrims continued to pour into Rome in great numbers; but they looked upon the Eternal City as a religious and artistic center largely detached from its geographical and political context. For centralization alone was unable to create a modern state, one capable of making an impression beyond its borders. It has often been said, and justly, that the frequent change of popes, and therefore of administrative personnel, was the chief cause of the political weakness of the Papal State. [Yet the explanation is not wholly valid]

---

[38] Vatican Archives, Bandi, arm. IV, bk. 70, *Poste*, esp. the edicts of 1592.

[39] By contrast, neither Charles V nor Philip II succeeded in getting the Spanish state to buy the alum mines of Mazarron. On this question see F. Ruiz Martín, *Les aluns espagnols* (Paris: S.E.V.P.E.N., 1967).

[40] G. Zippel, "L'allume di Tolfa e il suo commercio" in *Archivio della R. Società di Storia Patria*, xxx (1907). I have just now finished a work on the Tolfa mines from 1462 to 1797 [which has since been published—see introduction to this chapter].

for the popes changed no more rapidly than did the viceroys of Sicily or Catalonia.[41] And such changes avoided one of the causes of the political weakness in France: the sale of offices with the right of passing them on to the heirs of the incumbent.[42] For in the Papal State venal offices were sold only to ecclesiastics, and thus they reverted to the pope whenever the incumbent died or was promoted to a higher position, like the cardinalate. Finally, the popes never had to face opposition from constitutional bodies like the French *parlements*.

The principal weakness of the Papal State lay rather in the social and economic order. A comparison with the United Provinces of the Netherlands is illuminating in this regard. On one hand, a theocratic government which confers on the prince an absolute power over the souls as well as the bodies of his subjects; on the other hand, a loose federation of autonomous provinces where important decisions must be taken by a unanimous vote in the Estates General, which resembles an assembly of ambassadors. On one hand, a Catholic monarchy administered largely by ecclesiastics, whose sovereign can not only remove them at will from their posts but also excommunicate them; on the other hand, a Calvinist republic of provincial estates and autonomous cities over which the central government has very little control. On one hand, an idle aristocracy, a depopulated countryside, an industry of mediocre stature, a great number of beggars, a commercial fleet composed mostly of small boats, an often arbitrary and seldom efficacious system of justice. On the other hand, an enterprising bourgeoisie interested in commerce and industry,[43] an active program of lake drainage,[44] a numerous population, prosperous towns and villages, the world's greatest fleet, a surprising degree

[41] Helmut Koenigsberger, *The Government of Sicily under Philip II of Spain* (London: Staples Press, 1951), p. 199.

[42] Cf. Roland Mousnier, *La vénalité des offices sous Henri IV et Louis XIII* (Rouen: Maugard, 1945), particularly pp. 63 ff. and 309 ff.

[43] Cf. Violet Barbour, *Capitalism in Amsterdam in the Seventeenth Century* (Baltimore: Johns Hopkins, 1950).

[44] G. L. Burke, *The Making of Dutch Towns* (London: Cleaver-Hume, 1956), pp. 108–12.

of safety in the cities and on the highways, a university (Leiden) at the forefront of European intellectual activity, schools of painting that rivaled those of Rome, and active and intelligent artisans capable of producing such fine work as Delft faience. On one hand, finally, economic stagnation—the sclerosis of a society in which work was incapable of producing new wealth and in which too many people got too heavily into debt. On the other hand, intense activity, an appreciation of work, a sense of thrift and of calculated risk.

What was lacking in the Papal State of the Catholic Reformation, then, was not an adequate administrative structure but a healthy society and a healthy economy. The Papal State enjoyed an excellent geographical position in the center of the peninsula and a famous capital. Had it been able to add to these advantages an active agriculture and an active industry, it might have been able to bring about the unification of Italy—and to have done so well before the nineteenth century.

13 Naples: The Insurrection in Naples of 1585[1]

ROSARIO VILLARI

Rosario Villari was born in 1925. He is now professor of modern history at the University of Messina and director of the journal *Studi storici* in Rome. He has written numerous articles on the history of southern Italy. Besides his most recent *La rivolta antispagnola a Napoli: Le origini (1585–1647)*, from which the essay here translated is taken, he has written three important books: *Mezzogiorno e contadini nell'età moderna* (*The South and the Peasants in the Modern Period*, 1961); *Il Sud nella storia d'Italia* (*The South in the History of Italy*, 1961, and three subsequent editions by 1966); and *Conservatori e democratici nell'Italia liberale* (*Conservatives and Democrats in the Age of Italian Liberalism*, 1963), all published in Bari by Laterza.

THE first signs of the formation of popular political movements in Naples[2] are to be found in the last two decades of the sixteenth century. Hunger riots, appeals to the example of Flanders, religious anxiety, banditry, messianic visions, freethinking, and libertinism

[1] "L'insurrezione cittadina," first published in *Studi storici*, VIII (1967), and then incorporated as Section 1, ch. 2 of Villari's *La rivolta antispagnola a Napoli: Le origini* (Bari: Laterza, 1967). Translated and slightly abridged by the editor with the approval of the author and the publisher, Giuseppe Laterza e Figli.

[2] [The terms "people" and "popular" in this article (*popolo* and *popolare*) are always used in their historical sense. They sometimes refer to the native inhabitants of the city who did not have titles of nobility. They sometimes refer to that class of citizens in between the nobles (both the urban aristocracy and the feudal landowners who more and more during the sixteenth century spent much of the year in the capital) on one hand and the "plebeians" (*plebi*) on the other. In the latter sense the terms indicate a juridical status roughly (but only very roughly) equivalent to the *popolo grasso* and the *popolo minuto* of the northern Italian communes. The term "barons" (*baroni*), similarly, refers not to a specific rank of nobility, as it usually does in English, but to all the feudal nobility in general.]

—all these are expressions of an extraordinary tension during these years. They are not individual aspects of a single historical process consciously directed toward a precise goal. But they do have something in common: their radical rejection of [the entire established order] and their reflection of a feeling of helplessness among the "oppressed."

The Insurrection of 1585 wore itself out without effecting any notable change in the structure of the state. But at the same time it brought about the first crack in the political and cultural hegemony maintained until then by the nobility. The nobles had been strengthened by the assimilation of Renaissance human-ism, and they had drawn up a program of "national" autonomy with which to confront their foreign monarchs.[3] Once the acute moment of violence and terror had passed, however, the political landscape was found to be somewhat different from what it had been during the first decades of Spanish domination. The pro-tagonists were no longer just the monarchy and the barons; and the barons were no longer the sole spokesmen for the political conscience of the kingdom. The insurrection, then, did have a lasting effect: it put into motion a wave of popular opposition to the monarchy that was to become stronger and stronger in the years following as it was reinforced from other sources.

Giorgio Spini has justly observed that the study of seventeenth-

[3] [Since the Norman conquest the crown of Naples had passed first to the Hohenstaufen, then, in the second half of the thirteenth century, to the house of Anjou, and then, in the fifteenth, to a lateral branch of the house of Aragon. The individual rulers, even those of foreign origin, all resided at Naples; hence the period is usually referred to as *Il Regno*—or at least it is by Benedetto Croce in his classic *Storia del Regno di Napoli*, 4th edn., from the first of 1924 (Bari: Laterza, 1953), though more recent historians have proposed a completely different system of periodization: see ch. 1 of Giuseppe Galasso, *Mezzogiorno medievale e moderno* (Turin: Einaudi, 1965). After the union of the main line of the Aragonese with the crown of Castile through the marriage of Ferdinand and Isabella, and after the crisis provoked by the French invasion of 1494, Naples became a part of the empire; and its "kings" during the sixteenth century were the Emperor Charles V and, after his abdication, King Philip II of Spain. The "king" was thus no longer resident, and Naples was governed by a viceroy. Hence the appellation of the next "Crocean period," lasting until the accession of Carlo di Borbone in 1734, *Il Viceregno*.]

century Italian authors requires "an arduous labor of deciphering a sort of secret writing," a kind of writing imposed either by the "need to defend oneself against Inquisitorial persecution" or by the "interior complexity and uncertainty of the hard-working discoverers of unknown spiritual continents."[4] Spini's remark can be extended not only to texts, but also to the practical attitudes and political positions. There is a key to the cipher, however: it is to be found in the extremist movements that preceded the full triumph of the Counter Reformation. The hopes that were then expressed under the illusion that radical political changes could in fact be brought about continued to be present thereafter, more or less modified by the experience of defeat and by adaptation to the new political, cultural, and religious situation.

The Insurrection of 1585 marks a division between two phases in the history of the viceroyalty[5] and in the relations between Naples and the Spanish crown. This event inaugurated a period of agitation which ended in the failure of Campanella's revolt [of 1599], but which at the same time led to widespread questioning of the whole constitution of the kingdom and its political and cultural tradition.

The two greatest conflicts between subjects and the crown had occurred during the tumults of 1510 and 1547. Both conflicts were provoked by attempts to introduce the Spanish Inquisition into Naples. But both were in reality shocks brought about by the settling of the political equilibrium upon which Spanish dominion rested. The role played by popular forces in these conflicts was essentially that of transferring to a lower social plane the political program of the aristocracy, which traditionally had sought to balance the power of the crown with the influence of Rome.[6]

[4] Spini, *Ricerca dei libertini*, p. 12.

[5] [This is the nearest English can come to the term *Viceregno*—which in Italian means almost always nothing more than Naples in this period, just as the *Regno* ("the kingdom") often refers specifically to the kingdom of Naples (in all periods, not only in the period before the advent of the Spanish). Hence I use the term "the kingdom" in English when the author uses *Regno* in this sense.]

[6] [Ever since the Norman conquest Naples had been technically a feudal dependency of the papacy. This dependency was usually more theoretical than actual; but it frequently afforded domestic dissenters an opportunity to seek outside support.]

That program would have been wrecked by the establishment of an Inquisition dependent upon the crown alone. Even so, the aristocracy did not welcome this assistance from the people. Tristano Caracciolo showed a decided repugnance for the short-lived alliance between the two classes in 1510. His *Commentaries*[7] are much less preoccupied with the appearance of extraneous elements in the revolt than they are with the fear that popular initiative might diminish the values and the dignity of action of the nobles. Other contemporary manifestations of discontent— most of them brief and inconsequential outbursts, like the one brought on by the famine of 1508[8]—had seen "nobles and citizens animated by the same fear"[9] and lined up in mutual self-defense. In 1547, moreover, the attitude of the nobles was anything but consistent. "During the day they fraternized with the people; during the night with the viceroy."[10] Consequently for the first time there developed the germs of an autonomous popular movement. It was one directed against the *eletto*,[11] Alberto Terracina, and it was immediately stamped out.[12]

The Insurrection of 1585, on the other hand, revealed a disposition among some groups of the city bourgeoisie to present demands of their own. It is this new circumstance that explains the "memorable" quality of the event, "famous throughout the world," as one contemporary called it.[13] What gave it still more

---

[7] . . . *Opuscoli storici editi e inediti*, ed. G. Paladino; here cited on pp. 115–17 in *Rerum Italicarum Scriptores*, [3rd edn.], Vol. xxii (Bologna, 1934).

[8] G. Passero, *Prima pubblicazione in stampa, che delle storie in forma di giornali, le quali sotto nome di questo autore erano andate manoscritte, ora si fa a sue proprie spese da Vincenzo Maria Altobelli*, with preface by M. Vecchioni (Naples, 1785), p. 153.

[9] Michelangelo Schipa, *Masaniello* (Bari: Laterza, 1925), p. 24.

[10] L. Amabile, *Il Santo Officio della Inquisizione in Napoli* (Città di Castello, 1892), Vol. i, p. 210.

[11] [As becomes clear below, the city government, or council, was composed of elected representatives (called *eletti*—I maintain the Italian term) from each of six *piazze* in the city.]

[12] B. Capasso, "La Vicaria vecchia. Pagine della storia di Napoli studiata nelle sue vie e nei suoi monumenti," *Archivio storico per le province napoletane*, xix (1889–90).

[13] G. C. Capaccio, *Il forestiero* (Naples: Gio. Domenico Roncagliolo, 1634), p. 485.

fame, to be sure, was its reflection of the first great fracture to occur within the Spanish empire, namely, the revolt of the Netherlands.

Two main currents of opinion still dominated the political and cultural scene in Naples at the moment the revolt broke out. One of them derived from the ideas of the aristocracy. The other derived from the legalism [of the jurists]. The aristocratic tradition went back to the *Nobilitatis Neapolitanae Defensio* (*Defense of the Nobility of Naples*) of Tristano Caracciolo and to the platform he had defined in his speech for the coronation of Alfonso II of Aragon.[14] It was a tradition based on the principle of government "according to blood," a principle which admitted no action on the part of the monarchy that might be independent of the . . . barons. This is the position of Angelo Di Costanzo, whose works came out on the eve of the Insurrection of 1585.[15] In the *Apologia dei tre Seggi illustri di Napoli* (*Apology for the Three Illustrious "Seggi,"* [Venice, 1581]), he put several of the protagonists of the baronial revolt and of the aristocratic opposition to the monarchy in a gallery of "heroes."[16] He then edited one of the last and most suggestive works of Caracciolo, the *De Varietate Fortunae*. In his most important work, the *Historia del Regno di Napoli* (*History of the Kingdom of Naples*), he gathered the fundamental themes of the aristocratic tradition into an organic historical view with a precise political program. They were themes, to be sure, which had developed at the time of the Aragonese dynasty, when the monarchy was weak. But they were also themes which could still exert some pressure

[14] On the ideas and political program of Caracciolo's *Oratio*, published as "Oratio ad Alphonsum Juniorem" in *Opuscoli*, pp. 173–76, Eberhard Gothein, *Il Rinascimento nell'Italia meridionale*, Ital. tr. (Florence: Sansoni, 1915), and Tommaso Persico, *Gli scrittori politici napoletani dal 1400 al 1700* (Naples, 1912), p. 184, may still be consulted. See now also the recent *Tristano Caracciolo e la cultura napoletana della Rinascenza* (Naples: Armanni, 1957) by Mario Santoro.

[15] A part of his history of the kingdom was published in 1572 by Mattia Cancer in Naples. The entire work was published at Aquila by G. Cacchio in 1581.

[16] See particularly pp. 12–13 and 36. . . .

on public opinion, in spite of their anachronistic character.[17]

These extreme positions were not countered, either among Neapolitans or among official apologists of the Spanish governors, by any attempt to provide a rigid defense of centralism and monarchical absolutism. The regalist doctrines of the principal exponents of the Neapolitan juridical school—Matteo D'Afflitto, Jacopo De Franchis, and Marino Freccia—had accepted the viewpoint of the aristocracy; and they thus contributed more toward an eventual accord between the crown and the barons than to a defense of the rights of the former.[18] D'Afflitto appealed to the example of Catalonia and the "political liberty" it enjoyed through the limitations exerted by local laws and institutions upon the authority of the king.[19] His position was not unique. And he contributed to a convergence of ideas and policy regarding the constitution and the relations between the kingdom and Spain. The basis of this convergence was the concept of autonomy, conceived of as the respect for the traditional "liberties" and prerogatives of the nobility. The position of another regalist, Camillo Porzio, was substantially the same. It was based upon a reciprocal autonomy between nobility and crown. In his report [*Relazione*] to the marchese di Mondejar of 1577–79, he demanded that "the offices and benefices that had been theirs in the time of the Aragonese kings" be reserved to Neapolitans. The importance of this request lay in its reference to a historical period that the nobles looked back to with nostalgia. Thus Porzio echoed many of the

---

[17] B. Croce, "Angelo Di Costanzo poeta e storico" in *Uomini e cose della vecchia Italia*, Series 1 (Bari: Laterza, 1927). On Di Costanzo and the historiographical environment of Naples in his time, see also the preface by Ernesto Pontieri to Camillo Porzio, *La Congiura de' Baroni del Regno di Napoli contra il re Ferdinando Primo e gli altri scritti*, ed. Pontieri (Naples: Edizioni Scientifiche Italiane, 1959).

[18] Freccia bases his argument upon history (rather than upon abstract law); and his investigation of Neapolitan feudalism emphasized, therefore, the peculiarities of Naples with respect to feudal institutions in other parts of Italy and Europe. See C. Ghisalberti, "Marino Freccia e la storia del diritto feudale," *Clio*, 1 (1965), No. 4.

[19] *Decisiones Sacri Regii Consilii Neapolitani* (Venice: "Ad Signum Concordiae," 1588), pp. 209–10.

elements typical of the aristocratic antimonarchical attitude: "The barons also are dissatisfied because they are burdened with 'donations' beyond their ability to pay and because royal officials give their subjects such pride that they cannot be controlled."[20] On a more general level Scipione Ammirato affirmed the principle that the sovereign is obliged not to alter the constitution of a kingdom when that kingdom has submitted to him on the condition that its subjects' privileges be respected.[21]

The relations between crown and nobility were eventually established on just such principles as these; and they were established so firmly that neither occasional quarrels between viceroys and barons nor vestiges of nostalgia among the nobility could infringe upon them any longer.

The immediate cause of the Insurrection of 1585 was the decision of the *eletti* to increase the price of bread in the capital.[22] Shortly before they had authorized the exportation of more than 400,000 *tomoli* of grain to Spain.[23] Speculative operations of this kind were not new in the history of the city government, although they had usually been smaller in scope. Indeed, they formed an integral part of the mechanism of the grain trade, which was largely controlled by those in political power. These two measures were thus a normal consequence of an alliance between the city aristocracy and the great provincial grain-producers.

This decision, however, came at a moment when the balance of social classes throughout Mediterranean Europe was dangerously threatened by an increasing divergence between prices and real wages. The divergence had started as early as 1520; but the wage curve had suddenly taken a sharp turn downward toward the low

[20] In *La Congiura de' Baroni*, p. 376.

[21] *Discorsi sopra Cornelio Tacito* (Florence: Filippo Giunti, 1598), Book I, Discourse v. [On Ammirato, see above ch. 2.]

[22] [See the testimony of] T. Costo, in *Giunta di tre libri [Appendix of Three Books to the] Compendio dell'Istoria del Regno di Napoli* . . . "in which is contained everything worthy of memory that has occurred in the kingdom from the beginning of 1583 to the end of 1586" (Venice: Barezzo Barezzi, 1588), p. 135.

[23] G. A. Summonte, *Historia della Città e Regno di Napoli*, ed. G. D. Montanaro (Naples: Giacomo Gaffaro, 1643), Vol. IV, pp. 446–47 . . . [quoted at length in n. 17 to p. 38 of the original].

level that was to be reached in the decade 1590–1600.[24] This downward turn was the result of a process affecting the whole social structure: a disequilibrium between the increase in productivity and the increase in population. This disequilibrium acted directly upon wages; and it was reflected in the demographic and social structure of the city,[25] particularly in the efforts, from

[24] See Earl Hamilton, *American Treasure and the Price Revolution in Spain* (Harvard University Press, 1934), pp. 262–82. In Catalonia the price of grain went up threefold during the century, while agricultural wages seem to have remained stationary: John Huxtable Elliott, *The Revolt of the Catalans: A Study in the Decline of Spain, 1598–1640* (Cambridge University Press, 1963), p. 59; and it is precisely in the last thirty years of the century that the increase in grain prices at Barcelona was the sharpest: E. Giralt Raventós, "En torno al precio del trigo en Barcelona durante el siglo XVI," *Hispania*, XVIII (1958), 38–61, and Pierre Vilar, *La Catalogne dans l'Espagne moderne: Recherches sur les fondements économiques des structures nationales* (Paris: S.E.V.P.E.N., 1962), Vol. I, pp. 558–59 . . . [a table follows]. The fall of real wages in Languedoc has been analyzed with great finesse and considerable documentation by Emmanuel Le Roy Ladurie, *Les paysans de Languedoc* (Paris: S.E.V.P.E.N., 1966), Vol. I, pp. 263–80: prices of grain went up sevenfold between the periods 1480–1500 and 1585–1600, while wages of the basic categories of workers went up only threefold. For the entire Mediterranean, see Braudel, *La Méditerranée*, Vol. I, pp. 534–64. The data already published for southern Italy confirm the hypothesis of a depression of wages at the time; but they do not permit the establishment of a detailed line of development. See N. F. Faraglia, *Storia dei prezzi in Napoli dal 1131 al 1860* (Naples, 1878) [who concludes generically that wages remained unchanged while the price of food rose], p. 145. See also C. Massa, "I salari di mestieri in Terra di Bari dal 1449 al 1732," *Giornale degli economisti*, XLII (1911), 553–76; and for a different judgment, G. Coniglio, "Annona e calmieri nella Napoli spagnola," *Archivio storico per le province napoletane*, LXV (1940), 105–96, and "La rivoluzione dei prezzi nella città di Napoli nei secoli XVI e XVII," *Atti della IX riunione scientifica della Società Italiana di Statistica* (Rome, 1952). See also the general considerations in the preface by R. Romano to the anthology *I prezzi in Europa dal XIII secolo a oggi* (Turin: Einaudi, 1967), which includes selections from the volume of F. Parenti, *Prime ricerche sulla rivoluzione dei prezzi a Firenze* (Florence: C. Cya, 1939).

[25] See B. Capasso, *Sulla circoscrizione civile ed ecclesiastica e sulla popolazione della città di Napoli dalla fine del sec. XIII* (Naples, 1882), p. 31: Giuseppe Pardi, *Napoli attraverso i secoli. Disegno di storia economica e demografica* (Milan, Rome, Naples, 1924). Some description, with a dose of moralizing, in Schipa, *Masaniello*, pp. 23–24. By the end of the century the parish organization of the city was wholly insufficient and had to be expanded and reorganized. The archbishop, Alfonso Gesualdo, who worked out an interesting plan in this regard, noted that the antiquated structure of the Church made impossible an exact knowledge of the number of souls in the city. It also made it difficult

mid-century on, to halt immigration from the country[26] and to classify all "vagabonds" as delinquents.[27] The demand upon the labor market was shrinking rapidly.

On the other end of the social scale the fall in wages ... was one of the principal factors in the dynamics of the relations between the two upper classes. What social groups succeeded in inserting themselves most profitably in the "scissors" between wages and prices? [The question can to some extent be answered by noting] a parallel between two phenomena: the fall in wages and the increasing separation between the representatives of the people in the city government on one hand and the artisans and "plebeians" on the other. At the end of the sixteenth century the function of representing the people was completely in the hands of the privileged bourgeoisie—the tax-farmers, the rentiers, and the grain merchants. The separation of the *eletto del popolo* from the electoral basis of the office—the *Seggio di Sant'Agostino* and the ancient organizations in the quarters of the city (*piazze* or *ottine*)— had begun during the first years of Spanish dominion. It was furthered by two "reforms" adopted toward the middle of the century. In 1548 the viceroy, Toledo, ordered after the dismissal of the *eletto* Francesco di Piatto that henceforth the *Seggio di Sant'Agostino* should not elect its representative directly, but rather present him a list of six names from which to choose the representative.[28] Shortly afterward the *piazze* of the nobles were given the

---

for religious authorities to exercise control over the inhabitants, especially foreigners: Archivio Vaticano, Rome, Congregazione del Concilio, Relationes ad limina (Naples, 1595): "Discorso sopra le reforme della parocchie della città di Napoli. . . ."

[26] Under the viceroy Mendoza (1555) and his successors, Toledo's urban policy was completely reversed. See Capasso, *Circoscrizione di Napoli*. At the end of the century, indeed, a *Commissario contro i forestieri* ("Commissioner against Outsiders") was set up: A.S.N., Consiglio Collaterale, Curiae, Vol. XXXII, 28 November 1591.

[27] In the decree of the duke of Ossuna of 20 March (Biblioteca della Società Napoletana di Storia Patria [hereafter cited as B.S.N.S.P.], MS IX, A.9) this treatment is extended also to "those who work in the shops of several masters one or two days a week, and by this [subterfuge] escape the title of vagabond, even though they really are that."

[28] Summonte, *op. cit.*, Vol. IV, p. 215.

power to carry any measure in the council upon the affirmative vote of any four of them, even in the absence of the representative of the people. These "reforms" further reduced the ability of the *eletto del popolo* to influence the general policies of the kingdom through the city government. They diminished the control of the people over urban magistrates and practically eliminated the presence of popular organizations in public life. Finally, they favored the gradual absorption of the privileged bourgeoisie into the aristocracy. The aristocracy thus maintained its monopoly of city government, which was one of the most important bases of power in negotiations with the crown.[29]

All the autonomous popular organizations, on the other hand, underwent a profound crisis from which they were never to recover. The same thing happened in the governments of the urban centers in the provinces, though there the situation was somewhat less complex and the assimilation of the middle-class oligarchy into the local nobility was more rapid.[30]

[29] M. Schipa, in "Nobili e popolani in Napoli nel Medioevo," *Archivio storico italiano*, Ser. VII, Vol. III (1925), 4–44, 187–248, arrives at a different conclusion. As a result of the reforms [of the sixteenth century], he says, "nobles, professional men, and merchants united." The *eletto del popolo* thus became "largely an instrument of the viceroy, controlling the nobles in the interests of absolutism." A clear sign of the decadence of popular organizations can be found in the dispersal of the statutes and public acts that regulated the complex functions of the *Seggio del Popolo*, with its tribunal, its district captains, its role in particular sectors of the life of the city, and its prerogatives with respect to the nobility. An attempt to track down the documents was made, without success, after 1547 by the notary Castaldo, a historian and the secretary of the *Seggio*. The weakening of connections between the *Seggio* and its popular base and the decline of the prestige of the *eletto* is also evident in Summonte's particularly heart-rending judgment of the qualities of the various representatives. According to one chronicler, good *eletti* had become as rare as "white flies." For the history of Neapolitan institutions, see Schipa, "Contese sociali napoletane nel Medio Evo," published serially in *Archivio storico per le province napoletane*, XXXI (1906)–XXXIII (1906–1908), and "Il popolo di Napoli dal 1495 al 1522," *ibid.*, XXXIV (1909), 292 ff., as well as the summary in the first paragraph of "La mente di Masaniello," *ibid.*, XXXVIII (1913), 655–80, and XXXIX (1914), 95–431.

[30] The case of Teramo, fully illustrated by F. Savini in *Il Commune di Teramo nella sua vita intima e pubblica* (Rome, 1895), pp. 331–455, can be considered typical (the "oligarchical reform" of the commune took place in 1562). For

It is not surprising, then, that the high point of the Insurrection was the lynching of the *eletto del popolo*, Giovan Vincenzo Starace, in the course of an unruly public meeting on 9 May.[31] For the next few days the city remained in arms, "wondering whether worse was still to come, should the people in other cities wish to imitate the example of Naples."[32] Popular fury was also directed against other members of the class to which Starace belonged, many of whom fled for safety to the castles.[33] The Insurrection thus revealed an organizational capacity among the lower classes

---

Calabria, see Galasso, *Economia e società nella Calabria del Cinquecento* (Naples: L'Arte Tipografica, 1967), pp. 293–324. The collection of the statutes of Molfetta, edited by Luigi Volpicella as *Gli statuti dei secoli XV e XVI intorno al governo municipale della città di Molfetta* (Naples, 1875), makes it possible to follow the evolution of the laws of the commune over a whole century, from 1474 to 1574. The general lines of the development are set forth by N. F. Faraglia in his *Il commune nell'Italia meridionale, 1100–1806* (Naples, 1883).

[31] The son of a rich silk merchant who had been "master" of the corporation (merchants' guild), Starace had accumulated considerable wealth and had given up his father's profession to "live like a nobleman." He was a typical exponent of the privileged bourgeoisie that had monopolized the representation of the people in the city, and he frequently had held the position of *eletto*. He was accused of having favored a deal with the merchants charged with supplying the city with grain for the purposes of private speculation. "Everyone seems to be happy," wrote the Venetian ambassador on 16 May, "with the death of Starace. No one has yet said a word in his defense, and the people moved against him with great force because of his pride and because of the riches he has accumulated while in office. He has held the office twice before; and the preceding day he had greatly infuriated the people by telling them that if they rose up, he would make them eat dirt for bread." F. Mutinelli, *Storia arcana ed aneddotica d'Italia raccontata dai veneti ambasciatori* (Venice, 1856), Vol. II, p. 144.

[32] A. Bulifon, *Giornali di Napoli dal 1547 al 1706*, ed. N. Cortese (Naples: Società Napoletana di Storia Patria, 1922), Vol. I, p. 58.

[33] "Il tumulto napoletano dell'anno 1585," an anonymous report ed. N. F. Faraglia in *Archivio storico per le province napoletane*, XI (1886), 433–41; Costo, *Giunta* (Naples: Orazio Salviani, 1591), p. 181. Among others who were pursued by popular fury were the wine merchant Leonardo Andrea de Lione and the grain merchants Pietro Aniello Cimino and Solaro. The first of these was held responsible for "having created a shortage of wine in the whole kingdom, and then having it sold in Naples only in bottles at retail—a usage convenient to some but very hard on the mass of people, particularly the poor." Cimino had made a "deal" (*partito*) for importing 40,000 *tomoli* of grain into the city.

of the city that struck contemporaries with amazement.[34] It was not simply an explosion of wild anger. The masses followed the plans and intentions of their leaders with rigorous precision. Indeed, the real significance of the event lies in its careful organization.[35] The drama began with a meeting in the church of Santa Maria la Nova, where the *eletto* was to meet with the captains of the *ottine* for the purpose of sending a delegation to the viceroy. But the captains had gathered together a much greater crowd than the *eletto* had expected. Thus they prevented the formation of a delegation and instead forced the *eletto* to take part in a public debate at the headquarters of the *seggio* in the monastery of Sant'Agostino. Starace was put into the "chair" (*seggia*) in which he had come and carried, "with his shoulders turned and without his hat", toward Sant'Agostino.... It was a sort of triumph in reverse,[36]

[34] Some of this amazement is apparent in the baroque verses of G. C. Capaccio, an eyewitness of the event. [The author quotes a long stanza from B.S.N.S.P., MS xxix, E. 6, in n. 28 to p. 42 of the original.]

[35] The first account of the revolt to be published was that of Costo in the *Giunta* (1588). It was reproduced, with some modifications, in the Neapolitan edition published by Salviani in 1591 and in the Giunti edition of Venice, 1613. Several years later, toward the end of the century, G. A. Summonte dedicated to the Insurrection the final chapter of his *Historia*, but the last volume, which contained it, was published only in 1643. Interesting information is also given by Capaccio in *Il forestiero* and in the *Vitae Proregum Regni et Urbis Neapolis*, ed. Angelo Mai in *Spicilegium Romanum* (Rome, 1840), and then in *Diurnali di Scipione Guerra*, ed. G. de Montemayor (Naples, 1891), pp. 177–82. Jacques Auguste de Thou reconstructed the events in his *Historiarum Sui Temporis ab Anno Domini 1543 ad Annum 1607 Libri CXXXVIII* (Geneva: Pierre de la Rovière, 1620), Book LXXXII, exclusively from the pages of Costo, although he emphasizes certain aspects that are given merely as chronicle in his source and furnishes the first attempt at a historical explanation. Nothing new with respect to these authors is to be found in the account of D. A. Parrino, *Teatro eroico e politico dei governi de' vicere del Regno di Napoli* (Naples, 1692–94), or in Giannone's *Istoria civile*. Bulifon transcribes almost literally Summonte's narrative in his *Giornali*. Several eyewitness accounts are important: the dispatches of the Venetian ambassador, almost completely published by Mutinelli, *op. cit.*; the above-mentioned anonymous report published by Faraglia in 1886 (another published in the *Archivio storico per le province napoletane* in 1876 with the title "La morte di Giovan Vincenzo Starace" is less significant); and the *Diurnali di Scipione Guerra*, pp. 35–44.

[36] De Thou, *loc. cit.*: "inter mediam multitidinum quasi in triumphum ductus." On de Thou's work as a historian, see the excellent pages in Corrado

a symbol of rejection of authority, which was directed not only toward a particular person but toward the whole social class he belonged to.

The crowd took this event as a sign of revolt. As the parade went by, bystanders hurled insults: they shouted, "serra, serra," and plundered the stores in search of arms. The symbols of revolt then became more complex. Starace was killed. His body was then dragged through the streets, mutilated, and castrated; and the pieces were sold as if to be eaten. Finally, his house was sacked. To have been perfectly consistent, the rites should have culminated in the burning of the house, so that the women of the family might serve as "a sacrifice to God." Instead, all the furnishings were removed (to the value, according to the papal nuncio, of some 25,000 *ducati*). But even this gesture had a symbolic value. "They did not sack the house for the purpose of robbing it." Instead, they gave the furnishings to the monasteries. This gesture was not lost on contemporary observers, who fully understood what it meant: not just the killing of the *eletto*, but a declaration of rebellion, a disavowal of respect and "reverence for the master."[37] The rich were duly terrified: "All well-to-do persons were very much displeased, not so much by the tragedy of the *eletto* Starace as by the uprising of the people, particularly of the irrational and desperate plebeians, whose wrath they feared would soon be turned against them and their possessions."[38]

The event, then, was the manifestation of a will to overthrow the whole social order, and it was expressed in a language that the masses could immediately comprehend. At the same time it provided a formula which could serve, even at an elementary level, as a principle of organization. The very itinerary of the "body-dragging" ceremony is significant: first through the most popular

Vivanti, *Lotta politica e pace religiosa in Francia fra Cinque e Seicento* (Turin: Einaudi, 1963).

[37] "The duke had good reason to be angry, and the *plebe* was very wrong to show so little respect for its master. What it did was worse than homicide and assassination": Capaccio, *Il forestiero*, p. 495. The viceroy says much the same thing in A.S.N., Collaterale, Curiae, Vol. XXIX, 2 September 1585. . . .

[38] Costo, *Giunta*, p. 142ᵛ.

quarters of the city, the Selleria (as if to gain its solidarity with the action); then along the principal streets of the city; and finally, once the consent of the population had been obtained, before the palace of the viceroy—as if to provide the demonstration with a full political complement.

Where did the rebels learn this ritual, and what experiences enabled the people to comprehend it? The most fundamental precedent was certainly the procedure for administering capital punishments—a procedure which varied according to the social position of the victim.[39] Applying, therefore, the treatment reserved for lowborn criminals to someone of Starace's rank could mean nothing else, to the rich as well as to the poor, than a call for revolution. Other symbolic elements derived from the daily practice of recognizing social distinctions by outward gestures—gestures which were rigorously observed in the sixteenth century but which were to survive through the seventeenth only in the rural areas of the kingdom. To stand bareheaded before another person meant to recognize the superiority of his social class—not just the superiority of that particular individual.

The movement thus took over formulas that had been elaborated by the aristocracy and then turned them upside down. In so doing, however, it demonstrated its dependence (on a psychological and intellectual plane first, and only subsequently on a political one) upon "official" culture. But other signs were independent of that culture, though they had roots in the life and customs of the people. They may have expressed simply the exasperation of the poor. For the same signs appear again

---

[39] In the "Contesa graziosissima tra un nobile di Villa ed un Napoletano del popolo" ("Most Gracious Dispute between a Villa-Owning Nobleman and a Neapolitan of the People"), one of the liveliest chapters of the *Fuggilozio* o Tommaso Costo (Naples: Gio. Jacopo Carlino e Ant. Pace, 1598), this is the final argument used by the provincial noble to demonstrate his superiority to the man of the people: "Can you deny that nobility, even if it did me no other good, would at least have this benefit, that if I were brought to court for a capital crime, I would have my head cut off; whereas you, who are not a gentleman, would not have this privilege?" (p. 480.)

in all subsequent uprisings—though the chroniclers may well have exaggerated their more brutal aspects.[40]

The elementary reaction to the established order expressed by the Insurrection was not one which led to concrete political results. But some of the precise instructions passed through the mob and the obvious part played by the captains of the *piazze* convinced many observers that the movement had been fomented by persons who had clearer and more limited political objectives. The meeting at which the Insurrection started was composed, after all, not only of plebeians, but also of men of the *cappanera*—representatives of the professions and the magistracy. "Even though only persons of the lowest rank and of bad condition took part in the 'dragging,' it cannot be said that the 'people' [—the lower and middle bourgeoisie—] did not approve of the murder nor make use of the plebeians as an instrument for doing what would have been improper for themselves to do."[41]

The cry of "Death to bad government! Long live justice" that rose from the mob before the palace of the viceroy had a general political meaning. So also the specific demand for the abolition of the new sales taxes (*gabelle*) implied, in a somewhat rudimentary form, an opposition to the monarchy and the privileged bourgeoisie. Much more explicit in this sense was the demand for equalizing the votes of the nobility and the people in the city government. The demand was formulated in terms taken from the petition presented by the people's *seggio* to Ferdinand the

[40] L. Torraca, "A proposito di un recento episodio di antropofagia," *Atti dell'Accademia Pontaniana*, N.S., Vol. II (1963). The expression *morire strascinato* ("die by being dragged") was part of popular jargon when G. B. del Tufo wrote the verses of his *Ritratto o modello delle grandezze, delizie e marviglie della nobilissima città di Napoli* (1588), published in large part by S. Volpicella in "G. B. del Tufo, illustratore di Napoli del secolo XVI," *Atti della R. Accademia di Archeologia, Lettere e Belle Arti* (Naples, 1881), and then completely by C. Tagliareni (Naples: La Zagara, 1959). [The author here quotes at length (p. 46, n. 36) from the verses.]

[41] Costo's judgment that the Insurrection was promoted and organized by the *popolo*—by the lower and middle bourgeoisie, that is—is explicit in the Venetian edition of his *Giunta* of 1588. It is watered down, however, in the later editions of 1591 and 1613. [The author here quotes parallel passages from the 1588 and the 1613 editions.]

Catholic in 1507; and the ideal of independence was rendered current by direct references to the revolt of the Low Countries.

The demand for equalizing the votes was formulated at the moment when the viceroy was attempting to "postpone consideration of the matter until a later date" for fear of "some new and dangerous trouble."[42] Probably it was transmitted to him by the captains of the *ottine*, who were in close contact with the popular quarters of the city and were thus in a position to understand the reasons for the adherence of the lower middle classes. The testimony of the Venetian ambassador leaves no doubt as to the direction taken by the movement after the first few days: "New humors are being stirred up," he noted in his report of 26 May,

> humors that may cause even greater troubles; for the people have made known that they want re-established some privileges that they say have been abrogated. Among other things, they want [a reform of] the six *piazze* of this city, which control the city income and take charge of seeing that the population is properly supplied with food. Five of the *piazze* now belong to the nobles and one to the people, and each of the *piazze* has for many years had but one vote. They now want the single *piazza* of the people to have five votes—as many, that is, as have all five of the nobles together—so that with only one of the *seggi* ("seats"), the people can determine every resolution.

At the same time there appeared signs of an anti-Spanish orientation in the movement. It was said that some persons went around spying on the activities of the troops occupying the capital and that secret meetings were being held and arms were being collected in various parts of the city. Some posters were even put up that explicitly called for a rebellion against the Spanish. One of these posters suggested that the rebellion had just begun and set a time-table for its completion: "Oh insensitive people! You have begun, but you have not finished! On Corpus Christi let every man prepare. On St. John's day let him drop his bread and

42 Mutinelli, *op. cit.*, p. 148 [from which the next long quotation is also taken].

grab his gun."[43] Others threatened to create a second Flanders: "When it was let out that the viceroy would punish the leaders of the Insurrection, some persons went so far as to tell him to be careful and to keep in mind the affairs of Flanders."[44]

The first measures adopted [to calm the disturbance] were aimed at attenuating the economic crisis that had provoked it: 493,714 *tomoli* of grain were bought in Sicily and sold at the "political price" of $1\frac{1}{2}$ *ducati* per *tomolo* (the price had been $2\frac{1}{4}$–$2\frac{1}{3}$ *ducati*). The difference, which amounted to $368,695\frac{1}{3}$ *ducati*, was recovered by laying a tax upon the whole kingdom on the basis of a project carefully drawn up by the viceroy himself:[45] one-third was to be paid by the capital and two-thirds by the provinces, according to a sliding scale which diminished in proportion to the distance of a given province from Naples. This expedient was justified in that the importation of Sicilian grain had lowered the price of grain on the mainland, and particularly in the areas nearest to the capital. All those responsible for the administration of the city supported these measures, and they succeeded in overcoming much of the problem of food supply.

Two months after the end of the tumult ... forty galleys arrived in Naples with many companies of soldiers under the command of Don Pedro de Toledo. The viceroy, the duke of Ossuna, took the opportunity to embark upon a vast operation of repression. [He had reason to be nervous.] For the whole course of the revolt, as well as the reference to "the affairs of Flanders," had made it apparent that ideas of political independence, which the aristocracy had gradually abandoned, were now beginning to spread among the people. ... These ideas were not yet clearly formulated in terms of a political program. But they were already

43 *Il tumulto*, ed. Faraglia. On June 14 a young man who during a quarrel with a soldier had hollered: "When are we going to make salad out of these dirty Spaniards!" was arrested, publicly whipped (before an imposing array of Spanish soldiers), and sent to the galleys.

44 Mutinelli, *op. cit.*, p. 145.

45 B.S.N.S.P., MS XXVII, C.3: Il vicerè alla Sommaria, 12 June 1586. In November of 1585 the price of bread in the capital leveled off at 4 *grana* for 48 ounces.

capable of providing a framework for protests and criticisms such as those that were now directed against the privileged orders.

The task of searching out and bringing to trial those responsible for the Insurrection was given to a special commission composed of Annabile Moles as president, the regents of the *Consiglio Collaterale*, Antonio Cadena and Giovanni Antonio Lanario, the counsellor Ferrante Fornaro, and the public prosecutor Geronimo Olcignano. Moles had taken part in the examination of the event previously undertaken by the Council of Italy in Madrid and was thus informed of the decisions of the sovereign. Olcignano, a member of the Royal Council (*Sacro Regio Consiglio*), was selected because of the experience he had gained at Brussels as fiscal advocate in the cases against the counts of Horn and Egmont. One of the most well-tried Neapolitan generals, Carlo Spinelli, a veteran of numerous campaigns, was appointed regent of the *Vicaria*, with the job of assuring order in the city and organizing the arrest and execution of the culprits. During the second half of July "498 men" were seized "in three or four successive nights, without any notice or outcry. . . . And in three and a half months not only the 498, but 320 others were identified 'in contumacy'; and 820 trials were instituted."[46] Of these, 32 were condemned to death "with diverse sorts of torture"; 71 were condemned to the galleys, and 300 were exiled from the kingdom "with great fines and with the death penalty prescribed if caught within the borders."[47] At the same time, about 12,000 citizens who had in some measure taken part in the uprising fled the city—one last proof of its widespread character.[48]

The action of repression was made as terrifying as possible by the revival of spectacular punishments rarely used any longer in

[46] Summonte, *op. cit.*, Vol. IV, p. 462.

[47] Mutinelli, *op. cit.*, p. 152, and *Diurnali di Scipione Guerra*, pp. 37–41, in the notes.

[48] Mutinelli, *op. cit.*, p. 152; *Il tumulto*, ed. Faraglia; and *Diurnali di Scipione Guerra*, p. 41, n. 1. Among those condemned to death were two master artisans, one cloth merchant, two secretaries of the *Sommaria*, one secretary of the archdiocesan chancery, one citizen of Brussels (Georges Olivier), and numerous artisans and shopkeepers.

penal practice. These were the original models of the rites of the
Insurrection itself; but they became much crueler [in the hands of
the government], for they were applied not to a dead body but
to live men.[49] "Such is the terror among the people," commented
the Venetian ambassador, ". . . that I do not think anyone will try
anything new for any reason whatsoever."[50]

The investigations of the Consiglio Collatrale sought also to
uncover those leaders who had attempted to give the Insurrection
a political overtone. Thirty-three persons were exempted, accordingly, from the amnesty which "put an end to the numerous acts
of injustice committed since July" on 4 December. One of these
persons was the pharmacist Giovan Leonardo Pisano, the captain
of the Piazza della Selleria who was indicted as the "principal
author" of the uprising. He was the brother of a noted professor
of medicine at the university and a teacher of none other than
Giambattista Della Porta.[51] It is probable that he had contacts
with the lively political and social circles of the "Naturalists,"
either through Della Porta himself or through Ferrante Imperato,
then his colleague as captain of the Piazza di Nido. It was said that
his "laboratory" (*officina*) had been the meeting place for many
citizens "who engaged in various conversations concerning the
viceroy."[52] He had fled [immediately afterward] with his son,
probably to Venice; and he never again returned. But the conclusion of the affair followed the ritual of the Insurrection. In
February 1586, by order of the viceroy, his house was torn down.
A monument was erected on the site. The heads and the hands of

[49] Summonte, *op. cit.*, Vol. IV, p. 470: "condemned to be tortured with red-
hot pincers [while being drawn through the streets in] a cart; and when they
have arrived before the Church of S. Agostino, to have their right hands cut
off; then to be brought before the Tribunal of Justice of the Court of the
Vicaria and have their left hands cut off; then to be dragged to the market place
to be hung and then quartered. And so it was carried out."
[50] Mutinelli, *op. cit.*, p. 153 [I considerably abbreviate the long quotation on
p. 51 of the original].
[51] On Giovan Antonio Pisano, see L. Amabile, *Fra Tommaso Campanella; la
sua congiura, i suoi processi e la sua pazzia* (Naples, 1882), Vol. I, p. 35, and
N. Cortese, *Lo Studio di Napoli nell'età spagnola* (Naples, 1924), p. 131.
[52] Capaccio, *Vitae Proregum*, in *Diurnali*, p. 182.

those executed were set into a corresponding number of niches. And an inscription was placed over them which named Pisano as the promoter of the movement.

The monument remained standing for several months as a stern warning to the citizens. The popular revolt had been crushed. But it lived on in myth, in legends that turned the hope of justice and the sorrowful consciousness of defeat into apocalyptic visions: "A cart of fire has been reported running about the city; and a man on horseback with black torches has been seen coming out of the *Vicaria*; and the heads in the niches scream as he passes the monument."

Social tension, similarly, was far from overcome. The repression of the Insurrection had taken place during a pause in the usual crisis of food supply. A few of those condemned to the galleys shouted, as they were being taken through the streets to the port, "You now have bread and wine. You keep quiet, and we are going to our death." But the pause was not long lasting. The price of bread continued to rise; and by August 1586, 250,000 *tomoli* of grain were acquired in Puglia for 4 *ducati* per *tomolo*.[53] In 1591 an uprising in the Piazza della Selleria was barely avoided. In 1592, "with the price of food and all other things remaining high," posters reappeared in the streets calling on the people to revolt.

Bad as conditions were, these appeals were ineffective. An uprising could give only precarious results. It could alleviate poverty only for a short time—and then at the cost of immense suffering. The resistance to falling wages and rising prices thus took on new forms and developed permanent organizations. The unemployed and the vagabonds continued to be the objects of persecution. But the "confraternities" brought together for religious and charitable functions among the various categories of artisans were transformed into associations for the defense of current wage levels. Confraternities had multiplied in the period following the Council

[53] A.S.N. Collaterale, Partium, Vol. XXXII, 26 August 1586. In the next years "One could not walk through the streets because of the great number of poor people" (in *Il tumulto*). . . .

of Trent;[54] and they soon acquired a class consciousness that they were to maintain right down to recent times. This consciousness was usually expressed in internal solidarity, in participation in religious rites, ecclesiastical feasts, and civic ceremonies, and in the defense of certain forms of popular culture. It generally was not expressed in antagonism toward higher social classes. But this moment was an exceptional one. Outside of the normal corporate apparatus controlled by the bourgeoisie, these artisan associations now attempted to establish minimum wages and to oblige the members not to accept pay individually at rates inferior to those established by them collectively.[55] Ecclesiastical authorities denounced this danger and renewed the older prohibitions against considering anything [in the confraternities] other than questions of religious piety. Those who created such associations without proper authorization were threatened with excommunication.[56] Even the *seggi* reacted violently. In a memorandum addressed to the king they asked that political power be exerted to dissolve the artisan "congregations," which they said were centers of sedition and which they held responsible "for making prices of manufactured goods rise suddenly from one day to the next."[57] But the

[54] [See above, ch. 9.]

[55] [See below, ch. 14.] Mutinelli, *op. cit.*, pp. 189–90; Vatican Archives, Relationes ad Limina, Napoli 1599 (Arcivescovo Gesualdo): "Confraternities and congregations have multiplied in this city under the pretext of doing charitable works."

[56] *Decreta et Constitutiones Edita a Fabricio Gallo Neapolitano Episcopo Nolano in Synodo Diocesana Celebrata Nolae sub Die Sexto Mensis Novembris Anno MDLXXXVIII* (Naples: Oratio Salviano, 1590): "Let no one dare to erect any kind of confraternity without our knowledge under penalty of anathema" (p. 142); *Sinodo diocesana celebrata dal reverendissimo Mons. Antonio del Tufo, vescovo di Mileto, nella sua cathedrale a gli otto e nove d'aprile 1587* (Messina: Fausto Bufalino, 1588): "Laymen should not dare to institute lay confraternities or other charitable foundations without our license" (p. 144); *Constitutiones Editae in Diocesana Synodo Hostunensi Anno Domini MDLXXXVI ab Illustrissimo et Reverendissimo Domino Julio Caesare Carafa Episcopo Hostunensi* (Rome: Jacobo Ruffinelli, 1588), pp. 165–67.

[57] Mutinelli, *op. cit.*, p. 190. Analogous attempts to transform artisan charitable institutions into centers for the defense of wage scales are found in other European countries. See Frédéric Mauro, *Le XVIe siècle européen. Aspects économiques* (Paris: Presses Universitaires de France, 1966), p. 228.

phenomenon was fairly widespread, and because of its largely underground organization it was very hard to track down. It was blocked, therefore, not so much by the threats of the nobles and the prelates as by demographic pressures upon the labor market, which were too strong to permit them to prevent effectively a further fall in wage scales. There were still only two alternatives: revolt or resignation.

At the same time some popular political groups attempted to utilize the experience of the Insurrection in another way. They spread [subversive] opinions—that the Pisano monument was "not shameful but honorable to his memory," and that the Insurrection had been providential in preventing much graver troubles, "di estrema considerazione," by forcing the adoption of an emergency importation of food. Such interpretations sought to provoke discussion about reform of the city government. For they presented the Insurrection as an inevitable consequence of political disequilibrium and maintained the necessity of reform in the interest of the sovereign and of internal peace. Thus they anticipated arguments that were to become ever more prominent in later years.

When in June 1586 the viceroy acquiesced in the insistent requests that the macabre monument be removed, the popular "party" proclaimed that "in taking away the heads of the condemned and the monument in which they were placed, His Excellency has done a greater favor to himself than to the people; for otherwise the monument would have perpetuated the memory of the bad government which, after all, had caused the uprising by [permitting] the grain supply to diminish."[58]

The idea of "bad government" (*mal governo*) implied a criticism not only of certain individual speculators, but of the whole system of government. This idea was now enriched, though in fragmentary form, with new elements. In 1586 a Doctor Franceschiglio wrote a memorial against the sale of offices. He was condemned to death for his pains, as was a certain Martino Siciliano; and a Doctor Lerma died for the same cause after six years in prison.

[58] Archivio di Stato, Venice, Dispacci del residente veneto a Napoli, 4 July 1586.

Yet these memorials expressed, probably for the first time, the concept that merit should prevail in the assignment of offices; and they seem to reflect a rebellion of minor magistrates against the "bureaucratic rentiers"—those who acquired offices and then leased them out to men able to exercise them. But the terror produced by Ossuna's repressive measures prevented the substitution of this moderate position for those which were much more radical and decidedly anti-Spanish. The prevailing sentiment among the people remained that of an invective written on the occasion of Ossuna's retirement:[59]

> You who've killed us with your noose,
> With red-hot irons and like abuse,
> Who've left us hungry here to die
> Or frightened to the Turk to fly;
>
> We'll say that you've done all you could,
> That you've been fair and kind and good,
>   Providing that you leave!
>
> This pride of yours, this cruel flood
> Of avarice and people's blood,
>   Can never us deceive.
>
> Who follows, always, some proclaim,
> Is much more bad than who'd remain;
>   This ne'er will we believe.
>
> For worse than you we'll never find,
> Mid devils, Turks, or all mankind!

[59] The verses [which I render somewhat inelegantly but with care to preserve the original form and rhyme scheme] were written by Paolo Pacelli and published by Montemayor in the *Diurnali di Scipione Guerra*. They come from a manuscript in the Biblioteca Nazionale of Naples. Pacelli also wrote an *Oratione, nella quale si rallegra a nome publico coll'Illustrissimo e Reverendissimo Monsignor Conte Giorgio Manzuolo da Bologna, creato Vescovo d'Aversa* (Naples: Gio. Battista Cappelli, 1587). The testimony of the Venetian ambassador gives further evidence on the attitude of the population: "The whole city cannot wait for the present [viceroy] to go": Archivio di Stato, Venice, Dispacci del residente veneto a Napoli, 7 November 1586.

The "great disorder of '85," as it was called, had revealed much more than a plebeian disturbance. It had revealed a new spirit of opposition and a demand for independence distinct from the traditional defense of the "constitutions" of the kingdom. Those who "boasted of a thorough knowledge of past events" affirmed that an event of this nature had never occurred in Neapolitan history: and they thus were led to underline the political positions that accompanied the social protest. T. Costo observed a few years later that "there was no good left in the kingdom" thereafter,[60] recognizing thereby that the movement had not been exhausted in a single flash of protest.

Indeed, a still more detached consideration of absolutism and Spanish hegemony in Naples was favored by two occurrences in the international sphere that profoundly shocked public opinion: the defeat of the Invincible Armada and the assassination of Henry III (1589). The first led, as the Flemish War had not, to serious discussion about the "decline" of Spain;[61] and by the time of the death of Philip II, ten years later, the belief in the imminence of a new period in Spanish and European history was already widespread. Discussion about the second occurrence may well have served to introduce the ideas of the monarchomachs into Neapolitan culture. Giovanni Antonio Summonte wrote them into his *History of the City and Kingdom of Naples*—[a work that contributed much to] the formation and development of a current of popular opposition [to the government]. The *History* was published at a moment (1601) when revolutionary tendencies were ebbing, when the extremist phase was giving way to a reforming or "monarchical" phase. But it still reflects the flowering of extremist positions and revolutionary illusions that had been

---

[60] *La apologia istorica del Regno di Napoli contro la falsa opinione di coloro che biasimarono i Regnicoli d'incostanza e d'infedeltà* (Naples: Gio. Domenico Rocagliolo, 1613), p. 159.

[61] Giannone, *Istoria civile del Regno di Napoli* (I cite the edn. of The Hague, 1753), Book XXXIV, ch. V: The defeat of the Invincible Armada "ruined Spain and threw all her designs to the wind, along with her vast and ill-conceived ideas." Naples took part in the expedition with four *galeazze* and ten companies of soldiers: Costo, *Memoriale delle cose più notabili accadute nel Regno di Napoli dall'Incarnazione per tutto l'anno 1617* (Naples: Scipione Bonino, 1617), p. 66.

current in the 1590's. Commenting on the rebellion of the Count of Caserta against King Manfredi, Summonte states that "it is permitted the vassal to harm a lord who oppresses him excessively" and to refuse to obey a lord "in an unjust war." In certain cases, indeed, "it is permissible, even meritorious, for a vassal to kill his lord."[62] These ideas are put into a context of "democratic" ideals, and hence they are particularly significant novelties in Neapolitan culture. They were justified by reference to the medieval jurists—Baldo, Curzio, Giacomo di Belviso, Andrea d'Isernia—and to St. Thomas Aquinas; for such references served well as a means of circumventing the censors. But actually they were much closer to the spirit of the *Vindiciae contra Tyrannos* of Duplessis Mornay and of the other texts of the Protestant monarchomachs who inspired the rebellion of the French Huguenots and the Flemings, as well as the "inspired fanaticism" of the assassin of Henry III.[63] One of the last apologists of the Neapolitan nobility, R. M. Filamondo, was well aware of this similarity when, a hundred years later, he dedicated a violently polemical appendix of his *Genio bellicoso di Napoli* (*The Warlike Spirit of Naples*) to these pages in Summonte.[64]

There is nothing abstract or purely literary in these ideas. They represent rather an attempt to provide a political outlet for real and deeply felt sentiments. But how to apply these ideas in practice was quite another question. The chief obstacle lay not so much in the vigilance of the authorities and the violence of repressive measures as in the concrete conditions of the country. The distance between the subversive spirit of the Neapolitan plebeians and the incipient demands for independence among the middle classes was great enough. But it was small compared to the distance that divided the city from the country, the capital from the provinces. During the Insurrection "many bandits came together and threatened to move suddenly into the city." It was this threat that

[62] *Historia*, Vol. II (1601), pp. 183–84.

[63] The expression is L. Firpo's, in "Il pensiero politico del Rinascimento e della Controriforma," which I read in offprint from the *Grande antologia filosofica* (p. 505).

[64] Naples: D. A. Parrino, 1714.

led the viceroy to order the representatives of the city "to consider themselves as a republic"[65]—to make arrangements, that is, for controlling communications with the provinces, for closing the gates and organizing the defense of the walls. Nobles and bourgeoisie had answered the call with unanimity.[66] For they were convinced that an intrusion of external forces would turn a protest movement into a sack. This threat did much to water down the enthusiasm of those groups who might otherwise have sought to use the uprising as a way of provoking a serious discussion about institutional reform. . . .[67]

[65] *Diurnali di Scipione Guerra*, p. 37.

[66] One of the popular representatives who were charged with guarding the gates was the "Naturalist" Ferrante Imperato. See Francesco Imperato, *Discorso intorno all'officio di Decurioni, hoggi detti Capitani d'Ottine, seu Piazze populari della Città di Napoli*, printed in *Privilegi, capitoli e gratie concesse al fedelissimo populo napolitano et alla sua piazza* (Naples: Roncagliolo, 1624), p. 76.

[67] [This concluding sentence leads on to the next section on bandits and banditry, which is even more exciting than the one here translated on the city.]

14 Venice: The Rise and Fall of the Venetian Wool Industry[1]

DOMENICO SELLA

Domenico Sella has written a number of long articles on Italian economic history and has published two books: *Gli studi di storia religiosa negli Stati Uniti* (*Studies in Religious History in the United States*; Florence: Sansoni, 1956), and *Commerci e industrie a Venezia nel secolo XVII* (*Commerce and Industry in Venice in the Seventeenth Century*; Venice and Rome: Istituto per la Collaborazione Culturale, 1961). He holds degrees from the University of Notre Dame and the University of Milan; and he taught at the University of Genoa and at the Bocconi University in Milan before accepting the position he now holds as professor of history at the University of Wisconsin. His *Salari e lavoro nell'edilizia lombarda* has since been published (Pavia: Fusi, 1968).

I

THROUGHOUT the sixteenth century Venice remained one of the leading economic centers of the Italian peninsula and indeed of Western Europe. Difficulties and even partial losses no doubt there were. Early in the century the rich spice trade had slipped from Venetian hands; and for over fifty years it was to bring prosperity to Atlantic rather than to Mediterranean merchants and seamen. In the 1530's France, traditionally an important

[1] "L'industria della lana in Venezia nei secoli sedicesimo e diciassettesimo," a revised version of the earlier article in French published in *Annales E.S.C.*, XII (1957), 29–45, and republished in Italian in the anthology *Storia dell'economia italiana*, ed. Carlo M. Cipolla (Turin: Einaudi, 1959), pp. 533–56. Revised, with numerous modifications of the original thesis in the light of subsequent research, and then translated into English by the author for inclusion in the forthcoming volume *Crisis and Change in the Venetian Economy*, ed. B. S. Pullan (London: Methuen & Co.), and altered slightly for the purposes of this volume by the editor.

customer of Eastern commodities supplied from Venice, began to build her own commercial and shipping organization with the avowed aim of by-passing the Venetian middleman; and in the 1570's England followed suit. In 1571 the handsome colonial possession of Cyprus was lost to the Turks, and in the last quarter of the century the commercial fleet flying the banner of St. Mark lost ground before the competition of English and Dutch merchantmen, on whose services Venetian traders themselves became increasingly dependent.

Yet in spite of all these setbacks the economic record as a whole was still bright. For one thing, Venice retained control of the trade between the eastern Mediterranean and Germany, the largest market for Turkish cotton, Persian silk, and a variety of Mediterranean goods. For another, in the second half of the century spices, which had seemed irretrievably lost after the opening of the Cape route, began to flow again through the caravan routes of the Levant, at whose terminal points of Cairo and Aleppo they were purchased by Venetian merchants. Moreover, the ancient reputation of Venetian luxury industries—silks, glassware, mosaics, leatherwork—remained unblemished, while a commanding position was acquired in newer fields, such as printing and sugar refining. Lastly, in the course of the sixteenth century clothmaking was added to the city's industrial spectrum, and the new addition, as will be seen, was an impressive one indeed. Starting nearly from scratch, Venice was able to turn out, by the latter part of the century, over 25,000 pieces of high-quality wool cloth a year, thus ranking among the largest single textile centers in Europe.

Venice's economic prosperity, however, came to an abrupt end at the threshold of the seventeenth century: from about 1603, and more rapidly after 1620, the city was swept by a prolonged, disastrous crisis which affected both her commercial and industrial posture, with the wool industry as one of the chief casualties in the débâcle. Only after about 1670 were signs of recovery to be seen in the city of the doges, as shipping, commercial activity, silkmaking, sugar-refining, and a number of luxury handicrafts entered a period of unmistakable, if slow, revival. The one conspicuous exception was cloth-making. This industry, which had done so much to strengthen the Venetian economy in the previous century, failed to share in the general improvement of the late seventeenth century. Even after 1670 its output continued to shrink, until, by the close of the century, it had gone back to the negligible level of two hundred years before.[2] It is this remarkable and intriguing story of the rise and fall of a great industry that the present essay will attempt to sketch.

II

The course of the Venetian wool industry in the sixteenth century has been known for some years, thanks to a precious document edited by Pietro Sardella.[3] We are now in a position to trace its path for another century on the basis of new evidence found in the Venetian State Archives.[4] The broad picture is simple enough: annual cloth output in Venice soared from a paltry 2,000 pieces in the second decade of the sixteenth century to a peak of 28,729 pieces in 1602. Thereafter the trend was reversed: with striking symmetry output tumbled, until by the opening of the eighteenth century it was back to roughly the same level of 2,000 pieces where it had stood two hundred years before.

[2] Cf. Gino Luzzatto, "La decadenza di Venezia dopo le scoperte geografiche nella tradizione e nella realtà," *Archivio veneto*, LIV–LV (1954), 162–81. Further evidence in Sella, *Commerci e industrie a Venezia nel secolo XVII.*

[3] Sardella, "L'épanouissement industriel de Venise au XVIe siècle," *Annales E.S.C.*, II (1957), 196. See also Fernand Braudel, *Civiltà e imperi del Mediterraneo nell'età di Filippo II*, Ital. tr. [from the French original, *La Méditerranée*] (Turin: Einaudi, 1953), p. 458.

[4] Archivio di Stato, Venice (hereafter cited as A.S.V.), *Inquisitorato alle Arti*, busta 45. This is a printed document giving the year-by-year (from 1516 to 1712) number of pieces of cloth brought to the *Camera del Purgo* to be washed, finished, and stamped with the official seal. The same figures (but only as far as 1667) are in a manuscript document in A.S.V., Senato Rettori, filza 72, *sub dat.* 4 January 1669. [Additional information from the 1957 version of this article:] The exact dimensions of the pieces of cloth varied from one center of production to the other. Probably, however, the Venetian pieces were roughly the same length as those produced elsewhere: 56 *braccia* (= 38.24 meters), as compared to 40–45 *braccia* in Brescia, 56–60 in Verona, 50–52 in Como, and about 50 (= 30 meters) in Milan.

On closer scrutiny, however, the output curve reveals some interesting variations in its upward and downward slopes.[5] From about 1520 to 1569 figures climb dramatically at an annual pace of roughly 9 per cent, while over the next three decades the trend is one approaching stability. After the peak of 1602, on the other hand, output falls at the average rate of 1 per cent a year until the 1620's, and then at a slightly faster pace over the next forty years. From the mid-sixties till the end of the century contraction of output proceeds at the accelerated pace of about 2 per cent a year.

The main phases we have just outlined include, of course, a sequence of short-run fluctuations. Some of these can be easily ascribed to major disturbances, such as the plagues of 1525, 1576, and 1630, the Cyprus war of 1570–73, or the great crises that hit Europe in the 1620's and 1680's. It is more difficult to determine the origin of other fluctuations, and only a close study of the business cycle in the sixteenth and seventeenth centuries will be able to throw light on the precise mechanism responsible for them.

But let us go back to the long-run movements: one century of growth and one of decline, each subdivided into phases spanning several decades. What can be known about the forces and circumstances behind the bare quantitative record?

[5]

Peak Years	Number of Pieces	Average Annual Rate of Change Between Peaks
1521	4,701	
		+ 9.60%
1569	26,541	
		+ .25%
1602	28,729	
		− 1.10%
1620	23,000	
		− 1.25%
1665	9,975	
		− 2.00%
1701	2,803	

III

The Venetian wool industry, whose origins go back to the thirteenth century, remained a negligible segment of the city's economy until the great upsurge of the sixteenth century. Traditionally it had specialized in the making of high-grade fabrics, and notably of scarlet carded cloth woven of fine English wool.[6] In the late Middle Ages annual output never rose, so far as is known, beyond 3,000 pieces[7]—a very modest production as compared to that of other Italian towns from which, according to Doge Mocenigo, around 1420 Venice used to purchase as many as 48,000 pieces a year, largely for re-export to the Levant.[8] This absolute predominance of foreign over local fabrics in Venetian export trade need not surprise us. Medieval Venice owed her prosperity to trade and shipping. It was in these, rather than in manufacturing, that capital was mainly invested. Moreover, the city of Venice was poorly fitted to serve as a manufacturing center, except for a variety of luxury handicrafts or for an industry such as sugar–refining which required proximity to the dockyards. Scarcity of space on the crowded Lagoon islands, lack of water streams to operate the fulling mills,[9] a wide range of activities competing for the available labor supply—all of these were factors likely to discourage the development of a large wool industry manned by thousands of artisans.

[6] N. Fano, "Ricerche sull'Arte della Lana a Venezia nel XIII e XIV secolo," *Archivio veneto*, Ser. v, Vol. XVIII (1936), 73–213. In the sixteenth century fine Spanish wool was gradually substituted for English wool.

[7] A.S.V., Senato, Deliberazioni miste, reg. 59, decree of 15 September 1433: "Est impossibile quod in hac civitate possint laborari panni 3,000 et ultra [...] qui sunt necessarii pro nostra draparia."

[8] Cf. Luzzatto, *Storia economica dell'età moderna e contemporanea*, 4th edn., (Padua: A. Milani, 1954), Vol. I, pp. 89–90. [See also Luzzatto's *Storia economica di Venezia dall' XI al XVI secolo* (Venice: Centro Internazionale delle Arti e del Costume, 1961) and *Studi di storia economica veneziana* (Padua: C.E.D.A.M., 1954). Luzzatto's *Storia economica d'Italia* is available in English translation by Philip Jones (New York: Barnes & Noble, 1961).]

[9] Venetian-made cloth had to be sent to the mills at Treviso for fulling (Fano, *op. cit.*, p. 119).

Nevertheless, as we have seen, from the second decade of the sixteenth century cloth production suddenly entered a long period of phenomenal expansion. What forces stimulated this unexpected rise? What new opportunities attracted growing investments into a new field—one which must have long seemed unpromising to a city of traders and seamen but one which was soon to form one of the pillars of the city's economy?

The answer is to be found in the exceptional circumstances obtaining in the first half of the sixteenth century. On one hand, there was the sudden diversion of the rich spice trade to the Atlantic sea route as a result of the Portuguese voyages around Africa. For Venice the loss was a serious one, and its psychological impact was even more serious. "The news [of the Portuguese exploit]," a chronicler wrote in 1509, "has been received as a real catastrophe [. . .] and some of our wisest men were inclined to regard it as the beginning of the ruin of the Venetian State." Ten years later the rerouting of the spice trade to Lisbon was a fact which "everyone took for granted." But a deep-seated malaise still hung over Venice: "Merchants [. . .] are very much dissatisfied and even desperate about [Portugal's] seaborne trade."[10] It is conceivable that, confronted with shrinking commercial opportunities, many a Venetian merchant chose to shift to some other kind of business.

The long sequel of troubles and disturbances generated by the Italian wars in the early decades of the century offered Venice a set of unique and unexpected opportunities in the field of cloth-making. At various times in that period the leading textile centers in northern and central Italy were crippled by war, political turmoil, and foreign occupation. As a result of the devastations she suffered in 1512, Brescia lost many of her drapers and artisans and, with them, her flourishing wool industry.[11] As late as 1540 Brescian annual cloth output was down to 1,000 pieces, as against

[10] R. Fulin, "I Portoghesi in India e i Veneziani in Egitto (dai Diarii di Girolamo Priuli)," *Archivio veneto*, XXII (1881), pp. 162 and 264.

[11] A. Zanelli, "La devozione di Brescia a Venezia e il principio della sua decadenza economica," *Archivio storico lombardo*, Ser. IV, Vol. XVII (1912), 31.

8,000 a generation before.[12] Como, to whose workshops foreign merchants had traditionally brought raw wool from Germany, Provence, Spain, and England to have it woven into cloth, was threatened in 1507 by the war then raging between Emperor Maximilian and King Louis XII. Normal trade connections were temporarily disrupted, and cloth production ground to a stop.[13] In Milan the roll of new members joining the Drapers' Guild bluntly reflects the dimensions of the crisis in war-ridden Lombardy: as against 158 new entries in the second decade of the century, only 50 are recorded in the 1520's, and 59 in the following decade.[14] In that same period Pavia suffered heavy losses too: her population dropped from 16,000 at the opening of the century to 7,000 in 1535.[15] Desolation spread over much of Lombardy in those years. "Pavia," reported the English envoys on their way to Bologna in 1529, "looks miserable; along the highways children cry and die of hunger. [. . .] Vivevano is nothing but ruins. [. . .] Never has Christendom seen a like desolation. [. . .] It will be years before Italy recovers her former prosperity."[16]

Four years later the Venetian envoy in Milan wrote in much the same terms about a region that was well known as one of the most prosperous in Italy: "The State of Milan is full of misery and ruins. [. . .] Nor will it be possible to restore things as they used to be in a short time; for with so many houses destroyed and so many people missing, there are no more industries."[17]

[12] A.S.V., Senato, Miscellanea dispacci antichi, Rettori: Report from Brescia, 3 May 1540.

[13] G. Mira, "Provvedimenti viscontei e sforzeschi sull'Arte della Lana a Como (1335–1535)," *Archivio storico lombardo*, N.S., Vol. III (1937), 397 and 399.

[14] C. Santoro, *Matricola dei mercanti di lana sottile di Milano* (Milan, 1954), p. 38. Cf. also Aminatore Fanfani, *Storia del lavoro in Italia*, Vol. III (Milan: Giuffrè, 1953), p. 99.

[15] G. Aleati and Carlo Cipolla, "Il *trend* economico nello Stato di Milano durante i secoli XVI e XVII: Il caso di Pavia," *Bollettino della Società Pavese di Storia Patria*, N.S., Vol. III[4] (1951).

[16] Cf. Corrado Barbagallo, *Storia universale*, Vol. IV[1], *L'età della Rinascenza e della Riforma* (Turin: U.T.E.T., 1936), p. 497.

[17] Albéri, *Le relazioni degli ambasciatori veneti*, Ser. II, Vol. V, p. 333.

Florence did not escape the general disaster either. As the Venetian ambassador reported in 1529: "In Florence there used to be a great deal of business going on. Among other things, the city used to turn out every year over 4,000 pieces of fine cloth known as cloth of San Martino, besides 18 to 20,000 pieces known as *garbi* made of Spanish wool. Nowadays production is practically at a standstill."[18] Of the 270 draper's shops in existence in 1480,[19] only 63 were still open in 1537.[20] Population figures clearly reflect the economic collapse: 72,000 people in 1510, but only 59,650 twenty years later.[21]

In those dreadful years "only one Italian state managed to weather the storm that submerged all the rest, and that one state was Venice."[22] The city's population rose steadily: nearly 115,000 people in 1509, 130,000 by 1540, 158,000 in 1552, and 168,000 a decade later.[23] Safe from direct war damage, unaffected by domestic strife, ready to welcome refugees from the troubled Italian mainland, still in full control of a commercial network that reached deep into eastern Mediterranean countries, Venice found her own fortune in the very crisis then sweeping the Italian peninsula. As the traditional Italian sources of supply ran dry, the Venetians stepped in to fill the vacuum. Theirs was a striking success: for nearly fifty years the output of fine cloth kept rising; and in 1569, with over 26,000 pieces, it was roughly ten times as large as it had been at the start.

[18] *Ibid.*, pp. 430–31. [It should be remembered, however, that Florence at that moment was in the throes of civil discord and pestilence, and that many citizens had already gone into voluntary exile. Many more were to follow during the radical democratic regime and the siege of 1529–30.]

[19] Luzzatto, *Storia economica*, Vol. I, p. 101.

[20] Riguccio Galluzzi, *Istoria del Granducato di Toscana* (Florence, 1781), Vol. I, p. 288.

[21] G. Pardi, "Disegno della storia demografica di Firenze," *Archivio storico italiano*, LXXIV (1916), pp. 192 and 195.

[22] Barbagallo, *op. cit.*, p. 507.

[23] Daniele Beltrami, *Storia della popolazione di Venezia dalla fine del secolo XVI alla caduta della Repubblica* (Padua: C.E.D.A.M., 1954), p. 59.

IV

By 1569, however, the great upswing was over: for the next three decades, and more precisely until the new peak of 1602, progress was slight—less than 1 per cent a year on the average, as against 9 per cent in the preceding half-century of rapid growth.

Two facts seem to account for this abrupt deceleration. On one hand, in the second half of the century, as is now well known,[24] there was a revival of the spice trade along the overland routes of the Levant, and Venetian capital presumably felt once again the powerful attraction of commercial enterprise. On the other hand, and more importantly, as peace was restored to the Italian peninsula after 1559, industrial production in a number of towns gradually picked up, with the result that Venetian clothmakers found themselves confronted with a host of competitors.

Around 1580 the wool industry in Como was reported as booming.[25] In 1596 Bergamo could boast an output of 26,500 pieces as against 7–8,000 in 1540.[26] In Florence recovery was equally impressive: 14,700 pieces in 1553, 20,000 in 1560, and 33,312 in 1572; and much of her growing output found its way to the Levant. A memorandum submitted in 1573 by the Florentine drapers to their ruler shows them full of confidence, optimistic, ready—to use their own words—"to step up production even further in view of the fact that all their cloths have sold out and that Alexandria and other Turkish ports are free and safe."[27] Clearly the commercial agreements with the Ottoman empire of 1557, which ensured the Florentines the same privileges as the Venetians had traditionally enjoyed in the Levant, were bearing

[24] Cf. Luzzatto, "La decadenza di Venezia," and his discussion of Frederic C. Lane's well-known articles on the revival of the Venetian spice trade.

[25] Bruno Caizzi, *Il Comasco sotto il dominio spagnolo* (Como: Centro Lariano per gli Studi Economici, 1955), p. 84.

[26] A.S.V., Senato, Miscellanea dispacci antichi: Report from Bergamo, 25 April 1540; A.S.V., Sindici inquisitori di Terraferma, busta 63, "Descrittione ... del 1556."

[27] Galluzzi, *op. cit.*, Vol. III, p. 418.

fruit; and, of course, the War of Cyprus, by temporarily disrupting trade between Venice and the Turks, played into Florentine hands too.

It was not long before the Venetians became painfully aware of the mounting tide of Italian competition in the Levant. As early as 1578 the Republic's representative in Constantinople sent an alarming report:

> There have begun to appear in this city cloths after the Venetian style brought here by the Florentines, and they are of excellent stuff and fine colors. [. . .] There is thus reason to fear that, owing to their competition, our own industry will lose both its reputation and its profits. Our merchants are very worried indeed.[28]

Twenty years later the Venetian Board of Trade (*Savi alla Mercanzia*) made similar complaints about cloth produced in Spanish-ruled Lombardy; and for the first time they put their finger on the crucial problem of costs:

> A great deal of fine Spanish wool is wrought into cloth in foreign states, and notably in Como and other towns in the State of Milan, where cloth is being produced in increasing quantities in perfect imitation of our own fabrics, but with great advantages as regards wages and other things pertaining to production. Those foreign fabrics are then shipped to the Levant by way of Ferrara and Ancona and are sold more cheaply than ours.[29]

Disturbing though it may have been to Venetian exporters in the later part of the sixteenth century, Italian competition did not have disruptive effects on the Venetian wool industry. It certainly set a ceiling on its expansion, but it did not prevent it from holding its own. It is reasonable to assume that, despite its well-known handicaps, the Venetian industry managed to survive that early challenge thanks to its widely recognized reputation for quality[30]

[28] A.S.V., Senato, Dispacci Costantinopoli, filza 12, 6 July 1578.
[29] A.S.V., Cinque Savi alla Mercanzia (hereafter referred to as S.M.), Risposte, reg. 139, 5 December 1597.
[30] See, for instance, Fynes Moryson, *An Itinerary* (Glasgow: MacLehose & Sons, 1908), Vol. IV, p. 123.

and to Venice's well-established commercial organization in the Levant—an organization which other Italian states could hardly match.

V

Things changed suddenly, and for the worse, after the year 1602. From then on Venetian cloth production began the long, irreversible descent, at the end of which, a century later, it was on the same low level from which it had surged upward in the 1520's.

No blame could be put this time on Italian competitors, for in the seventeenth century they fared no better than the Venetians. In the first half of the century Como saw her cloth output tumble from 8,000 to a paltry 100 pieces,[31] and Milan suffered serious losses as well.[32] As for the Florentine industry, whose competition had given Venetian producers so much concern in the 1570's, it too was losing ground: it produced only about 15,000 pieces in 1616; and it produced less than 6,000 by 1640.[33] What, then, were the difficulties besetting Venice from the beginning of the new century? Why did she fail to benefit once again from her neighbors' troubles by filling the vacuum they had left?

So far as we can tell, there were three main reasons for this. One was the deterioration of normal transport services between Venice and the Turkish ports. Another was the contraction in the demand for cloth in the Levant. And a third was the entry of new competitors—England, Holland, and, in the latter part of the century, the Venetian mainland.

In the last quarter of the sixteenth century, as English and Dutch ships began to ply Mediterranean waters in growing numbers, they quickly asserted their superiority over local carriers—so much so, indeed, that by the close of the century a large portion of

[31] Caizzi, op. cit., pp. 104–5.

[32] Cipolla, "The Decline of Italy," Economic History Review, Ser. II, Vol. V (1952–53), 178–79.

[33] Ruggiero Romano, "A Florence au XVIIᵉ siècle: industries textiles et conjoncture," Annales E.S.C., VII (1952), 508.

Venice's maritime trade came to be handled by northern ships, whose superior performance was candidly recognized by Venetian merchants and authorities.[34] In 1602, however, a drastic measure had been passed which, in order to protect Venetian shipping interests, imposed severe restrictions on the use of foreign carriers between Venice and the Levant. As a result of this ill-fated "Navigation Act" seaborne communications with the eastern Mediterranean ports were seriously hindered, and Venetian exporters were forced to rely, as a rule, on the less efficient ships flying the banner of St. Mark.[35]

Early in the seventeenth century, on the other hand, disquieting reports began to reach Venice that the demand for cloth in the Ottoman empire was slackening. "Turkey has lost so much of her population and wealth on account of internal strife," a Venetian consul wrote in 1611, "that she now imports a third of what she used to." The poorer people apparently turned away from imported woolens and increasingly turned to "padded cottons" produced locally.[36] Later on, at the time of the Turco–Persian war (1623–38), conditions deteriorated even further; and it was noticed that consumers in the Levant tended to adopt fabrics that were "greatly inferior, both in quality and in price," to those traditionally supplied from Venice.[37]

Diminishing market opportunities in the East were likely, of course, to affect all cloth suppliers. This was true of the Venetian and other Italian industries; but it was true, in part, of the English wool industry as well. The latter had traditionally supplied the

[34] Alberto Tenenti, *Naufrages, corsaires et assurances maritimes à Venise, 1592–1609* (Paris: S.E.V.P.E.N., 1959), pp. 13–27; Lane, "La marine marchande et le trafic maritime de Venise à travers les siècles" in *Les sources de l'histoire maritime en Europe du Moyen-Age au XVIIIe siècle*, ed. M. Mollat (Paris: S.E.V.P.E.N., 1962), p. 13.

[35] For a detailed discussion of the new policy and its negative effects on Venetian trade, see Sella, *Commerci e industrie*, pp. 34–45.

[36] Guglielmo Berchet, *Le relazioni dei consoli veneti nella Siria* (Turin, 1896), p. 131.

[37] Nicolò Barozzi and G. Berchet, *Relazioni degli ambasciatori veneti: Turchia*, Vol. I, p. 386 [in *Relazioni degli Stati europei lette al Senato degli ambasciatori veneti...*, 10 vols. (Venice, 1856–78)].

Levant countries with cheaper and coarser woolens known as "kerseys,"[38] intended for low-income consumers, while higher-grade cloth had come mainly from Italy. In the first decades of the seventeenth century shipments of English kerseys dropped precipitously, and by about 1630 kerseys had practically disappeared from the Levant.[39] Their place was taken, we can presume, by locally produced substitutes such as "padded cottons."

The English, however, managed to offset the loss of their traditional exports by entering the cloth market traditionally serviced by the Italians. In the late 1590's a few hundred pieces of English broadcloth made their first appearance in the Levant. By the 1620's an average of 6,000 pieces were annually shipped there from England, and for the next forty years broadcloth exports stabilized around that figure.[40] This new development was particularly disturbing to Venetian interests on two scores. In the first place, here was a product which, unlike kerseys, directly competed with Venetian cloth. Secondly, coming as it did at a time when demand was sluggish, whatever market English broadcloth was able to win was obviously at the expense of Venetian sales.

[38] Kerseys (carisse) appear among Venetian re-exports to the Levant at least as early as the fifteenth century (cf. A.S.V., Senato, Deliberazioni miste, reg. 58, 18 September 1430). The tariff of 1545, which slightly increased import rates on foreign fabrics, explicitly exempted kerseys (see Salvatore Cognetti de Martiis, "I due sistemi della politica commerciale veneziana, Vol. I of Biblioteca dell'economista, Ser. IV (Turin: U.T.E.T., 1900), p. ccxxxvi). According to Braudel, op. cit., p. 456, in the late sixteenth century Mediterranean countries "were literally flooded" by English kerseys; cf. also W. Brules, "L'exportation des Pays-Bas vers l'Italie par voie de terre au milieu du XVIe siècle," Annales E.S.C., xiv (1959), 475–79. At the opening of the seventeenth century, in the Levant, kerseys were worn by the poor. The well-to-do dressed in broadcloth (Samuel Purchas, His Pilgrimes [Glasgow: MacLehose & Sons, 1905–7], Vol. III, p. 86). From a Venetian source we learn that kerseys "do not compete (non fanno concorso) with Venetian cloth" (A.S.V., S.M., Risposte, reg. 147, 26 June 1626).

[39] Barry Emanuel Supple, Commercial Crisis and Change in England, 1600–1642 (Cambridge University Press, 1959), p. 160 n. See also R. Davis, "Influences de l'Angleterre sur le déclin de Venise au XVIIe siècle" in Aspetti e cause della decadenza economica veneziana nel secolo XVII (Venice and Rome: Istituto per la Collaborazione Culturale, 1961), p. 205.

[40] Davis, loc. cit.

The success scored by English textiles was mainly ascribed, in the first half of the century, to one thing: they sold more cheaply than Venetian fabrics. Admittedly, English cloth was of a somewhat inferior quality. But this did not seem to affect their popularity at a time when Levantine customers were reportedly reluctant to spend as much as they used to. In 1612 the Venetian ambassador in Constantinople could write that the English "bring hither [. . .] large quantities of kerseys and broadcloth and sell them very cheap to the great prejudice of our own trade."[41] Thirty years later another Venetian diplomat spoke of "the great profit" English merchants reaped "by selling inferior cloth at such low prices as to spoil the trade of every other nation."[42] In the second half of the century, when English cloth exports to the Levant rose to new heights[43] and when Dutch fabrics made deep inroads into the Turkish market as well, their success was explained not only in terms of lower prices but also in terms of their being lighter and more attractive. The English, it was claimed, "offer cloth that looks better and costs less than ours, and the Turks more and more grow fond of it."[44] "It is well known," reads another document, "that Dutch woolens have displaced ours. Being pleasant, light, and inexpensive, they have infected the mind of the Turks (*hanno corrotto il genio de Turchi*), so that [. . .] the latter no longer appreciate our draperies, which are heavy both to buy and to wear (*pesanti tanto nel comprarli quanto nel portarli*)."[45] To restore the tottering fortunes of the Venetian cloth manufacture, it was deemed imperative not only to cut prices but also "to experiment with new styles and patterns and to cater to the changing whims of fashion."[46]

[41] Barozzi and Berchet, *op. cit.*, p. 213.

[42] *Ibid.*, p. 386.

[43] Davis, *loc. cit.*: as against an annual average of 6,000 pieces for the period 1620–60, English broadcloth exports fluctuated between 12,000 and 20,000 pieces a year in the next forty years.

[44] A.S.V., Senato Rettori, filza 72, 30 December 1668.

[45] A.S.V., Provveditori di Comun, busta 7, 5 January 1673 O.S.

[46] Barozzi and Berchet, *op. cit.*, p. 178 (report from Turkey for 1676).

VI

The decline and eventual collapse of the Venetian wool industry is evidence enough of its failure both to lower its prices and to innovate. How can this twofold failure be explained?

As far as industrial conservatism is concerned, the blame would seem to belong to the rigid set of technical rules and prescriptions imposed on the industry in 1588 and strictly enforced, with occasional and limited exceptions, until 1677.[47] And yet even after the old manufacturing code was lifted the wool industry failed to recover.[48] Far from being reversed in the last quarter of the century, its downward course was accelerated—and this is the more surprising since at the time a number of other industries in Venice were making substantial, if slow, gains.[49] The real trouble was that the wool industry, whether it was regimented or not, had to grapple with the problem of costs—and costs apparently grew increasingly intractable as time went by.

One early source of difficulties may have been the "Navigation Act" of 1602, which, as will be recalled, forced Venetian exporters to use national carriers, however inefficient these might be. A document of 1640 reads: "The obligation imposed on our merchants to load in Venetian ships puts them at a disadvantage as compared with other nations, since our merchants are compelled to place their goods where they are the least safe. This way they are forced to give up their trade."[50]

Later in the century another grievance was taxation, notably the intricate web of excise and export duties levied both on raw

[47] A.S.V., S.M., N.S., busta 126, fasc. "Cesarotti."

[48] The making of cloth "after the English and Dutch style" was authorized in 1673 (A.S.V., Provveditori di Comun, busta 7, 28 March 1673); the annual output of "foreign draperies" in Venice between 1678 and 1698 was negligible and never rose beyond a few hundred pieces (A.S.V., S.M., N.S., busta 139, fasc. "Processo n. 3, Camera del Purgo."

[49] There was progress in the silk industry, glass-making, sugar-refining, and a variety of luxury handicrafts, and also in trade and shipping: see Sella, *Commerci e industrie*, pp. 55, 72, 83, 86, 109, and 131.

[50] Barozzi and Berchet, *op. cit.*, p. 403. See also A.S.V., S.M., Risposte, reg. 146, 29 December 1625, and reg. 152, 12 September 1640.

materials and finished products. Petitions for tax reductions were frequently submitted by disgruntled clothmakers and merchants, and government officials themselves conceded at times that the cloth manufacture was "exceedingly burdened" and that "if some of the burdens were lifted, prices would fall and sales would increase accordingly."[51]

But by far the most common complaint was about labor costs. After the great plague of 1630 it was asserted that "weavers' rates have gone up by as much as one third";[52] and thirty years later an official report could still claim that "our merchants have received great damage as a result of wages rising at the time of the plague and remaining high thereafter."[53] In 1671 a local merchant publicly denounced "the excessive price" fetched by Venetian cloth. He went on to state that "the rates our drapers must pay the workers are truly exorbitant; if they be lowered [. . .] cloth will sell more cheaply and the vent thereof will be augmented."[54] Wage rates, however, could not be easily adjusted down to competitive levels because they were rigidly fixed by law: "The old policy which ensured the workers a given pay [. . .] has caused the ruin of our wool industry."[55] Government approval was required to alter the wage schedule (*limitazione delle mercedi*), but the government itself may have been reluctant to take a step which, however necessary, was bound to be unpopular.[56]

[51] A.S.V., S.M., N.S., busta 136, 29 March 1689. Numerous petitions for tax reductions in A.S.V., Provveditori di Comun, busta 57 and reg. 7.

[52] A.S.V., S.M., busta 467, 29 September 1636.

[53] A.S.V., Senato Rettori, filza 72, 30 December 1668.

[54] *Scrittura inedita di Simon Giogalli* (1671), ed. Emanuele Antonio Cicogna (Venice, 1878), p. 16. A similar opinion was expressed by a group of merchants who claimed that the Venetian cloth industry could be salvaged only by lowering prices and that "this can be easily done by lifting some fiscal burdens and correcting extravagant labor costs" so as to make Venetian cloth competitive. English and Dutch textiles, they claimed, "sell at very low prices" (A.S.V., Senato Rettori, filza 82, 21 January 1671, O.S.).

[55] A.S.V., S.M., N.S., busta 126/62, 15 June 1689.

[56] At the close of the century, for instance, the Board of Trade yielded to a request for a wage rise submitted by the silk weavers, in spite of the fact that the request itself was considered "unfavorable" to the interests of the industry (A.S.V., S.M., busta 477, 25 September 1696).

In the documents, however, the problem of excessive labor costs is often envisaged in a somewhat different light. Rather than high wage rates, the target of criticism is the workers' inefficiency relative to the pay they are entitled to. "The workers," we are told in one place, "being legally entitled to a given wage (*sicuri, per i decreti, di una determinata mercede*), care little about doing a good job, for they get paid anyway regardless of their performance."[57] From another source we learn that the draper "has little say in the making of the cloth, although, as owner of the capital and anxious to get a good product in order to improve his sales, he ought to be free and absolute master." Everything is rather left to the discretion of the artisans working for him, and these "work as they please with little concern for the perfection of the product."[58]

Responsibility for this sorry state of affairs would seem to lie, in turn, with the powerful craft guilds in which Venetian spinners, weavers, and dyers were compulsorily enrolled. By setting their own standards of workmanship and by denying the employers a free hand in the choice of the artisans as well as direct control over the artisans' performance, the guilds allegedly acted as a powerful drag on the efficiency of labor. To remedy these evils the drapers on one occasion petitioned the government (in vain, as it turned out) for "complete freedom in hiring workers of their choice," claiming that guild members refused "to follow the drapers' instructions in their work."[59] A similar request was submitted in 1696 by an enterprising Fleming who had come to Venice some years earlier "with fourteen highly trained artisans" to launch the manufacture of "cloth after the Dutch style" but who had been "discouraged by the spirited opposition he had met in the city and been forced to betake himself to the Treviso area."[60] This time he asked for, and actually secured, "permission to keep the

[57] A.S.V., S.M., N.S., busta 126/62, 29 March 1689.
[58] A.S.V., Provveditori di Comun, ref. 7, 5 January 1673 O.S.
[59] A.S.V., S.M., N.S., busta 126/62, 18 March 1690. The Board of Trade, after conceding that the matter was "very serious," ruled it "unadvisable for the time being to alter traditional practices."
[60] A.S.V., S.M., busta 467, petition submitted by Pietro Comans in 1683.

workers on his own premises, to hire and pay them without any conceivable outside interference"; and he insisted upon "his manufacture and workers being in no way molested by the Venetian guilds."[61]

Naturally enough Venetian entrepreneurs made envious comparisons with conditions prevailing outside their own city. On the Venetian mainland, for instance, where the cloth industry was doing well late in the century,[62] they claimed that "artisans work for lower wages [. . .] and are free from the guilds' fetters."[63] In England, Holland, and France they saw "nothing but freedom"— and they meant "freedom to reward the artisans according to their skill and merit and at rates that have been freely agreed upon."[64]

VII

It is, of course, far from easy to decide how much truth there was in the various complaints about taxation, the wage schedule, and the guilds' interference, since we have no direct way of comparing conditions in Venice with those obtaining elsewhere.

[61] A.S.V., S.M., N.S., busta 125/63, 16 January 1696 O.S. This second petition was favorably received on 1 February 1696 O.S. (A.S.V., S.M., busta 467).

[62] A.S.V., Provveditori di Comun, busta 7, 26 March 1687: the progress of clothmaking in the Republic's mainland dominions is here considered as "one chief cause of the decline of cloth production in Venice." Total output on the mainland for 1686 was reported at 49,944 pieces. Of these, 34,116 were reported for the district of Bergamo and, next in order, 10,042 for Treviso. Production in these areas, however, consisted primarily of low-grade woolens (*panni bassi*). As such, it may have been a less serious threat to the Venetian industry than was claimed at the time. The situation possibly changed in later years as the mainland industries succeeded in producing cloth in imitation of English and Dutch fabrics (A.S.V., S.M., Risposte, reg. 165, 22 June 1697). Woolens produced on the mainland sold largely on the domestic market. But they also sold in Spain (A.S.V., Provveditori di Comun, busta 7, 15 February 1673 O.S.), in the Levant (A.S.V., S.M., *loc. cit.*), and in Germany (see G. Canali, "Il Magistrato Mercantile di Bolzano e gli Statuti delle Fiere," *Archivio per l'Alto Adige* [1942–43], p. 102).

[63] A.S.V., Arte della Seta, busta 110/209, 13 May 1675, and 16 January 1685 O.S.

[64] A.S.V., S.M., Risposte, reg. 159, 3 June 1678.

Moreover, those complaints, and notably those about the guilds, reflected, as might be expected, the merchants' viewpoint, and they are not entirely above suspicion. Lastly, it is certain that the situation abroad was not so idyllic as disgruntled Venetians were inclined to think. That the Venetian wool industry was undersold by its foreign rivals is clear enough. That differences in labor costs in particular played a decisive role is quite plausible in view of the intensive character of the industry. What is really debatable is the claim so often made by contemporaries that labor costs were too high in Venice, either because they were pegged by law at excessive levels or because the guilds stood in the way of any attempt to use manpower more productively. For this would amount to arguing that, had it not been for a misguided wage policy or for the guilds' obstructive practices, the Venetian wool industry would have survived the challenges of the seventeenth century.

This is unlikely. After all, the spectacular rise of cloth production in Venice had occurred at an exceptional moment—at a moment, that is, when most Italian textile centers were crippled, when competition from northern Europe still lay far ahead in the future, and, in short, when the Venetian wool industry enjoyed a virtually monopolistic position. On the other hand, that rise came to a stop and eventually gave way to an irreversible decline as soon as that exceptional position was lost. Nor did the belated adoption of more liberal policies succeed in reversing the trend.[65]

The conclusion seems inescapable that conditions in Venice were basically unfavorable to the life of a large cloth industry, except in the exceptional circumstances such as obtained for a time during the sixteenth century. A wiser wage policy, more flexible labor contracts, and a freer hand for the merchant-drapers might conceivably have retarded the industry's downfall

[65] Various privileges (implying the right to imitate foreign fabrics) were granted in the 1670's to individual clothmakers. In 1679 "the manufacture of Dutch cloth" was permitted to all interested drapers (see Sella, *Commerci e industrie*, pp. 119-20). In 1696, as mentioned above, P. Comans was even exempted from the control of the guilds. The results, however, were disappointing (*ibid.*, p. 120).

in the seventeenth century. But they could hardly have overcome the disadvantages built into the very structure of the city itself.

Not only, as mentioned before, did Venice lack certain facilities, such as ample space and water streams; we have every reason to believe that the city was, and continued to be in the seventeenth century, at a serious disadvantage as regards the labor supply—guilds or no guilds. The presence in the city of scores of wealthy households, whose lavish spending the baroque age is well known and is attested to this day by their magnificently built and sumptuously furnished palaces, was bound to keep living costs high and thus set a relatively high floor for wages. In conjunction with the enduring, if reduced, vitality of the harbor and of a number of luxury and other industries, it was also bound to insure a considerable range of employment opportunities. It thus kept the labor force in a strong bargaining position and made it less docile than the drapers would have liked.

It is no mere coincidence that the manufacture of cloth held its ground and even expanded on the Venetian-ruled mainland, where cheap rural labor was available. But neither is it a coincidence that Venetian cloth output fell most sharply in the last three decades of the century—at a time, that is, when the old harbor experienced a marked revival and when the making of elaborate silks and delicate glassware as well as the refining of sugar prospered. Clearly Venetian capital, enterprise, and manpower were being channeled once again into traditional fields in which either the city's locational advantage was crucial or in which exquisite workmanship and artistic taste were far more important assets than an abundant supply of cheap labor.

PART FIVE

Toward a New Age

15 Venice, Spain, and the Papacy: Paolo Sarpi and the Renaissance Tradition[1]

WILLIAM BOUWSMA

Born in 1923, William Bouwsma received a Ph.D. from Harvard University in 1950. He taught at the universities of Nebraska, Indiana, and Illinois before being appointed professor of history at the Berkeley campus of the University of California. In 1969 he returned to Harvard as professor of history. His first major book was *Concordia Mundi: The Career and Thought of Guillaume Postel*, published by the Harvard University Press in 1957. He has since become interested chiefly in Late-Renaissance Venice and in historiography—two fields which come together in Paolo Sarpi. His "Three Types of Historiography in Post-Renaissance Italy" appeared in *History and Theory*, IV (1965), and his "The Venetian Interdict and the Problem of Order" in the volume *Histoire, Philosophie, Religion*, published by the Institute of Philosophy and Sociology of the Polish Academy of Sciences in 1966. The essay here published is a preparatory study for a second major book, *Venice and the Defense of Renaissance Liberty: Renaissance Values in the Age of the Counter Reformation* (University of California Press, 1968).

Paolo Sarpi (1552–1623) was a man of insatiable curiosity and immense learning who was recognized by his contemporaries as a master in mathematics, Scotist philosophy, alchemy, astronomy, history, classical literature and languages, law, and theology. He entered the Servite Order in 1566; and after a brief period as preacher at the court of

[1] "Paolo Sarpi e la tradizione rinascimentale," *Rivista storica italiana*, LXXIV (1962), 697–716. Translated by Catherine Enggass and corrected by the editor with the approval of the author. The article is used with permission of the Italian publisher, Edizioni Scientifiche Italiane.

Mantua, he was ordained to the priesthood at the age of twenty-two. He returned to Venice after a brief residence respectively in Rome and Milan (where he became an admirer of the archbishop, Charles Borromeo); and there he was received, along with Galileo, Bruno, and other leading intellects of the age, as a welcome guest in the *Ridotto Morosini*—the meeting place of the party of the Young Nobles who were seeking to revivify the Republic by freeing it from its Spanish and papal connections. When Pope Paul V, in an effort to defend ecclesiastical immunities, laid Venice under an interdict in 1606, Sarpi was made official theologian of the Republic; and this office launched him into a busy career of public service that was to last until his death. Between 1612 and 1615 he composed his most famous work, the *History of the Council of Trent*, which was published under a pseudonym in London in 1619.

ALTHOUGH Paolo Sarpi is one of the great figures of the seventeenth century, not only of Italy, but of all Europe, and although many historians, Italian and non-Italian, have studied his career and thought, he remains an enigma and a subject of controversy. It is true that we have good editions of his most important writings and an increasing body of information concerning his life and surroundings. Yet there is still no satisfactory general work on Sarpi, nor is there any generally accepted interpretation of his personality, his thought, and his purposes.

In the past, attempts to interpret his career have taken two main directions. On one hand, they have tried to ascertain whether Sarpi's hostility to the papacy and his loyalty to his native Venice were chiefly religious or political in motivation. On the other, these interpretations have sought to establish whether he was, as he protested, a loyal Catholic, or whether he was rather a secret sympathizer with Protestantism and a heretic at heart.[2] These

[2] One example, among many, appears in the *Consiglio in difesa di due ordinazioni della Serenissima Repubblica*, published in *Istoria dell' Interdetto e altri scritti* of Sarpi, ed. M. D. Busnelli and G. Gambarin (Bari: Laterza, 1940; hereafter referred to as *Scritti*), Vol. II, p. 16: "Just as until the present I have put forward

questions, however, have too often led to mere polemics, and Sarpi has chiefly been exploited by both sides in the great controversies that continue to divide Italy. Largely for this reason the endeavor to answer these questions has been inconclusive. Some scholars have even come to believe that Sarpi himself was singularly evasive and enigmatic regarding his true position and purposes.[3] I should like to suggest, rather, that not Sarpi but the questions have been at fault. They are based, in my opinion, on certain modern distinctions that are hardly applicable to Sarpi and his times.

The first problem, whether Sarpi's motives were essentially religious or political, depends on a tendency to distinguish between religion and politics, and hence between church and state. That distinction is characteristic only of more modern times. For Sarpi, as for the supporters of the pope, the struggle between Venice and the papacy was only one more chapter in the age-old debate about the location of supreme authority in Christendom.[4] It is important to recognize (as we too often fail to do) that this debate was not, after all, between the rival powers of church and state. As Pope Nicholas the Great wrote in the ninth century, "The Church is the world"; and this famous definition meant that the struggles between popes and emperors were always seen as taking place within the Church. The issue was not between church and state or between politics and religion (although each

in my writings only clear and unquestioned doctrine, so in the future I will be able to state quite simply all that I know to be Christian and Catholic doctrine." Cf. Luigi Salvatorelli, "Paolo Sarpi" in *Contributi alla storia del Concilio di Trento e della Controriforma*, pp. 142–43.

[3] On Sarpi as a problem in historiography, see Giovanni Getto, *Paolo Sarpi* (Rome, 1941) [but now republished, substantially unaltered, by Olschki in Florence, 1967], pp. 7–43 [pp. 1–52 of the Florentine edition]; Vincenzo M. Buffon, *Chiesa di Cristo e Chiesa Romana nelle opere e nelle lettere di Paolo Sarpi* (University of Louvain, 1941), pp. 31–32; Federico Chabod, *La politica di Paolo Sarpi* (Rome and Venice: Istituto per la Collaborazione Culturale, 1962), pp. 13–18; Gaetano Cozzi, "Paolo Sarpi: Il suo problema storico, religioso e giuridico nella recente letteratura," *Il diritto ecclesiastico*, LXIII (1952), 52–88; and Giovanni Gambarin, "Il Sarpi alla luce di studi recenti," *Archivio veneto*, L–LI (1953), 78–105.

[4] Cf. Chabod, *La politica di P. S.*, p. 48.

side accused the other of mere worldliness), but between two rival conceptions of church order and between two religious agencies.[5] For Sarpi the state was a religious institution with divinely appointed responsibilities and a major role in the Church. In promoting the cause of Venice against the papacy, he was defending an ancient religious position; and as historians we have no reasonable grounds to doubt his sincerity. The distinction between a political Sarpi and a religious Sarpi thus seems to me false: the political Sarpi does not exclude, but rather helps to explain, the religious Sarpi.[6] The second problem, whether Sarpi was truly a Catholic, seems to me equally anachronistic. For several generations before the appearance of Martin Luther a rich doctrinal ferment, both various and free, had permeated Western Christendom; and this variety persisted among men who continued to think of themselves as Catholics long after the last session of the Council of Trent. What true Catholicism was, what the authority of the Council was, and what its decrees meant, were still open questions for many thoughtful Catholics in Sarpi's time.[7] If doubts about these matters were displayed less openly in Italy than in France, the reason was as much lack of opportunity as religious conviction.[8] From this point of view it was therefore quite legitimate to attack Tridentine Catholicism as a merely factional position which did not adequately reflect Catholic tradition, and even, without any disloyalty toward Catholicism, to share certain Protestant formulas. We are not justified in assigning the consolidated, monolithic Catholicism [of the nineteenth and early twentieth centuries] to the early seventeenth century. Nor are we justified in imputing subversive

[5] See the penetrating book by Henri X. Arquillière, *L'Augustinisme politique: Essai sur la formation des théories politiques du Moyen-Age* (Paris: Vrin, 1934).

[6] Cf. Salvatorelli, "Paolo Sarpi," p. 139.

[7] Cf. Hubert Jedin, *Das Konzil von Trient: Ein Ueberlick über die Erforschung seiner Geschichte* (Rome: Edizioni di Storia e Letteratura, 1948), pp. 62 ff. [I have reviewed much of the recent literature on this subject in "New Light on the Italian Counter Reformation," which will appear in *Catholic Historical Review* in 1970.]

[8] Arturo Carlo Jemolo, *Stato e Chiesa negli scrittori politici italiani del Seicento e del Settecento* (Turin: Bocce, 1914).

Protestant intentions to Sarpi.[9] Sarpi must be taken literally. He was struggling against what he considered a false Catholicism in favor of a true one.

Since the study of Sarpi by way of these questions has not proved fruitful, I should like to put the problem on a different basis. It seems to me that one must start by identifying in Sarpi a certain *forma mentis* and certain fundamental attitudes that correspond to a particular political situation and to a related moment in the history of culture. This observation, however commonplace it may appear, will be far more helpful in our endeavor to understand Sarpi than any effort to seek the origin of his thought in particular literary sources. Books and ideas are important historically not because of their intrinsic value and abstract force, but because of the fertile ground they find in certain readers; and the historian's major problem is that of determining not the lineage of a position, but the reasons for its attraction for a specific individual or group. It is in this sense, for example, that we must interpret Sarpi's preference for the philosophy of William of Ockham over that of any other Scholastic.[10] Sarpi was not identifying himself with a school. He was simply reporting his discovery of a kindred spirit.

For this reason we must approach Sarpi by way of a certain context of sympathies and values. These alone, I believe, will bring us to the heart of the question. First of all, it seems to me that Sarpi is best understood as a representative of certain attitudes prevalent in the late Middle Ages and the Renaissance. These attitudes have been variously described. Georges Delagarde has defined them as "l'esprit laïque" and has given particular attention to their expression in the thought of Marsilio of Padua and

---

[9] Cf. Buffon, *Chiesa di Cristo e Chiesa Romana*, p. 32. On this point I agree with Getto, *op. cit.*, pp. 116–17, and I agree still more with Salvatorelli in his penetrating study *Le idee religiose di fra Paolo Sarpi*, Classe di Scienze Morali . . . Memorie, Vol. v (Rome: Accademia Nazionale dei Lincei, 1953), p. 338.

[10] Letter to François Hotman, 22 July 1608, in Sarpi, *Lettere ai Gallicani*, ed. Boris Ulianich (Wiesbaden: F. Steiner, 1961), p. 173. Cf. Buffon, *Chiesa di Cristo e Chiesa Romana*, p. 185.

William of Ockham.[11] Eugenio Garin and Hans Baron have defined them somewhat differently and have preferred to associate them with the Italian humanistic tradition, especially in Florence.[12] Notwithstanding the differences between them, both positions insist upon the relationship of these tendencies in philosophy to the attempts of townsmen to free themselves from certain medieval forms of thought and social organization. It is against this general background that I wish to consider Sarpi, though without placing him too precisely within any particular tradition. If in the course of this discussion I make frequent allusions to the Renaissance, my intention is only to suggest a general framework of values. I do not claim, for example, that Sarpi was a humanist in any exact sense. He had no interest in rhetoric; and although he received a classical education, he did not attach much importance to ancient models of thought and expression. Nevertheless, profound influences from the Renaissance can be discerned in him.

Whatever else may be said about them, the republican communes of Renaissance Italy clearly provided an atmosphere favorable to the development of wide interests and broader spiritual horizons; and the responsibilities of civic life stimulated both patriotism and a new historical consciousness. Local tyranny and the Spanish domination eventually destroyed this political framework in most of the Italian states, and the Counter Reformation generally suppressed what was left of the culture that the older political order had supported. But Venice, as has been too little recognized, was a unique exception to the rule. Venice retained the liberty that was lost by the rest of Italy.[13] At the same

[11] Georges Delagarde, *La naissance de l'esprit laïque au déclin du Moyen-Age*, 6 vols. (Paris, 1942–48; but see now the new edn. in 5 vols. published by Nauwelaerts at Louvain, 1956 *et seq.*).

[12] Cf. in particular Eugenio Garin, *L'umanesimo italiano* (Bari: Laterza, 1952 [now in a Universale Laterza paperback, 1965]); and Hans Baron, *The Crisis of the Early Italian Renaissance* (Princeton University Press, 1955 [but now see the revised edn. of 1966, also issued in paperback]).

[13] Gaetano Cozzi, *Il doge Nicolò Contarini* (Venice and Rome: Istituto per la Collaborazione Culturale, 1958), p. 81.

time, she jealously guarded her religious autonomy in the face of all attempts at centralization by Rome: and neither the Inquisition nor the Index managed to acquire much power within her dominions.[14] Thus, however much the world around her had changed, Venice remained the unwavering champion of Renaissance values as late as the first decade of the seventeenth century.[15] And the serious threat to these values posed by the papal offensive of 1606, which was encouraged by Spain, had almost the same effect on the Venetians, and on Sarpi in particular, as the Milanese aggression against Florence had had on Bruni's generation two centuries earlier.

Much of Sarpi's position is rooted in these circumstances and events. His youthful openness to all human thought and experience is typical of the varied and stimulating life of the Italian city. Endowed with an inexhaustible curiosity, he cultivated every branch of natural sciences. He actively participated in the philosophical inquiries of the University of Padua. He studied law and history. He talked with everyone, Italian or foreign, who could feed his curiosity about *le cose humane* ("the affairs of men"). And he longed to travel in order to see with his own eyes what his foreign acquaintances reported.

The variety of Sarpi's interests is one of the most significant aspects of his personality.[16] But the way in which he dealt with these interests is even more suggestive. What is more impressive in Sarpi is his directness, his concreteness, and his flexibility in the

[14] Cf. Chabod, *La politica di P. S.*, p. 119, and Clemente Maria Francescon, *Chiesa e Stato nei consulti di fra P. S.* (Vicenza, 1942), p. 251. The Republic's protection of Cesare Cremonini from the Inquisition is of special interest in this regard. See Spini, *Ricerca dei libertini*, pp. 146–47.

[15] Cf. Salvatorelli, "Venezia, Paolo V e fra P. S." in *La civiltà veneziana nell'età barocca* (Venice and Rome: Istituto per la Collaborazione Culturale, 1959), p. 91.

[16] This is the impression that emerges very forcefully from the first biography of Sarpi, the *Vita* by Fulgenzio Micanzio [first published at Leiden in 1646 and more readily available in the Milan, 1824, or the Florence (Barbèra), 1958, editions of the *Istoria del Concilio Tridentino*], here cited in the 1658 edition (no place); see p. 178 for Sarpi's interest in travel. See also Chabod, *La politica di P. S.*, p. 32.

face of any kind of experience. Perhaps the central conclusion of his early philosophical speculation was that the mind can return again to the real world of immediate experience.[17] This conclusion seems to be reflected in aspects of his later thought as well. For Sarpi, man must always start from the concrete and the particular, since general principles are deceptive. And it is his constant attachment to this conclusion that explains the rigidity of the positions he subsequently took.

After Romano Amerio's investigations, Sarpi's scientific empiricism and his positive conception of law can no longer be open to question.[18] It will therefore be more useful to illustrate this attitude in other aspects of his thought. The attitude underlies his work as a historian. The historian, he says, must avoid general principles and base his work on concrete situations and the accumulation of particular detail.[19] At one point in his *History of the Council of Trent* Sarpi suddenly seems to realize that his meticulous attention to particulars might bore his readers. He therefore stops to explain: "To someone reading this report, its attention to trivial things and causes may seem excessive. But the writer of the history, taking a different view, has thought it necessary to show what tiny rivulets caused the great lake that occupies Europe."[20] Thus the flow of time seems to be composed of innumerable tiny droplets, each of which requires individual attention. This same attitude is manifested in Sarpi's view of

[17] Cf. Romano Amerio, *Il Sarpi dei Pensieri filosofici inediti* (Turin, 1950), pp. 13–15, and the citations in Sarpi, *Scritti filosofici e teologici*, ed. Amerio (Bari: Laterza, 1951).

[18] In *Il Sarpi dei Pensieri filosofici inediti*. Notable examples of Sarpi's empiricism are to be found in his letters to Jérome Groslot de l'Isle of 6 January and 12 May 1609, in *Lettere ai Protestanti*, ed. Manlio Duilio Busnelli (Bari: Laterza, 1931; hereafter cited as *Lettere*), Vol. I, pp. 58 and 79. For his juridical thought, see "Consiglio in difesa di due ordinazioni" and "Consiglio sul giudicar le colpe di persone ecclesiastiche," both in *Scritti*; see especially pp. 6 and 52–53.

[19] [See ch. 4 above].

[20] *Istoria del Concilio Tridentino*, ed. Giovanni Gambarin (Bari: Laterza, 1935), Vol. I, p. 187. [This text has now been issued in paperback with a new introduction by Renzo Pecchioli (Florence: Sansoni, 1966); and in two large volumes at the modest price of 3,000 *lire* ($5), it is now accessible to the general public.] Cf. Getto, *P. S.*, pp. 175–76.

education, as his friend and collaborator Fra Fulgenzio Micanzio tells us. Sarpi resolutely refused to deal systematically in his teaching with any author, because he held that this method was in general followed "not [to gain] knowledge or to improve the mind, but to speak with subtlety, to show one's cleverness, and to make oneself more pertinacious than sincere as an investigator of the truth." He preferred instead to teach "in the Socratic and obstetric manner," that is, to employ that method which emphasized particular human insights and the immediate and concrete response of the student.[21]

I have insisted on Sarpi's concrete and direct method because I think it crucial to our understanding both of the man and of his place in the development of Western culture. Efforts have been made to identify this tendency in Sarpi with particular systems of thought—with nominalism, for example.[22] I will not deny certain affinities between Sarpi's thought and that of Ockham. But I think that the attempt to classify Sarpi in this way obscures the essential quality of his mind. He did not have a system of his own, and he deeply opposed all systems as falsifications of reality. We must look first of all at Sarpi himself, at his concern with all things human and at his refusal to be constrained by any intellectual construction that he believed might cut him off from the richness and paradoxes of human experience.

This interpretation of Sarpi as a Renaissance man gains substance when two other aspects of his career are considered: his view of history and his connections with the Venetian Republic. Sarpi's view of history reveals the same sense of discontinuity between his own age and antiquity that had been characteristic of the Florentine historians; and his writings likewise reveal how well he had learned, like them, that institutions develop and change in time by natural processes. But in one way Sarpi went further than they: he applied this insight systematically to the Church. He did so with regret, since he believed that the Church ought to

[21] *Vita*, pp. 79–80.
[22] Cf. Buffon, *Chiesa di Cristo e Chiesa Romana*, p. 10. Getto, on the other hand (*P. S.*, pp. 68–69 and 92), sees Sarpi as a "Stoic sage."

be identical and continuous with its primitive forms. In this sense he was a foe of history: he saw time as the great corrupter.[23] Nevertheless he recorded the changes that he observed; and though dealing with that institution to which some superiority over history was generally attributed, he noted the relativity of particular arrangements and pronouncements in terms of the concrete historical circumstances in which they occurred.[24] His extension of this Renaissance theme to the Church is perhaps Sarpi's greatest technical contribution to Western historiography.

But Sarpi's major link with the Renaissance tradition appears in his attitude toward society and in his political thought and activity. His career falls naturally into two parts. Until 1605 he devoted himself to study, although his *vita contemplativa* was interrupted from time to time by the demands of his Order.[25] But with the crisis provoked by the Interdict, he was suddenly called to take part in the affairs of the world; and from then until his death he was strenuously committed to the *vita activa*. Thus Sarpi in his own life was forced to grapple with a problem that had been crucial to the development of Florentine humanism. He was not the only one of his circle to be so involved. The problem had been faced by his close associate Nicolò Contarini;[26] and the comment of Fra Fulgenzio on this abrupt change in Sarpi's life shows us the traditional way in which Venetians regarded this central problem of the Renaissance circle. "At this period," Fulgenzio wrote, "it might be said that he terminated

[23] "Considerazioni sulle censure," in *Scritti*, Vol. II, p. 209: "Many things which in their beginnings are good become pernicious as they then change."

[24] See his discussion of the Council as an institution in Christian history: *Istoria del Concilio Tridentino*, Vol. I, pp. 5–6 and 214–18; of the cult of the Virgin, *ibid.*, Vol. I, pp. 287–90; of ecclesiastical government, *ibid.*, Vol. I, pp. 350–52; and of ecclesiastical benefices, *ibid.*, Vol. I, pp. 400–3. Naturally I do not exclude the importance of Protestant historiography in Sarpi. [Indeed, he mentions Johannes Sleidanus on the very first page of the *Istoria*.]

[25] [I.e. the Order of the Servites—an order founded by the Florentine Filippo Benizi in the Middle Ages and still centered in the Church of the Annunziata in Florence. The name of Sarpi, the greatest Servite of his age, is carefully omitted from the official history of the Order, the *Monumenta Ordinis Servorum Sanctae Mariae* (Rome, 1737–50).]

[26] Cozzi, *Contarini*, pp. 56–57.

his tranquil studies and his private life; and from then until the end of his life he entered into another world, or rather into the world. And it pleased God to call him to labors to which he would never have thought to apply himself. But man is not born for himself. [He is born] principally for his country and for the common good."[27] It is interesting to observe the ardor with which Sarpi threw himself into the fray and what little regret he felt for the serene life of study he had forsaken. He seems, indeed, to have been waiting all his life for this moment.[28] Indeed, as though this activity corresponded to some profound personal need, his health, which had always been poor, suddenly improved.[29]

Yet even in action Sarpi did not base himself on general principles. What attracted him was not the abstract moral obligation of social duty but service to a particular community. Sarpi loved Venice as Salutati and Bruni had loved Florence; and his pride in the political achievements of the Republic and in the long duration of her freedom frequently recurs in his writings, both public and private. For him the cause of Venice against the papacy was that of "our liberty, which Divine Providence has preserved inviolate for one thousand and two hundred years . . . amongst innumerable dangers".[30]

But under the pressure of papal attack Sarpi also developed a theoretical justification for the authority of the Venetian government. It was one which, in its glorification of the powers inherent in the community, suggests a radical extension of certain elements of Renaissance patriotism. The obvious feature of Sarpi's political thought is the large authority it attributes to the "prince," a term by which he seems to have meant administrative office in general as well as the person holding it. Like other

[27] *Vita*, p. 76.
[28] Note the conclusion of Sarpi's first formal *consulto*, the "Consiglio in difesa di due ordinazioni," in *Scritti*, Vol. II, p. 16. . . .
[29] Micanzio, *Vita*, pp. 93 and 145.
[30] "Risposta al Breve circa li prigioni" in *Scritti*, Vol. II, p. 71. Sarpi's words reflect a general Venetian ethos; see Ernesto Sestan, "La politica veneziana del Seicento" in *La civiltà veneziana nell'età barocca*, p. 54.

theorists of his time, Sarpi derived the sovereign authority of the prince directly from God;[31] and he attributed to sovereignty a remarkable comprehensiveness. Sovereignty, he declared, is necessarily indivisible and inalienable. Above all, it is absolute in its own realm. "Sovereignty is a power absolute by nature from which nothing can be exempted or excepted," he declared. "And the moment that it yields to any condition or exception, it loses its supreme being and becomes dependent."[32]

This sentiment may suggest that Sarpi was only another of the many exponents of seventeenth-century absolutism. But such a suggestion should be corrected in the light of another important aspect of his political thought. Although Sarpi's term "prince" is applicable to every supreme political authority, from the French monarchy to the Venetian *dogato*, he was thinking primarily of his own Republic. Absolute sovereignty of divine derivation is for Sarpi evidently consonant with republican government; it would therefore be somewhat misleading to associate him too closely with conventional theories of divine right. In reality Sarpi was concerned with the duty of the prince to the community; and this duty had for him a meaning very close to the function of government for Locke. "The prince and the senate have not sinned," Sarpi maintained; "they have rather obeyed the commandments of God in seeing to the preservation of the lives, honor, and property of His subjects."[33] Sarpi's absolutism, then, is not an unregulated and arbitrary power but unlimited authority to be exercised for the common good.[34]

If Machiavelli is the only touchstone of Renaissance political thought, this association of Sarpi's politics with the Renaissance

[31] As in "Scrittura sopra la forza e validità della scommunica," in *Scritti*, Vol. II, pp. 38–39.

[32] From the *consulto*, *Della giurisdittione temporale sopra Aquileia*, cited by Francescon in *Chiesa e Stato nei consulti di fra P. S.*, p. 114. Cf. also "Consiglio in difesa di due ordinazioni," in *Scritti*, Vol. II, pp. 12, 14, and 15, and "Consiglio sul giudicar le colpe di persone ecclesiastiche," *ibid.*, p. 46.

[33] "Considerazioni sopra le censure," in *Scritti*, Vol. II, p. 251.

[34] Note the skill with which Sarpi contrasts the authoritarianism of Pope Paul V and the free deliberations of the Venetian Senate in "Istoria dell'Interdetto," *Scritti*, Vol. I, pp. 15 ff. *et passim*.

would be quite unconvincing. As Chabod has emphasized, Sarpi's political philosophy has little in common with Machiavelli's, and it reveals rather more affinity with that of the French jurists of the period.[35] Sarpi's divergences from Machiavelli are many. The most notable is his insistence that the moral and religious obligations of the prince are greater than those of the ordinary citizen.[36] But Sarpi's intention was to defend what he considered the ancient rights of a free republic and not, as was Machiavelli's, to propose extraordinary remedies to halt a process of degeneration. So conservative a purpose really somewhat resembles that of those French theorists who were trying to bolster the position of an established monarchy. On the other hand, Sarpi's aim had also some precedent in a more vital period of Florentine history; his real spiritual precursor seems to me to be Salutati, who loved and served Florence and who praised the laws of his community as instruments of God's will.[37]

To identify Sarpi with the Renaissance past may appear somewhat anachronistic, and it therefore calls for some further elaboration. The seventeenth century is certainly not the fifteenth; the world had altered greatly since the time of Bruni and Salutati. But to establish Sarpi's relationship with the Renaissance will provide a point of departure for the next stage in our investigation. We must now examine how the Renaissance motives in Sarpi were adapted to new conditions and how they were modified in the process. Indeed, this appears to me to be the unique value of Sarpi, and indeed of the whole Venetian episode, for the historian. The special political conditions basic to Renaissance culture no longer existed in other parts of Italy, and what remained of it was defensive or merely academic. In Venice alone at this late date can we find central attitudes of the Renaissance still alive and engaged in an encounter with a changing world. Sarpi was the major Venetian exponent of these values, and because of a

---

[35] *La politica di P. S.*, p. 72.
[36] "Considerazioni sopra le censure," in *Scritti*, Vol. II, p. 249.
[37] Cf. Garin, *L'umanesimo italiano*, pp. 31 ff.

mentality extraordinarily open and sensitive to change, he was also the outstanding witness to their transformation.

The changes that had taken place since the "golden age" of the Renaissance were of several kinds; and it will be useful to distinguish here two major sorts of alteration, both of which deeply affected Sarpi and gave a particular direction to those of his characteristics that I have associated with the Renaissance. The first of these changes was political; and it resulted from the altered relation of Venice, as of the rest of Italy, to the powers of Europe. The emergence of a system of well-organized and ambitious states able to determine the destiny of Italy had made her role in European affairs increasingly passive. Venice's own field of action was more and more restricted, and her very existence as an independent state often seemed to depend on developments and decisions elsewhere.[38] With his broad interests and clarity of vision, no one realized this better than Sarpi.[39]

Sarpi recognized that the impotence of Italy came in part from her political division.[40] But he also saw that her principal problem was of a moral nature. For that reason he included even his beloved Venice, during the years after the Interdict, in his indictment of Counter-Reformation Italy. Echoing Machiavelli, he wrote sorrowfully of his native city: "Now we have breathed out all our virtue; . . . we have drunk some opiate from the vessel that puts everyone to sleep."[41] On the other hand, all was not yet lost for Sarpi as long as Venice retained her freedom. But she needed powerful allies, such as France or the Netherlands,[42] and Sarpi would not have rejected an alliance even with the Turks. When a Turkish attack on Rome seemed in prospect, he com-

[38] Cf. Sestan, "La politica veneziana," pp. 45 ff.

[39] Cf. Chabod, *La politica di P. S.*, p. 135.

[40] Thus in the "Istoria dell'Interdetto," *Scritti*, Vol. I, p. 57, Sarpi speaks of the Spanish view that "the distrust between the two greatest Italian [states] made their affairs more stable; and by having the pope conquer the Republic, they would also increase their temporal jurisdiction. . . ."

[41] Letter to Groslot, 23 October 1607, in *Lettere*, Vol. I, p. 4.

[42] Cozzi, *Contarini*, pp. 133–34; letter to Groslot, 25 September 1612, in *Lettere*, Vol. I, p. 244.

mented: "It causes sorrow here, people fearing the Turk in Italy; but it would be a universal salvation."[43]

But however conscious Sarpi might be of Venice's weakness and vulnerability, he retained his sense of the dignity of the Republic and his pride in the political values she represented. For Sarpi, Venice was the courageous defender of a common cause: "She alone upholds the dignity and true interests of an independent prince."[44] As such she merited the respect and assistance of the great powers; but she should beware of being absorbed by them. Therefore, the first rule for a state that "wanted an understanding with the Republic" would be "to demonstrate the desire for associates, not dependents."[45] In spite of all her vicissitudes, Venice continued to represent for Sarpi a complex of values that had to be preserved at any cost.

Closely connected with [his estimate of] the political situation was Sarpi's doctrine of "opportunity" (*opportunità*), a doctrine which helped him to solve a very serious problem. In a world so menacing, so inimical to the development and even the survival of everything most dear to him, how was a man or a government to act? To struggle openly and continuously against superior force would only ensure destruction. Yet to do nothing was unthinkable. Sarpi resolved this dilemma by proposing a policy of alert vigilance, of patient waiting for the opportune moment which would be presented by Divine Providence, and then of striking with vigor.[46] The doctrine of "opportunity" reveals how much the mood of the Renaissance had changed since the time of Machiavelli. In so far as the doctrine counseled shrewdness and

---

[43] Letter to Groslot, 23 October 1612, *ibid.*, Vol. I, p. 248.
[44] "Istoria dell'Interdetto," in *Scritti*, Vol. I, p. 4, *et passim*.
[45] Letter to Groslot, 27 April 1610, in *Lettere*, Vol. I, p. 119.
[46] This doctrine appears in many of his works. Note, for example, the letter to Groslot of 25 November 1608, *ibid.*, Vol. I, p. 50: "But in all things the occasion is the chief matter, without which all goes not only fruitlessly, but even with loss. When God shows us the opportunity, we must believe it to be His will that we take it. When [He does] not, we must await silently the time of His good pleasure." The doctrine is carefully examined by Salvatorelli in *Le idee religiose di fra P. S.*, pp. 312 ff. and 358 ff., and by Cozzi in "Fra P. S., l'Anglicanesimo e la 'Historia del Concilio Tridentino,'" *Rivista storica italiana*, LXVIII (1956), 569-71.

flexibility, it may have precedents in Machiavelli. But for Sarpi it became a measure of human impotence. *Virtù* could no longer even hope to triumph over *fortuna*. Man is not incapable of controlling events. At the most he can only cooperate with the opportune moment. The wise man, therefore, must patiently resign himself to long periods of inactivity. Indeed, there is no certainty that God will even present him with a genuine *opportunità*. Sarpi himself began to suspect that it would not come in his generation and that, at best, he could work only for posterity. "It is well to instruct posterity," he pointed out, "at least with writings, so that when the evil of the present changes, they can regain liberty if it should be lost to us . . . ."[47]

A pessimism bordering on desperation with regard to the limits of human action is obviously not a characteristic generally associated with the Renaissance; and we are entitled to attribute Sarpi's gloom in great measure to altered political circumstances. Yet even here I think that his position was a natural development of the Renaissance emphasis on particular, concrete experience and of its rejection of all-embracing intellectual systems created by men. For the Renaissance mentality had two rather different aspects. On one hand, it tended to liberation and bold adventures of the mind; and this positive tendency could seem most prominent in a time of relative hope. But on the other hand, it rejected adventure in the present and withheld confidence in the future; and it manifested a profound skepticism concerning the limits of the human understanding and a resignation to man's imprisonment in the chaotic immediacy of direct experience. It is hardly surprising that for Sarpi this second tendency reflected the real truth about man's position in the universe. Indeed, notwithstanding his persistent pessimism regarding the probable course of events, he steadfastly refused to predict the future,[48] thereby

[47] Letter to Groslot, 25 September 1612, in *Lettere*, Vol. I, p. 243.

[48] See, for example, the letter to Groslot of 26 October 1610, *ibid.*, Vol. I, p. 149: "I, however, have observed many times that matters thought to be without hope turn out well and those that appear to have every chance of success turn out badly. I thus prefer to wait to see what happens and make no predictions."

revealing a deeper pessimism than would have been suggested by the certainty of disasters ahead. For Sarpi the world would always present surprises. He was convinced not only that all human calculation was useless but also that events usually turned out completely opposite to man's expectations.[49] Man, for Sarpi, was helpless in a world he could never hope to comprehend.

With this aspect of Sarpi's thought we have come to the other large set of changes that had altered the world since the time of the Renaissance, those released by the Reformation. If the political scene justified one kind of pessimism, the Christian view of man suggested another, though the two were closely related. The religious tendencies of the period were also reflected in Sarpi's thought. His most important writings, including his great *History*, are works in which he tried to present the values and attitudes we have just examined within a religious context. He did not sacrifice these values to a religious perspective. Indeed, it seems to me that the key to an understanding of his religious position is to be found precisely in his effort to preserve these values and to reconcile the demands of Christian belief to all that he held most dear. For Sarpi, as for each of us in some sense, the validity of a religious position was to be tested by its consistency with what he otherwise knew to be true.

It seems to me, therefore, that Sarpi's religious position was based on the same renunciation of the general in favor of the particular that we have observed in other aspects of his thought— on the pessimism implicit in this point of view, and especially on the feeling of the helplessness of man as a moral being, which in some degree parallels and in some degree underlies his helplessness to understand and to control events. For Sarpi, the weakness of man was, among other things, certainly moral. "Every human action," he wrote, "lacks perfection";[50] and this gloomy vision seems to pervade the *History of the Council of Trent*, a work

[49] So the letter to Groslot of 14 September 1610, *ibid.*, Vol. I, p. 135: "As to predicting the future, I dare not do it, because of the experience I have had with things that always turn out contrary to expectations."

[50] Letter to Groslot, 4 August 1609, *ibid.*, Vol. I, p. 88. Cf. Micanzio, *Vita*, p. 173.

singularly lacking in heroes and one which appears at times to be almost a deliberate demonstration of the depravity of man. But this vision does not exclude all consolation. Sarpi also saw that man's moral deficiencies implied his dependence on divine grace, and this explains the attraction he felt for extreme forms of the Pauline-Augustinian tradition.[51]

Sarpi's sense of human limitations is equally evident in his attitude toward Christian doctrine. Here his affinities with the thought of the Renaissance are even clearer. I have in mind something more general than the influence of that evangelism which was so deeply rooted in sixteenth-century Venice. Regarding human reason as incapable of passing from particulars to general truth, and considering all intellectual conclusions as possessing a merely operational validity and as being incapable of final verification, Sarpi considered reason irrelevant to salvation. The truths of Christianity could only be approached by faith:[52] hence his bitter criticism of the systematic theological discussions which produced the doctrinal formulations of Trent. This aspect of the *History*, although it has been little noticed, is almost as important as his antagonism to Rome for the comprehension of his work.[53] To apply the subtle definitions and distinctions of human reason to the content of the faith was for Sarpi a shocking contamination of heavenly with earthly things, the product of human vanity, contentiousness, and presumption. It was therefore doomed to futility.[54]

[51] Cf. Boris Ulianich, "Sarpiana: La lettera del Sarpi allo Heinsius," *Rivista storica italiana*, LXVIII (1956), 425–46, and Cozzi, "Fra P. S., l'Anglicanesimo e la 'Historia del Concilio Tridentino'" [n. 46 above]. Micanzio, *Vita*, p. 73, speaks of Sarpi's special interest in St. Augustine.

[52] Cf. Amerio, *Il Sarpi dei Pensieri filosofici inediti*, pp. 13–15.

[53] Note, for example, the debates on systematic theology in the *Istoria del Concilio Tridentino*, Vol. I, pp. 298–99, 318, 343–44, 365, and 380–81. Cf. Cozzi, "Paolo Sarpi tra il cattolico Philippe Canaye de Fresnes e il calvinista Isaac Casaubon," *Bollettino dell'Istituto di Storia della Società e dello Stato Veneziano*, I (1958), 98–99, on Sarpi's attitude with regard to speculative theology among the Protestants. See also Chabod, *La politica di P. S.*, pp. 149–50.

[54] [This is the position taken subsequently by Galileo and the Galileans, and it may be traced to the close personal ties between Galileo and Sarpi.]

The same skepticism also underlies Sarpi's tolerance of religious difference and his aversion to persecution. Since a precise, systematic, rational, and coherent definition of the faith is so far beyond human capabilities, diversity of opinion must be permitted, and condemnation should be slow. For Sarpi, the doctrinal cleavages of Europe were largely verbal;[55] and since words cannot penetrate to the heart of reality, they were also essentially frivolous. This position, rather than an expression of *politique* indifference or the consequence of a direct inspiration from Protestant doctrines, explains his willingness to collaborate, for both political and religious ends, with Lutherans, Calvinists, and Anglicans. These "heretics" could not be excluded from the Church of Christ on dogmatic grounds, for no human authority could be considered intellectually competent to determine their orthodoxy.

We have thus arrived at another fundamental element in Sarpi's religious position: his theory of the Church.[56] Here his emphasis on the particular as the exclusive reality in human experience merges with the other major Renaissance element in his thought, to which it is closely related: affection for a particular social community. Sarpi's concept of the Church is based on his insistence upon the fundamental importance of the individual believer. The Church thus becomes merely an aggregation of individuals, *convocatio fidelium*.[57] Moreover, Sarpi insisted on the right and duty of individual judgment in religious matters, which he held to be superior to the collective judgment of the Church as expressed by ecclesiastical authority. The Venetians might

[55] Letter to Groslot, 7 July 1609, *Lettere*, Vol. I, p. 86.

[56] For a more complete documentation on what follows, see Buffon, *Chiesa di Cristo e Chiesa Romana*, and Boris Ulianich, "Considerazioni e documenti per una ecclesiologia di P. S." in *Festgabe Joseph Lortz* (Baden-Baden: B. Grimm, 1958), Vol. II, pp. 363–444.

[57] See for example the "Apologia per le opposizioni fatte dal cardinale Bellarmino," *Scritti*, Vol. III, p. 69: "What is meant by 'Church'? If we follow the meaning of the word itself and the Holy Scriptures, [it is] the congregation of the faithful. . . ." For precedents of Sarpi's position among the medieval canonists, see Brian Tierney, *The Foundations of Conciliar Theory* (Cambridge University Press, 1955).

therefore in good conscience defy the papal ban.[58] Obviously, this theory also implied a revision in the relations between layman and priest. If the authority of the Church resided in the individual believer, then the priest was only a delegate [of the faithful], and [the authority] of the clergy was based on consent.[59] In this way Sarpi was evidently attempting to supply a historical and theoretical foundation for the secular and anticlerical lay spirit that was so deeply rooted in the civic consciousness of the late Middle Ages and Renaissance. But the essence of his position is that the clerical conception of the Church is a violation of the true structure of reality, which resides in individuals rather than in comprehensive systems.

The basis of authority in the Church thus resided in the individual believer. But the believer in turn belonged to a national and confessional community. Hence, Sarpi saw the universal Church Militant essentially as the sum of all individual churches—Roman, Gallican, Greek, Anglican, and even Lutheran and Reformed.[60] His ideal, in fact, was not an organizational unity but a loose confederation of autonomous units. For this reason he showed little enthusiasm for any formal reconciliation and institutional unification between Catholics and Protestants.[61] Unity savored too much of authoritarian uniformity, and it was therefore the

[58] "Scrittura sopra la forza e validità della scommunica," *Scritti*, Vol. II, p. 21: "And the theologians give as a certain and infallible rule that when a man is sure in his conscience of not having sinned mortally in the action for which he has been excommunicated, he can have a sure conscience about having no damage in his soul and of not being excommunicated [in the eyes of] God, nor deprived of the spiritual assistance of the Church. . . ." For Sarpi's opinion on the Jesuit doctrine of obedience, see "Istoria dell'Interdetto," in *Scritti*, Vol. I, p. 107 [and on the troubles of the Jesuits during the Interdict crisis, see Pietro Pirri, S. J., *L'Interdetto di Venezia del 1606 e i Gesuiti* (Rome: Institutum Historicum S. I., 1959)].

[59] Thus Sarpi's approval of the electoral principle in ecclesiastical office. See the letter to Groslot of 17 February 1608, *Lettere*, Vol. I, p. 65.

[60] For Sarpi, the cause of Gallican autonomy was also the cause of the Universal Church. See letter to Groslot of 22 July 1608, *ibid.*, Vol. I, p. 24.

[61] Note the texts presented by Cozzi in "Sarpi, L'Anglicanesimo e la 'Historia . . . ,'" pp. 613-15, and "P. S. tra il cattolico Philippe Canaye . . . ," pp. 123-24, n. 284.

absolute negation of that freedom to which he so much aspired. Sarpi's idealization of division in the Church was perhaps the primary reason for his approval of the Protestant Reformation.[62] Papalism as a theory of ecclesiastical government was obviously contrary to his conception of the proper organization of the Church. Moreover, the papal concept of monarchy as the imposition of a general principle of authority over all particular churches and persons was radically opposed to Sarpi's almost instinctive location of essential reality in the individual.

For Sarpi, just as truth is inaccessible to man, who can know nothing but the particular, so the Holy Spirit does not function through institutions or other visible and tangible entities. There is no meeting point between the ultimate and the immediate, the spiritual and the worldly. Sarpi therefore insisted on the exclusively spiritual character of the Church: "It is called the kingdom of heaven, not only because it will attain perfection in heaven, but because while yet on earth it reigns and governs not by rules and worldly interests but by completely spiritual ordinances. By another name this is called the Church. . . ."[63] He conceived of the clergy as a spiritual body that by its nature is far removed from laws, government, property, or questions of an earthly character in general.[64]

When the clergy concerns itself with such matters, another serious inversion of values occurs. His position here offers Sarpi the opportunity for another attack on Rome. In his view the papacy was generally guilty of confusing the temporal with the spiritual, thus contaminating spiritual things;[65] and the Roman Church had degenerated into a political instrument employed

---

[62] He represented [Protestant doctrine] as a radical remedy for "extinguishing tyranny" in the letter to Groslot of 22 July 1608, *Lettere*, Vol. I, p. 23.

[63] Cited in Buffon, *Chiesa di Cristo e Chiesa Romana*, p. 42, from the "Sommario di una considerazione sulla libertà ecclesiastica," Biblioteca Marciana, Venice, MS It., cl. XI, cod. 176, fol. 171.

[64] Note Sarpi's caustic reply to the pope in "Nullità nelli brevi del pontefice," *Scritti*, Vol. II, p. 90.

[65] See the summary of this position in Amerio, *Il Sarpi dei Pensieri filosofici inediti*, pp. 35–36.

by shrewd rulers to govern the masses for their own interest.[66] To this extent Sarpi was Machiavellian. He accepted the "Averroist myth,"[67] and hence a political interpretation of papal policies. The political efficacy of religion, he held, was demonstrable.

Feeling strongly that such a Church did not serve the Christian faith, however, Sarpi wished for something better. Yet how could a purely spiritual Church function in the world? With his reply to this question we have come to what, in the more religious atmosphere that followed the Reformation, I would describe as a religious expression of the civic spirit of the Renaissance. Sarpi attributes a wide responsibility to the civil authority, or "prince," as he calls it, both for what concerns the institutional and secular aspects of the Church and for what relates to its spiritual life. The institutional direction of the Church naturally belongs to the prince, since he is the legitimate ruler of all temporal things.[68] But its spiritual direction also belongs to him. If the authority of the Church definitively resides in the lay community and is merely delegated to the clergy, the head of the Church is unquestionably the representative of this community. Therefore it is the prince who in the last analysis determines both spiritual and material matters.[69] Thus Sarpi was able to declare that the Venetian Republic and other political governments have frequently and rightly intervened in ecclesiastical matters, "not as princes and political authorities, but as believers and representatives of the whole body of believers."[70] The prince has been delegated by God to govern both the spiritual and temporal orders on behalf of the community. If we keep in mind his pre-

[66] "Consulto sui rimedii . . . ," *Scritti*, Vol. II, p. 159: "It becomes just and legitimate to reject and oppose those pontiffs who adopt any means (even though wicked and impious) in order to conserve and increase their temporal authority. . . ."

[67] Note Spini, *Ricerca dei libertini*, pp. 15 ff.

[68] Note the texts assembled with regard to this point by Francescon in *Chiesa e Stato nei consulti di Fra P. S.*

[69] See Micanzio, *Vita*, pp. 161–62.

[70] "Consiglio sul giudicar le colpe di persone ecclesiastiche," *Scritti*, Vol. II, p. 49.

dilection for Venice, Sarpi's position evidently serves to combine civic and religious impulses; his radical ecclesiology expresses patriotic devotion and faith in his own community. From this point of view citizenship is the only social condition of importance, and the clergy themselves are first of all simply citizens like other men.[71] In this sense the Republic of Venice was not a secular state at all. It was in the fullest sense the Church itself, in so far as the Church impinges on man's experience in this world. The exaltation of the Renaissance city-state could go no further.

It is not my intention either to claim systematic consistency for Sarpi's views or to maintain that they have much intrinsic ecclesiological interest. Nevertheless, I think that the historians can discover in him more than a curious renewal of the doctrines of Marsilio of Padua or a late expression of the "Byzantinism" so often attributed to Venice. No doubt Sarpi's doctrine owes something to both these sources. But his importance comes rather from the concrete historical circumstances that elicited his position. Sarpi was the champion of the values inherent in a particular community, values that were seriously menaced; and to defend them he attributed to the community a set of religious sanctions that went far beyond the patriotic affirmations of the Renaissance, even though they were moving in the same direction and serving the same ends. Sarpi reveals the persistence at a remarkably late date of a fundamental motif of the Renaissance; and he helps us to see its development and transformation under the pressure of new historical conditions. He succeeded in being both a patriot and a realist, and in his radical glorification of the state he suggests an important contribution of the Renaissance to the absolutism of early modern Europe.

But even deeper than his attachment to Venice was Sarpi's aversion to the general and the rigidly systematic and his preference for the particular and the immediate. Two rather different historical impulses may be seen converging in this aspect

---

[71] *Ibid.*, p. 50: "Ecclesiastics are citizens and members of the republic. But the republic is governed by the laws of the prince. Hence [ecclesiastics] are subjects; and in disobeying [the law] they sin before God no less than the laity."

of his thought. One is the reflection of a previous era; the other is an anticipation of much that was most fruitful for the later development of Western thought. Living in a less happy age, he recognized the darker implications of these impulses, and he adapted them to the construction of a more religious world view. There is no question here of a calculated and cynical exploitation of religious values for political and secular ends, as in the case of Machiavelli. Sarpi was a product of the Reformation as well as of the Renaissance, and one of the most striking features of his thought is precisely the way in which it so honestly combines two movements frequently considered antithetical. If, indeed, Sarpi's religious position appears finally closer to Wittenberg and Geneva than to Rome, it is not because he was attracted by Protestantism as such, but rather because the position expressed in the Protestant creeds seemed to him more consonant with the values he held so deeply as a free citizen of a free republic. In this way Sarpi can perhaps provide some insight into major tendencies of both the Renaissance and the Reformation, and above all into their profound connection.

16 Baroque Poetry: New Tasks for the Criticism of Marino and of "Marinism"[1]

FRANCO CROCE

Born in 1927, Franco Croce is now professor *incaricato* of modern and contemporary Italian literature at the University of Genoa. He writes the regular "Seicento" column in the bibliographical portion of the *Rassegna della letteratura italiana* and is author of three major monographs on Seicento literature: *Carlo de' Dottori* and *Federico Della Valle* (both Florence: La Nuova Italia, 1957 and 1965), and *Tre momenti del barocco letterario italiano* (Florence: Sansoni, 1966), as well as an anthology of Baroque literature, soon to appear in a Zanichelli edition in Bologna.

Giovan Battista Marino, a poet as famous in his own day as he is little-known in the English-speaking world today, was born in Naples in 1569, and he began his literary career as the secretary to a Neapolitan noble family. An unfortunate love affair landed him in prison in 1598, whence he escaped shortly afterwards to Rome. After several years as secretary to the nephew of Pope Clement VIII, Cardinal Pietro Aldobrandini, he moved to Turin, having already acquired a considerable reputation as a writer. In 1611 he was back in prison again, and in 1615 he moved to France as a favorite of Queen Marie de' Medici. These were his years of greatest productivity: the *Sampogna*, the *Galleria*, and the *Adone* followed in rapid succession. But pressed by a disappointment

---

[1] "Nuovi compiti della critica del Marino e del Marinismo," *Rassegna della letteratura italiana*, LXI (1957), 456–73, translated and somewhat abridged by the editor with the approval of the author. For a good biographical sketch of Marino, and for a critical judgment somewhat different from the one stated in this essay, English-speaking readers are referred to James V. Mirollo, *The Poet of the Marvelous, G. M.* (Columbia University Press, 1963).

with court life and by a nostalgia for his native country, he returned, first to Rome in 1623, and then to Naples in 1624; and there he died the following year.

NOW that a half-century has gone by since scholars first became interested in studying the world of the Baroque, it is perhaps time to reconsider what is still valid in the old Romantic interpretation of Italian Marinism and what new lines of research have opened up above and beyond those traced out by the critics of Romanticism during the first half of the present century.

The Romantic interpretation maintained its basic vitality right up through the time of Croce himself, and in its time it was a fairly rich and articulate position. It accepted, of course, the negative and rather summary judgment inherited from the Arcadians;[2] but it gave the judgment a different motivation. It provided a broader historical framework for what the Arcadians had called a "crisis" in the Italian literary tradition and what they had attributed to the abandonment of the good, sound school of Petrarch. On one hand, it saw this crisis (like Salfi,[3] for instance, though he was a critic somewhat marginal to the main currents of Romanticism) in relation to the tension provoked in all parts of the culture of the age by the prospect of new developments— a tension which had productive results in the sciences but which was sterile, through an error in the way they were presented, in poetry. On the other hand, like the greater part of Risorgimento literary historiography, it explained the aesthetic poverty of Marino and of his imitators by the political decadence of Italy. Still, within the limits of this harsh judgment the Romantics

[2] ["Arcadia" was a literary movement that arose in the last decades of the seventeenth century in opposition to what later came to be called "Baroque" and what at the time was called "Marinism." The name comes from the Academy of the Arcadia, founded in Rome among the frequenters of the circle of Queen Christina of Sweden under the leadership of Giovan Maria Crescimbeni. The express purpose of the academy was "to exterminate the bad taste [of the present century] and chase it down . . . into the most remote castle or villa [of the peninsula]."]

[3] [On Francesco Salfri, see B. Croce's article in his *Nuovi saggi sulla letteratura italiana del '600* (Bari: Laterza, 1949).]

succeeded in bringing together many important characteristics of Marinist literature under a single formula—a formula which remained more or less the same from Sismondi's *esprit et volupté*[4] to Croce's "sensualism and ingenuity." It had the unquestioned merit, first, of underscoring (if only to draw attention to its qualitative defects) one of the central sentimental themes of the seventeenth century, and second, of connecting it (if only, in most cases, to put the connection in terms of a simple opposition) with the strain of "wit" fundamental to Marinist poetics.

Certainly the most vulnerable and the most ingenuous element of this system of criticism, the one most infected by the now discounted Risorgimento polemics and at the same time the one most undermined by the modern awareness of the European scope of the "Baroque" phenomenon, is its conviction that Marinism must be explained by the moral, cultural, and political crisis of Italian society. And yet it seems to me, now that the critical revision of the Romantics' position has been largely concluded, that even this element ought in some ways to be taken once again into consideration. I have in mind not so much the partial resumption of Salfi's suggestions in Calcaterra's attempt to reconnect Marinism with an epistemological crisis.[5] I am thinking, rather, of the interest in the political and social background of *Secentismo* that has begun to appear in more recent works of criticism—in Francastel,[6] for example, who is concerned, in the figurative arts, with characterizing the phenomena of taste according to time, place, and structure, or in Morpurgo Tagliabue,[7] who is interested in what he calls the "sociology of the concept."

[4] [On Sismondi, see above, ch. 1, n. 37.]

[5] [Carlo Calcaterra's principal work on this subject is his *Il Parnaso in rivolta* (Milan: Mondadori, 1940), as well as his subsequent article, "Il problema del Barocco" in *Questioni e correnti di storia letteraria* (Milan: Marzorati, 1949), pp. 481 ff.]

[6] Pierre Francastel, "Limites chronologiques, limites géographiques et limites sociales du Baroque" in *Retorica e barocco* (Rome: Bocca, 1955), pp. 55–61.

[7] Guido Morpurgo Tagliabue, "La retorica aristotelica e il barocco" in *Retorica e barocco*, pp. 119–96, here referred to on pp. 142–43.

This is a new interest, one that has arisen in part from the internal exigencies of the work of criticism itself and in part from recent changes in [literary and artistic] taste. It has arisen in Francastel, for instance, from his fight against *la mystique Wölfflin*.[8] Naturally, it cannot lead us back to a pure and simple acceptance of the generous but superficial historical criticism of the Risorgimento. But it can lead us to take up again, with greater sensitivity and with a broader background of [historical] data, the problem put by the Romantics regarding the social and political situation that conditioned the Baroque. The new critical approach will have to abstain from the facile schemes of the Romantics and from their tendency to look for immediate connections between civil and poetic decadence. And it will not be able to insist on equations between literary taste and the preferences of a particular social class, following the theme of an aristocracy that becomes worldly—equations which are valid, if at all, only within the precise limits [established by] Morpurgo Tagliabue. We must look in Marinism for the imprint, not just of one single aspect of Seicento society, but more generally of a particular [historical] situation—and of a situation which was not simply one of national crisis, as nineteenth-century historiography would have it, even though it was one very different from that of the early Renaissance. It was a world in which the importance of civic life is strongly diminished. It was less middle-class, more plebeian on one hand and more aristocratic—or feudal-capitalistic—on the other.[9] It was quicker to align itself with the usages of Europe as a whole, and at the same time less mercantile, more fragmented, and more divided up into closed regional areas.

[8] "Le Baroque," in *Atti del V. Congresso Internazionale di Lingue e Letterature Moderne* (Florence, 1955), pp. 165-77. Heinrich Wölfflin's *Renaissance und Barock* (Munich, 1888) was in large part responsible for stimulating a new and more favorable judgment of the period in the late nineteenth and early twentieth centuries.

[9] [Such terms as "feudal-capitalism" may be shocking to American university students, who have all read a good bit of Karl Marx; but they are somewhat more common in Italy, where the writings of Marx do not ordinarily form a part of the school curriculum.]

Taking account of this situation will avoid returning to the Romantics' thesis of a direct relationship between literary frivolity and a political crisis. It will help us, moreover, to understand some of the basic elements in Seicento culture. It will help us to understand, for instance, the extraordinary international success of Marino, the greatest exponent of the new taste. It will help us to understand also the varied fortune of his followers, the Marinists, who were united by their intense fervor for the new poetry, it is true, but whose reputations, controversies, and discussions . . . seldom passed the provincial boundaries within which they were confined once the brilliant parabola of their master had been completed. Finally, it will help us to understand why the most active opposition to orthodox Marinism took place in those better-organized urban societies that least resembled the norm of Seicento culture—in those that reproduced some of the social conditions of the Renaissance, like the court of Urban VIII in Rome, and in those that anticipated the conditions of early Settecento culture, like the Florentine scientific and literary groups around Redi and Leopoldo de' Medici.[10]

The importance of political and economic structures must be evaluated with greater caution, however, when we consider the substance of Marinism rather than its reception. These structures are elements that must filter through a great quantity of speculation about poetic theory and flow along a long and purely literary course before they finally open out into concrete works of literature. But attention to them can be useful—in helping us, for example, to comprehend the odd convergence of a very elegant repertory of stylistic inventions on one hand, and on the other, a

[10] [Prince, and then Cardinal, Leopoldo de' Medici, brother of the Grand Duke Ferdinando II (1621–70), was the patron and one of the principal participants of the Academy of the Cimento, founded among Galileo's disciples in 1657. Redi (1626–97) was a lexicographer, critic, and poet (his *Bacco in Toscana* is a minor classic of Italian literature), as well as one of the leading scientists in late seventeenth-century Italy—the one who first demolished the theory of spontaneous generation. On the importance of the Florentine literary circles in preparing the anti-Baroque reaction of the end of the century, see Walter Binni, "La formazione della poetica arcadica e la letteratura fiorentina di fine Seicento" in his *L'Arcadia e il Metastasio* (Florence: La Nuova Italia, 1963).]

rather poorly articulated sentimental context, generally lacking in a sense of moral and political commitment. . . .

As far as the second part of the Romantic evaluation of Marinism is concerned, modern critics cannot, certainly, accept the insistence on sensual delight as its single sincere emotional inspiration without considerable reservation. For one thing, they can no longer share the sense of moral revulsion that the thesis inevitably evokes. For another, they cannot overlook the many equally important characteristics of Marinism that have come out of the studies of the post-Romantics. They cannot forget, that is, the detailed attention to reality, which Croce noted in Marino's descriptive passages, and particularly to the reality of luxurious objects (Getto), as well as the love of appearances (Rousset) and literary sensuality (Flora), the predilection for emblems (Praz), the taste for violent caricatures (Marzot), the interest in punctilious romantic gallantry and in unexpected occurrences (which, according to Morpurgo Tagliabue, correspond in the plot to what the trope is in the aphorism), and, finally, the feeling of the transitoriness of things and of universal metamorphosis (which Getto has found in the Marinists).[11]

And yet the theme of sensual delight can still today be regarded as a symbol of what is new in the Baroque sentiment. For it actually was new, even though it was won at the cost of minimizing and exteriorizing the patrimony of the Renaissance, from Petrarch through Tasso.

[11] These elements have been noted in other literary figures of the age who have no connection with the Italian Baroque—particularly by Fritz Strich in his comments on the preoccupation with the present, with the particular moment, with immediacy, and with the theme of vanity, in "Der lyrische Stil des siebzehnten Jahrhunderts," *Abhandlungen zur deutschen Literaturgeschichte* (*Festschrift Franz Muncken*) (Munich: Beck, 1916), pp. 21–53. [The critics and historians mentioned in the text are: (1) Giovanni Getto in the introduction to his edition of *Opere scelte di Giovan Battista Marino e dei Marinisti* (Turin: U.T.E.T., 1949; 2nd edn., 1964); (2) Jean Rousset, in his *La Littérature de l'âge baroque en France* (Paris: J. Corti, 1953); (3) Francesco Flora, in his *Storia della letteratura italiana* (1942; but the author cites the 7th edn. by Mondadori of 1955), Vol. II; (4) Mario Praz, in his *Studi sul concettismo* (Florence, 1946), as well as in his *Studies in Seventeenth Century Imagery*; and (5) Giulio Marzot in "Il Seicento," *Classici italiani* (Florence: Sansoni, 1940).]

The lines that [Luigi] Settembrini brought forth to illustrate the transition from Armida's love [in Tasso's poem by that name] to Marino's sensual delight ("It is an incident from the *Gerusalemme* stretched out into a poem and diluted") can be re-examined for other nuclei of Marinist inspiration that were nourished by a preceding literary tradition. They may, for instance, reveal the search for greater and more external variety in the Renaissance casuistry concerning [the nature of] love (Getto's "multiple predication" of woman in the Marinists),[12] the exteriorization of the pathetic in the amatory vicissitudes of Tasso and of Late Renaissance romances and dramas, the refinement of Tasso's melancholy and of his sense of the transitory in the more open, prestigious—and facile—Seicento poetry on life's fleeting course.

Yet what Settembrini regarded only negatively, as a reduction and a dilution, may actually be considered as an original contribution. The themes of the Renaissance and of Tasso may have become less restrained and less profound as they passed into Marinism. But they also became more explicit, more uninhibited, and more stimulating; and in their very violence, they acquired something of youth and of freshness. Hence De Sanctis's interpretation of the Baroque as nothing more than a degeneration of the Renaissance is no longer acceptable. Yet the assertion of another Romantic, one whose sensitivity was rather different from that prevailing in the nineteenth century, is still valid, namely, that of Carrara, when he spoke of *Secentismo* as a healthy breath of air on the "luke-warm ashes" of fantasy.[13] I would say, in fact, that the more its sentimental content is manifest, sumptuous, and fancifully capricious, the more the Baroque experience turns out to be important culturally, and the more disposed it is to get rid of its negative elements and to provoke creative reactions.

[12] Getto, in the *Opere scelte* cited in the preceding note, Vol. II, p. 22. Luigi Settembrini's judgment is in his *Lezioni di letteratura italiana* (Naples, 1881), Vol. II, p. 273.

[13] [Francesco De Sanctis, that is, in ch. 18 of his *Storia della letteratura italiana*, and Enrico Carrara in *La poesia pastorale* (Milan: Vallardi, 1909).]

From this point of view, Marino, whom the critical anthologies of the twentieth century have judged to be somewhat marginal in respect to his subtle imitators, must be restored to the central position given him by earlier historiography.[14] If the experiments of certain of the Marinists often attained more pleasing results, and if at times they touched more intimate chords and stimulated greater emotions of sensuality and melancholy, it is precisely in the uninhibited founder of their school that the healthy externalizing breeze is most clearly felt. To observe Marino from the point of view of his contemporaries can be an effective guarantee against the temptation to encumber Marinism with subtle meanings which were not germane to it but which reflect rather [the critic's] experience with modern changes of taste or with other phases of the Baroque in other parts of Europe.[15] . . .

Marino is relatively free of complications. Most of what he wrote is easy and clear, as self-confident and intelligent as it is at times somewhat inarticulate and superficial. Just for that reason, indeed, it is fresher and more decisively, if also more facilely, rebellious. It is difficult to give an adequate explanation for such vivacity and such lack of scruples without engaging in a concrete reconstruction of the formation of the style and sentiment of the vigorous and frivolous leader of the Baroque poets. But what is clear already is the strong consciousness he himself had of the originality of his work and of the break it marked in the Italian literary tradition.

Marino was not the first of the Baroque poets because he was the inventor of new modes of expression. In that sense the first of them was another, and a much greater, poet, Tasso, as Getto has pointed out in indicating the author of the *Gerusalemme* as the true ancestor of the Baroque all over Europe. Rather Marino was the first of the Baroque poets because he was the first of them to

[14] Without, of course, going to the extremes of Theodor Elwert, who sees Marino as an explorer in the realms of the spirit not inferior to Galileo: "Zur Charakteristik der italienischen Barocklyrik," *Romanistisches Jahrbuch*, III (1950), 421–98, p. 433.

[15] [This warning is issued to literary critics, needless to say, not to historians, for whom it is just stating the obvious.]

be completely free of doubts concerning the novelty and the originality of his work and concerning the [element in it that we call] Baroque.[16] Tasso was both proto-Baroque and Late Renaissance at the same time; and standing at the transition from one age to the next, he was capable of much greater richness and novelty [in regard to his predecessors] than was Marino after him. True, he also was aware of the autonomous value of his own poetry, though under attack he often lost his self-confidence and was willing to compromise. But this awareness became fully manifest only when spurred by the enthusiastic admiration of a Camillo Pellegrino, on one hand[17] (the same Pellegrino who was to become a herald of the still further novelties of Marino's conceits), or, on the other, by the intelligent and lucid opposition of the reactionary Salviati.[18] Marino instead was completely sure of himself and serenely ostentatious about the way he wrote. Indeed, it is this very quality in him that indicates his vitality and his modernity.

The consciousness in Marino of an opposition to his predecessors reinforced his unrestrained aspiration for novelty. So also did certain characteristics of his personality, characteristics that fit very well with the requirements of his poetic theory. Cold, calculating, and intelligent, Marino enjoyed turning himself into a "personage" and transforming every event of his life, many of which were indeed troublesome, into a pretext for capricious showing-off. We need only consider certain of his letters—the one full of bizarre pleasantries to d'Aglié,[19] for example, written

[16] [Croce has *del proprio barocco*; but I use the paraphrase to avoid giving the impression that Marino himself ever used such a term, which is, of course, of much later coinage.]

[17] [First of all in *Il Carrafa, o vero, Della epica poesia* of 1584. See Weinberg, *A History of Literary Criticism*, pp. 991 ff.]

[18] [Lionardo Salviati (1540–89) is the spokesman for the Accademia della Crusca in the literary war described fully by Weinberg, *op. cit.*, ch. XIX. His most important polemical work on this question was *Lo 'nfarinato secondo, ovvero . . . Risposta al libro intitolato "Replica di Camillo Pellegrino"* . . . (Florence, 1588). See above, ch. 2.]

[19] [To Lodovico d'Aglié, 10 February 1612, now in *Lettere*, ed. Marziano Guglielminetti (Turin: Einaudi, 1966), pp. 526 ff.]

from his prison in Turin[20]—to understand the coincidence between his sentimental nature and his taste for gratuitous violence of expression. Thus while noticing his facility of rhyme and invention, we will also do well to remember the observations of his contemporaries, Chiabrera among others, concerning the extraordinary *natural* poetic gifts of the author of the *Adone*.[21]

Marino's fortunate career as a man of the world, finally, can also help us to understand his work as an example of Baroque splendor. He took advantage of the most attractive aspect of the social situation of his era, namely, the facility with which it permitted an Italian to acquire a reputation all over Europe. His success in this regard strengthened his "Seicento" arrogance by freeing it from the doubts and the resentments to which he otherwise would have been exposed in the closed provincial environment many of his compatriots were forced to live in. We need only compare his own nonchalance with the irritable malignity of another supporter of the "Moderns," Tassoni. Better yet, we can compare it with the arrogance of an extreme Marinist like F. F. Frugoni, or with the hesitations of an orthodox follower like [Girolamo] Preti—of one, that is, who hesitated to smash all the bridges with the past even while accepting the superiority of the *Adone* to the *Gerusalemme*.[22]

---

[20] The situation in which Marino finds himself is truly wretched, but the literary result of it is not dramatic. It is almost a symbol of what Morpurgo Tagliabue observed (*op. cit.*, p. 194): "The Seicento is tragic; the Baroque is not. It is merely the frivolous aspect of the century."

[21] The eulogy of Marino is in *Elogi di uomini illustri*, published in Gabbriello Chiabrera, *Dialoghi dell'arte poetica con altre sue prose e lettere* (Venice, 1830), pp. 167–69. [Chiabrera (1552–1638) was almost as much applauded in his time as was his contemporary and friend Marino. But since his poetic efforts were directed largely toward adapting the forms of Greek verse to Italian, and since he did not renounce the Petrarchan tradition, he became a hero among those Arcadians who were bent upon finding at least one stream of "good taste" in the midst of an otherwise corrupt age (as explained in the "To the Reader" of the first comprehensive edition of his works, published by the Roman Arcadia at the beginning of the eighteenth century and many times thereafter).]

[22] [Alessandro Tassoni (see above, ch. 1, n. 13) wrote a comic epic, or rather an epic poem intended to make fun of epic poems, called *La secchia rapita* (*The Stolen Bucket*), about a war between Bologna and Modena, which was first

Marino boasted about his fortunate career in accordance with his proud nature and with his love of boldness in poetry. Nonetheless his career did have at least one negative aspect. It did not provide him with the experience of discontent and uneasiness that made some of his more provincial imitators less sincere, it is true, but also, at times, more intimate and more thoughtful. In this sense the first of the Baroque poets was also the most antiquated. He was the one most convinced, for instance, of the superiority of Italian culture just at the moment when such a conviction was becoming ever less justified, and he was the one least apt to appreciate the more serious elements in the European Baroque, partly because his rise to fame outside Italy was so rapid.

Finally, there is the third theme of the Romantic synthesis: *esprit* and ingenuity. And this one is still squarely in the center of critical research today.

On this theme, indeed, twentieth-century criticism has worked with much greater continuity and consistency. It has elaborated, in a dense and fruitful discussion, the premises of Romanticism up to the point of the sharp conclusions taken from Elwert ("Gaity and humor are not merely signs of liberation from the Baroque; rather they belong to its very essence"),[23] which to me seem perfectly valid. The merry atmosphere of Marinism, so frequently a product of its exasperation in a search for conceits, is not foreign to the Baroque. It is not an involuntary result of an excessively serious use of *fiori*.[24] Nor is it (in the sense of caricature) a comic liberation from the Baroque. It is rather an integral part of its nature, a jesting tone fundamental to its style—a part

published in 1622 and then, in an edition supervised by the author, in 1624. The standard modern edition by Pietro Papini (1912) reproduces the 1624 text and has recently been republished by Giulio Cattaneo (Florence: Sansoni, 1962). Francesco Fulvio Frugoni wrote, in his own or assumed names, a series of *Ritratti critici abbozzati e confrontati* (1669) and of stories entitled *Del cane di Diogene* (*Diogenes's Dog*; 1687–89). Preti of Bologna (1582–1622), who ended up in the service of Cardinal Francesco Barberini, wrote a volume of lyric poems often reprinted after the first edition of 1614.]

[23] [In the article cited above at n. 14.] p. 478.

[24] [*Fiori*: the equivalent of the sixteenth-century English term meaning rhetorical ornamentation in general.]

of the constant ambiguity of *Secentismo* so well revealed by Flora.

The main task of this line of criticism from now on will be that of specifying more completely the ways in which this fundamental tone is manifested. On one hand, it must look further into the nature of the episode—which is less a characteristic of Marinism than of a more moderate branch of the Baroque—of the episode, that is, in which ingenuity seeks to become the bearer of moral values, in which sharpness seeks to become pithy, and in which the conceit seeks to become operative, of the episode, finally, which has a varied history and which comes out at times even in poetry that goes beyond the Baroque, like the *Aristodemo* of Dottori.[25] On the other hand, criticism must avoid pushing too far Elwert's thesis about Marinism as objective poetry deprived of sentiment. It must rather re-examine more precisely the relationship made by the Romantics between wit and what there really was of sentiment in the Seicento.

The scholar who has best pointed out the path to follow is still Flora. It is he who has insisted on the function of the Marinist smile, the smile that attenuates, though without denying it, the clear sentimental content, be it sensual, or be it full of gloomy pessimism and intimations of death. "That smile at the cleverness of what is being said or at the contradiction contained in it, is not an invitation to arrive at a moral conclusion contrary to the one just proposed (as in the case of logical or moral irony). It is rather a comment, in the form of a joke, an expression of modesty, or an exoneration of vanity of expression, twisted words, and harsh meanings. It is a form of emphasis that is 'corrected' by a beckoning gesture—one, in other words, that is toned down or modified rather than being stated explicitly."[26]

---

[25] [On Carlo de' Dottori (1618–87), see the author's own book cited in the introduction to this chapter. *Il Parnaso* has recently been edited by Carlo L. Golino and published by the University of California Press (1957).]

[26] *Storia della letteratura italiana*, p. 240. [I put "correct" here and elsewhere in quotation marks to preserve the un-English connotation of Croce's *corretto*. The Italian meaning of the word is explained here in the phrase I add at the end of the sentence, and which readers familiar with Italian know in the common expression *caffè corretto*—coffee with a shot of brandy in it.]

For the Marinists, indeed, wit has an ornamental function. This ornamentality, however, is one without which the raw emotive nucleus would be formless—one similar to the decorations admittedly used by some modern architects as a way of "correcting" errors in the construction. It is not as it is in Dottori (where we are outside of Marinist ornamentality), a strongly felt expression of strongly felt sentiments, but rather a very elegant literary justification for sentiments which in themselves alone would be too superficial or too crude.

Thus I do not consider as fruitful the search, so long conducted in the work of the Marinists, for "oases" of clearer and more limpid sentiments [amid what is held to be a wholly unsentimental and merely capricious style]. The aspiration for more explicit and more fully explained motives typical of the Baroque (the aspiration for sensuousness rather than love, according to the categories of the Romantics), is certainly a positive element, one leading to greater modernity. But it is also one that has very serious risks, for it leads to poorly articulated forms whenever the smile of wit is missing. If separated from the usual ingenious and playful treatment, for example, the sensuousness of the Marinists falls into pornography, their pessimism into troublesome and unrelieved gloom, their taste for reality into unbearable descriptive minutiae. On the other hand, the *fiori*, the ingenious cavils, the very linguistic intarsia, animate the superficial and violent material with something that is without doubt an important addition, even though it must not be overrated. This is not the "spiritual aura that radiates from the Empyrean nerve center" that Calcaterra spoke of, but the reduction of the new world that had been discovered with so much superficial capriciousness to the proportions of a very civilized game of allusions, and its refinement by means of the "urbane jesting" so dear to Tesauro.[27] It is an equilibrium won not in the intimacy of a well-ordered conscience but through the juxtaposition of two distant poles: the witty *fiori* and the crude new sentiments.

[27] [Emanuele Tesauro (1592–1675) in his *Il cannocchiale aristotelico*, written in 1654 and republished in his *Opera omnia* at Turin in 1670.]

It is an unstable equilibrium, one more often (if not always) purely literary rather than poetic. And the task of the critic must indeed be that of looking amid the production of the Seicento for the various ways in which this equilibrium is realized—not that of establishing the moments in which the sentiment alone is manifested, that is, but that of finding those in which its "correction" through the use of "ornaments" is truly effective.

In this search the position of the leader of the school will again become central. This is not because the author of the *Adone* actually realized the more valid literary, or worse, poetic, accomplishments of the whole of Marinism. It is rather because he undoubtedly offers the greatest variety of formulas by which the equilibrium was subsequently sought out, and because we can most conveniently find in him the pathways through the forest of his imitators. First of all, it is in Marino, and precisely in some of his most celebrated and representative poems, that we can find some of the clearest examples of the "corrective" function of the witty superstructure—of the way, that is, in which it modifies what otherwise would be an excessively strong sentimental content.

The sonnet "Tu, che i miei brevi sonni allor che il core,"[28] for example, written in honor of Adriana Basile, has a lyrical nucleus of no little vitality. It is pervaded by a sense of wonder and ardor that cannot be reduced to a mere literary commonplace. The song rises in the "high silence" and in the "tranquil peace" of the "nocturnal horror"; and to the poet it seems to have a supernatural power to "inebriate sweetly with love . . . the waves, the air, and the sky when it is the stillest." It is like a "strange poison" that "knows and sucks" at the heart and that possesses both sweetness and bitterness at the same time—in accordance with the Seicento taste for composite realities and for the convergence of opposites.

> Pasce l'aure di dolce, e me d'amaro . . .
> m'empie di gioia e poi m'ancide e strugge.[29]

---

[28] [This sonnet has not been found worthy of inclusion in any of the modern anthologies.]

[29]   ["(It) feeds the winds with sweetness, but me with bitterness;
It fills me with joy, and then destroys and kills me."]

This, indeed, is one of the most vivid testimonies of Marino's capacity for sentiment. And the judgment of Damiani is not wholly unjustified when, in line with his general interpretation of Marino as a poet of decadence,[30] he sees there transfused "the infinite desire that the song raises up in the human spirit." And yet even in this extreme case, here when Marino's sensibility shows an exceptional delicacy, the risk typical of what is new in the sentiment of the Baroque is still present. The theme, that is, seems at moments to be less than profoundly felt, as if it were on the point of lapsing into facile emphasis ("novo del mar sei certo angel verace"). A reading of the poem that isolated the quatrains and the first tercet in search of a more ambitious and romantic design would certainly lead to an unfavorable judgment of it— of an end not realized, that is, and of a sentimental reality that is merely mentioned but not completely expressed.

Hence the utility of the "correction" in the elevated conclusion. Indeed, the last tercet:

> al tremolar del dolce canto e caro
> l'anima trema, alle sue fughe fugge
> da' suoi sospiri a sospirare imparo[31]

seems, in the abstract, with its ingenious structure, with its witty correspondence between the movements of the voice and those of the listener's spirit that is carried over even into the small play on words ("alle sue fughe fugge"), to conflict with the gentle melancholy of the first part. But actually this tercet is beneficial to the composition, for it brings it back to its more proper dimensions as a clever and affectionate compliment ("dolce canto e caro"—"sweet, dear song") to the lovely Adriana. Some of the more exaggerated themes ("strange poison") become less lofty. That which seemed a not too well expressed shiver of fear ("the waves, the air, and the sky") turns out to be what it is in reality, a

---

[30] [Guglielmo Felice] Damiani, *Sopra la poesia del cavalier Marino* (Turin: Clausen, 1899), p. 83.

[31] ["At the trembling of the sweet, dear song,
The soul trembles; from its flights it flies,
Unable to sigh at its sighs."]

short, dreamy movement, softly and sweetly represented. The ingenious final structure, which the poet uses to justify a lyrical élan that is not sustained by a Romantic faith in the autonomous value of spiritual states, can also help the reader to grasp the brief span in which the enchantment that the poet has invoked succeeds in being poetic. . . .

When the sentimental content is delicate, as it is in the sonnet "Tu, che i miei brevi sonni," the "correction" of the emphasis can be entrusted to a bit of ingenuity that is not very deeply felt, without bothering to search about for more deceptive marvels. When, on the other hand, the sentimental elements are tauter and more realistic, the wit is livelier. One of the best examples of this characteristic is another of Marino's celebrated poems, the "Trastulli estivi" ("Summer Pastimes").[32]

Marino here follows a composition of Ovid, the first Elegy of Book I of the *Amores*; and he does it in the characteristic Baroque manner of making an "improved" translation. The "improvement" consists in an amplification according to the Marinist taste for more abundant and more ornate writing and according to a different sentimental point of view.

From the very beginning Marino elaborates extensively upon the elements in his model, leaving aside certain ornaments that no longer serve his purpose (like the references to Semiramis and Laïs) and drawing out a single verse (like Ovid's description of a summer afternoon) into an entire strophe. But at the same time he adds some new themes of his own: that of violated innocence, for instance (Ovid's Corinna becomes "Lilla the little virgin"). He introduces sensuous details ("Corinna comes clad in a veiled tunic" gives way to a more attentive description of the *candidetto velo* "whence the members that honesty covered and hid as in white snow still appeared nude though they remained enveloped"). He replaces the rapid "Deripui tunicam" ("I tore off the tunic") with a slower, more punctuated account ("I pressed her in my arms and received her in my embrace; with hurried hand I untied and undid the precious habit of perfumed linen"). He develops

[32] [In Ferrero's anthology (n. 38, below), pp. 388–91.]

and insists upon the malicious observation—so that the simpler
"Quae cum ita pugnaret tamquam quae vincere nollet—victa est
non aegre proditione sua" becomes:

> Vidi per prova allor, si come e quanto
> mal volentier contrasta
> o ritrosetta o casta
> virgine, qual sia l'ira e quale il pianto:
> falso pianto, ira finta.[33]

These are themes that prepare the reader for the somewhat
different conclusion of the poem. In Ovid, the joy before the
beauty of the girl that at last has been uncovered . . . amounts to
a somewhat gluttonous delight in the pleasure that comes of it.
In the Baroque poet, the solution is more complex—a lengthening
of Lilla's malicious resistance, a sensuous description of the lover's
first advances, an insertion of the virgin's laments as she is on the
verge of yielding ("What are you doing, O cruel one"), and an
announcement, after the final hesitation, with a triumphal sense
of conquest, that the "sweet goal" has been reached.

All this is in the line of a coherent development, so that the
slower pace of the first part, which is closer to the Ovidian model,
corresponds perfectly to the stronger sensuous tension of the
conclusion. Marino attains his originality in his greater insistence
upon the sensual texture, and his autonomous lascivious images
are more belligerent and more modern than Ovid's gluttonous
precipitation. And yet even here the sentimental content runs into
the danger of over emphasis and of an overfacile, obscene
rhetoric. To be acceptable in themselves, Marino's forms need to
be rooted in a more authentically disturbed sensibility, one where
the central theme of violated innocence (so minutely unfolded) is

[33] ["So, while she fought as if she wished not to conquer, by her own betrayal
she was conquered without difficulty": Ovid, *Amores*, I, v, 13 ff.
"I then saw from experience how unwillingly
She opposed an assault on her virginity,
And remained retiring and chaste, and
What anger and tears she was capable of:
It was false tears and a false anger." (56–60)]

backed up by more convincing motives, such as decadent sexual exasperation, and not just Seicento exuberance.

The clever turn of phrase at the end is thus necessary and easily takes the place of the linear departing wish in Ovid. . . . The different sentimental charge in Marino requires something more deeply felt than the ingenious correspondence between the "flights" (*fughe*) of music and the "flights" in the soul of whoever listens to the sonnet for Adriana. It requires a more genuine joking movement, an arrogant justification of the violation that disperses with a smiling paradox the erotic tension that otherwise would be too urgent and too down-to-earth:

> Canzon, lasciar intatta
> da sé partire amata donna e bella
> non cortesia, ma villania s'appella.[34]

Thanks to this ending, the sensual vulgarity is lightened into what Tesauro would call an "urbane caviling," a "pleasant laugh." The obscene details in the description of the sexual act are passed through an atmosphere of ambiguity and joking allusions, and they thus become easier to accept. . . . The result is a successful literary caprice rather than a still formless outlet for a strong voluptuous passion. The sense of exasperation proceeds, indeed, not from a passion within the poet himself, but from the requirements of poetics—from the demanding conditions, that is, of a poetic contest with Ovid (improving on Ovid's sensuality by introducing the theme of violated virginity). It proceeds, in other words, from a situation of paradoxical ingenuity; and to this ingenuity the details themselves have to remain subordinate. The final *pointe* therefore is a fundamental element in the equilibrium of the composition. It is that which restores to the poem the tone appropriate to it, the Baroque tone of capriciousness. . . .[35]

---

[34]   ["Oh song, let the beautiful, beloved lady depart intact;
For (not to do so) would be a villainy, not a courtesy."
(133–35)]

[35] [Here Croce analyses several other works according to the same categories. I pass directly to his analysis of the best-known of them.]

In the *Adone*, finally, the play between sentiment and wit is expanded to the point of including the most varied kind of ornaments—to the point of transforming the slender myth into an immense encyclopedia of poetic devices. We are now at the opposite pole with respect to the better lyrics of his youth. In these we find a minute and clever intertwining of refined sensuality and elegant conceits—a thematic content restricted within the confines of the gallant idyll. In the *Adone* we find rather a grandiose and heterogeneous mixture, a thematic content that embraces everything and that seems to be extremely ambitious. However, the vaster and more complex formula does not lead to a more energetic core of lyricism, and the immeasurable ornamental paraphernalia finds (when it succeeds in doing so, which it does not always do) an equilibrium only in the Baroque manner of ambiguous, joking allusions and in a capricious delight in ingenious literary variations. It is the usual Marinist formula projected onto a bigger scale. And just for this reason it reveals so much more clearly its artificial quality and the short breath of its anxious pursuit of novelty.

There is an illuminating example of this characteristic in one of the episodes in the *Adone*: in the meeting between *Amore* and *Morte* (Love and Death) in Canto VI, which is exceptionally brief in comparison to the usual length of Marino's episodes, but which is typical of the way in which the poem is generally written. It begins with a joking allegory of facile nonchalance. *Amore* beats his nurse, *Speranza* (Hope). Venus throws him out of home. He wanders furiously through the world until he gets involved in a game with *Interesse* (Interest), to whom he loses and must surrender his bow and arrows. This event is followed, as occurs so frequently in the *Adone*, by a brusque shift in tone. *Amore* gets his arms back and then, led by *Infausta Sorte* (Bad Luck), he suddenly is found walking "among the tombs of Menfi"; and there he meets *Morte* (Death). The terrible aspect of this dark divinity is described in gloomy detail. His head is "meagre and hairless," a horrible "framework of bones and joints." He has "sunken eye sockets," a "flattened nose," "two rakes" in his "toothless mouth," and "horrid fissures" in his "open belly." All this lugubrious descriptive virtuosity does not, however, serve to prepare for the expression of any kind of grave sentiment—which, if it were there, would contrast sharply with the excessive emphasis on details in the preceding description. It serves merely to exhibit a new type of ornamentation—that prepared on the more ample palette of the *Adone*. And in fact the horror of the appearance of *Morte* is immediately dispersed by the behavior of *Amore*, who at the sight of him "could hardly keep from laughing." The gloominess of the episode thus reveals its true nature. It is not a tragic theme, but a Baroque grotesque element, one meant to arouse not terror but laughter.

At this point a "bitter fight" flares up between the two divinities. Here again we might be led to expect a great novelty—a sublime duel between Love and Death. But nothing of the sort occurs. The duel is a rapid, ingenious *trouvaille* that ends up in a play on words ("vibrando ella la falce, egli la face"),[36] without any further consequences. The two divinities are reconciled. They pass the night together and on the morrow they exchange their arms. The conclusion of this complicated allegorical apparatus is therefore rather disappointing. Each with the other's arms,

> Morte induce ad amar l'alme canute.
> Amor tragge a morir la gioventute.[37]

I have not been able to find in these verses any kind of "pre-Romantic lightning flashes," even when I try isolating them from their context according to the suggestions of Ferrero.[38] They are nothing but a clever joke, one which terminates the episode with a witty figure and discharges the tension, half grotesque and half symbolic, with a bitter smile. The meeting between the charming youth and the horrible skeleton and the "bitter fight" and the

[36] ["Death brandishing his sickle, Love his halo." This passage is not to be found in Ferrero's anthology either.]

[37] ["Death leads white-haired souls to love. Love leads the youth to die."]

[38] [Giuseppe Ferrero, in *Marino e i marinisti* (Milan: Ricciardi, 1954). Ferrero recognizes, however, that this procedure is somewhat arbitrary: p. 107.]

reconciliation are all very modest. They are simply some of the many eccentricities of the world, where old people fall in love and young people die. This is not a pre-Romantic "sorrowful meditation on the anxiousness of Love as He sees life fly by," etc., but a chuckling, Baroque consciousness of the extravagances of the lot of men. The equilibrium between the opposite tones of the brief episode (horror and laughter) is thus placed once again in wit—wit which here is not all gratuitously capricious, but which is enriched by a touch of bitterness. Nevertheless, the wit is introduced above all for the sake of the autonomous pleasure in the "marvelous" contradiction (old people who fall in love, young people who die) and not for the sake of expressing, by means of the contradiction, a protest or a sense of discomfort. The recourse to what seem like more ambitious figurations, in other words, does not carry us even in the *Adone*, and even in this scene that is thematically so promising, outside of the usual ingenious and committed atmosphere of the Baroque.

In fact, I would say that the wider scope of the poem makes Marino's limitations all the more evident. For in its attempt to embrace a reality much greater than the more modest amorous and idyllic reality of the minor works, it ends by reducing the reality it embraces to the proportions of ingenious wit. Yet it is precisely in this coincidence between a less restrained ambition and an equally unrestrained renunciation of strong moral and sentimental commitments that gives importance to the "royal poem" in the context both of the entire work of Marino and in the Baroque as a whole. The *Adone* does not contain the best of Marino; but it does contain what is most typical of him—the Marino who is both voracious and superficial, extremely literary and yet at times somewhat inarticulate, the Marino who exemplifies a brief and not really great season in the history of taste, but one that is still lively and stimulating.

The proof of the importance of the *Adone* at the time is given by the vast polemic it aroused in all Seicento culture. Not so the more adroit and refined investigations of the early lyrics, which seemed to favor the kind of compromise reached by the moderate

Baroque—a lyric, that is, which can indulge in a wit prohibited to more serious forms of literature. They thus offered a contribution of considerable historical significance in furthering the general affirmation of Baroque innovations—hence their favorable reception by someone like Stigliani,[39] for example, and by the moderates of the mid-century. They retained their influence even later, indeed, in encouraging the occasional compromises of Arcadian poetry with certain elements of the Baroque. . . . But they did not contribute to that passionate discussion of poetics that is among the most important ingredients of Baroque culture, and precisely that ingredient that was most to affect the culture of succeeding periods.

With the *Adone* however—with its explicit aim of surpassing all other poems and with its attempt to represent the whole of reality by reducing it to the proportions of ornamental witticism —no compromise is possible. On one hand there are the enthusiastic admirers like Aleandri.[40] On the other hand there are the furious opponents like Stigliani, those who in the heat of the discussion were led to reconsider their initial Baroque or pre-Baroque positions and who then discovered new and better-founded reasons for defending the Italian literary tradition and for denouncing the crisis of the Seicento. Finally, there are those like Villani,[41] who accepted Marino's call to innovation but who rejected the specific form of innovation he himself realized. For they considered it an untrue expression of emotion and an only apparent improvement on the patrimony of the classics; and from the experience of Marino and the Moderns they drew, not the haughty self-satisfaction of the Marinists, but encouragement to

[39] [Tommaso Stigliani (b. 1573) had met Marino during his years in Naples and corresponded with him frequently from 1603 on. But growing bad relations between the two ended in an open break after the publication of the *Adone*, which Stigliani was the first to attack, in his *Occhiale*. On the fight that followed, see Mirollo, *op. cit.*, pp. 92 ff.]

[40] [Girolamo Aleandri (1574–1629) was a classicist and a Latin poet. He defended the *Adone* against Stigliani in his *Difesa dell'Adone* of 1629.]

[41] [Nicola Villani's *Uccellatura* and *Considerazioni* were published in 1630 and 1631.]

try out still further, more serious and more committed innovations, with a moderation that was no longer a compromise.

This work, then, monotonous and boring as it is, turns out to be a very provocative one, a sort of touchstone by means of which the various aspirations of Seicento literature are clarified and become conscious of themselves. Close attention to it will save modern critics as well from facile compromises. It will oblige them above all not to attribute to Seicento literature a spirit and an accomplishment that belong rather to later ages. For the more fully developed structure of the *Adone* will reveal as merely apparent the similarities that may be noticed in other works. A study of the *Adone* will also encourage them to trace out a more varied picture of the world of the Seicento, one no longer reduced to a few great denominators, but one rich in the internal tensions (which become particularly apparent in the contemporary discussion of the *Adone*), in the diverse episodes, in the various results, and in the different personalities that distinguish it.

We have thus arrived at the last of the new tasks that the critics, in my opinion, are called upon to assume in complementing the work of Romantic historiography and of the twentieth-century rediscovery of the Baroque. It is the last and, I should say, the most important of those indicated in this rapid sketch: the task, that is, of substituting for grand generalizations and for texts appropriate to anthologies a more careful reconstruction of individual works, of the environment in which they were created, and of the personality of the authors.

I am not speaking of a commitment, interesting though it may be, to periodize the Baroque,[42] or to list its various sub-species in the manner of D'Ors.[43] I am speaking rather of a desire for the

---

[42] As in Helmut Hatzfeld, whose lucid outline is proposed in his "The Baroque from the Viewpoint of the Literary Historian," *Journal of Aesthetics and Art Criticism*, XIV (1955), 156–64. [This whole issue of the journal is dedicated to the definition of the Baroque from the point of view of different fields. See also Hatzfeld's "L'Italia, la Spagna e la Francia nello sviluppo del Barocco letterario" in *La critica stilistica e il barocco letterario* (Florence: Le Monnier, n.d.).]

[43] [Eugenio D'Ors y Rovira, in *Lo Barroco* (Madrid, 1944), first published in French translation in 1935.]

historically concrete, one which is more complex and less given
to cataloguing, and one which can be realized only by using
many different instruments, from rigorous stylistic analysis (like
that, so stimulating even with its many limitations, conducted by
Pozzi on Orchi)[44] and from a well-documented exposition of
Seicento poetics (of which the essay of Morpurgo Tagliabue,
already cited,[45] is a good example), to a study of the formation and
experience of the various writers.

This, I think, is the best way to realize fully the need of which
the critics of the early twentieth century were particularly aware—
the need, namely, to do justice to the Seicento. To do justice, no
longer by means of risky confrontations of taste, but by casting
a full and objective light on the century and by ridding it of the
confused myths that have since been cast upon it—both the negative myth of black decadence created during the Risorgimento
and the various positive myths created during the anti-Romantic
reaction of a half-century ago. In other words, we must enrich
the generalizations of the last 150 years, which, to be sure, once
had a considerable historical validity. We must recognize, above
and beyond the overall framework of the Baroque, the many
different faces, passions, relationships, and experiences of the
individual authors and moments of the age.[46]

[44] [Giovanni da Locarno] Pozzi, *Saggio sullo stile dell'oratoria sacra nel Seicento
esemplificata sul P. Emanuele Orchi* (Rome: Inst. Hist. O.F.M. Capp., 1954).

[45] [Above, n. 7.]

[46] [A small addition to Marino bibliography: Marziano Guglielminetti's
Tecnica e invenzione nell'opera di G. B. M. (Florence and Messina: D'Anna,
1964), reviewed at length by Edoardo Taddeo in *Giornale storico della letteratura
italiana*, CXLIII (1966), 279–88, and by Croce himself in the 1965 volume of *La
rassegna della letteratura italiana*.]

17 Music—How Opera Began: An Introduction to Jacopo Peri's *Euridice* (1600)[1,2]

HOWARD MAYER BROWN

Howard Mayer Brown taught at Wellesley College before coming to the University of Chicago, where he is now professor of music. Among his more important publications are *Music in the French Secular Theater* (1963) and *Instrumental Music Printed Before 1600: A Bibliography* (1965), both published by the Harvard University Press. He is also director of the Collegium Musicum of the University of Chicago; and in this capacity he was responsible for a performance in January 1967 of Jacopo Peri's opera *Euridice*, the score of which he is now preparing for publication.

MUSICIANS in the Renaissance began to study Greek culture in detail rather later than their counterparts in other disciplines. Franchino Gafori was apparently the first to have Greek musical treatises translated into Latin for him at the end of the fifteenth century, and the Swiss Heinrich Glareanus, whose *Dodecachordon* was published in 1547, was the first musician to know the Greek language.[3] Moreover, the nature of classical studies in music was different from studies in other fields, since very few specimens of actual Greek music were known during the Renaissance, and

---

[1] [From a manuscript provided directly by the author and slightly emended for the purposes of this anthology, by the editor with the author's approval.]

[2] This essay was originally read at a session of the Renaissance Seminar of the University of Chicago as an introduction to a performance of Peri's *Euridice*, given by the Collegium Musicum of the University of Chicago in January 1967.

[3] See Edward E. Lowinsky, "Music of the Renaissance as Viewed by Renaissance Musicians," *The Renaissance Image of Man and The World*, ed. Bernard O'Kelly (Ohio State University Press, 1966), pp. 171–72. The most recent edition of the *Dodecachordon* is an English translation by Clement A. Miller, 2 vols. (American Institute of Musicology, 1965).

those few examples that had been discovered could not be deciphered. Scholars were thus forced to speculate about the true nature of Greek music on the basis of theoretical treatises, some of which began to be generally known only toward the middle of the sixteenth century.

D. P. Walker, whose series of articles on musical humanism in the sixteenth and early seventeenth centuries is the most complete résumé to date of the ideas about Greek musical thought current during the Renaissance, makes clear how universal the interest in Greek music was.[4] Almost all sixteenth-century treatises pay at least lip service to the Greeks, and many writers made a serious attempt to understand the character of their music. Surprisingly enough, in spite of the lack of classical sources, sixteenth-century scholars all arrived at very much the same general conception of ancient music, even though there were important details about which they differed. Quite aside from these details, though, they were in basic disagreement about the extent to which modern music ought to be reformed according to ancient precepts. Some humanists took a purely scholarly interest in Greek music. Others believed modern music to be vastly inferior and wished to change the music of their own time radically. Still others, notably Gioseffo Zarlino and, perhaps, most of the more humanistically inclined composers, took a middle position: sixteenth-century music, they thought, had reached a new state of perfection—they believed in progress— but it could be improved still more, since it was in certain ways inferior to that of the Greeks.

One of the chief defects of modern music, in the view of some

---

[4] D. P. Walker, "Musical Humanism in the 16th and Early 17th Centuries," *The Music Review*, II (1941), 1, 111, 220, 288; and III (1942), 55. The essay is also published separately (Cassel and Basel: Bärenreiter, 1949) in a German translation. The summary of sixteenth-century attitudes toward Greek music is taken from Walker (German translation, p. 9), who cites Franchino Gafori, Giovanni Artusi, Francisco Salinas, and Domenico Pietro Cerone as representatives of the conservative, scholarly approach; Pontus de Tyard, Vincenzo Galilei, Girolamo Mei, and Giovanni Battista Doni as representatives of the radical, reforming approach; and Heinrich Glareanus, Nicola Vicentino, Gioseffo Zarlino, and Marin Mersenne as moderates.

sixteenth-century theorists, was that it could not produce the powerful psychological, and sometimes even miraculous, effects on listeners that Greek music was supposed to have been capable of producing. Writers on music describe the miracles said to have been worked by Orpheus, Amphion, Arion, Timotheus, and various other Greek musicians. Zarlino, for example, writes that although ancient music was imperfect, the ancient musicians were able to arouse in the human soul many different kinds of emotions. They could move the soul to anger and then change that anger to gentleness and docility. They could also induce tears, laughter, and other similar passions. Their ability to move men, he writes, is all the more incredible, since modern music is incapable of producing such effects, even though it seems so perfect that one could scarcely hope for improvement. It may be, he suggests, that modern music, rather than ancient music, is imperfect.[5] Edward E. Lowinsky has recently shown this fascination of the Renaissance with the effects of music to be a symbol of the transformation of music from a handmaid of theology to the most human art imaginable—to one, indeed, that can affect men's souls more profoundly and more immediately than any other art; and he connects this interest in Greek effects with the beginnings of "expression" in the music of Josquin des Prés and his contemporaries.[6]

A great deal of sixteenth-century speculation and discussion about ancient music centered on a variety of theoretical problems; the Greek diatonic, chromatic, and enharmonic genera, the nature of the Greek modal system, and the various tuning systems proposed by ancient theorists. But discussions of these theoretical problems were often subservient to the larger aim of attempting to understand the sources of the Greek effects: how they were produced and how they could be revived. In the long run, speculation about genera, modes, and tuning systems did have an influence

[5] Gioseffo Zarlino, *Istitutioni harmoniche* (Venice, 1573), Part II, ch. IV (pp. 73 ff. of the 1966 reprint).

[6] Lowinsky, *op. cit.*, pp. 151–52. See there for a more extended discussion of humanists' references to the effects of Greek music.

on composers, albeit an indirect one. Much of Nicola Vicentino's provocative discussion of the ways to create expressive music in his treatise *L'antica musica ridotta alla moderna prattica*, published in 1555,[7] was stimulated by speculation on just such questions. And stylistic innovations, like the rise of chromaticism in sixteenth-century music, for example, can be linked with humanistic study, even though the more historically oriented experiments, like those of Vicentino with Greek genera, were of no far-reaching practical consequence. But the avenue of approach that proved the most fruitful to composers, right from the beginning of discussions about Greek music at the end of the fifteenth century, was the exploration of means for connecting the music more closely with the text to which it was set. The importance of the text, and of good text declamation, was realized from the time of Josquin des Prés. Adrian Willaert perfected the technique for matching natural text accent to musical accent by the middle of the sixteenth century. And madrigal composers from at least the middle of the century were all preoccupied with the relationship of text to music and with the problem of expressing the meaning of the words in their music.[8] The theorists, too, were fully aware of the importance of text in reproducing emotion in music. Zarlino, for example, states that melody, rhythm, and speech, plus a well-disposed listener, are the requisites for expressive effects, and that melody alone is incapable of moving an audience to laughter or to tears.[9] Vincenzo Galilei is more extreme in his evaluation of the

---

[7] Facsimile edition by Edward E. Lowinsky (Cassel and Basel: Bärenreiter, 1959).

[8] The most complete study of Vicentino is Henry W. Kaufmann, *Nicola Vicentino (1511–1576), Life and Works* (American Institute of Musicology, 1966). The most succinct statement on Willaert's crucial position in the history of text setting may be found in Edward E. Lowinsky, "A Treatise on Text Underlay by a German Disciple of Francisco de Salinas," *Festschrift Heinrich Besseler* (Leipzig: Deutscher Verlag für Musik, 1961), pp. 245–46. Alfred Einstein's monumental study *The Italian Madrigal*, 3 vols. (Princeton University Press, 1949), remains the best exposition of the increasingly close connection between literary meaning and musical style in the Italian madrigal as the sixteenth century wore on.

[9] *Istitutioni* (1966 reprint), p. 84.

power of words. The noblest and most important part of music is the conception of the soul expressed by means of words, according to Galilei, and modern musicians have made reason a slave of their appetites in pretending that the way in which all the parts of polyphonic music come together is more important than that expression.[10] The notion that music ought not to be mistress of the words, but rather the servant of the words, was thus current long before Monteverdi expressed this sentiment in 1607.[11]

Not many theorists took as extreme a position on the inferiority of modern music as Vincenzo Galilei. Galilei, the father of the famous Galileo, was a lutanist, singer, and lute teacher in Florence and Pisa from the middle of the century until his death in 1591; and for many years he was the companion and protégé of Giovanni de' Bardi, count of Vernio, the patron of the Florentine Camerata. In his *Dialogo della musica antica et della musica moderna*, published in Florence in 1581, Galilei was outspoken in his condemnation of modern polyphonic music. He rejected Zarlino's moderate position that sixteenth-century composers could improve their music by making it more expressive, even though they were much more skillful than their predecessors.[12] The

[10] Vincenzo Galilei, *Dialogo della musica antica et moderna* (Florence, 1581; facsimile edition by Fabio Fano, Rome, 1934), p. 83.

[11] In the foreword to *Il quinto libro de' madrigali*, as published with commentary by Claudio Monteverdi's brother in Claudio's *Scherzi musicali* (Venice, 1607). A facsimile of the foreword is printed by Malipiero in his edition of Monteverdi's works, Vol. x, pp. 69–72. Oliver Strunk, *Source Readings in Music History* (New York: Norton, 1950), pp. 405–15, includes a complete English translation of the foreword and its commentary.

[12] On Galilei, see Fabio Fano, *La Camerata Fiorentina: Vincenzo Galilei (1520?–1591), la sua opera d'artista e di teorico come espressione di nuove idealità musicali*, "Istituzioni e monumenti dell'arte musicale italiana," Vol. iv (Milan: Ricordi, 1939); Henriette Martin, "La 'Camerata' du comte Bardi et la musique florentine du XVIe siècle," *Revue de musicologie*, xvi (1932), 63, 152, 227; and xvii (1933), 92 and 141; Nino Pirrotta, "Temperaments and Tendencies in the Florentine Camerata," *The Musical Quarterly*, xl (1954), 169; Claude Palisca, *Girolamo Mei: Letters to Vincenzo Galilei and Giovanni Bardi* (American Institute of Musicology, 1960), "Vincenzo Galilei's Counterpoint Treatise: a Code for the Seconda Pratica," *The Journal of the American Musicological Society*, ix (1956), 81, and "Vincenzo Galilei and Some Links between 'Pseudo-Monody' and

Dialogo begins with a long discussion of the tuning system in current use for *a cappella* singing, in which Galilei tries to refute Zarlino's contention that the Ptolemaic, that is, just, intonation was quite properly employed. Then he compares Greek theory with modern theory and sharply attacks both Zarlino's and Glareanus's ideas about the Greek modes. After a section criticizing modern polyphonic music (the section of greatest interest to us), the *Dialogo* concludes with a history of musical instruments and notation and a very brief critical exposition of the instrumental music of the sixteenth century.

Galilei's point of departure for his criticism of modern polyphonic music is the attitude typified by Zarlino's statement that the true aim of music is to perfect the intellect, to dispose man to virtue, and to pass the time in a noble manner apart from the vulgar necessities of daily life.[13] This attitude Galilei counters with a statement reminiscent of what Vicentino had written in 1555.[14] "The practice of music," he insists, ". . . was introduced among men to express the passions with greater effectiveness in celebrating the praises of the gods, the genii, and the heroes, and, secondarily, to communicate these passions with equal force to the minds of mortals for their own benefit and advantage." Sixteenth-century music, he maintains, is completely incapable of achieving this end. It therefore needs to be reformed completely.

His principal argument against polyphonic music is that the expressive power of any one musical element is canceled out when two or more events are occurring simultaneously.[15] If high

---

Monody," *The Musical Quarterly*, XLVI (1960), 344. A facsimile edition of Galilei's *Dialogo* was published in 1934 (see n. 10 above). An English translation of pp. 80–90—the section attacking modern polyphonic music—appears in Strunk, *Source Readings*, pp. 302–22. [See also above, ch. 2, where some of these titles are also cited.]

[13] *Istitutioni*, (1966 reprint), p. 84.

[14] *Dialogo*, 1934 edn., p. 81. The English translation is from Strunk, *op. cit.*, pp. 306–7. The passage in Vicentino, *L'antica musica*, 1959 edn., fol. 10ᵛ, is discussed in Edward E. Lowinsky, *Secret Chromatic Art in the Netherlands Motet*, 2nd edn. (New York: Russell & Russell, 1967), pp. 88 ff.

[15] The summary of Galilei's views in this and the next paragraphs is from the *Dialogo*, pp. 80–90.

sounds express one thing and low sounds another, then combining a low sound with a high sound will neutralize the emotion.
If certain rhythmic patterns conjure up certain kinds of passions,
then combining different patterns at the same time will destroy
the expressive power of any one of them. And since in polyphonic music different parts of the same sentence are sung
simultaneously, the affective quality of the text is lost completely.

Galilei argues that Greek music was originally monodic, but
that gradually instrumentalists devised rules of harmony and
counterpoint in order to make their own parts more interesting.
The composers of polyphony consider these rules excellent and
necessary for the mere delight that the ear takes in the variety of
harmonies. But for the expression of conceptions, they are
pestilent: they are fit for nothing but making the *concentus* varied
and full. Polyphonic music is appropriate and even good for
instruments. But its rules were never meant to apply to those
harmonies which are combined with words and with the passions
conveyed by the words, and which thus express the conceptions
of the mind. Moreover, when polyphonic composers attempt to
imitate such conceptions, their techniques turn out to be naïve and
childish. Galilei is bitingly sarcastic in condemning the literal
imitation of words in sixteenth-century music. The habit of
illustrating words like "flee" with rapid notes, "disappear" or
"die" with an abrupt rest in all voices, and "heaven" or "hell"
with ascending or descending melodies, seems to Galilei a per-
version of the true aim of music, even though such imitation had
become a part of the standard stylistic vocabulary of the composers of his age, especially the composers of madrigals. These
absurd "madrigalisms" were intended merely to delight the ear,
not to induce in another the same passion that one felt oneself.
Galilei recommends that composers go to the theater to hear how
one quiet gentleman sounds when he speaks with another: how
high or low his voice is pitched, what volume of sound he uses,
what sorts of accents and gestures he adds to his speech, and how
slowly or rapidly he pronounces each word. Composers should
note how these things change when a gentleman speaks with his

servant, when a prince addresses his subjects, when a lover pleads with his mistress, and when an infuriated, excited, lamenting, timid, or exultant person vents his emotions.

Music needs, in other words, to express more directly the sense of the text, rather than stylizing emotions by means of conventional, but basically abstract, musical formulas. But beyond this general advice Galilei offers no very specific suggestions about the reform of music. He seems to be in little doubt that one of the key factors in reviving the emotional power of Greek music involved a return to the simpler, monodic state of earlier music; and this is perhaps his most revolutionary suggestion. He can hardly have intended that composers go the whole way and write literally monophonic music. The *Dialogo* is not clear on this point; other evidence shows that he was aware that any reform would need to take into account the advances—whether or not he would have called them that—of modern music. A new music, he sensed, would have to be nonpolyphonic. But it would nevertheless have to be harmonic—some sort of compromise between polyphony and monophony.

To be sure, Galilei was not wholly new in these proposals. Others had already written that the text was the most important element in the expressive power of music, and others had already criticized the naïveté of "madrigalisms." Indeed, Nicola Vicentino's *L'antica musica ridotta alla moderna prattica* of 1555 is a much more brilliant exposition of the same thesis, even though the thesis is then applied not to the abolition but to the reformation of polyphony. Most of what Galilei says about Greek monody in particular and Greek music in general, moreover, came not from his own researches but from those of Girolamo Mei. Mei was a Florentine philologist resident in Rome, one of the most learned men of his time on the subject of Greek music, whose pioneering work has only recently been correctly evaluated.[16] Even though he was not a musician himself, he might be called the first historical musicologist, for he devoted himself to an objective reconstruction and evaluation of Greek music theory. He sought,

[16] Palisca, *Girolamo Mei*.

that is, to discover exactly what Greek music had been, rather than proposing a new synthesis of ancient and modern styles on the basis of the incomplete knowledge then available. And he passed on the results of his discoveries in the letters he began writing to Galilei as early as 1572.

Still, it is not at all clear from the *Dialogo* exactly what sort of music Galilei had in mind when he advocated his sweeping reforms. Claude Palisca has shown that he did make some practical suggestions in several treatises written toward the end of his life and never published.[17] In these treatises Galilei favors the sort of popular airs that had been written throughout the sixteenth century, which he praises for the same qualities of simplicity, naturalness, economy, and direct expression that he saw in Greek music. Apparently Galilei urged composers to take over such popular forms as the *villotte*, the *napolitane*, the *canzonette*, and airs on traditional harmonic patterns, and adapt them to their humanistic purposes. Filippo Azzaiolo's *villotta* "Ti parti cor mio caro" (Example 1), for instance, is one of these native Italian songs, untainted by northern counterpoint, that Galilei singles out for praise.[18] With its simple melody, its repetitive dance rhythm, and its one accentual blunder ("l'aníma" instead of "l'ánima"), the song hardly seems a suitable model for a dedicated humanist, let alone an example of music's power to express noble sentiments. But simple, melodious airs, in simple, homophonic settings actually had more in common with the aims of the humanists than many more complicated polyphonic pieces. A part, at least, of Galilei's polemic may thus have been directed toward a re-evaluation of native Italian music.

But whatever Galilei may have proposed later in life, he probably had in mind some genuinely new and more declamatory kind of melody when he wrote the *Dialogo*, even though he

[17] See Palisca, "Vincenzo Galilei's Counterpoint Treatise" and "Vincenzo Galilei and Some Links."

[18] The Azzaiolo example, first published in 1557, is taken from Palisca, "Vincenzo Galilei and Some Links," p. 349. The original sources of the composition are given there.

EXAMPLE I "Ti parti cor mio caro", Filippo Azzaiolo

defined it very imprecisely. He did, in fact, experiment in a new
style that was to be a model for other composers. He set one
sacred text, a part of the Lamentations and Responds for Holy
Week, and one secular text, the lament of Count Ugolino from
the *Divine Comedy*, for solo tenor and consort of viols. These two
examples would have made clear the direction of Galilei's
thoughts in the early 1580's, but unfortunately they are both lost.
Apparently they were not entirely successful artistically, for they
were said to have had a certain roughness and an excessive
"antiquity."[19]

The *Dialogo della musica antica et moderna*, as fanatical and
vague as it is in many ways, is the most complete theoretical statement that we possess from any member of the Florentine
Camerata.[20] But its thoroughness does not mean that we should
accept it uncritically as the official program of the group. Indeed,
I have dwelt on it at such length because it represents an extreme
statement of ideas current in the second half of the sixteenth
century, and because it comes from the same artistic milieu as the
music of Jacopo Peri. It is therefore symptomatic of the trend of
thought of the men in the Camerata, even if each member of the
group did not feel obliged to incorporate every particular into
his own program. Galilei was undoubtedly the most learned
member of the Camerata in musical matters; but it may be signi-

[19] The source for the thesis that Galilei composed these pieces and for the
value judgment about them is Pietro de' Bardi, "Lettera a G. B. Doni sull'origine
del melodramma (1634)," printed in Angelo Solerti, *Le origini del melodramma*
(Turin: Bocca, 1903), pp. 143 ff.; translated into English in Strunk, *Source
Readings*, pp. 363 ff.

[20] It is difficult to reconcile Galilei's activities as a radical reformer with the
fact that he wrote polyphonic music, a treatise on counterpoint, and a volume
largely concerned with teaching lutanists how to arrange polyphonic compositions for their instruments (*Fronimo*, [Venice, 1568]). Bernard Weinberg of the
University of Chicago has pointed out to me that Italian Renaissance authors
of literary treatises in dialogue form customarily represent actual people expressing their own and not the authors' opinions. Since Giovanni de' Bardi,
count of Vernio, is the principal speaker in Galilei's *Dialogo*, it may well be that
Galilei was presenting Bardi's views rather than his own. The treatise was
dedicated to Bardi, and it is clear from the dedication that Bardi had subsidized
Galilei's studies for some time.

ficant of their evaluation of him that he was not asked to contribute in any way to the elaborate celebrations held in Florence in 1589 for the wedding of the Grand Duke Ferdinando I and Cristina of Lorraine, even though every other member of the Camerata did make some contribution.[21]

Whatever the relationship of Galilei's *Dialogo* to the thinking of the Florentine Camerata may have been, a complete history of their work in detail will probably never be possible. The Camerata was not a formal academy, complete with set papers, but merely an informal group of men with similar interests—a kind of literary salon, which discussed music as only one aspect of Greek culture.[22] This circle of musicians and humanists met under the patronage of Giovanni de' Bardi from the late 1570's, just at the time when the *Dialogo* was taking shape, until 1592, when Bardi left Florence to take a position in the papal court in Rome. Thus its most celebrated accomplishment, the invention of opera, did not even take place until long after the original group had stopped meeting.

Nino Pirrotta has warned us against conceiving of the Camerata as a unified group.[23] There was a great diversity of temperament among the various men. Giovanni de' Bardi, an old aristocrat, playwright, and author of a treatise on football as well as one on Greek music, was the model of a Renaissance man. Jacopo Corsi, who was only too eager to assume Bardi's leadership after 1592, was another aristocrat, one whose house was always open to artists and musicians; and he himself, like Bardi, composed a bit. Ottavio Rinuccini, who grew up at the Medici court, was a poet

[21] All of the music for the 1589 *intermedii* is printed in *Les Fêtes du Mariage de Ferdinand de Médicis et de Christine de Lorraine, Florence 1589*, Vol. I, "Musique des intermèdes de 'La Pellegrina,'" ed. D. P. Walker (1963; cited above, ch. 2, n. 67). On the festivities, see also Angelo Solerti, *Musica, ballo e drammatica alla corte medicea dal 1600 al 1637* (Florence: Bemporad, 1905), pp. 12 ff.; A. M. Nagler, *Theatre Festivals of the Medici, 1539–1637* (Yale University Press, 1964), pp. 70 ff.; and Federico Ghisi, *Feste musicali della Firenze medicea (1480–1589)* (Florence: Centro Nazionale Studi sul Rinascimento, 1939), pp. xvi ff.

[22] For studies of the Camerata, see n. 12 above.

[23] The following paragraph is taken mostly from Pirrotta, "Temperaments and Tendencies."

of rather conventional courtly lyrics; and only later did he display his full talents in the series of elegant pastoral plays that he wrote to be set to music: *Dafne*, *Euridice*, and *Arianna*. Jacopo Peri, director of the Medici court music from 1591, was a pupil of Cristofano Malvezzi and well known as an organist as well as singer and composer. His archrival, Giulio Caccini, less learned a musician, was also a virtuoso singer, and performances by both men are highly praised by many contemporary writers. Numerous clashes of personality mark all of the events in Florentine music history connected with their names.

The main artistic activities of the members of the Camerata centered about the musical life at the Medici court. And so it is to music at that court that we must look in order to find out what happened in the twenty years between the first discussions of the group and the first performance of Jacopo Peri's *Euridice*. How did Peri and his colleagues work out the musical problems posed in the discussions of the Camerata and in Galilei's *Dialogo*? Some first attempts at a solution may be found in the music for the celebration of the wedding of the grand duke in 1589. Bardi was in charge of all the celebrations, and responsible especially for their literary programs; Emilio de' Cavalieri, a nobleman from Rome and another important figure in the early history of opera, supervised the music; and Bernardo Buontalenti directed the costumes and staging. Bardi asked not only the official court composers, Alessandro Striggio, Luca Marenzio, and Cristofano Malvezzi, but also his younger friends, Peri, Caccini, and Cavalieri, to contribute music for the wedding; and he himself also composed several pieces. The chief musical event of the occasion was the *intermedii*, first performed between the acts of Girolamo Bargagli's comedy *La Pellegrina*.

By 1589 the *intermedio* tradition was firmly established in Florence. Comedies with musical *intermedii* were the principal entertainments at almost every official celebration, and, indeed, Florence was already famous for the sumptuousness and high quality of these theatrical spectacles. The music for the *intermedii* consisted mostly of big, concerted compositions performed by large and varied consorts of voices and instruments; and it was usually coupled with spectacular theatrical effects achieved by elaborate stage machinery. Normally there were six *intermedii* for each comedy, one before the prologue and one before each of the five acts. The *intermedii* had no spoken parts; a more or less elaborate pantomime explained the subject matter of the one or two compositions; and all the *intermedii* for a given play were related to some general theme, although they almost never achieved any artistic unity. For the 1589 celebrations Bardi chose as his theme for the six *intermedii*, significantly enough, the power of ancient music. Various tableaux dealt with the harmony of the spheres, the rivalry between the Muses and the Pierides, Apollo victorious over the python, the story of Arion, and the descent of rhythm and harmony to earth. Only one scene, the one in which the age of gold that was to follow the royal marriage is foretold to the spirits in hell, breaks the thematic unity of the production, and it was probably included merely to conform with the *intermedio* tradition that there must always be at least one scene in the underworld. Each tableau was more elaborate than usual: four, five, or six compositions accompanied each one of them, and the scenic effects were unparalleled in their magnificence. The music for the event, most of it preserved in a souvenir edition published a year or two after the wedding, is of the most diverse kinds: there are polyphonic madrigals, compositions for solo voice with instrumental accompaniment, purely instrumental interludes and *sinfonie*, polychoral pieces, and some quite simple homophonic pieces.

Disappointingly, there is not much that is startlingly new in the music. Much of it, far from being more expressive than ever before, has that blandness of sound and simplicity of texture characteristic of much music written for the theater in all periods —a music, in other words, that is simple enough to carry across the footlights. There is, for example, an almost complete lack of dissonance in much of the music and an excess of vocal virtuosity, both features inimical to expression. Two of the pieces for solo voice and instrumental accompaniment are, it is true, slightly different from usual *intermedio* music. The opening composition,[24] sung by the famous Vittoria Archilei, and an echo song sung by Peri,[25] are both printed with an extremely simple, mostly homophonic texture for four instrumental parts, while the vocal line is an elaborately ornamented version of the highest accompanying line. But this striking vocal display negates any effective expression, for the running passages almost invariably obscure the words. Bardi's composition for the hell scene,[26] for solo voice, trombones, viols, and a *lira da braccio*, might also be singled out for its homophonic texture and its expressive sonorities, but it falls squarely into one of the *intermedio* traditions that can be traced back at least fifty years. One is forced to the conclusion that the first experiments of the Camerata members in attempting a music fully expressive of the text resulted in compositions not so very different from much courtly entertainment music of the mid-century: homophony was to replace polyphony, and the top voice, which could be distorted by passage work, was to dominate.

Music for *intermedii*, while theatrical, is seldom genuinely dramatic. The Florentines, in fact, seem not to have thought of setting an entire play to music until Emilio de' Cavalieri, a Roman, did so about 1590. Galilei, it should be remembered, had not discussed Greek drama. Even though he recommended that composers study diction in the theater, his aim was a reform of all music. Moreover, even in 1590 Florence was by no means the first place where the possibilities of a new and humanistically inspired music for the stage were explored. There was, for example, the performance of *Oedipus* with choruses by Andrea Gabrieli which opened the Teatro Olimpico in Vicenza in 1585— a performance of the utmost historical importance, in spite of the fact that the musical problems it posed defeated the composer's attempts to write artistically significant music.[27]

[24] *Les Fêtes du Mariage*, pp. 2 ff.   [25] *Ibid.*, pp. 98 ff.   [26] *Ibid.*, pp. 85 ff.
[27] Gabrieli's music for *Oedipus*, and a study of the first performance in Vicenza, is printed in Leo Schrade, *La Représentation d'Edipo Tiranno au Teatro Olimpico* (*Vicence 1585*) (Paris: Centre National de la Recherche Scientifique, 1960).

The first dramatic music in Florence consisted of settings for three plays, a part of Tasso's *Aminta* and two short pastoral plays by Cavalieri's friend Laura Guidiccioni, *Il Satiro* and *La Disperazione di Fileno*.[28] Since the music for all of them is lost, it would be feckless to speculate on its style. The librettist's mother, hardly an impeccable authority, did write that the manner of singing was different from the ordinary one ("altro modo di cantare che l'ordinario"); but she may have referred only to its manner of performance.[29] Giovanni Battista Doni reported[30] that it consisted only of simple airs, an observation that would be consistent with the notion of Cavalieri's style gained from his masterpiece, the *Rappresentazione di Anima e di Corpo*,[31] performed in Rome in 1600, for much of that music resembles the popular homophonic airs praised by Galilei or the homophonic *intermedio* music of 1589 more than the declamation of Peri. In any case Cavalieri deserves the credit for channeling the energies of at least some of the Florentines into dramatic productions, a debt that Peri acknowledges in the preface to *Euridice*.

Since Cavalieri's works are lost, and since their real character therefore remains unknown, we are justified in considering the first opera to be the setting of Ottavio Rinuccini's pastoral play *Dafne*. The play is an expansion of one of the episodes from the *intermedii* of 1589. The music for it was begun by Jacopo Corsi and completed by Peri.[32] It was first performed at Corsi's palace in the 1590's and was performed again several times during the following carnival seasons, both at court and in Corsi's private

[28] On these three plays with music, see Angelo Solerti, "Laura Guidiccioni Lucchesini ed Emilio del Cavaliere," *Rivista musicale italiana*, IX (1902), 817, and Claude Palisca, "Musical Asides in the Diplomatic Correspondence of Emilio de' Cavalieri," *The Musical Quarterly*, XLIX (1963), 339.

[29] Solerti, *op. cit.*, p. 813.

[30] *Ibid.*, p. 821.

[31] Rome, 1600. A facsimile edition was issued by the Gregg Press in 1968.

[32] All of the surviving music for *Dafne* is printed in William Porter, "Peri and Corsi's *Dafne*: Some New Discoveries and Observations," *Journal of the American Musicological Society*, XVIII (1965), 170. See also Federico Ghisi, *Alle fonti della monodia* (Milan: Bocca, 1940). The libretto is printed in Andrea Della Corte, *Drammi per musica* (Turin: U.T.E.T., 1958) Vol. I, p. 45.

circle of friends. Most of the music is lost. But some idea of its general layout and its style can be gathered from the libretto and from the surviving fragments, which consist mostly of formal set pieces, strophic songs, and some of the choruses that closed each of the five short scenes. Like all the first Florentine operas, and unlike the more directly classical dramatic experiments in other cities, *Dafne* more closely resembles a comedy, that is, a dramatic pastoral with *intermedii*, than it does any Greek play. Indeed, its libretto, like that of *Euridice*, falls into a literary tradition that begins with Agostino Beccari's *Sacrificio* of 1554 and includes Tasso's *Aminta*.[33] The surviving formal numbers from *Dafne* do not differ markedly in style from the *intermedio* pieces of the earlier Florentine tradition. Some of them go further in the direction of the melodic style found in *Euridice*. It can only be assumed, in the absence of the complete score, that the dialogue was written in an early version of the declamatory style which Peri was to perfect in his *Euridice*.

The experiment of *Dafne* was apparently successful, for Rinuccini and Peri were asked to collaborate again in a work written to celebrate the marriage of Maria de' Medici and Henry IV of France in October 1600. For this occasion they produced the *Euridice*.[34] By 1600 the Camerata had pretty much fallen apart.

[33] The most recent study of this tradition is an article soon to be published by Henry W. Kaufmann, "Music for a *favola pastorale* (1554)." I am grateful to the author for allowing me to read the article before publication.

[34] On the festivities of 1600 in general, see Solerti, *Musica, ballo*, pp. 23 ff.; and Nagler, *Theatre Festivities*, pp. 93 ff. Many of the details about the first performance of *Euridice* are taken from Claude Palisca, "The First Performance of 'Euridice,' " *Twenty-fifth Anniversary Festschrift (1937–1962)* (Queens College of the City University of New York, Department of Music, 1964), pp. 1–23. See also Palisca, "Musical Asides." The libretto of *Euridice* is printed in Angelo Solerti, *Gli albori del melodramma* (Milan: Sandron, 1904), Vol. II, pp. 114 ff.; in Della Corte, *Drammi per musica*, Vol. I, p. 69; and, with an English translation by Howard Mayer Brown, in a private edition (Chicago, 1967). The preface by Ottavio Rinuccini to the libretto is printed in Solerti, *Origini*, pp. 40 ff., and in an English translation in Strunk, *Source Readings*, pp. 367 ff. The first Florentine edition of 1600 of Peri's music for *Euridice* was reprinted in a facsimile edition (Rome, 1934). *L'arte musicale in Italia*, ed. Luigi Torchi (Milan: Ricordi, 1906), Vol. VI, contains a modern edition of the music. I am now preparing a

Bardi had been living in Rome for almost ten years. The rivalry between Peri and Caccini had become so intense that Caccini refused to allow his singers to perform any music composed by Peri. Here Peri, singing the role of Orfeo, was answered at the first performance of the opera by Euridice singing music by Caccini. Cavalieri, who had Bardi's former job as supervisor of the festivities, was not able to bring all of the rival factions together, nor to complete all of the necessary preparations for the celebration. The scenery for *Euridice*, for example, had not been entirely finished in time for the performance. In fact, Cavalieri was quite disgusted with the way things had gone, and almost immediately after the wedding he left for Rome, resolved never to return. In Rome there were plenty of malicious remarks about the performances, and these remarks, more than anything else, have given Peri's work a bad name. The Romans, at least partly for reasons of chauvinistic nastiness, said that the music was tedious—that it seemed like the chanting of the Passion. Ironically, Bardi himself, whose fame rests at least partly on the first Florentine operas, was also scornful. He compared the music at the 1600 wedding unfavorably with the music that he had arranged in 1589, and he declared himself to be amazed that tragic texts and objectionable subjects (he was referring to the now lost *Il Rapimento di Cefalo*, with music by Giulio Caccini, as well as to the *Euridice*) should have been used for so happy an occasion.[35] Actually, the *Rapimento* was credited with being still less successful than the *Euridice*. It was thought to be an inappropriate medium for Caccini, who, during the years in which Peri was developing his declamatory style, had been working on the sort of intimate chamber music that was later to bear fruit in his

---

new performing edition of the score. Peri's preface to the score is printed in Solerti, *Origini*, pp. 43 ff., and in an English translation in Strunk, *Source Readings*, pp. 373 ff. The libretto for *Il rapimento di Cefalo* is printed in Solerti, *Gli albori*, Vol. III, pp. 29 ff. Excerpts from the music may be found in Giulio Caccini, *Le nuove musiche* (Florence, 1601; facsimile edn., Rome, 1934).

[35] For a discussion of these criticisms and the text of the letter in which they are found, see Palisca, "Musical Asides," pp. 351 ff.

famous collection *Le nuove musiche*.[36] Yet the *Rapimento* was the principal musical event of the wedding. It was performed before an audience of 3,800 people in the great hall over the Uffizi, with spectacular stage-sets designed by Buontalenti. The *Euridice*, on the other hand, was performed in a small room on one of the upper floors of the Pitti Palace for no more than 200 specially invited guests; the production was quite simple and probably used no stage machinery.

Rinuccini's libretto for *Euridice* resembles his *Dafne* very much in structure and general layout. In both, rhymed dialogue, in freely alternating seven- and eleven-syllable lines interspersed with occasional more regular strophic verse, leads at the end of each of the five scenes to a formal chorus in strophes of four or six lines, in the manner of an *intermedio*. *Euridice* is longer than *Dafne*, more varied, and more dramatically successful; for the plot, while draped in the most florid, courtly language, traces its course without interruption from beginning to end. This arrangement, obviously reminiscent of the festival plays with *intermedii*, is in fact a hallmark of all the earliest Florentine operas. Already by 1607, when Monteverdi's *Orfeo* was first performed in Mantua, the structure of opera was different and more complex, even though Monteverdi's work still owes much to the sixteenth-century festival tradition.

The plot of *Euridice*, similarly, is very simple. Tragedy sings a prologue explaining that she has abandoned her usual attributes in order to present a happier story in honor of the royal wedding. In the first scene nymphs and shepherds rejoice at the thought of the forthcoming marriage between Orpheus and Euridice.[37] Euridice appears, expresses her happiness, and suggests that she and her companions pass the time by singing and dancing in the woods. In the second scene Orpheus enters, delivers a monologue

[36] Florence, 1601; facsimile edn., Rome, 1934.

[37] To my knowledge, no one has previously noticed that the line which climaxes the shepherds' rejoicing in Scene I and immediately precedes Euridice's entrance, "Non vede un simil par d'amanti il Sole," is from Petrarch's sonnet "Due rose fresche e colte in paradiso" (*Canzoniere*, no. 245, ed. Emilio Bigi [Milan: Ugo Mursia, 1963], p. 178).

apostrophizing nature, and explains to the trees, plants, flowers, and wild beasts why they will no longer hear him lament. The rustic Tirsi interrupts the ensuing conversation between Orpheus and his friend Arcetro in order to sing, play his panpipes, dance, and thus show his joy over the wedding. But he has scarcely finished his song when Dafne bursts onto the stage to recount the tragic death of Euridice. Orpheus, grief-stricken, sings a lament and then rushes off-stage to find his beloved, followed by Arcetro, who goes to comfort him. The nymphs and shepherds trail back from the woods, bewailing the loss of their mistress. The third scene consists mainly of a monologue in which Arcetro describes how Orpheus threw himself down on the spot where Euridice died and wept, when suddenly a goddess—she later turns out to be Venus—descended in a golden chariot and carried him away. In the fourth scene Venus has led Orpheus to the gates of hell, where he sings a lament for Euridice. The intensity of his passion finally forces open the gates of hell and, after a prolonged argument, Pluto, moved by Orpheus's pleas, agrees to return Euridice to him, without, be it noted, any reservation about his not looking back. The opera, performed at a wedding, had, after all, to have a happy ending. In the fifth scene, the shepherd Aminta announces the happy news to the other nymphs and shepherds, Orpheus and Euridice arrive, and the opera closes with an elaborate chorus of rejoicing.

Apart from the choral finales and Tragedy's prologue, there are also two other strophic songs: Tirsi's in Scene II, and Orpheus's welcome to the shepherds in Scene v. But the main part of the opera is written in the declamatory style that Peri devised to mimic speech in music, the so-called *stile recitativo*. To be precise, the first and fifth scenes are set as a dialogue among shepherds, nymphs, Orpheus, and Euridice; and the core of the second, third and fourth scenes is a series of monologues: Orpheus's opening apostrophe to nature, Dafne's narration followed by Orpheus's lament, Arcetro's recital of Venus's rescue of Orpheus, and Orpheus's plea before the gates of hell. The *stile recitativo*, in which most of the opera is written, then, was Peri's solution to the problem of reinstating the emotional power that music was said to have in ancient times. It was an attempt to make music fully expressive of the text.

But the opera contains two quite distinct styles: song and recitative. Although these are not the two poles they were to become later in the history of opera, the distinction must be made in order to separate those parts that more closely resemble the earlier Italianate popular songs, simple and homophonic, from those parts that are written in a genuinely new style. Just as the sections in song can be separated into solo and choral textures, so the recitatives can be divided into those dialogues that are comparatively neutral emotionally and those dialogues and especially monologues in which peaks of emotion are reached. This distinction is followed in the music.

I stress variety in the *Euridice*, variety in the song textures and variety in the style of the declamatory parts, because Peri has often been accused of failure on just this point. Historians of music have often dismissed his recitative as unrelieved and dry, and, paraphrasing the malicious Romans of Peri's age, they have said in effect that it resembles the chanting of the Passion.[38] In my opinion, however, *Euridice*'s bad press is undeserved. It has resulted in part from a rather uncritical acceptance of the accusations made at the time, usually on other than aesthetic grounds. But it has also resulted from the failure to see the opera in its historical context—to compare it carefully, that is, with Caccini's musical setting for the same text of Rinuccini, which was published the same year as Peri's was put on the stage.

Caccini's work may well be the only "spite opera" in the history of music. The score shows signs of haste.[39] It is a badly executed

[38] See, for example, Paul Henry Lang, *Music in Western Civilization* (New York: Norton, 1941), p. 338; Donald Jay Grout, *A History of Western Music* (New York: Norton, 1960), p. 279; and Alec Harman and Wilfrid Mellers, *Man and His Music* (New York: Oxford University Press, 1962), p. 373.

[39] Caccini's score was published in a modern edition in *Publikation älterer praktischer und theoretischer Musikwerke*, ed. Robert Eitner (Berlin: Trautwein, 1881), Vol. x. The preface to the score is printed in Solerti, *Origini*, pp. 50 ff., and in an English translation in Strunk, *Source Readings*, pp. 370 ff.

work, inferior in every way to Peri's, and unworthy of the composer of *Le nuove musiche*. Obviously it was rushed off to the press in order to beat Peri's version to the draw; and it succeeded, then and for centuries afterward, in obscuring the merits of its rival.

Both works are among the first to use the new *basso continuo* texture, in which the composer indicates only the vocal line and the bass line. In performance the bare two-part texture is filled out at sight by instrumentalists, who realize the harmonic implications of the bass by playing chords and sometimes more elaborate passage work. Neither Peri nor Caccini invented the *basso continuo*. It is a technique that became so widespread during the last decade of the sixteenth century and the first decade of the seventeenth that a single inventor will never be identified. Indeed, some such technical change was almost bound to have occurred in view of the very common practice of the later sixteenth century in accompanying vocal music by keyboard and other instruments. But it is significant that both composers adopted this technique as the solution to the problem implied in Galilei's *Dialogo*: the problem of a new, nonpolyphonic music which still took into account one of the chief virtues of modern music, harmony.

Caccini's chamber-music style using the new *basso continuo* texture can best be illustrated by a few phrases from his most famous monody, "Amarilli mia bella" (Example 2).[40] Caccini has simply eliminated all of the contrapuntal inner parts, leaving as framework only the top line and the bottom line. Thus the words are not obscured, and the composer is free to compose a melodic line which is, in Caccini's own words, "a kind of music by which men might, as it were, talk in harmony, using . . . a certain noble neglect of the song."[41] The result is a two-part composition that is different from the typical sixteenth-century

---

[40] The complete composition can be found in *La flora*, ed. Knud Jeppesen (Copenhagen: Hansen, 1949), Vol. I, p. 12.

[41] Strunk, *Source Readings*, p. 378. The quotation is from the foreword to *Le nuove musiche*.

EXAMPLE 2 "Amarilli mia bella" (beginning), Giulio Caccini

A - ma - ril - li mia bel - la! Non cre - di, o, del mio cor dol - ce de - si - o: d'es - ser tu___ l'a-mor mi - o. *etc.*

bicinium. The upper voice has greater independence and melodic freedom; its rhythm and pitch are more closely connected with the accents of natural speech. The lower voice has a more specifically harmonic function. The middle of the texture is filled not with contrapuntal lines but with chords. And finally, the singer declaims more simply and with an altogether different notion of good vocal technique.

Peri's use of the new *basso continuo* texture is slightly different. Compare Caccini's "Amarilli" with the first of Orpheus's three stanzas of pleading before the gates of hell in Scene IV of *Euridice* (Example 3).[42] While the texture of the two examples is very similar, Peri has slowed down the bass line. Caccini's bass line is rhythmically quite close to the top line; it still has some identity as a contrapuntal line. Peri's bass, on the other hand, is nothing but

---

[42] 1600 edn., pp. 29–30.

a series of notes that function exclusively as anchors for the chords they imply. This slow-moving bass line is, as far as I know, Peri's own invention. It is particularly well suited to dramatic expression rather than to the more lyric monodies of Caccini, for it leaves the singer freer to declaim. The value of this technique for stage works was recognized even by Caccini, and he also made use of it in his own setting of the *Euridice*.

Actually, these two slightly different varieties of *stile recitativo*

EXAMPLE 3 *Euridice* (excerpt from Scene IV), Jacopo Peri

ro - le   Men-tre con me-sti-ac - cen - ti   Il perdu - to mio

ben   con voi —— so - spi - ro   E

voi   deh per pietà del mio par - ti - ro   Che nel mi - sero

cor - di - mo - ra e - ter - no   La - cri -

ma - te al mio pian - to   om - bre d'in-fer - no

came about in different ways. Caccini simplifies the sixteenth-century contrapuntal texture by sweeping away all the inner voices, leaving only the bass and superius. Peri begins with the text he wants to set, and he writes a chord wherever there is a tonic accent in the sentence, not just where there is an accented syllable in a word. "I knew that in our speech," he writes in his preface to the opera, "some words are so intoned that harmony can be based upon them, and that in the course of speaking it passes through many others that are not so intoned until it returns to another that will bear a progression to a fresh consonance."[43] Thus Peri's music is completely sprung from its contrapuntal framework, and his technique, stressing the most important

EXAMPLE 4 *Euridice*, mm. 625–36, Jacopo Peri

43 Strunk, *op. cit.*, p. 374.

accents of a sentence and thus tying his music more closely to the natural cadences of speech, is genuinely revolutionary.

This explanation of Peri's technique is, needless to say, over-simplified. Actually, the technique is subtle enough to go against the metrical regularity of the music—to exploit, in fact, the metrical regularity—for dramatic effect. In Arcetro's first im-passioned response to Dafne's narration of Euridice's death, for example, his persistent off beat accents, along with the striking dissonances, heighten incomparably the poignancy of the situation (Example 4).[44]

Perhaps the most important element in matching text declama-tion to music, in attempting, that is, to imitate speech in song, which is the avowed aim of both Peri and Caccini, is a sensitive use of rhythm. Peri shows consummate skill in adjusting the rhythms of his recitatives to the requirements of the text. His skill becomes even more apparent when his setting of *Euridice* is compared with that by Caccini and with a typical sixteenth-century madrigal.

The superius of Cipriano de Rore's setting of Alfonso d'Avalos's poem "Ancor che col partire" (Example 5)[45] can serve as an example of a good sixteenth-century solution to the problem of matching text to music. It is one of the best-known compositions of a composer who was widely admired by sixteenth-century writers on music, including members of the Camerata, for his skill in handling words. Rore's is a subtle art; the way in which text accents coincide with musical accents is very sophisticated

[44] 1600 edn., p. 16.
[45] The complete madrigal appears in *The Madrigals of Cipriano de Rore for 3 and 4 voices*, ed. Gertrude Parker Smith, Smith College Music Archives, No. VI (Northampton, Mass., 1943), pp. 45 ff. The translation of the text given there reads:

Although whene'er we part
I feel death pressing on,
Each moment would I fain depart,
Such joy of life I win when I return.
So each day would I gladly part
From you a thousand times and more,
So sweet, so sweet my homings are.

EXAMPLE 5 "Anchor che col partire" (superius part), Cipriano de Rore

indeed.[46] Yet no one would mistake a performance of the superius part with an acceptable literary reading of the poem, let alone for an imitation of natural speech. There are unnatural repetitions of phrases, for instance, irrational changes in pace, strange pauses, and syllables that are excessively elongated for purely musical reasons. Even though the most important text accent in a sentence or complete thought does get the strongest musical accent of the phrase, the accent pattern, stylized to a degree, cannot be said to imitate realistically natural speech.

The opening speech of Scene 1 of *Euridice*, the shepherd's welcome to the nymphs, and his encomium of Orpheus and Euridice, is very different:

> Ninfe, ch'i bei crin d'oro
> sciogliete liete a lo scherzar de'venti.
> e voi, ch'almo tesoro
> dentro chiudete a' bei rubini ardenti,
> e voi, ch'all'alba in ciel togliete i vanti,
> tutte venite, o pastorelle amanti;
> e per queste fiorite alme contrade
> risuonin liete voci e lieti canti.
> Oggi a somma beltade
> giunge sommo valor Santo Imeneo.
> Avventuroso Orfeo,
> fortunata Euridice,
> pur vi congiunse il ciel: o di felice!

> "Nymphs, whose beautiful golden hair
> is loosened by the playful wind,
> and you, whose great treasure
> is hidden by beautiful burning rubies,
> and you, who are more glorious than the dawn,
> come all of you, pastoral lovers;
> in this dear countryside, covered with flowers

[46] See, for example, the praise given him by Giovanni de' Bardi in his "Discourse on Ancient Music and Good Singing," printed in English translation in Strunk, *Source Readings*, p. 295.

happy voices and happy songs resound.
Today to consummate beauty
blessed Hymen joins consummate valor.
Adventurous Orpheus,
fortunate Euridice,
heaven joins you together: O happy day!"

EXAMPLE 6   *Euridice*, (beginning of Scene I), Giulio Caccini

The rhythm of Caccini's setting of this speech (Example 6)[47] approaches natural speech much more closely than does Rore's. In spite of the puzzling misaccentuation of "avventuroso"—a blunder that a sympathetic and discreet singer can easily repair— and in spite of the lengthening of words at cadences, which is almost inevitable in setting words to music, Caccini's setting makes rhythmically a fairly plausible reading of the text as an actor might declaim it. The difference between Rore's solution and Caccini's to the problem of text setting should make absolutely clear the novelty of the *stile recitativo*.

Peri's setting of this same speech (Example 7)[48] is much more subtle rhythmically than Caccini's. Both versions agree in many details. But Peri has tightened the pace of the first six lines—there are not the pauses found in the Caccini setting that interrupt the

EXAMPLE 7   *Euridice* (beginning of Scene 1), Jacopo Peri

voi ch'all' al-ba in ciel to-glie - te i van - ti

Tut - te ven - i - te o pas-to - rel - le a - man - ti

E per ques-te fio - ri - te al - ma con-tra - de Ri -

suon in lie-te vo - ci e lie - ti can - ti. Og-gi a som-ma bel -

ta - de Giun-ge som-mo va - lor San-to I - me - ne -

o. Av-ven-tu-ro - so Or - fe - o for-tuna-ta Eu-ri -

6   4   3

(6)

thought—so that all the motion proceeds toward the first climax of the speech: "Tutte venite, o pastorelle amanti." Both Peri and Caccini isolate the two "e voi's" at the beginning of the third and fifth lines for emphasis. But Peri manages to isolate them without letting the impetus stop completely. Even when the two composers agree exactly on the rhythm, as in "Oggi a somma beltade/ Giunge sommo valor Santo Imeneo," Peri's is the more successful in context, for his rather square rhythm, ♩♩♩♫♩♩♩♫, comes after a more varied line with many shorter notes. Thus the line is, quite properly, stronger and more metrical, and it reflects the fact that a new thought has been introduced, one that demands greater strength. In many details Caccini's solution is at best dull and pedestrian. Why, for example, does he interrupt the motion in the middle of the second line, "Sciogliete liete—a lo scherzar de' venti?" Only a few changes, similarly, would suffice to turn Caccini's quite monotonous "Avventuroso Orfeo" into the exclamation that it is in Peri's version.

When the element of pitch organization is added to the rhythm, Peri's superiority is again obvious. Even considering how the high notes are distributed will reveal Peri's subtlety. Both examples cover almost the same range of notes. Caccini has reserved the highest note of all for the misaccented *a* of "avventuroso." Peri uses the same note more often. There is not one high peak in the section, but several, and they function in different ways: first, to underline the high point of the second line of text, "Sciogliete *liete* a lo scherzar de' venti"; second, to mark the arrival at the first larger point of destination, "Tutte venite, o pastorelle amanti." Three times afterwards it marks important words: in the line beginning "Oggi a somma beltade," for example, the high point on "Sant'Imeneo" is well focused, whereas Caccini's melodic sequence reaches its climax too soon and dissipates its energy by repetition. Peri's setting, in short, establishes a reading for the text with the greatest sensitivity in the same way that an actor interprets a speech in a play.

The criteria for building a melody were thus completely different from the qualities of balance and design characteristic of much sixteenth-century music. Peri's setting does make less abstract musical sense than the Rore madrigal, but his music imitates much more closely the way in which the words would be declaimed by an actor. The structure of the melody is not done away with completely. It is merely disguised; and to say, as some scholars have, that the music comes to a full stop at the end of every line is an oversimplification that distorts the real meaning of the music. Such an accusation is much closer to the truth about Caccini's setting. Peri organizes his melodies in larger sections, and a hierarchy of cadences can be discerned within any one longer speech or scene. In the shepherds' opening speech, for example, there is a half-cadence at the end of the second line, a full cadence on the dominant at the end of the fourth line, and finally, a full cadence on the tonic at the natural completion of the first thought—on the words "Tutte venite, o pastorelle amanti." Cadences on scale degrees other than the tonic end lines 8 and 10 (on "canti" and on "Sant'Imeneo"), and the last three lines are set as a unit. Thus the opening speech divides into two parts, the first destination being the completion of the first unit of thought. "E per queste fiorite alme contrade/risuonin liete voci e lieti canti," a new thought, gets a new phrase of music, as do the next two lines; and the musical unit completes itself by a return to the tonic for the last lines. A purely musical structure does, therefore, underlie the passage, although its individual segments are determined by the free play of concepts expressed by means of words rather than by any more abstract ideals of design.

But the crucial question in considering Peri's music is precisely the one that began the whole cycle of events leading to the first Florentine operas, namely, how does the music reflect the emotional content of the words? How does Peri change his style according to the changing passions of the characters? For the music must express not only the external characteristics of language and declamation but also the sense of the text.

The music itself can arouse only generalized emotions; words are required to give the emotion focus and a specific name. Thus Peri's techniques for imitating states of mind can be analyzed in two large categories: ways of arousing tragic emotions, and ways of arousing happy emotions. In my opinion, Peri is far better as a tragedian. To accomplish his aims, he employs a number of techniques: skillful dissonance treatment, sudden shifts of harmony, so-called forbidden melodic intervals, ametrical rhythms, striking juxtapositions of purely formal and highly emotional scenes, and control of melodic shape and phrase length.

Peri's most striking means of evoking tragic emotions is by his skillful use of dissonance. In the new noncontrapuntal *stile recitativo* the contrapuntal framework against which dissonance could be introduced and resolved has been removed. Without such a framework, and following sixteenth-century rules of counterpoint, a style with insufficient variety might easily result, the sort of bland sound that is characteristic, for example, of some of the 1589 *intermedii*. Caccini's *Euridice* falls into this trap, for the composer is quite timid about introducing dissonances that violate the older rules. Peri is much bolder, and he faces the problem squarely. If the old sorts of dissonances cannot be used, then a new sort must be introduced, and that is precisely what he does, although, to be sure, he retains certain formulas, such as four-three suspensions at cadences. But dissonant notes are also boldly introduced against the static basses, almost always to heighten a dramatic situation. In most cases they cannot be explained as a temporary conflict between two independent melodies, nor are they introduced as consonances and resolved regularly. Instead, they are motivated purely by his desire for intense expression. Many examples from *Euridice* leap to mind, most of them more daring even than the famous "Cruda Amarilli" dissonance of Monteverdi that so incensed Artusi.[49] There is, for example, Dafne's leap of a fourth from A to E over a G minor triad on the

EXAMPLE 8   *Euridice*, mm. 505-8, Jacopo Peri

words "Si miserabil caso" (Example 8).[50] Less extreme, but more poignant, is the very first unprepared, accented dissonance introduced into Dafne's narration after she had spoken of the simple pleasures of Euridice's companions in the woods. On the words "Ma la bella Euridice," which introduce the account of Euridice's being bitten by a snake, Dafne sings an accented C against a

EXAMPLE 9   *Euridice*, mm. 558-60, Jacopo Peri

[49] Monteverdi's "Cruda Amarilli" is printed in the Malipiero edition of his complete works, Vol. v, p. 1. An English translation of Artusi's attack can be found in Strunk, *Source Readings*, pp. 393 ff.

[50] 1600 edn., p. 14.

B-flat triad (Example 9).[51] When Dafne then sings of the mortal sigh that came from Euridice, a freely introduced dissonance is combined with the forbidden interval of a diminished fourth

EXAMPLE 10   *Euridice*, mm. 585–6, Jacopo Peri

(Example 10).[52] And when she sings of Euridice's dying moment, Peri underlines the impression of Euridice's beautiful face be-

EXAMPLE 11   *Euridice*, mm. 616–19, Jacopo Peri

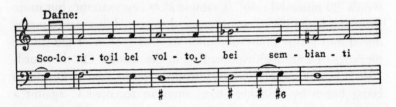

coming lifeless in the same way (Example 11).[53] Similar passages abound in the opera, but especially in the more "mournful and serious airs" of Dafne, Orpheus, and Arcetro.

Sudden and irrational shifts of harmony also help to intensify the moments of grief. When Dafne bursts upon the stage, for example, with her dreadful news, she enters on a G minor triad that follows immediately after an A major cadence. Almost overcome by her initial outburst, she exclaims "Ohimè," in a passage that combines a forbidden interval, a ferocious dissonance,

---

[51] 1600 edn., p. 15.   [52] *Loc. cit.*   [53] 1600 edn., p. 16.

EXAMPLE 12   *Euridice*, mm. 445–6, Jacopo Peri

and a sudden shift of harmony from G minor to E major (Example
12).[54] Dafne's sudden appearance is made all the more shattering
by contrast with the simple and sunny air of Tirsi, which almost
immediately precedes it. Her excitement and breathlessness is
imitated in the music by short, disconnected phrases. When she
finally collects herself and begins her narration, "Per quel vago
boschetto," her relative composure is expressed by longer and
structurally more coherent phrases and by the fact that she intones
the beginning of the narration on one repeated note.[55] As she
recalls every detail of the event, she becomes gradually more and
more agitated, and the range of her melodic line expands
accordingly.

Explaining Peri's means of evoking happier emotions is less
easy, and in my opinion he was less successful in this regard.
Many of the details of style that constitute his evocation of
happiness must be defined in negative terms. For these passages
Peri writes no dissonances, and he makes no sudden shifts of
harmony. The rhythm is not ametrical; on the contrary, it quite
markedly follows the meter. Sometimes, as in the finale of Scene I
and in Orpheus's welcome song in Scene V, dance rhythms pre-
dominate. But that by itself does not constitute evidence of happy
emotions; for both the serious chorus at the end of Scene III, "Se
de' boschi," and the moving "Sospirate" chorus that ends Scene II,
the emotional and musical climax of the entire opera, are also
written in regularly recurring rhythmic patterns, imitative of the

[54] 1600 edn., p. 13.
[55] Dafne's narration is printed in Arnold Schering, *Geschichte der Musik in
Beispielen* (Leipzig: Breitkopf und Härtel, 1931), pp. 187 f.

dance. The happier scenes are paced faster, for Peri takes care to imitate the speed at which people speak in various emotional states, following the convention that laments and mournful songs are slower than happier songs.

To be sure, most of Peri's techniques for evoking an emotional response are not new at all. Whereas none of his predecessors took such extreme care to imitate natural speech patterns, many of them had exploited dissonances, sudden shifts of harmony, forbidden melodic intervals, and the like for expressive purposes. What is new in his music is the combination of all these elements, along with the new static *basso continuo*, the sophisticated control of a novel sort of dissonance treatment, the concern for the pace of a speaker's words, and a musical structure that is justified not in terms of abstract design but in terms of its fidelity to the sense of the text and the free play of poetic concepts. The result is a work that comes close to the ideal envisaged by Galilei, one in which the composer, having learned either from real life or from the theater, writes a kind of music that naturalistically reflects the passion of the speaker (if the word "naturalistic" can refer to a work written in so elegant and artificial a poetic diction). Perhaps one should say that Peri's music accurately reflects the natural way in which Renaissance courtiers dressed as shepherds conversed on stage. *Euridice*, in other words, is quite literally a musical drama; it is not a strictly musical phenomenon, nor a strictly literary one, but a hybrid genre somewhere in between.

Peri's combination of all of these old and new technical elements results, in fact, in a continual psychological interpretation of the actions on stage. This point can best be illustrated by considering one short monologue, the lament of Orpheus after he has learned that Euridice is dead (Example 13).[56] Orpheus passes through three states of mind: his initial dumb shock gradually gives way to effusive grief, and his grief is in turn supplanted by his resolution to join Euridice, wherever she is. Orpheus's inarticulate shock is expressed at the beginning of his speech by the static quality of the music. His melodic line only

[56] 1600 edn., p. 17.

EXAMPLE 13   *Euridice* (Orfeo's lament), Jacopo Peri

gradually expands from a single note, to a range of a minor third, to a diminished fifth, over static harmony. The poignancy is underlined by the simple expedient of a bald dissonance on "e non sospiro," physically palpable when sung against the sustained note of the organ. As grief takes over, the melodic line jumps suddenly upward to exploit a completely new range, and at the same time it covers a much larger amount of musical space. Orpheus enters on an irrational dissonance for "O mio core, o mio speme." The harmonic rhythm speeds up, and the harmonies become more chromatic and less rational. The sudden shift of mood from grief to resolution just before "Tosto vedrai" is marked by a sudden shift of harmony, and Orpheus's melodic line, harmonized in a relatively clear and stable F major, speeds up slightly and becomes markedly more metrical.

Such an analysis may shock the modern musician, for it smacks more of Sigmund Spaeth than of Heinrich Schenker. But, in truth, one cannot analyze *Euridice* in abstract musical terms, for much of the music is without a meaning independent of the words. Even though the phrase structure is often planned in larger sections that correspond with the dramatic structure, the complete scenes are not designed as musical units. They are not tonally organized, for example, and a single unit, like Orpheus's lament, often ends in a different key from the one in which it began. These negative qualities have discouraged musicians from examining the work more closely and thus from discovering in it those remarkable positive qualities that it does possess.

From what I have said already, it should come as no surprise to learn that I think Peri's *Euridice* succeeds remarkably well in fulfilling the aims of its composer. It is a work that deserves repeated hearings and study, not merely for its historical significance as the first extant opera, but because it is capable of moving listeners even today. If I hesitate to rank it among the acknowledged masterpieces of early opera—and they are only two: Monteverdi's *Orfeo* and his *L'Incoronazione di Poppea*—it is because I feel that Peri's *Euridice* is really *hors de concours*, a "special" work, lacking perhaps the breadth and universal appeal of a genuine masterpiece, but nevertheless brilliantly succeeding in the more limited goals the composer set for it.

Index

P